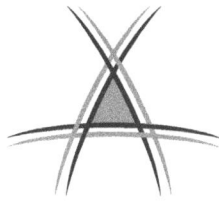

ASCENT®
CENTER FOR TECHNICAL KNOWLEDGE

CATIA V5-6R2017:
Sheet Metal Design

Learning Guide
1st Edition

ASCENT - Center for Technical Knowledge®
CATIA V5-6R2017: Sheet Metal Design
1st Edition

Prepared and produced by:

ASCENT Center for Technical Knowledge
630 Peter Jefferson Parkway, Suite 175
Charlottesville, VA 22911

866-527-2368
www.ASCENTed.com

Lead Contributor: Scott Hendren

ASCENT - Center for Technical Knowledge is a division of Rand Worldwide, Inc., providing custom developed knowledge products and services for leading engineering software applications. ASCENT is focused on specializing in the creation of education programs that incorporate the best of classroom learning and technology-based training offerings.

We welcome any comments you may have regarding this learning guide, or any of our products. To contact us please email: feedback@ASCENTed.com.

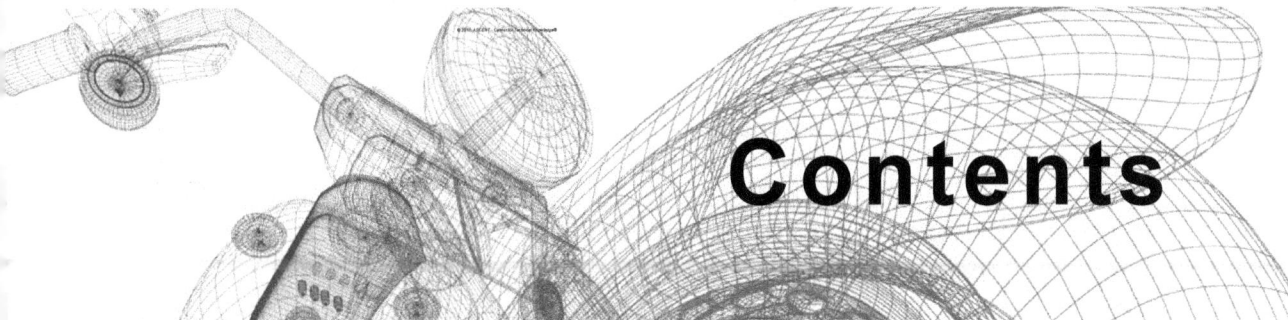

Contents

Preface

The *CATIA V5-6R2017: Sheet Metal Design* learning guide enables students to create features that are specific to the sheet metal modeling process. Students are provided with a process-based approach to creating sheet metal models. Each step in the process is discussed in depth using lectures and several hands-on practices. This learning guide focuses on the Generative Sheet Metal Design workbench.

Topics Covered:

- Generative Sheet Metal Design workbench

- Sheet Metal terminology

- Sheet Metal process

- Sheet Metal parameters

- Primary wall creation – Profile, Extruded, Rolled, and Hopper

- Defining walls

- Secondary walls – Wall on edge (automatic and sketch based), Tangent, Swept

- Cylindrical bends

- Bends from flat

- Unfolded view

- Corner relief

- Point and curve mapping

- Creating standard stamps – surface stamp, bead, curve stamp, flanged cutout, louver, bridge, flanged hole, circular stamp, stiffening rib, dowel

- Punch and die

- Punch with Opening Faces

- Sheet Metal features – Corners, chamfers, cuts and holes

- Feature duplication

- Patterning – rectangular patterns, circular patterns

- User patterns

- Converting a solid part to sheet metal

- Output to DXF and drawing

Note on Software Setup

This learning guide assumes a standard installation of the software using the default preferences during installation. Lectures and practices use the standard software templates and default options for the Content Libraries.

This course was developed against CATIA V5-6R2017, Service Pack 1.

Lead Contributor: Scott Hendren

Scott Hendren has been a trainer and curriculum developer in the PLM industry for over 20 years, with experience on multiple CAD systems, including Pro/ENGINEER, Creo Parametric, and CATIA. Trained in Instructional Design, Scott uses his skills to develop instructor-led and web-based training products.

Scott has held training and development positions with several high profile PLM companies, and has been with the Ascent team since 2013.

Scott holds a Bachelor of Mechanical Engineering Degree as well as a Bachelor of Science in Mathematics from Dalhousie University, Nova Scotia, Canada.

Scott Hendren has been the Lead Contributor for *CATIA: Sheet Metal Design* since 2013.

In this Guide

The following images highlight some of the features that can be found in this guide.

Practice Files

To download the practice files for this student guide, use the following steps:

1. Type the URL shown below into the address bar of your Internet browser. The URL must be typed **exactly as shown**. If you are using an ASCENT ebook, you can click on the link to download the file.

   Address bar

   `http://www.ASCENTed.com/getfile?id=xxxxxxx`

   File Edit View Favorites Tools Help

2. Press <Enter> to download the .ZIP file that contains the Practice Files.

3. Once the download is complete, unzip the file to a local folder. The unzipped file contains an .EXE file.

4. Double-click on the .EXE file and follow the instructions to automatically install the Practice Files on the C:\ drive of your computer.

   Do not change the location in which the Practice Files folder is installed. Doing so can cause errors when completing the practices in this student guide.

   http://www.ASCENTed.com/getfile?id=xxxxxxxx

   Stay Informed!
   Interested in receiving information about upcoming promotional offers, educational events, invitations to complimentary webcasts, and discounts? If so, please visit www.ASCENTed.com/updates/

   Help us improve our product by completing the following survey:
   www.ASCENTed.com/feedback
   You can also contact us at: feedback@ASCENTed.com

Link to the practice files

Practice Files

The Practice Files page tells you how to download and install the practice files that are provided with this guide.

Chapter 1

Getting Started

In this chapter you learn how to start the AutoCAD® software, become familiar with the basic layout of the AutoCAD screen, how to access commands, use your pointing device, and understand the AutoCAD Cartesian workspace. You also learn how to open an existing drawing, view a drawing by zooming and panning, and save your work in the AutoCAD software.

Learning Objectives in this Chapter

- Launch the AutoCAD software and complete a basic initial setup of the drawing environment.
- Identify the basic layout and features of AutoCAD interface including the Ribbon, Drawing Window, and Application Menu.
- Locate commands and launch them using the Ribbon, shortcut menus, Application Menu, and Quick Access Toolbar.
- Locate points in the AutoCAD Cartesian workspace.
- Open and close existing drawings and navigate to file locations.
- Move around a drawing using the mouse, the **Zoom** and **Pan** commands, and the Navigation Bar.
- Save drawings in various formats and set the automatic save options using the **Save** commands.

Learning Objectives for the chapter

Chapters

Each chapter begins with a brief introduction and a list of the chapter's Learning Objectives.

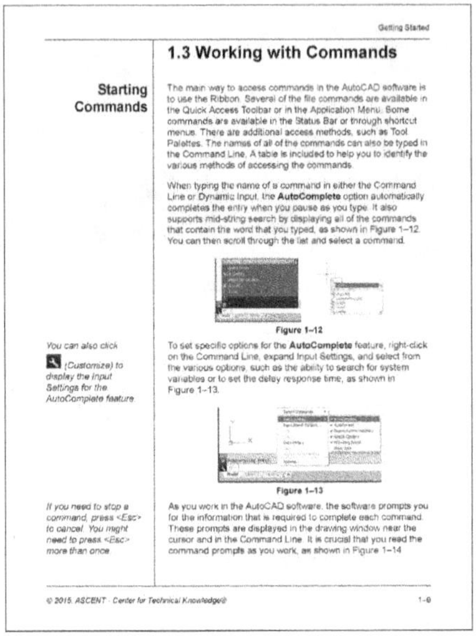

Getting Started

1.3 Working with Commands

Starting Commands

The main way to access commands in the AutoCAD software is to use the Ribbon. Several of the file commands are available in the Quick Access Toolbar or in the Application Menu. Some commands are available in the Status Bar or through shortcut menus. There are additional access methods, such as Tool Palettes. The names of all of the commands can also be typed in the Command Line. A table is included to help you to identify the various methods of accessing the commands.

When typing the name of a command in either the Command Line or Dynamic Input, the **AutoComplete** option automatically completes the entry when you pause as you type. It also supports mid-string search by displaying all of the commands that contain the word that you typed, as shown in Figure 1–12. You can then scroll through the list and select a command.

Figure 1–12

You can also click (Customize) to display the Input Settings for the AutoComplete feature.

To set specific options for the **AutoComplete** feature, right-click on the Command Line, expand Input Settings, and select from the various options, such as the ability to search for system variables or to set the delay response time, as shown in Figure 1–13.

Figure 1–13

If you need to stop a command, press <Esc> to cancel. You might need to press <Esc> more than once.

As you work in the AutoCAD software, the software prompts you for the information that is required to complete each command. These prompts are displayed in the drawing window near the cursor and in the Command Line. It is crucial that you read the command prompts as you work, as shown in Figure 1–14.

© 2015, ASCENT - Center for Technical Knowledge® 1-9

Side notes

Side notes are hints or additional information for the current topic.

Instructional Content

Each chapter is split into a series of sections of instructional content on specific topics. These lectures include the descriptions, step-by-step procedures, figures, hints, and information you need to achieve the chapter's Learning Objectives.

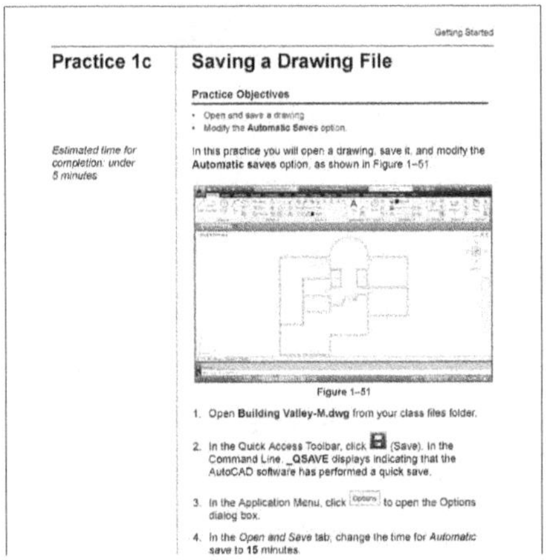

Getting Started

Practice 1c **Saving a Drawing File**

Practice Objectives

- Open and save a drawing.
- Modify the **Automatic Saves** option.

Estimated time for completion: under 5 minutes

In this practice you will open a drawing, save it, and modify the **Automatic saves** option, as shown in Figure 1–51.

Figure 1–51

1. Open **Building Valley-M.dwg** from your class files folder.
2. In the Quick Access Toolbar, click (Save). In the Command Line, **_QSAVE** displays indicating that the AutoCAD software has performed a quick save.
3. In the Application Menu, click Options to open the Options dialog box.
4. In the *Open and Save* tab, change the time for *Automatic save* to **15** minutes.

Practice Objectives

Practices

Practices enable you to use the software to perform a hands-on review of a topic.

Some practices require you to use prepared practice files, which can be downloaded from the link found on the Practice Files page.

Practice Files

To download the practice files for this guide, use the following steps:

1. Type the URL shown below into the address bar of your Internet browser. The URL must be typed **exactly as shown**. If you are using an ASCENT ebook, you can click on the link to download the file.

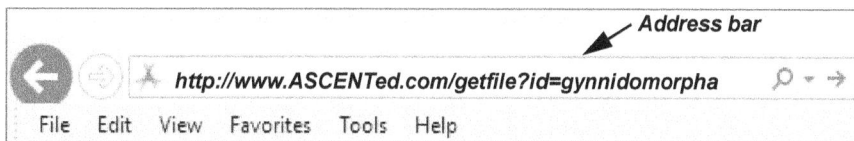

    Address bar

    http://www.ASCENTed.com/getfile?id=gynnidomorpha

    File   Edit   View   Favorites   Tools   Help

2. Press <Enter> to download the .ZIP file that contains the Practice Files.

3. Once the download is complete, unzip the file to a local folder. The unzipped file contains an .EXE file.

4. Double-click on the .EXE file and follow the instructions to automatically install the Practice Files on the C:\ drive of your computer.

    Do not change the location in which the Practice Files folder is installed. Doing so can cause errors when completing the practices.

http://www.ASCENTed.com/getfile?id=gynnidomorpha

Stay Informed!

Interested in receiving information about upcoming promotional offers, educational events, invitations to complimentary webcasts, and discounts? If so, please visit:

www.ASCENTed.com/updates/

Help us improve our product by completing the following survey:

www.ASCENTed.com/feedback

You can also contact us at: *feedback@ASCENTed.com*

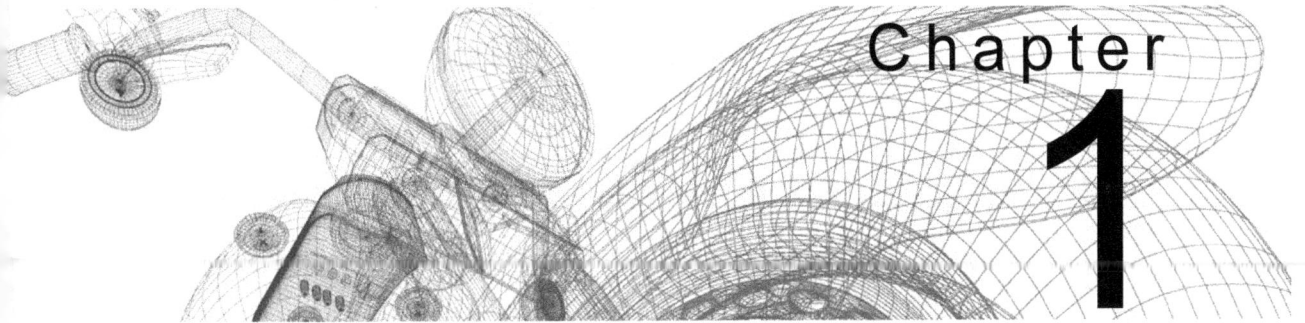

Introduction

The Sheet Metal Design workbench enables you to create features that are specific to the sheet metal modeling process. To design effective sheet metal parts in CATIA, you must become familiar with sheet metal tools and terminology.

Learning Objectives in this Chapter

- Review the Generative Sheetmetal Design Workbench.
- Review Sheet Metal Terminology.
- Understand the Sheet Metal design process.
- Review compatibility between Sheetmetal workbenches.

1.1 Generative Sheetmetal Design Workbench

To access this workbench, open a part model that was last saved in the Generative Sheetmetal Design workbench or select **Start>Mechanical Design>Generative Sheetmetal Design**, as

shown in Figure 1–1. The workbench symbol changes to [image].

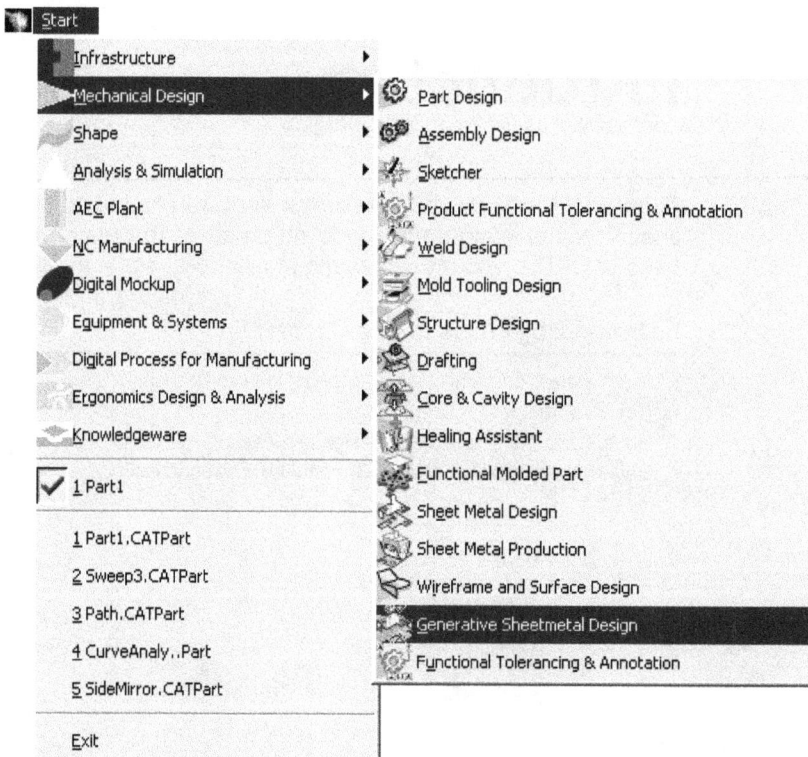

Figure 1–1

User Interface

Sheet metal parts in CATIA V5 have a *.CATPart file extension. The Generative Sheetmetal Design workbench is similar to the Part Design workbench, except that it includes a **Sheet Metal Parameter** icon and sheet metal-specific toolbars. The user interface is shown in Figure 1–2.

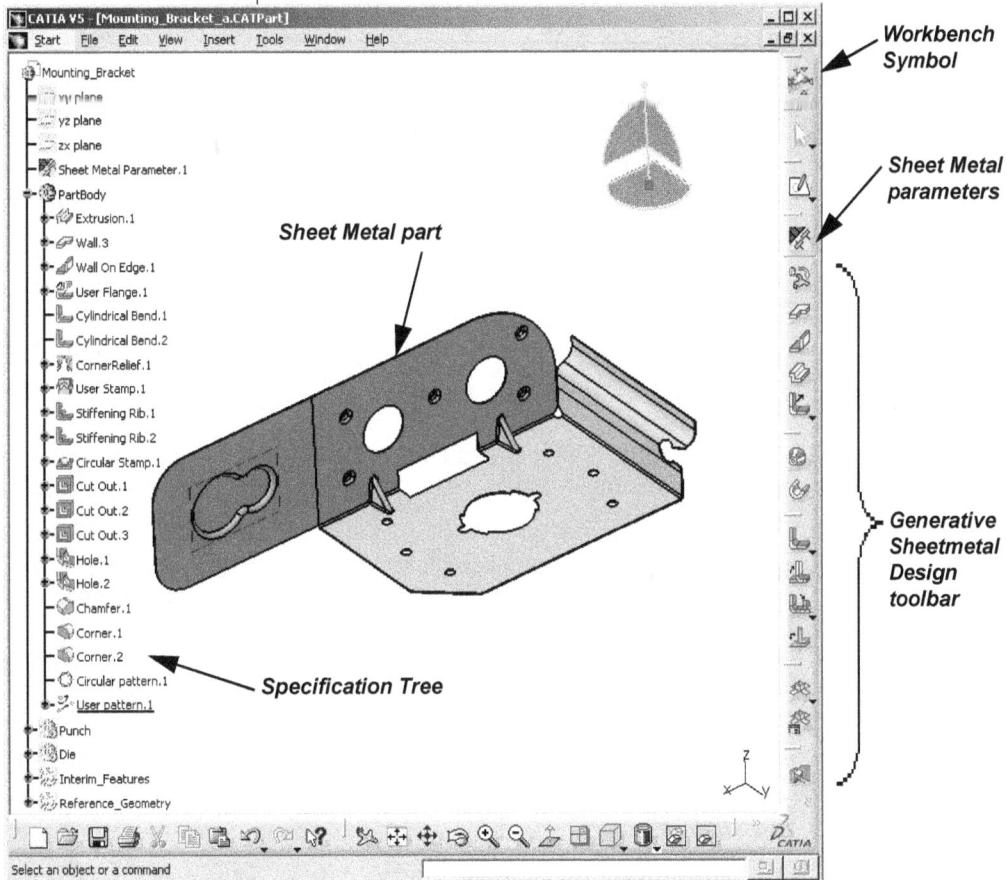

Figure 1–2

1.2 Sheet Metal Terminology

An example of the following terminology is shown in Figure 1–3.

Sheet Metal Parameters

Sheet metal parameters include a part's material thickness, default bend radius, and bend relief type.

Walls

Sheet metal parts consist of a first wall and multiple walls on edges.

Cutouts

Cutouts and holes remove material, similar to pockets and holes in the Part Design workbench.

Bends

Bend features in sheet metal parts join wall features with a circular radius.

Relief

Bend relief features can be defined to enable bends to be fabricated.

Sheet Metal Features

Various sheet metal class features can be produced such as a hem, flanged cutouts and holes, and various stamps as shown in Figure 1–3.

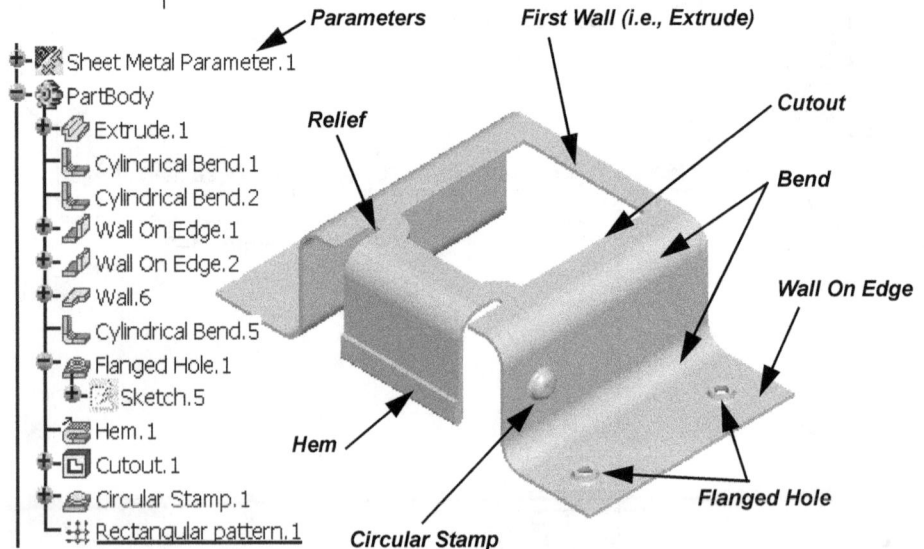

Figure 1–3

Flat View

An example of a flat view of a sheet metal part is shown in Figure 1–4. A flat view can be displayed in a drawing along with formed views of the part. This enables you to display the 3D shape of the model, while also displaying critical manufacturing dimensions on the flat view.

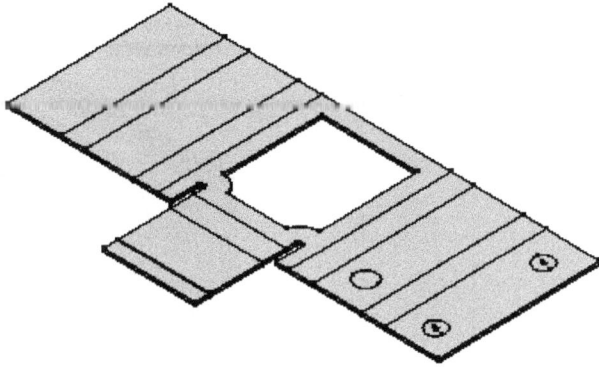

Figure 1–4

Sheet metal parts can be folded and unfolded as required throughout the design of the part. For example, a part can be unfolded to provide a planar face for sketching additional features, such as the cutout shown in Figure 1–5. When the part is folded, the resulting cutout takes the shape of the formed part.

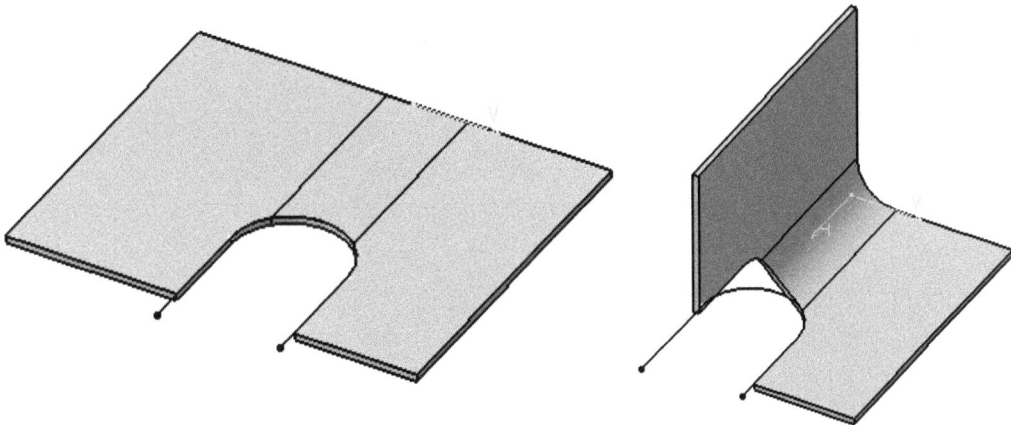

Figure 1–5

Just as feature creation order impacts solid model integrity in the Part Design workbench, toggling between the flattened and 3D views in the Generative Sheet Metal Design workbench affects the resulting geometry. The model view should be actively adjusted to ensure that your design intent is fulfilled.

For example, a cutout feature created in the unfolded view results in different geometry than a cutout created in folded view, as shown in Figure 1–6. Conversely, use of the folded view can assist in the creation of repeated features, such as a cutout that extends through multiple walls.

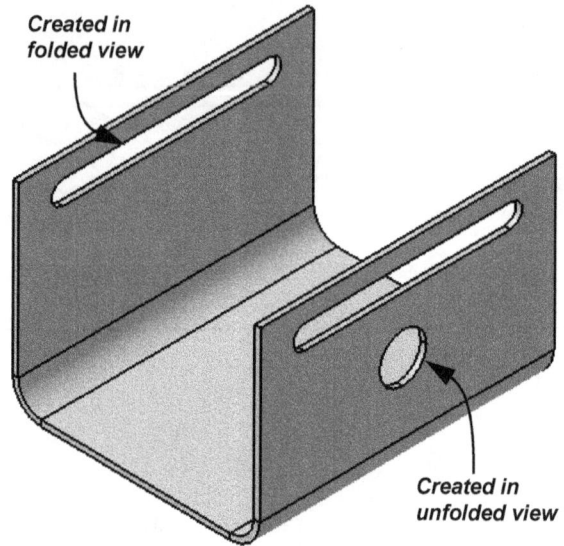

Created in folded view

Created in unfolded view

Figure 1–6

1.3 Sheet Metal Process

The process of creating a sheet metal model is very similar to the process of creating a solid part. Individual features are created in sequence and reference one another resulting in parent-child relationships.

General Steps

Use the following general steps as a guideline when creating a sheet metal part:

1. Assign the material parameters.
2. Create the first wall.
3. Create the secondary walls and bends.
4. Create the sheet metal features (cutout, stamp, etc.).
5. Create the deliverables (drawings).

Step 1 - Assign the material parameters.

When the Sheet Metal Design workbench is first activated, only the **Sheet Metal Parameter** and **Recognize** icons are available, as shown in Figure 1–7. No features can be created until the sheet metal parameters are defined. Sheet metal parameters define the default bend radius, bend thickness, bend relief, and bend allowance. Once these parameters have been defined, feature creation can begin.

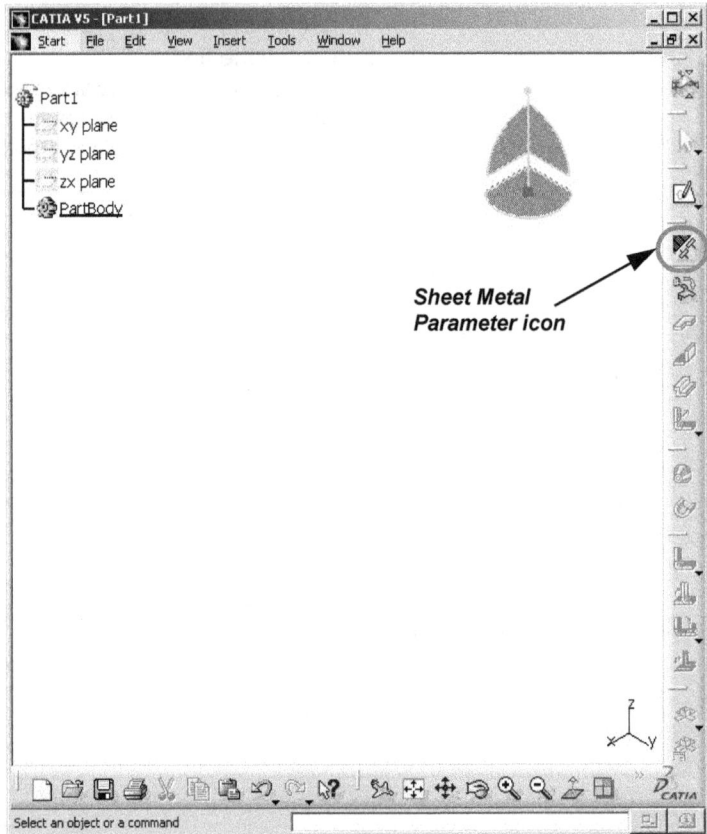

Sheet Metal Parameter icon

Figure 1–7

Step 2 - Create the first wall.

The first feature created in any sheet metal model is called the first wall, or primary wall. It is always created from a sketched profile and can be created using the Profile, Extrude, Hopper, or Rolled Wall operations.

The first wall becomes the fixed wall during an unfolding operation and therefore determines the orientation of the flattened part. If the first wall includes a bend, the first sketched edge defines the wall that is fixed during flattening. First walls can be as simple as a singular flat wall or made more complex to include several walls. Figure 1–8 shows a first wall that was created using the Profile Wall operation.

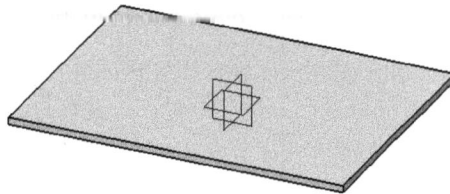

Figure 1–8

Step 3 - Create the secondary walls and bends.

Once the first wall has been created, additional walls and bends can be added. Additional walls can be created using the Profile, Extrude, and Wall on Edge operations. As well, flanges can be constructed using the Basic Flange, Hem, Tear Drop, and User Flange operations.

Figure 1–9 shows the sheet metal model started in the last step, with two walls and a tear drop flange added.

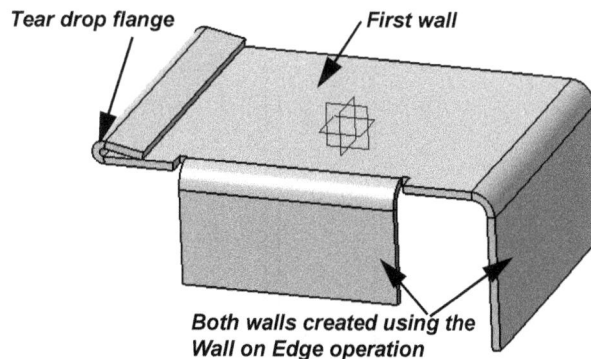

Tear drop flange   First wall

Both walls created using the
Wall on Edge operation

Figure 1–9

Step 4 - Create the sheet metal features (cutout, stamp, etc.).

Once the walls of the sheet metal part are created, additional features are created to complete the model. Sheet metal features consist of Stamps, Corners, Chamfers, Cutouts, and Holes. Figure 1–10 continues the example from the previous steps. Surface Stamps, Cutouts, Corners, and Chamfers have been added to the model.

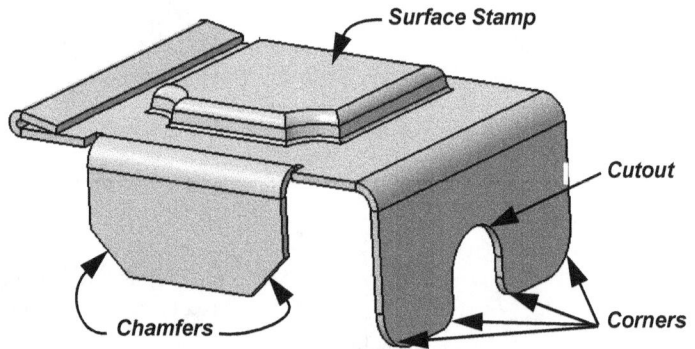

Figure 1–10

Step 5 - Create the deliverables (drawings).

Once the sheet metal model is completed, drawings and DXF files can be created to output the file for manufacture. Unfolded views can be created in a drawing to display the unfolded model, as shown in Figure 1–11.

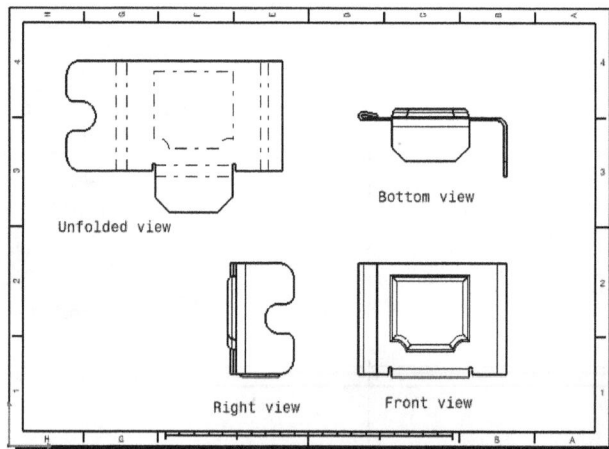

Figure 1–11

1.4 Workbench Compatibility

Sheet Metal Design

There are currently two sheet metal design workbenches available: Sheet Metal Design (SMD) and Generative Sheet Motal Design (GSMD). Since CATIA V5R14, sheet metal models can no longer be created in the SMD workbench. An error box opens when a primary wall is initialized, as shown in Figure 1–12.

This course focuses on the use of the Generative Sheet Metal Design workbench.

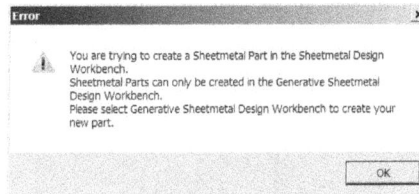

Figure 1–12

The SMD workbench is included in post-R14 releases as a legacy product; secondary features, such as walls and bends, can be added to original SMD models using the SMD workbench.

Generative Sheet Metal Design

The GSMD workbench is an upgraded version of the SMD workbench. It contains several new features and improved algorithms to create sheet metal parts. If you are unsure whether to use the GSMD or SMD workbench, please consult your company's CAD Administrator.

Part Design

No additional features can be created in the GSMD workbench when a Part Design workbench feature is applied to a sheet metal model. For example, if a Part Design feature is created on a sheet metal part, the error message shown in Figure 1–13 opens when the next sheet metal feature is created.

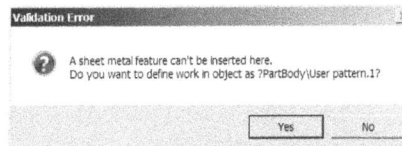

Figure 1–13

To resolve this, the Part Design feature should be removed. Solid models created in the Part Design workbench can be converted into a sheet metal part using the Recognize function. All features applied to sheet metal models should be created in the GSMD workbench to preserve model compatibility.

Chapter 2

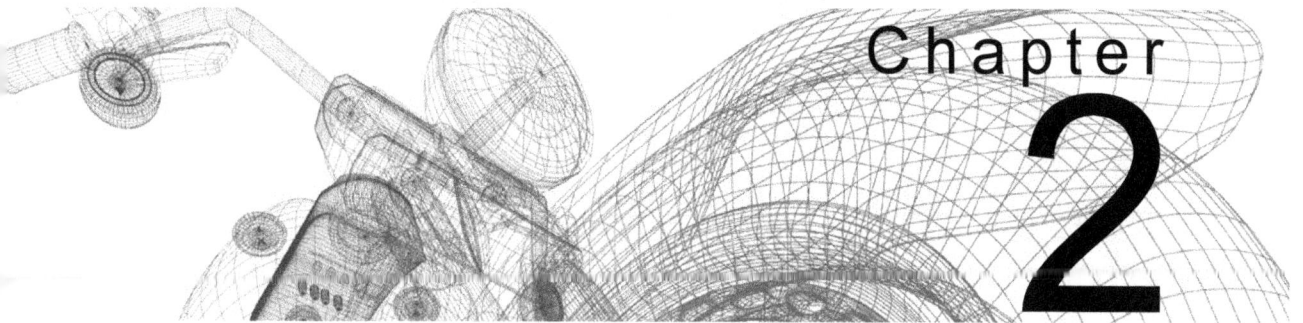

Primary Walls

The Generative Sheetmetal Design workbench contains two types of walls: the first wall (or primary wall), and secondary walls. The first wall is the first feature to be created in the sheet metal model and forms the foundation on which all other wall features are built.

Learning Objectives in this Chapter

- Understand the Sheet Metal Parameters
- Create the first wall in a model.
- Define additional walls.
- Create a Hopper.

2.1 Sheet Metal Parameters

Sheet metal parameters are the default settings for the sheet metal model. They include wall thickness, default bend radius, default bend relief, and bend allowance. When a sheet metal model is first created, all icons in the Generative Sheetmetal Design toolbar are grayed out, with exception of the **Sheet Metal Parameters** and **Recognize** icons, as shown in Figure 2–1. No features can be created until the sheet metal parameters are defined.

Figure 2–1

General Steps

Use the following general steps to set the sheet metal parameters:

1. Access the Sheet Metal Parameters dialog box.
2. Define the parameters.
3. Apply the parameters to the model.
4. Modify the parameters, if required.

Step 1 - Access the Sheet Metal Parameters dialog box.

Click  (Sheet Metal Parameters) in the Walls toolbar. The Sheet Metal Parameters dialog box opens as shown in Figure 2–2.

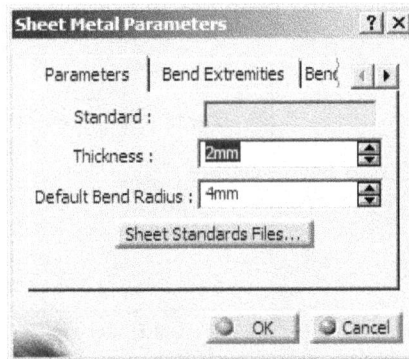

Figure 2–2

The dialog box contains the following tabs:

- *Parameters*: Define wall thickness and bend radius values.

- *Bend Extremities*: Define the type bend relief.

- *Bend Allowance*: Define the K-factor value.

Step 2 - Define the parameters.

Parameters Tab

Use the *Parameters* tab to enter values for **Material Thickness**, and **Default Bend Radius**, as shown in Figure 2–3.

Click **Sheet Standards Files** to browse to a design table (*.xls) to read in a company- or industry-standard bend table.

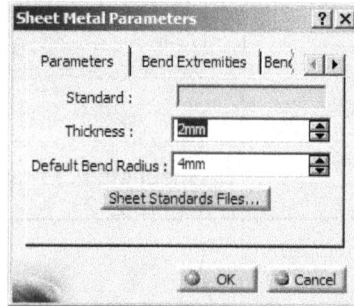

Figure 2–3

The fields in the *Parameters* tab are described as follows:

Parameter	Description
Thickness	The material thickness of the model. All features in the model are constructed using this thickness and it cannot be overridden by an individual feature.
Default Bend Radius	The default bend radius is the internal radius used during bend creation. This value can be overridden by an individual feature.

Bend Extremities Tab

Use the *Bend Extremities* tab to define the bend relief, as shown in Figure 2–4.

Figure 2–4

Use the **Text** or **Graphic** menu to select the type of relief. The bend relief types are described as follows:

Bend Relief	Image	Description
Square relief		Square relief is defined by specifying the height (L1) and width (L2) of the square notch.
Round relief		Round relief is defined by specifying the height (L1) and diameter (L2) of the rounded notch.
Linear	*Folded view* *Unfolded view*	Linear relief connects the two walls using a linear edge in the unfolded view. This type of relief does not have modifiable dimensions and displays deformed in the folded view.
Tangent	*Folded view* *Unfolded view*	Tangent relief uses a profile that is tangent to each wall edge at the bending line. This type of relief does not have modifiable dimensions and displays deformed in the folded view.
Maximum		Maximum relief extends the bend surface to the maximum width of the two walls. This type of relief does not have modifiable dimensions.
Closed	*Folded view* *Unfolded view*	Closed relief enables you to create a relief without overlapping by extending the wall to create a closed corner on the part. Closed relief should not be set as a default relief as not all design conditions enable it to be successfully created. However, closed relief can be set for a specific wall or bend feature.

| Flat joint | 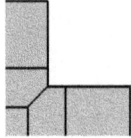 | Flat joint relief extends the wall edges so that they intersect to define the extent of the bend. |

Depending on the type of relief selected, the value fields might require additional input. A preview of how the dimensions are applied is shown on the left side of the Sheet Metal Parameters dialog box, as shown in Figure 2–5.

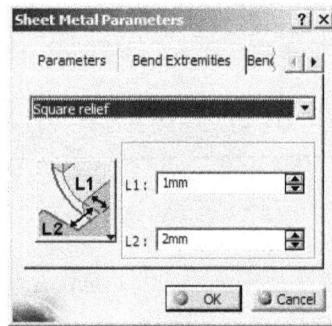

Figure 2–5

An example of a bend with square relief applied is shown in Figure 2–6.

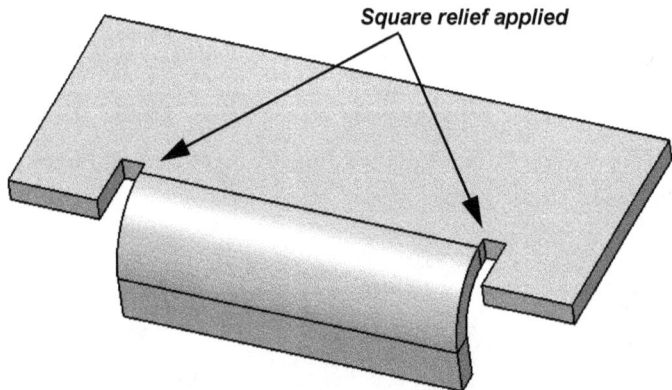

Figure 2–6

Bend Allowance Tab

When a sheet metal part is deformed, stretching and compression occur in the areas where the bends are located. CATIA accounts for this deformation by calculating the developed length or bend allowance. The calculation for bend allowance locates the neutral bend line (where neither stretching nor compression occurs) and measures its length for a given bend as shown in Figure 2–7. Mathematically, this equation considers material thickness, bend radius, bend angle, and other material properties.

The default formula used by CATIA to calculate bend allowance is:

$$W = \alpha * (R + k * T)$$

where:

 W is the bend allowance

 α is the inner bend angle in Radians

 R is the inner bend radius

 T is the sheet metal thickness

 k is the K Factor

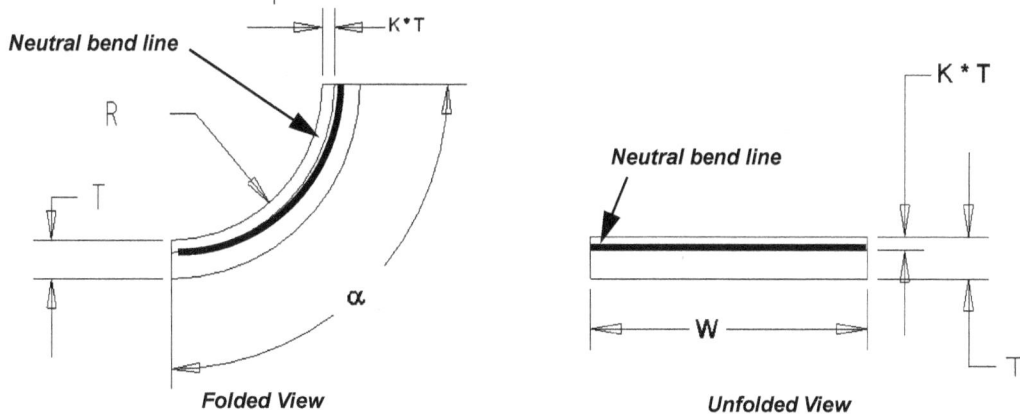

Folded View   Unfolded View

Figure 2–7

The K Factor is a ratio of the distance from the neutral bend line to the inside of the bend and the total thickness of the material. The *Bend Allowance* tab displays the system defined K Factor, as shown in Figure 2–8.

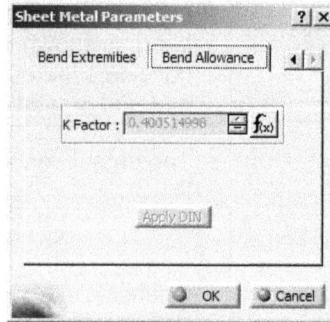

Figure 2–8

You can override the system defined K Factor by right-clicking on the *K Factor* field and selecting **Formula>Deactivate** as shown in Figure 2–9. You can edit the *K Factor* field once the formula has been deactivated.

*You can reactivate the system defined K Factor by right-clicking on the K Factor field and selecting **Formula> Activate**, or by clicking **Apply DIN**.*

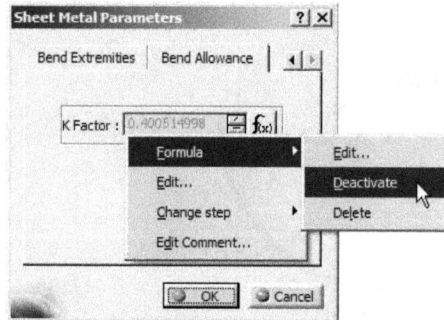

Figure 2–9

*To toggle on the parameters in the tree, select **Tools>Options> Infrastructure>Part Infrastructure>Display** and enable **Parameters** in the Display in Specification Tree area.*

Step 3 - Apply the parameters to the model.

Once all parameters have been entered, click **OK** to close the dialog box. All icons in the Generative Sheetmetal Design toolbar are now available, as shown in Figure 2–10.

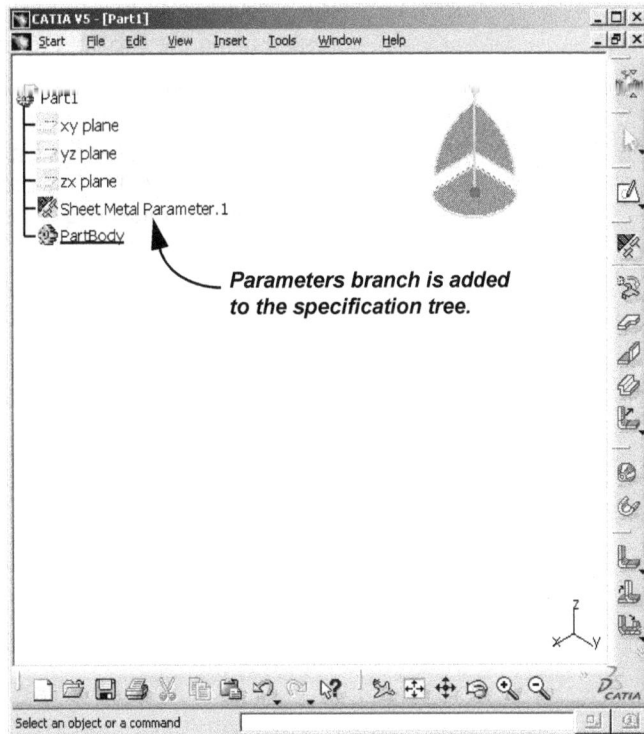

Figure 2–10

Step 4 - Modify the parameters, if required.

The sheet metal parameters can be changed at any time. To modify them, double-click on the **Sheet Metal Parameters** icon in the specification tree, as shown in Figure 2–10, or click

(Sheet Metal Parameters) in the toolbar.

Once the parameters have been modified, click **OK** to close the Sheet Metal Parameters dialog box. The model automatically updates to reflect the changes.

2.2 First Wall

Once sheet metal parameters have been defined, the first wall can be created. The first wall is similar to the base feature in a solid part. Both the base feature of a solid model and the first wall of a sheet metal model contain the basic shape of the object. The first wall must have a sketched profile and can be created using the Profile, Extruded, Hopper, and Rolled operations.

Profile Wall

A profile wall is created from a closed loop sketch, as shown at the top of Figure 2–11. This profile is then thickened to the default material thickness set in the sheet metal parameters, as shown on the bottom of Figure 2–11.

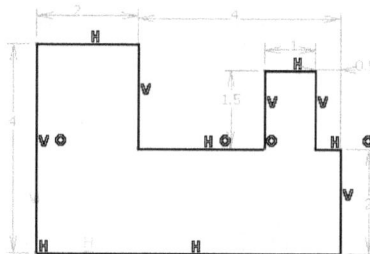

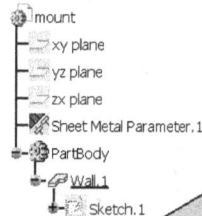

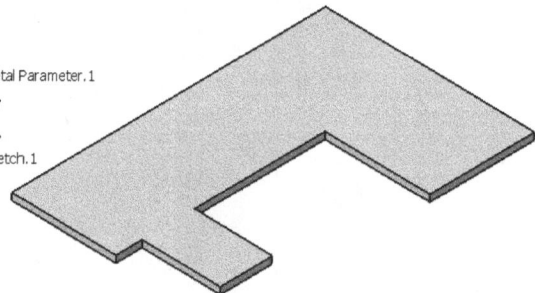

Figure 2–11

Extruded Wall

Extruded walls are created from open loop sketches. The profile is then thickened to the default material thickness and extruded, as shown in Figure 2–12. Extrusion options for an extruded wall are similar to those used to create a pad feature in the Part workbench. When switched to the unfolded view, an extruded wall unfolds onto the support plane of the first sketched element (effectively the first wall).

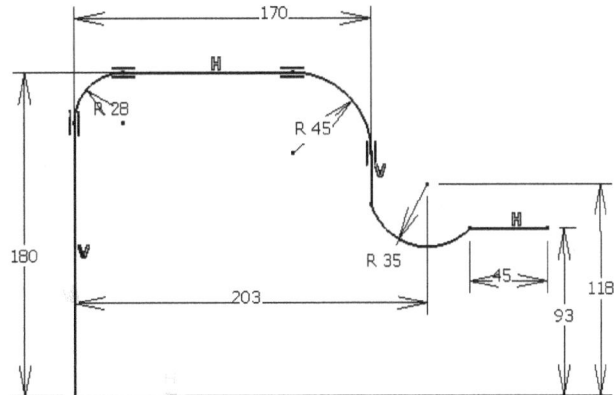

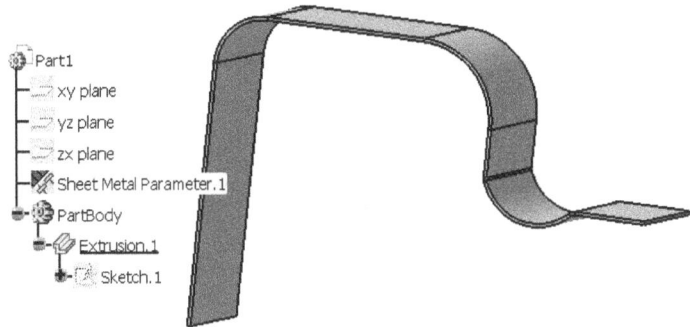

Figure 2–12

Rolled Wall

A rolled wall is created by extruding an open or closed circular profile as shown in Figure 2–13. Additional wall features can be added to the planar edges of a rolled wall; curved edges can only be combined with flange and cutout features.

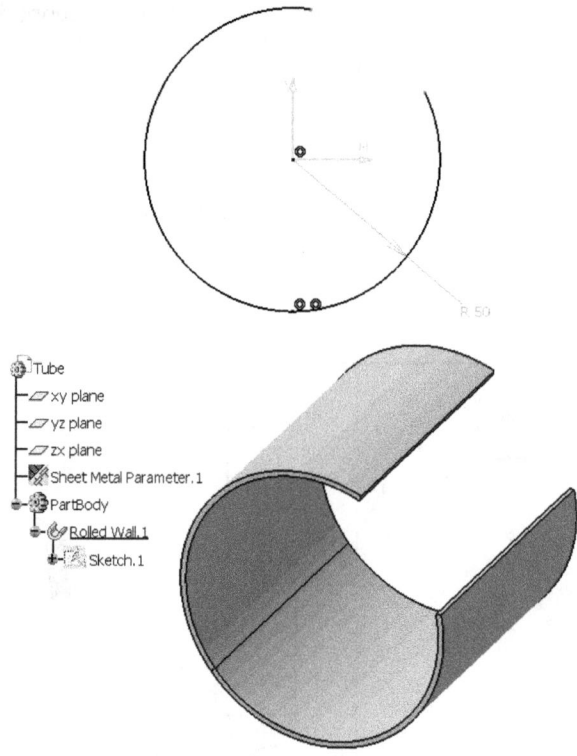

Figure 2–13

2.3 Defining Walls

General Steps

Use the following general steps to define the first sheet metal wall:

1. Create a sketch.
2. Select a wall type.
3. Define the material side.
4. Complete the feature.

Step 1 - Create a sketch.

Use one of the default reference planes as the support for the profile. Depending on the type of wall to be created, the sketch can be an open or closed loop.

Step 2 - Select a wall type.

Profile

With the closed loop sketch highlighted, click [icon] (Wall). The Wall Definition box opens as shown in Figure 2–14.

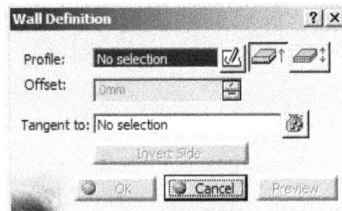

Figure 2–14

You can offset the wall from the sketch by typing in the required value in the *Offset* field.

The following icons, located beside the profile section, enable you to position the profile to the bottom or middle of the wall.

Icon	Image	Description
(Sketch at extreme position)		Places the sketch at the bottom of the wall.
(Sketch at middle position)		Places the sketch at the middle of the wall.

Extrude

Depth options for an extruded wall are similar to the pad feature in the Part Design workbench.

With the open loop sketch highlighted, click (Extrusion). The Extrusion Definition dialog box opens as shown in Figure 2–15.

These options are the same as the ones in the Wall feature.

Figure 2–15

To extrude in two directions, enter a different depth value in the *Limit 2 dimension* section or select the **Mirrored Extent** option to use the same depth as the **Limit 1 dimension**.

In *Fixed geometry* section, you can specify the face that remains fixed when the model is unfolded.

You can also explode the extrusion feature into several features by enabling the **Exploded mode** option as shown in Figure 2–16.

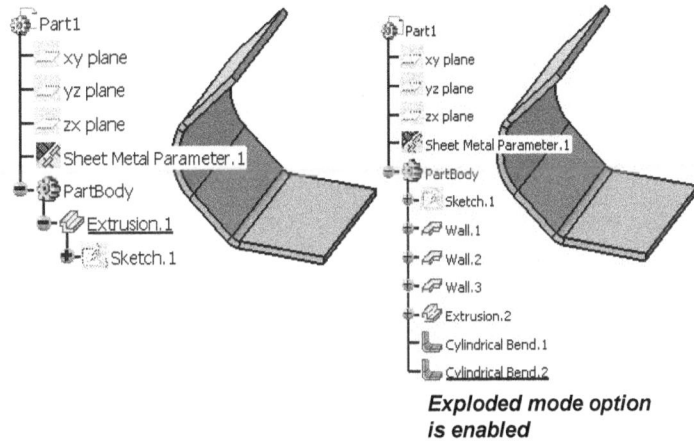

Exploded mode option
is enabled

Figure 2–16

Rolled

With the closed or open circular sketched profile highlighted,

click ⌑ (Rolled Wall). The RolledWall Definition dialog box opens, as shown in Figure 2–17.

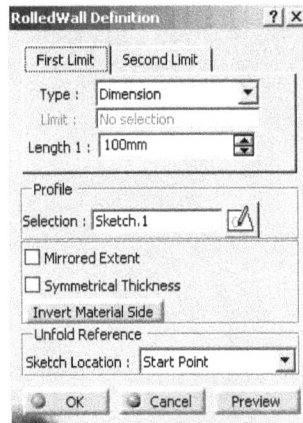

Figure 2–17

For closed sketches, you cannot control where the wall is split for unfolding.

The **Unfold reference** option enables you to select the location in the sketch from which the feature is unfolded. The reference can be the start point, end point, or middle point of the sketch.

Step 3 - Define the material side.

Material thickness for any feature is defined in the Sheet Metal Parameters dialog box.

For each type of wall, you can select the side of the profile to which to add the material thickness. The direction of the arrow indicates which side material is added to, as shown in Figure 2–18. To change the side to which material is added, click **Invert Material Side**.

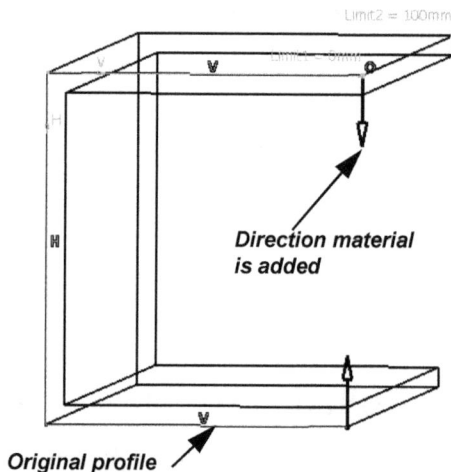

Figure 2–18

Rolled wall enable you to add material thickness equally to both sides of the sketched profile using the **Symmetrical Thickness** option, as shown in Figure 2–19.

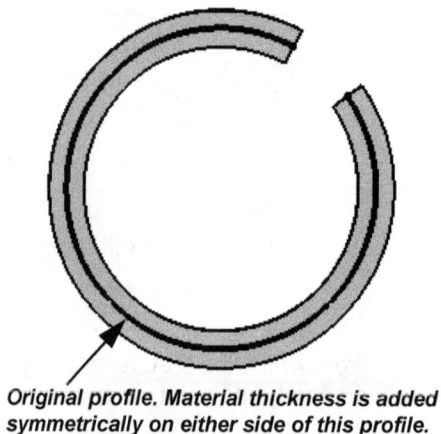

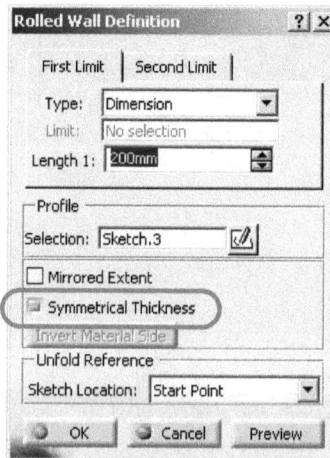

Figure 2–19

Step 4 - Complete the feature.

Click **OK** to complete the feature. Additional secondary walls, flanges, and sheet metal features can now be added to the first wall.

2.4 Creating a Hopper

A hopper feature is used when directive or converging sheet metal geometry is required. There are two modes of hopper creation: Surfacic and Canonic.

A surfacic hopper wraps sheet metal around an existing surface, whereas a canonic hopper fills in the space between two sketched profiles. At least two open or closed sketches of similar or corresponding geometry are required for both modes of hopper creation.

An instance of the two modes of hopper creation is shown in Figure 2–20.

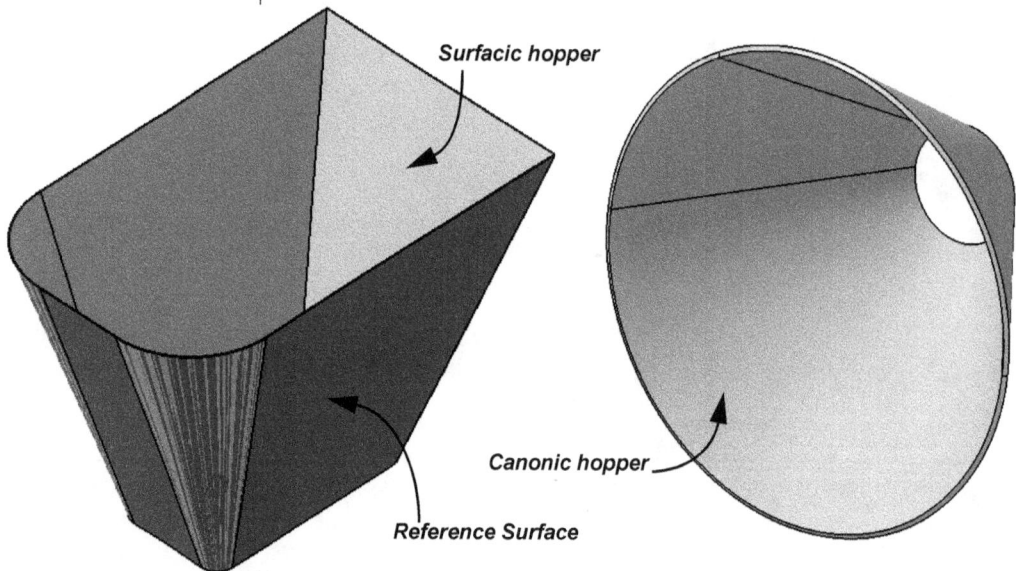

Surfacic hopper

Canonic hopper

Reference Surface

Figure 2–20

The advantage of the Surfacic Hopper mode is its ability to create advanced shapes. Complex hopper geometry can be created and controlled effectively using a multi-sections surface.

General Steps

Use the following general steps to define surfacic and canonic hoppers:

1. Prepare the reference geometry.
2. Initialize the hopper feature creation.
3. Provide the required inputs.
4. Complete the feature.

The profile sketches of a surfacic hopper can lie on non-parallel planes.

Step 1 - Prepare the reference geometry.

If the part does not contain any existing geometry on which to build the hopper, create two profile sketches. The sketches can consist of an open or closed loop. Ensure that the shape and number of vertices in the sketches correspond.

Step 2 - Initialize the hopper feature creation.

Click ![icon] (Hopper). The Hopper definition dialog box opens as shown in Figure 2–21. Select the type of hopper that you want to create (surfacic or canonic) in the menu at the top of the dialog box.

Figure 2–21

Step 3 - Provide the required inputs.

Surfacic Hopper

With Surfacic Hopper selected in the menu, the dialog box opens, as shown in Figure 2–22. If the support surface already exists, select in the *Selection* field and select the surface.

Figure 2–22

To create a new surface, right-click on the *Surface Selection* field and select **Create Multi-sections Surface**. The Multi-Sectons Surface Definition dialog box opens, enabling you to create the multi-sections surface on the fly. The resultant multi-sections surface is placed below the main hopper feature node in the specification tree.

A guide curve created during the multi-sections surface definition can also be used as the reference wire.

To designate the edge which remains fixed while unfolding, a reference wire must be specified. The reference wire is a line that lies on the multi-sections surface. Select an existing line or create a new one by right-clicking on the *Reference wire* field and selecting **Create Line**. Select two corresponding vertices in the defining profile sketches to create a point-to-point type line.

The invariant point lies on both the reference wire and multi-sections surface. Select in the *Invariant point* field and select one of the vertices used to create the reference wire. If the reference wire was created using an intersection or projection and no reference point is available, right-click on the *Invariant point* field and select **Create Point**. Create an On curve type invariant point on the reference wire.

The tear wire defines the opening line of the hopper. Although a default tear wire is selected during hopper creation, this reference is susceptible to failure during downstream modification. The tear wire should be explicitly defined during hopper creation to maintain model integrity.

Analyzing deformation of a non-ruled surface

The terms ruled surface and non-ruled surface are not unique to CATIA. These terms universally define the type of surface geometry.

A ruled surface has curvature in one direction, as shown in Figure 2–23.

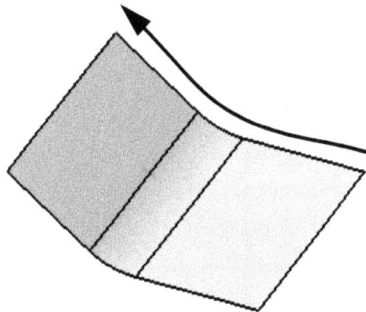

Figure 2–23

A non-ruled surface has curvature in two directions, as shown in Figure 2–24.

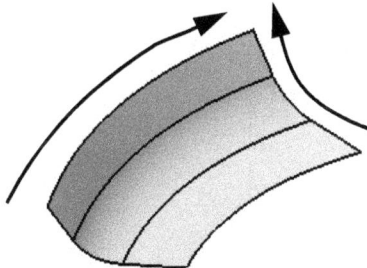

Figure 2–24

Sheet metal features defined by non-ruled surfaces typically experience more material deformation than ruled surfaces.

If an existing non-ruled surface is selected, you have the ability to analyze the deformation of the sheet metal.

First select the non-ruled surface as shown in Figure 2–25 and then click **Preview**.

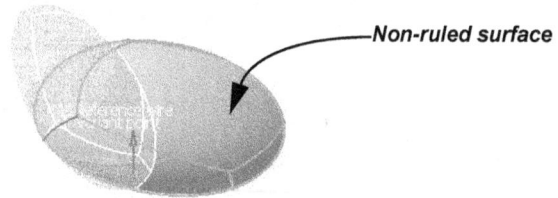

Non-ruled surface

Figure 2–25

The Hopper dialog box updates to display **Display distortions**. To analyze the deformation, click the button. A Flattened Surface Length Distortion dialog box opens displaying the distortions, as shown in Figure 2–26.

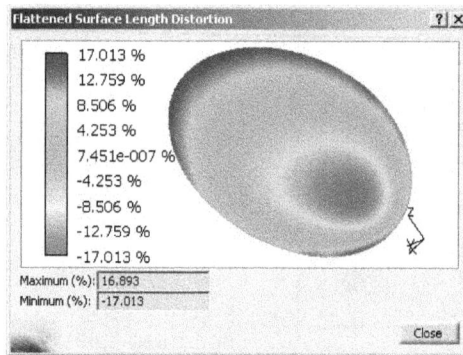

Figure 2–26

Canonic Hopper

With **Canonic Hopper** selected in the menu, the Hopper dialog box opens as shown in Figure 2–27.

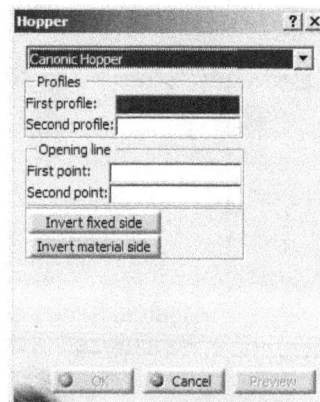

Figure 2–27

Select the two hopper profile sketches as the First and Second Profiles. To define the opening line, select two corresponding points lying on the defining profile sketches. The points cannot be created contextually or in the profile sketches. A point-to-point line is created automatically.

Step 4   Complete the feature.

Click **OK** to complete the feature. A hopper feature can only be created as a primary wall; additional hopper features must be created in new part bodies.

Practice 2a | Creating a First Wall

Practice Objectives

- Define Sheet Metal Parameters.
- Create an extruded first wall.

In this practice, you will create a sheet metal model, set up sheet metal parameters, and create a first wall. At the end of this practice, the model will display as shown in Figure 2–28.

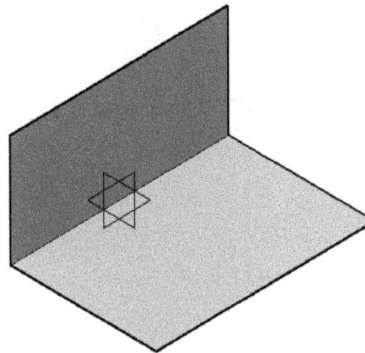

Figure 2–28

This extruded profile will be built on in later practices to create the mounting bracket as shown in Figure 2–29.

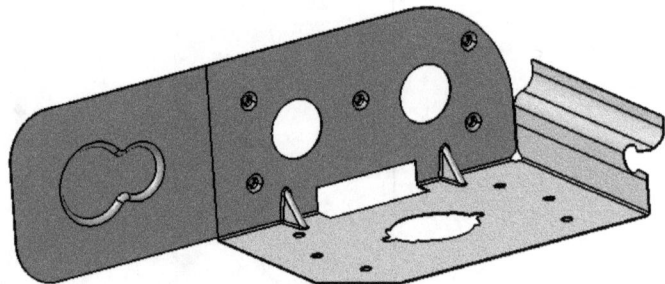

Figure 2–29

Task 1 - Enter the Generative Sheet Metal Design workbench.

1. Select **Start>Mechanical Design>Generative Sheetmetal Design**.

2. Ensure that the **Enable hybrid design** option is cleared.

3. Enter **Mounting_Bracket** in the *Enter part name* field, as shown in Figure 2–30.

Figure 2–30

4. Click **OK**.

Task 2 - Define sheet metal parameters.

In this task, you will define the sheet metal parameters. All sheet metal operations are unavailable until the parameters have been defined.

1. Click (Sheet Metal Parameters).

2. Select the *Parameters* tab and enter **1mm** in the *Thickness* field and **2mm** in the *Default Bend Radius* field.

3. Select the *Bend Extremities* tab and make the following selections, as shown in Figure 2–31:

   • Select **Square Relief** from the drop-down list.
   • *L1:* **2mm**
   • *L2:* **2mm**

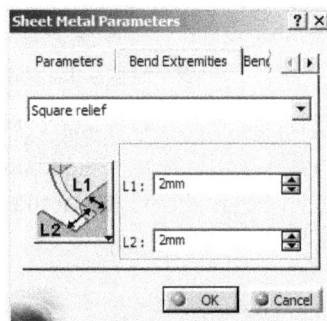

Figure 2–31

4. Click **OK** to close the Sheet Metal Parameters dialog box. The sheet metal operations are now available.

Task 3 - Create the profile for the wall.

In this task, you will create the profile of the first wall in the Sketcher workbench.

1. Highlight the YZ plane and click (Sketch).

2. Create the sketch shown in Figure 2–32. Create the Horizontal line first.

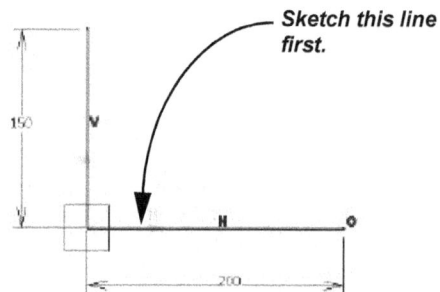

Figure 2–32

3. Click (Exit Workbench) to return to the Generative Sheetmetal Design workbench.

Task 4 - Create an extruded wall.

The sketched profile created in the previous task is extruded to become the First wall of the model in this task.

1. Highlight the sketch and click (Extrusion).

2. Make the following selection as shown in Figure 2–33:

  • *Limit 1 dimension:* **150mm**
  • Select **Mirrored extent**.
  • Clear the **Automatic bend** option.

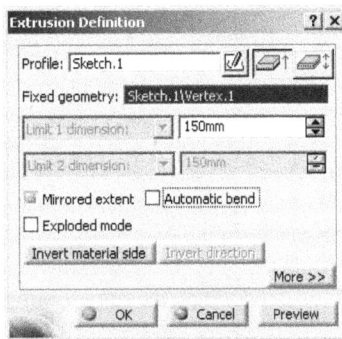

Figure 2–33

3. Verify that the material direction is inward as shown in Figure 2–34. To reverse the material direction, click **Invert material side** or click the material direction arrow.

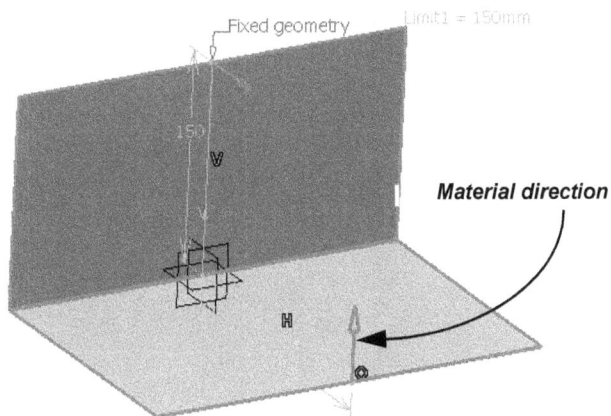

Figure 2–34

4. Click **OK**. The extruded profile displays as shown in Figure 2–35.

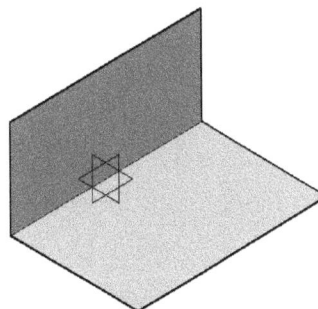

Figure 2–35

Task 5 - Save and close the file.

1. Click (Save).

2. Save the **Mounting_Bracket** model in the *SheetMetal Design practice Files* directory.

3. Close the file.

Practice 2b | Bracket

Practice Objectives

- Define Sheet Metal Parameters.
- Create a profile first wall.

In this practice, you will create a new sheet metal model, set up the sheet metal parameters, and create a first wall. At the end of this practice, the model will display as shown in Figure 2–36.

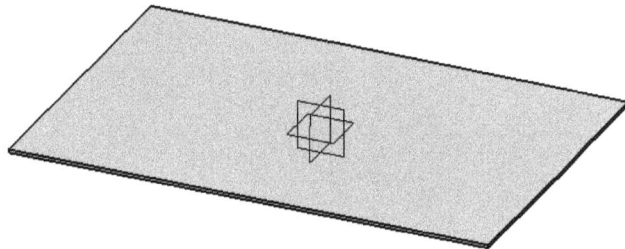

Figure 2–36

This model will be built on in later practices to create a bracket that is used to hold electronics equipment, as shown in Figure 2–37.

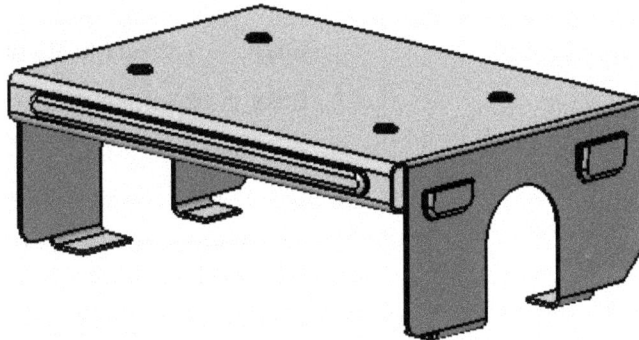

Figure 2–37

Task 1 - Open a new part model.

1. Select **Start>Mechanical Design>Generative Sheetmetal Design**.

2. Ensure that the **Enable hybrid design** option is cleared.

3. Name the part **Mount**, as shown in Figure 2–38.

Figure 2–38

4. Click **OK**.

Task 2 - Define sheet metal parameters.

1. Click  (Sheet Metal Parameters).

2. Enter the following parameters:

   • *Thickness:* **2mm**
   • *Default Bend Radius:* **4mm**

3. Select the *Bend Extremities* tab and make the following selections:

   • Select **Round Relief** from the drop-down list.
   • *L1:* **1mm**
   • *L2:* **2mm**

4. Click **OK** to close the Sheet Metal Parameters dialog box. The sheet metal operations are now available.

Task 3 - Create the profile for the first wall.

1. Select the XY plane and click ▱ (Sketch).

2. Create the sketch as shown in Figure 2–39.

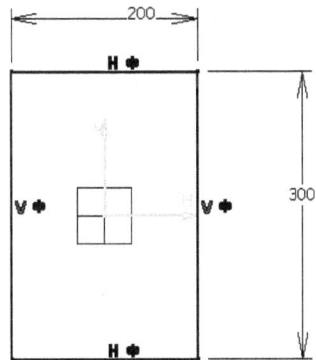

Figure 2–39

3. Click 🗁 (Exit Workbench) to return to the Generative Sheetmetal Design workbench.

Task 4 - Create a profile wall.

In this task, the sketched profile created in the previous task will be extruded to become the First wall of the model.

1. Highlight the sketch and click ▱ (Wall).

2. Create the wall so that the thickness is added upward, as shown in Figure 2–40.

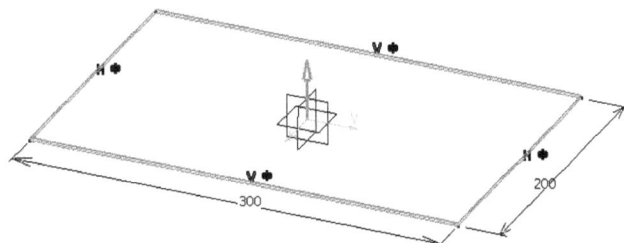

Figure 2–40

3. Click **OK** to complete the wall feature, as shown in Figure 2–41.

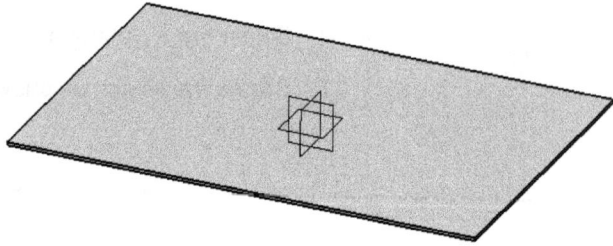

Figure 2–41

Task 5 - Save and close the file.

1. Click ▣ (Save).

2. Close the file.

Practice 2c | Creating a Hopper

Practice Objectives

- Create a surfacic hopper.
- Create a canonic hopper.

In this practice, you will create a hopper feature using the two hopper types, surfacic and canonic. At the end of this practice, you will have created the models shown in Figure 2–42.

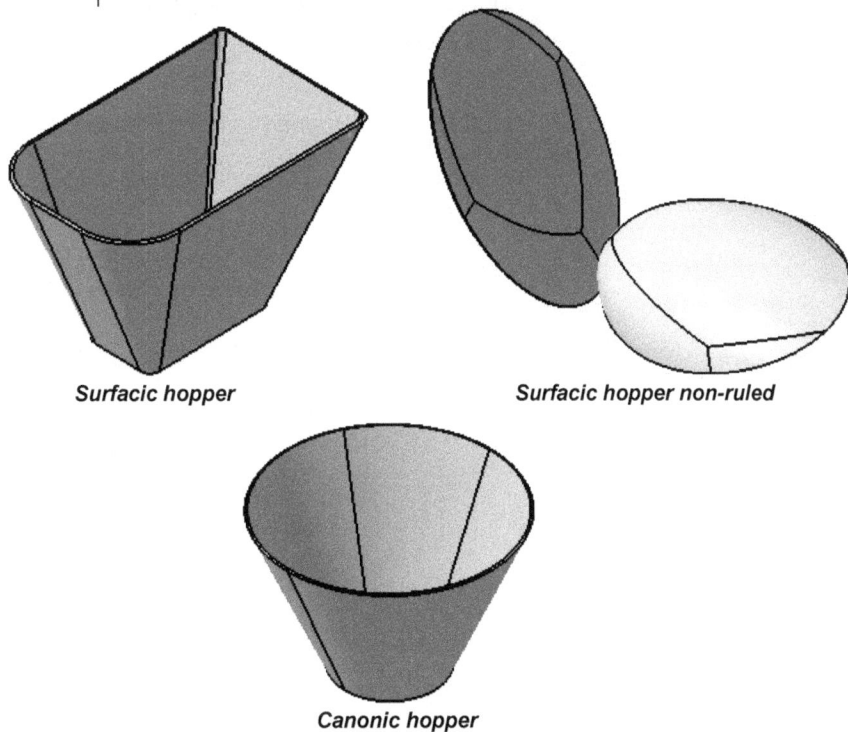

Surfacic hopper

Surfacic hopper non-ruled

Canonic hopper

Figure 2–42

Task 1 - Open a part file.

1. Open **HopperSurfacic.CATPart**. The model consists of two, parallel sketches: **BaseProfile** and **TopProfile**.

Task 2 - Create a surfacic hopper feature.

In this task, you will create the multi-sections surface that the hopper will be wrapped around on the fly. All reference geometry has been provided. You will then define the reference and tear wires, and the invariant point, to complete the sheet metal hopper feature.

1. Click (Hopper) to open the Hopper Definition dialog box.

2. Verify that the **Surfacic Hopper** option is selected as shown in Figure 2–43.

3. Right-click on the *Surface Selection* field and select **Create Multi-sections Surface**, as shown in Figure 2–43.

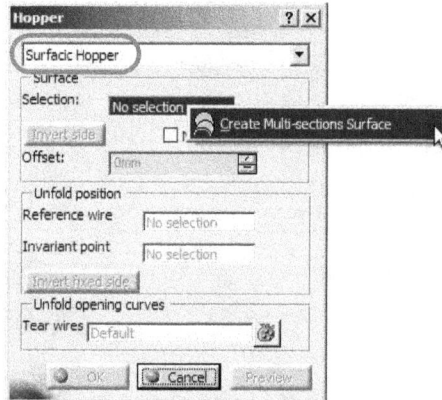

Figure 2–43

4. In the specification tree, in the **RefGeom** geometrical set, select **BaseProfile** and **TopProfile** as the first and second sections. The Multi-sections Surface Definition dialog box opens as shown in Figure 2–44.

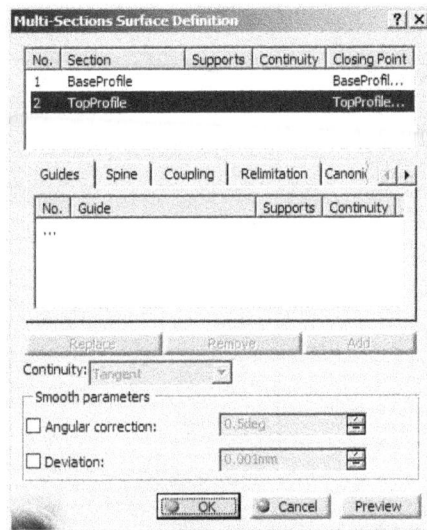

Figure 2–44

5. Ensure that the closing points and directions display as shown in Figure 2–45.

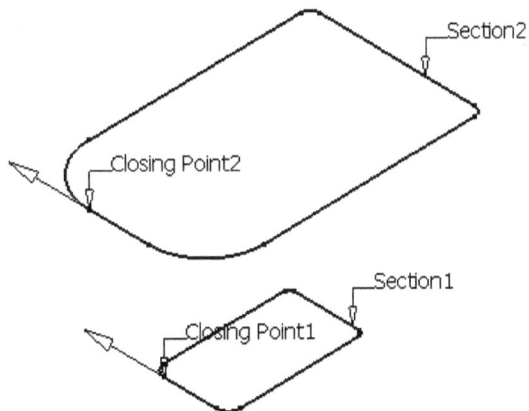

Figure 2–45

6. Switch to the *Coupling* tab and select **Vertices** in the Sections coupling drop-down list, as shown in Figure 2–46.

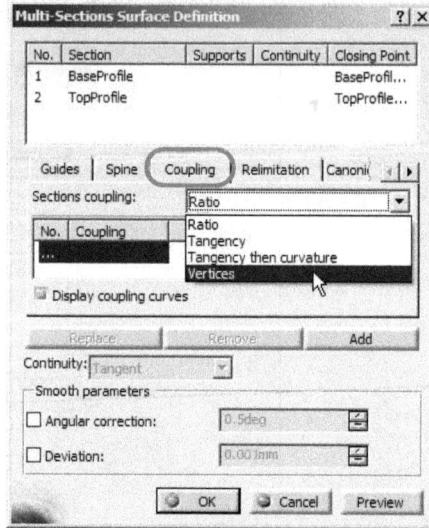

Figure 2–46

7. Click **OK** to complete the multi-sections surface feature.

8. Select inside the *Reference wire* field.

9. Select the edge as shown in Figure 2–47.

10. Define the Invariant point as shown in Figure 2–47.

11. Click inside the *Tear wires* field and define the Tear wire using the edge used for the Reference wire.

The edge and point specify the reference face of the model.

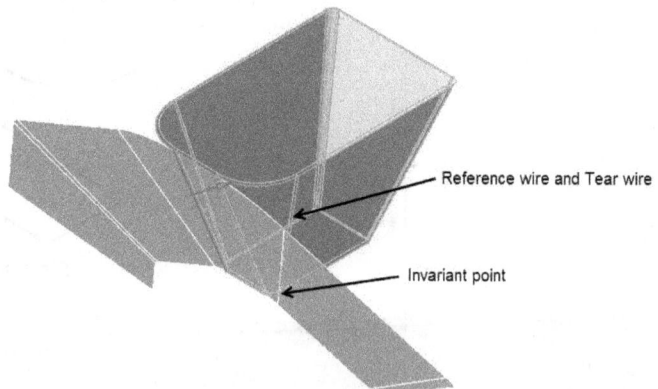

Reference wire and Tear wire

Invariant point

Figure 2–47

12. Click **OK** to complete the surfacic hopper feature.

13. Hide the RefGeom geometrical set. The completed model displays as shown in Figure 2–48.

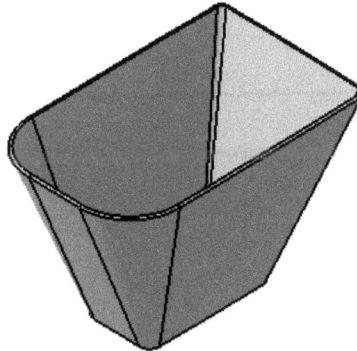

Figure 2–48

14. Click ✿▾ (Fold/Unfold). The plane onto which the model unfolds is defined by the face containing the reference wire, specified in the Hopper definition dialog box.

15. Save and close the file.

Task 3 - Create a surfacic hopper feature.

In this task, you will create a surfacic hopper using a non-ruled surface.

1. Open **SurfacicHopper_non-ruled.CATPart**. The model displays as shown Figure 2–49.

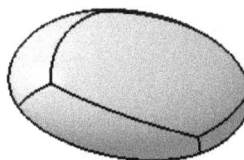

Figure 2–49

2. Click 🔘 (Hopper) to open the Hopper definition dialog box.

3. Select **Surfacic Hopper** in the Type drop-down list, if required.

---

4. Select **Non-ruled_Surface** in the specification tree or from the display.

5. Click **Preview**. The model and Hopper dialog box update as shown in Figure 2–50.

*If you receive a warning regarding the use of a default tear wire, click **Close** in the Warning dialog box.*

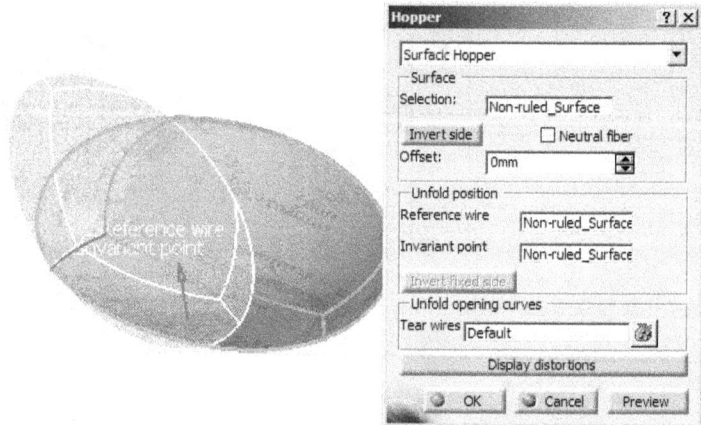

Figure 2–50

6. To analyze the deformation click **Display distortions**. The Flattened Surface Length Distortion dialog box opens. Orient the model in the dialog box as shown in Figure 2–51.

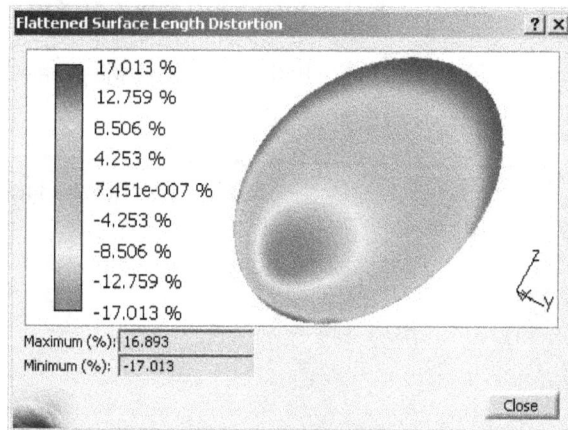

Figure 2–51

7. Close the Flattened Surface Length Distortion dialog box.

8. Complete the feature creation.

9. Click ![icon](Fold/Unfold). The model displays as shown in Figure 2–52.

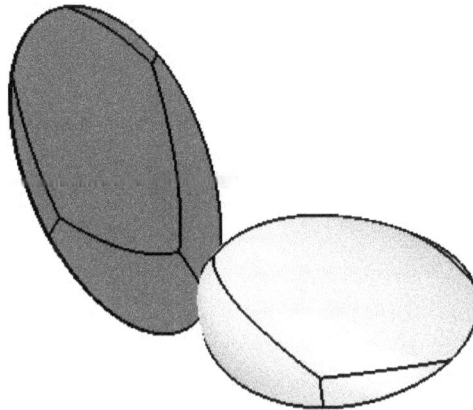

Figure 2–52

10. Save and close the model.

Task 4 - Create a canonic hopper feature.

In this task, you will use the provided reference geometry to construct a canonic hopper feature.

If you receive a warning that the model was created with an education license, close the Incident Report dialog box and continue.

1. Open **HopperCanonic.CATPart**.

2. Click to open the Hopper definition dialog box.

3. Select **Canonic Hopper** in the Type drop-down list.

4. Expand the **RefGeom** geometrical set and make the following selections in the Hopper definition dialog box:

   • *First profile:* **BaseProfile**
   • *Second profile:* **TopProfile**
   • *First point:* **ClosingPt01**
   • *Second point:* **ClosingPt02**

The Hopper dialog box opens as shown in Figure 2–53.

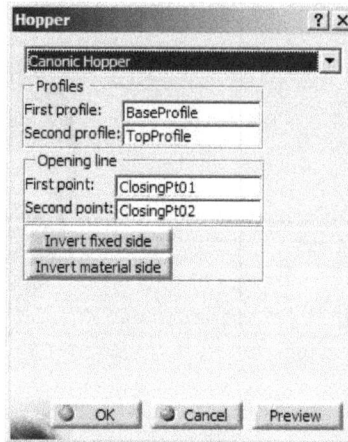

Figure 2–53

Design Considerations

The capabilities of a canonic hopper feature are limited compared to those of a surfacic hopper. The profile planes of a canonic hopper feature must be parallel. Also, when projected perpendicular to a profile plane, the centers of arcs in the profile sketches must be coincident.

5. Ensure that the material direction arrow points away from the model and click **OK** to complete the canonic hopper feature.

    The completed model displays as shown in Figure 2–54.

Figure 2–54

6. Click (Fold/Unfold). The model unfolds in the direction specified by the Fixed side arrow in the Hopper definition dialog box.

7. Save and close the file.

Practice 2d

Creating a Rolled Wall I

Practice Objectives

- Create a rolled wall.
- Apply different types of bend reliefs.

In this practice, you will create a rolled wall feature and apply different types of bend reliefs. At the end of this practice, the models will display as shown in Figure 2–55.

Figure 2–55

Task 1 - Open a part file.

1. Open **CoatHanger.CATPart**. The model displays as shown in Figure 2–56.

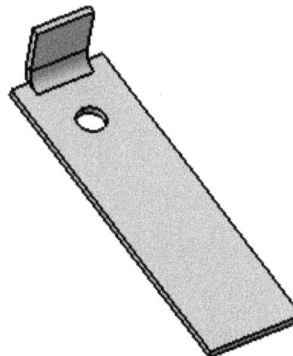

Figure 2–56

Task 2 - Create a rolled wall profile.

In this task, you will create the profile for a rolled wall.

1. Highlight the face shown in Figure 2–57 and click

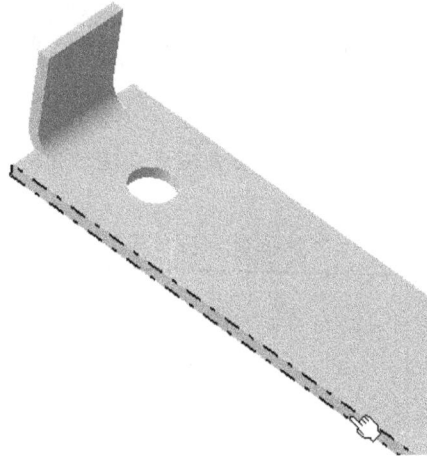

   ⬚ (Sketch).

Figure 2–57

2. Create the profile shown in Figure 2–58.

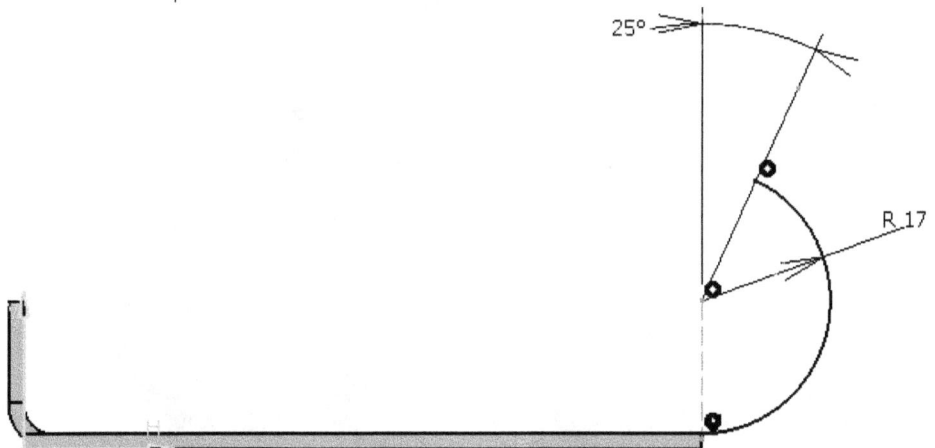

Figure 2–58

3. Click ⬆ (Exit Workbench) to return to the Generative Sheetmetal Design workbench.

Task 3 - Create a rolled wall.

1. Highlight the profile in the display or specification tree and click (Rolled Wall) in the Rolled Walls toolbar. The Rolled Wall Definition dialog box opens.

2. Select **Up To Plane** in the Type drop-down list.

3. Select the face shown in Figure 2–59 to set the extrusion limit.

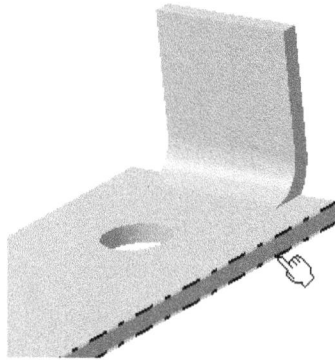

Figure 2–59

4. Ensure that the material direction is outward.

5. Click **OK** to complete the rolled wall feature.

6. The model displays as shown in Figure 2–60.

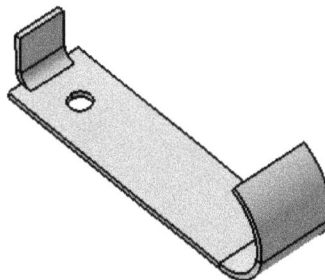

Figure 2–60

Task 4 - Apply different types of bend reliefs.

In this task, you will apply different types of bend reliefs.

1. Click (Sheet Metal Parameters) in the Walls toolbar.

2. Select the *Bend Extremities* tab and make the following selections as shown in Figure 2–61:

   - Select **Square Relief** from the drop-down list.
   - *L1:* **2mm**
   - *L2:* **3mm**

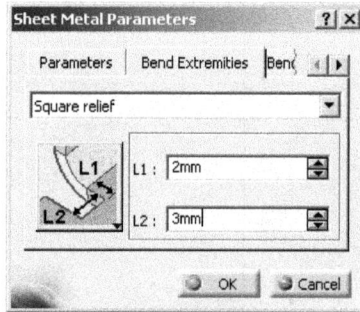

Figure 2–61

3. Click **OK**. The model displays as shown in Figure 2–62.

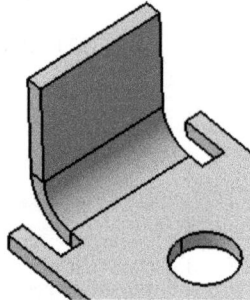

Figure 2–62

4. Use the previous steps to apply different types of bend reliefs to observe the impact on the model.

5. Apply a tangent bend relief on the model and it displays as shown in Figure 2–63.

Figure 2–63

6. Save and close the file.

| Practice 2e | # Creating a Rolled Wall II |

Practice Objectives

- Create a first wall.
- Create a rolled wall.

In this practice, you will create a first wall and a rolled wall feature without instruction. At the end of this practice, the models will display as shown in Figure 2–64.

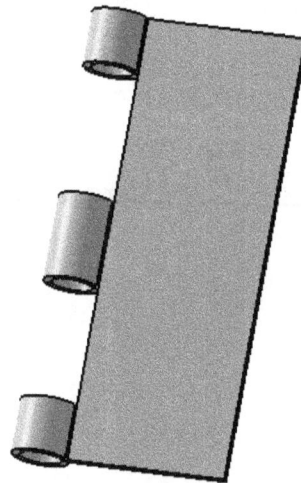

Figure 2–64

Task 1 - Create a part with no instruction.

1. Create a new part named **DoorHinge**.

2. Define the sheet metal parameters and create the part shown in Figure 2–65. There is a gap between the flat and rolled walls, which can be resolved by adding a bend feature. For now, leave the gap between the walls.

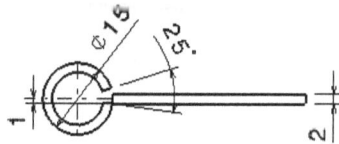

Bottom view
Scale: 1:1

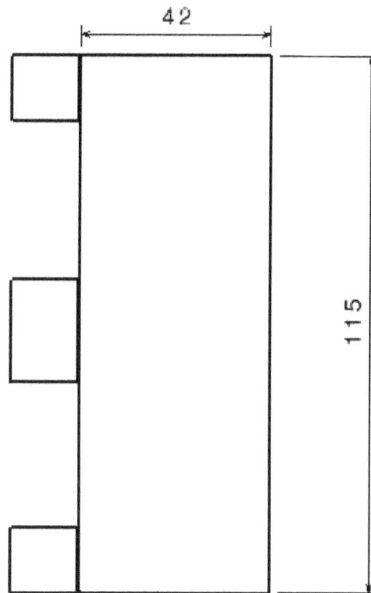

Front view
Scale: 1:1

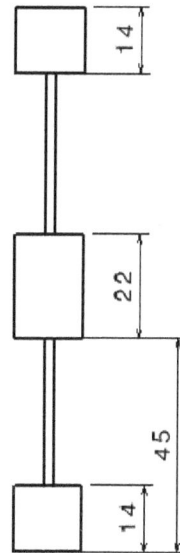

Left view
Scale: 1:1

Figure 2–65

3. Save and close the file.

Chapter

3

Secondary Walls

Just as secondary solid features are built by referencing the base feature, secondary walls are built by attaching them to the first wall. Secondary walls can be created from a profile, or by simply selecting an edge of an existing wall.

Learning Objectives in this Chapter

- Learn how to manually create a wall on an edge.
- Learn how to automatically create a wall on an edge.
- Create a sketch based wall on edge.
- Learn how to create walls tangent to other walls.
- Create swept walls.

3.1 Wall on Edge

The **Wall on Edge** tool is used to add secondary walls to a sheet metal part. There are two methods of creating a Wall on Edge:

*   Automatic

*   Sketch Based

The Wall on Edge dialog box opens as shown in Figure 3–1.

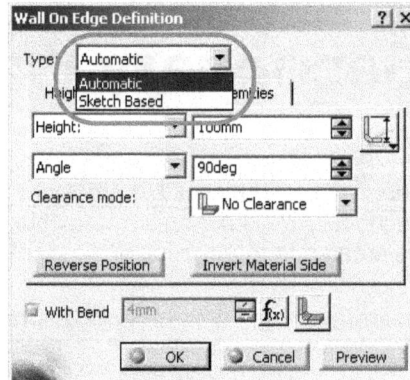

Figure 3–1

Automatic

An automatic wall on edge feature does not require a sketched profile; it only requires the edge of an existing wall for placement. An example is shown in Figure 3–2.

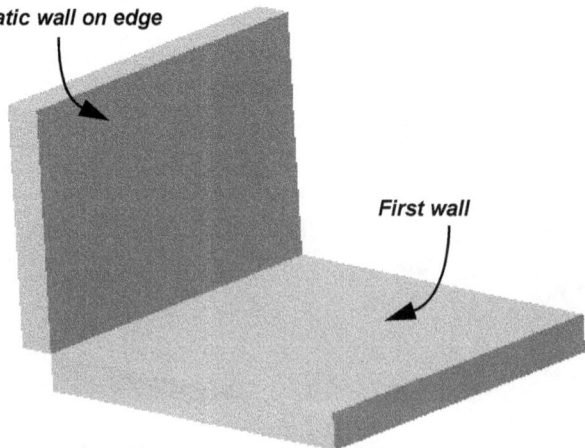

Automatic wall on edge

First wall

Figure 3–2

Sketch Based

The **Sketch Based** option enables you to define the profile of the wall using a sketch. You must define the attachment edge and the sketch to be used. An example of a sketch based wall on edge is shown in Figure 3–3.

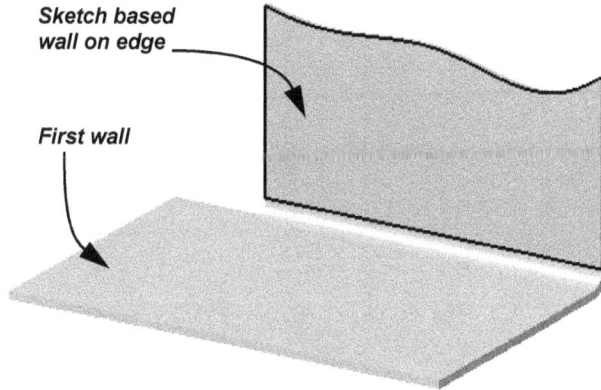

Sketch based wall on edge

First wall

Figure 3–3

3.2 Automatic Wall on Edge

General Steps

Use the following general steps to create an automatic wall on edge:

1. Select a reference edge and activate the **Wall on Edge** tool.
2. Define the wall type.
3. Define the height of the wall.
4. Define the angle of the wall.
5. Define additional parameters, if required.
6. Set wall limits, if required.
7. Complete the feature.

> ## Step 1 - Select a reference edge and activate the Wall on Edge tool.

Click [icon] (Wall on Edge) and select an edge to reference, as shown in Figure 3–4. By default, the wall is created normal to the wall containing the selected edge.

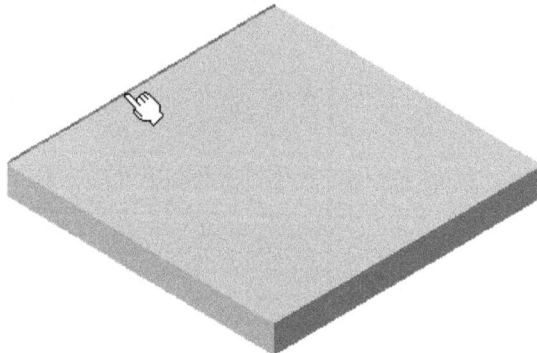

Figure 3–4

Edges can be selected from multiple support faces.

Additional edges can be selected to create several walls using a single Wall on Edge operation. To quickly select all of the edges on a face, select the first edge, right-click on the No Clearance annotation, and select **Auto Selection**, as shown in Figure 3–5.

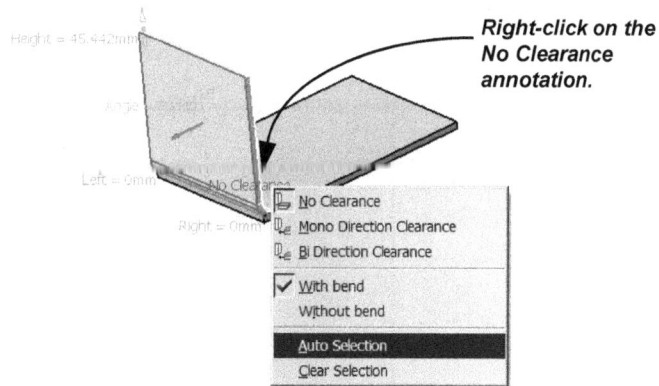

Figure 3–5

Step 2 - Define the wall type.

*Throughout this section, the **With Bend** option is cleared to improve visualization.*

There are two options for creating a Wall on edge: **Automatic** and **Sketch Based**. To create a wall without a sketch, select **Automatic** in the Type drop-down list, as shown in Figure 3–6.

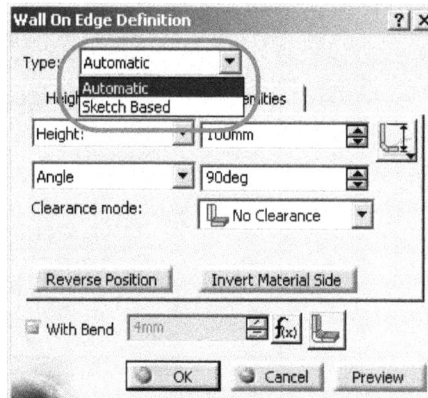

Figure 3–6

Step 3 - Define the height of the wall.

When multiple edges are selected, the height of the walls must be the same.

The size of the wall is defined using options in the *Height & Inclination* tab. These control the size and angle of the wall, as shown in Figure 3–7.

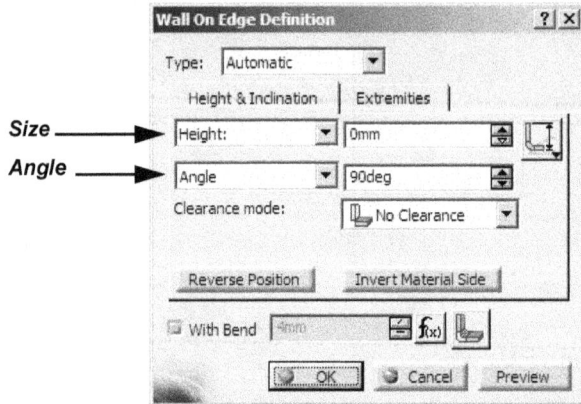

Figure 3–7

Wall size can be defined by selecting either **Height** or **Up To Plane/Surface** in the drop-down list, as shown in Figure 3–8.

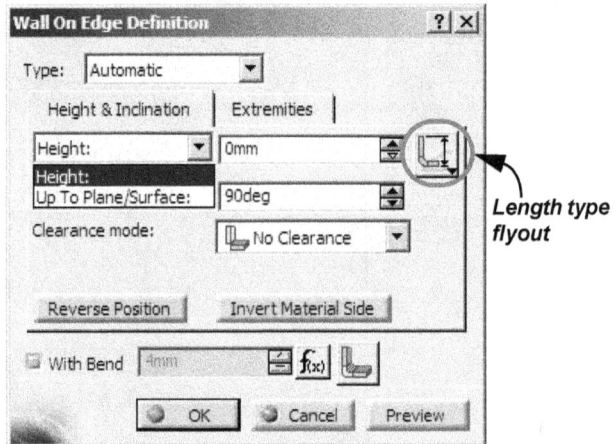

Figure 3–8

Height

The **Height** option is demonstrated in Figure 3–9.

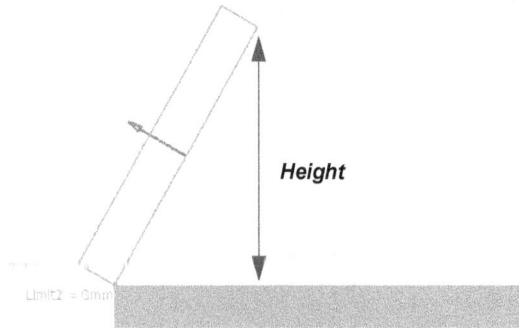

Figure 3–9

When the **Height** option is selected, you can select a reference type in the **Length type** flyout menu. Once the reference has been selected, enter the value for the height of the wall. The available reference types are described as follows:

Length Type	Description
	The height is measured from the top of the reference wall.
	The height is measured from the bottom of the reference wall.
	The height is measured from the upper edge of the bend.
	The height is measured from the mold line.
	The height is measured from the intersection between the top of the reference wall and the top of the wall on edge.

Up To Plane/Surface

When the **Up To Plane/Surface** option is selected, a plane or surface is used to define the length of the wall. If required, you can enter a dimension in the *Offset* field, as shown in Figure 3–10.

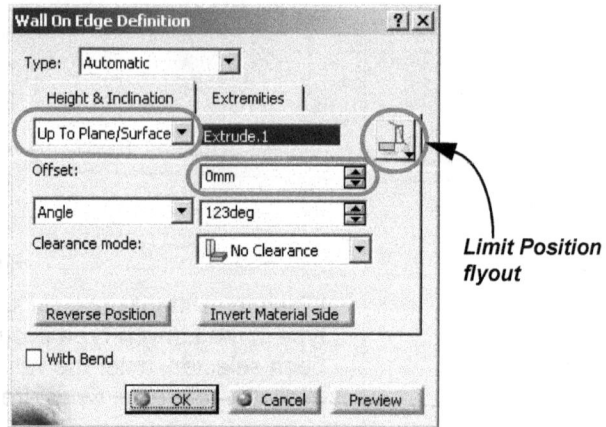

Figure 3–10

There are two different limit positions:

- Click ⬚ to use the inner edge of the wall as the limit.

- Click ⬚ to use the outer edge of the wall as the limit.

These options are demonstrated in Figure 3–11.

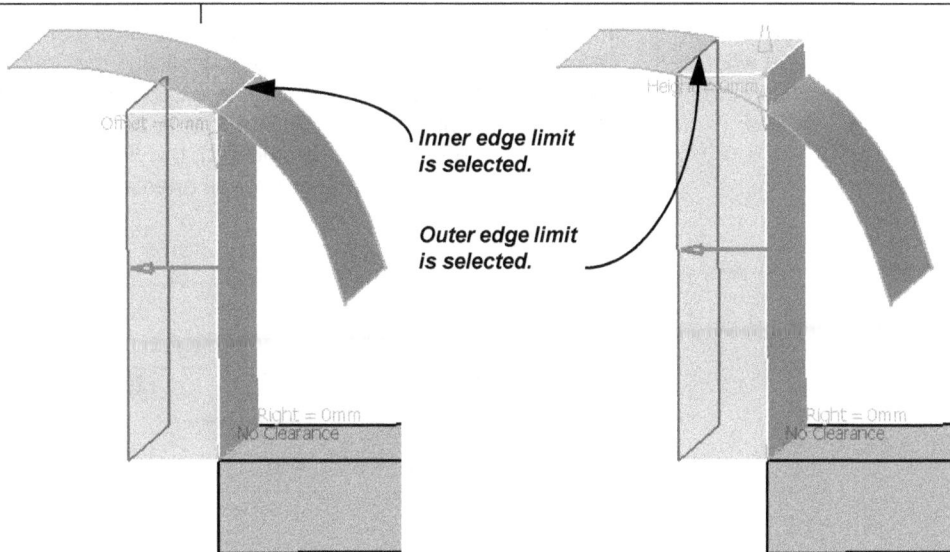

Inner edge limit is selected.

Outer edge limit is selected.

Figure 3–11

Step 4 - Define the angle of the wall.

When multiple edges are selected, the angle of the walls must be the same.

By default, the wall is created at a 90 degree angle from the reference wall. The angle can be changed to suit your requirements, as shown in Figure 3–12.

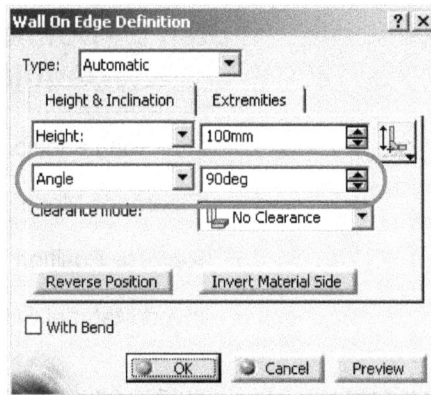

Figure 3–12

You cannot select an Orientation Plane when multiple reference edges are selected.

To drive the angle of the wall using a reference plane, select **Orientation Plane** from the drop-down list. A previously created plane can be selected, or a new plane can be created by right-clicking and selecting **Create Plane**, as shown in Figure 3–13. After a plane is selected, the *Rotation angle* field can be used to further define the wall orientation.

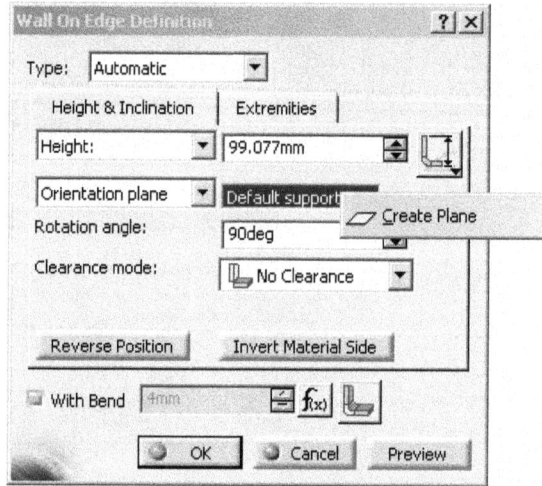

Figure 3–13

Step 5 - Define additional parameters, if required.

The following additional parameters can be configured:

• Clearance Mode

• Reverse Position

• Invert Material Side

Clearance Mode

Clearance enables you to specify a horizontal and vertical offset distance between the wall and the edge. Select one of the 3 different types of Clearance modes to apply the clearance. The available Clearance modes are described as follows:

Clearance Mode	Description
🔲 No Clearance	Select this option to create the wall on edge without a clearance.
🔲 Monodirectional	Select this option to create the wall on edge with an horizontal offset.
🔲 Bidirectional	Select this option to create the wall on edge with an horizontal and vertical offset. By default, Bidirectional clearance offsets by the default bend radius value. The system prompts you to create a formula relating this offset to the bend radius parameter.

When multiple edges are selected, the same clearance must be used for all edges.

Once the Clearance mode is selected, enter the offset value in the clearance value section as shown in Figure 3–14.

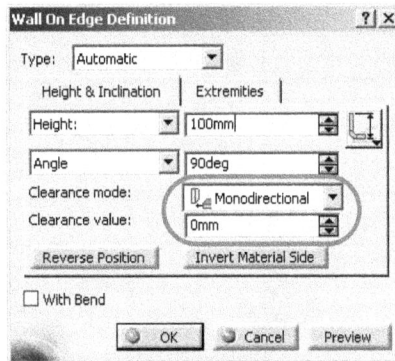

Figure 3–14

Reverse Position

The direction of the wall on edge is based on the selected edge. If the top edge of the reference wall is selected, the wall is created upward and the reverse is true if the bottom edge is selected. The direction of wall creation can be changed by clicking **Reverse Position**. Reversing the position does not change the referenced edge, as shown in Figure 3–15.

Reference edge does not change

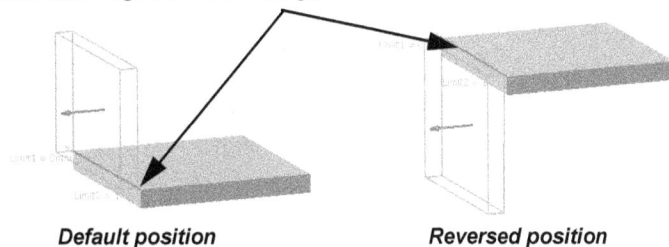

Default position   *Reversed position*

Figure 3–15

Invert Material Side

The material side is selected by default to maintain the continuity of the reference wall. This can be reversed by clicking **Invert Material Side** in the Wall On Edge definition dialog box or the red arrow in the model.

Step 6 - Set wall limits, if required.

By default, the wall on edge is created along the full length of the referenced edge. You can limit the width of the wall using the *Extremities* tab. The tab contains options to limit the left and right side of the wall, as shown in Figure 3–16. The wall can be limited by an offset value, reference plane, or surface.

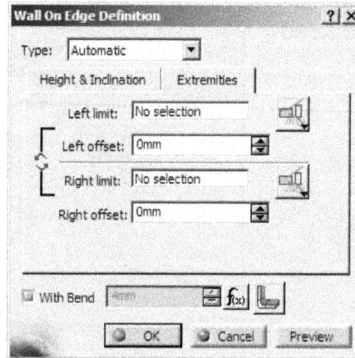

Figure 3–16

An example of a wall on edge that is limited by a negative offset value and a surface is shown in Figure 3–17.

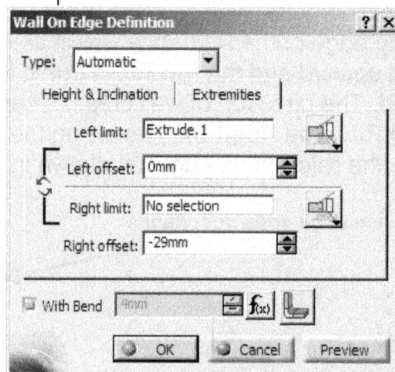

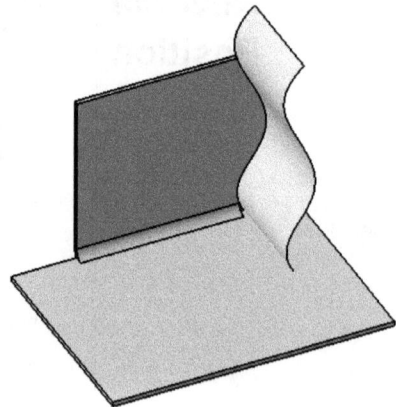

Figure 3–17

When multiple edges are selected, the *Extremities* tab displays as shown on the left in Figure 3–18. The **Left limit** and **Right limit** options available when a single edge is selected are no longer available. Use the *Gap Value* field to include a gap at any intersecting corner between the walls, as shown on the right in Figure 3–18.

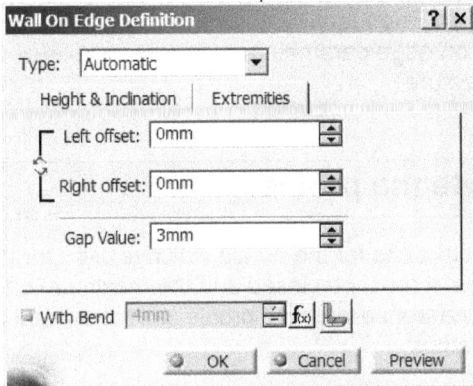

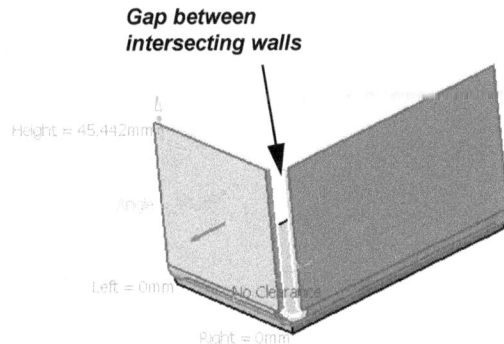

Gap between intersecting walls

Figure 3–18

Step 7 - Complete the feature.

A bend can be included with the wall, if required. Select the **With Bend** option to generate the bend with the wall on edge. This bend feature does not display in the tree. However, the feature name is changed from **Wall On Edge.#** to **Wall On Edge with Bend.#**. If you require the bend to be a unique feature, it can be created later using a bend feature.

Once all parameters for the wall on edge have been defined, click **OK** to complete the feature.

3.3 Sketch Based Wall on Edge

General Steps

Use the following general steps to create a sketch based wall on edge.

1. Create the profile.
1. Active the **Wall on Edge** tool.
1. Define the wall on edge parameters.
2. Complete the feature.

Step 1 - Create the profile.

There are some restrictions for the profile which is used for the wall on edge feature. It must be closed and the maximum offset value between the reference wall and profile cannot exceed the value of the bend radius.

An example of a sketch for a wall on edge is shown in Figure 3–19.

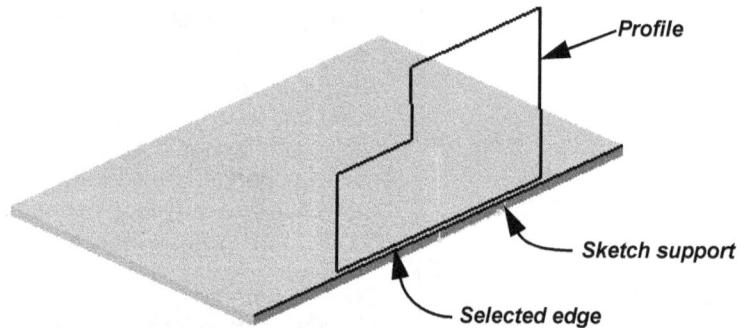

Figure 3–19

Step 2 - Active the Wall on Edge tool.

Click ![icon] (Wall on Edge) and select **Sketch Based** in the **Type** drop-down list. Select the sketched profile and select a reference edge from the support face. The Wall on Edge Definition dialog box opens as shown in Figure 3–20.

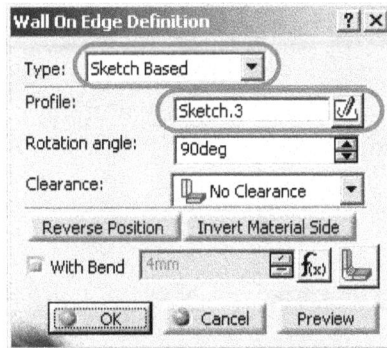

Wall On Edge Definition

Type: Sketch Based

Profile: Sketch.3

Rotation angle: 90deg

Clearance: No Clearance

Reverse Position   Invert Material Side

With Bend   4mm

OK   Cancel   Preview

Figure 3–20

Step 3 - Define the wall on edge parameters.

The following parameters can be defined:

*   Rotation angle

*   Clearance

*   Reverse Position

*   Invert Material Side

Rotation Angle

By default, the wall is created by adding material thickness to the sketched profile. The angle of the wall can be changed to suit your requirements. The 0 degree angle is defined by the angle between the plane in which the sketch was created and the selected reference edge. When the Rotation angle is modified, the wall is rotated about the reference edge.

Clearance Mode

Clearance enables you to specify a horizontal and vertical offset distance between the wall and the edge. Select one of the 3 different types of Clearance modes to apply the clearance. The following describes the available Clearance modes.

Clearance Mode	Description
No Clearance	Select this option to create the wall on edge without a clearance.
Monodirectional	Select this option to create the wall on edge with an horizontal offset.
Bidirectional	Select this option to create the wall on edge with an horizontal and vertical offset. By default, Bidirectional clearance offsets by the default bend radius value. The system prompts you to create a formula relating this offset to the bend radius parameter.

Reverse Position

The direction of the wall on edge is based on the selected edge. If the top edge of the reference wall is selected, the wall is created upward and the reverse is true if the bottom edge is selected. The direction of wall creation can be changed by clicking **Reverse Position**. Reversing the position does not change the referenced edge

Invert Material Side

By default, the material side is selected to maintain the continuity of the reference wall. This can be reversed by clicking **Invert Material Side** in the Wall On Edge definition dialog box or by clicking the red arrow in the model.

Step 4 - Complete the feature.

After all of the required options are applied, click **OK** to complete the wall on edge as shown in Figure 3–21.

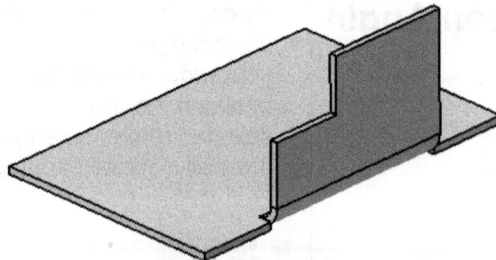

Figure 3–21

3.4 Tangent Walls

Tangent walls are created similar to profile walls, except that they must include information on the existing wall or flange to which they are tangent. This information is used to unfold the wall correctly. For example, a wall is created as shown in Figure 3–22 On the left side, the wall is created using a profile wall without specifying the tangency references. When the model is unfolded, the wall does not unfold correctly. On the right side, the same wall is created, but this time it is set tangent to an existing wall. When the model is unfolded, the wall unfolds as expected.

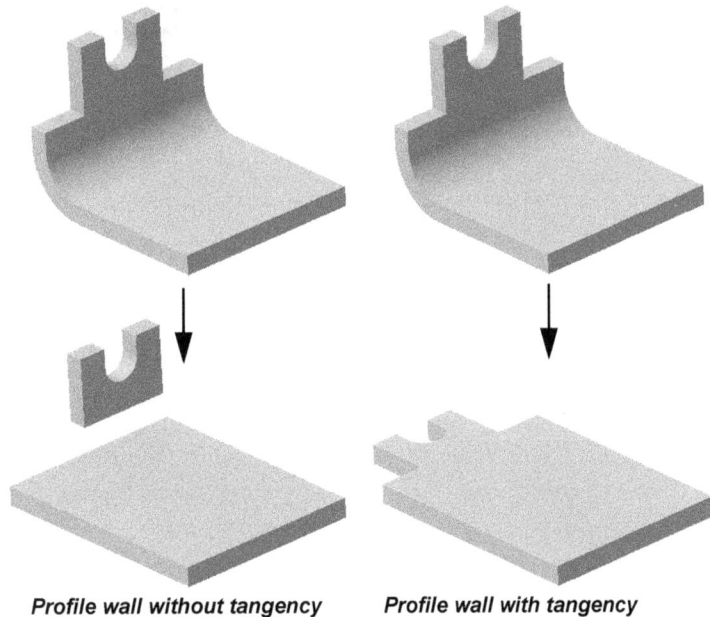

Profile wall without tangency　　*Profile wall with tangency*

Figure 3–22

General Steps

Use the following general steps to create a tangent wall:

1. Create the profile sketch.
2. Activate the **Profile wall** tool.
3. Define the tangent wall.
4. Complete the feature.

Step 1 - Create the profile sketch.

Like a profile wall, the profile for a tangent wall must be closed. The wall is created using the tangent wall as its sketch support. For example, a tab is required on top of a side wall. To create the tab, select the side wall as the sketch support, as shown in the top image of Figure 3–23, and create the profile of the tab, as shown in the bottom image of Figure 3–23.

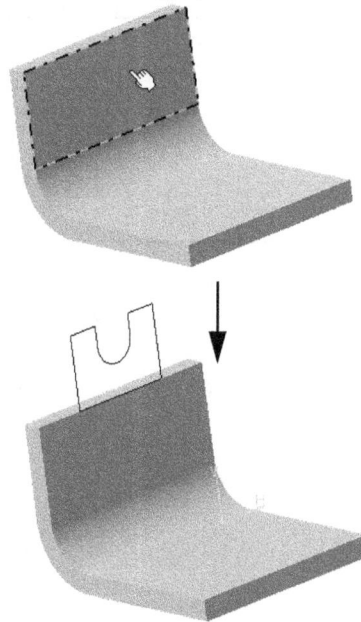

Figure 3–23

Step 2 - Activate the Profile wall tool.

Ensure that the profile to be used for the tangent wall is selected and click (Wall).

Step 3 - Define the tangent wall.

In the Wall definition dialog box, activate the *Tangent to Selection* field and select the tangency reference, as shown in Figure 3–24.

It is not required to change the material side. Once the tangent to wall is selected, the material side is automatically constructed to match.

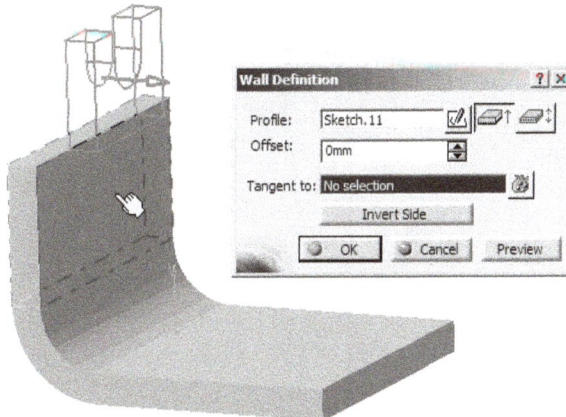

Figure 3–24

Step 4 - Complete the feature.

Click **OK** to complete the wall. The tangent wall is shown in Figure 3–25.

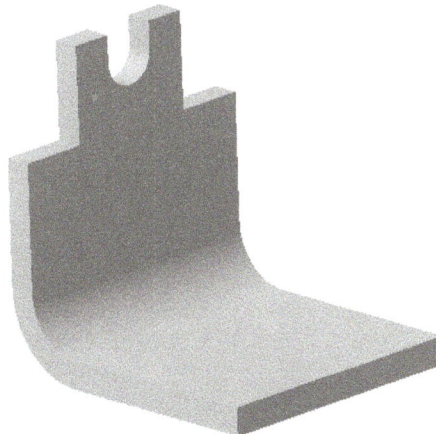

Figure 3–25

3.5 Swept Walls

Four types of swept wall features can be created in the Generative Sheetmetal Design workbench. They are found in the Swept Walls toolbar, as shown in Figure 3–26.

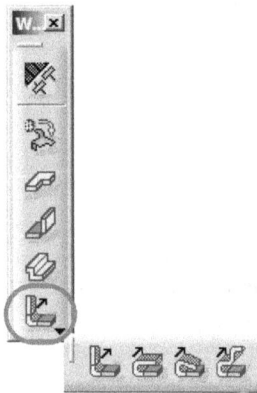

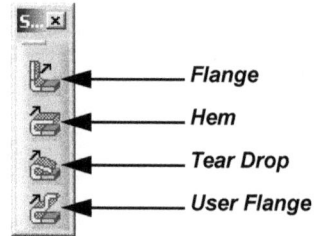

Flange
Hem
Tear Drop
User Flange

Figure 3–26

Examples of the types of swept walls are shown in Figure 3–27.

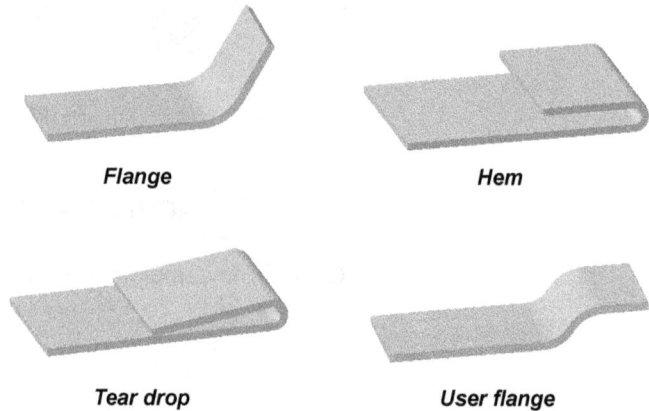

Flange   *Hem*

Tear drop   *User flange*

Figure 3–27

General Steps

Use the following general steps to create a sheet metal swept wall feature:

1. Select a reference edge.
2. Select the type of swept wall feature.
3. Enter parameter information.
4. Complete the feature.

Step 1 - Select a reference edge.

The swept wall feature requires an edge to be selected; it acts as the spine for the swept wall. Select a reference edge to start the creation of the swept wall, as shown in Figure 3–28.

Select this edge

Figure 3–28

Direction of Creation

The direction in which the Swept wall is created depends on which edge is selected. The Swept wall is created on the opposite side to the selected edge. For example, on the left side of Figure 3–29, the bottom edge of the reference wall is selected as the spine. On the right side of Figure 3–29, the top edge is selected as the spine.

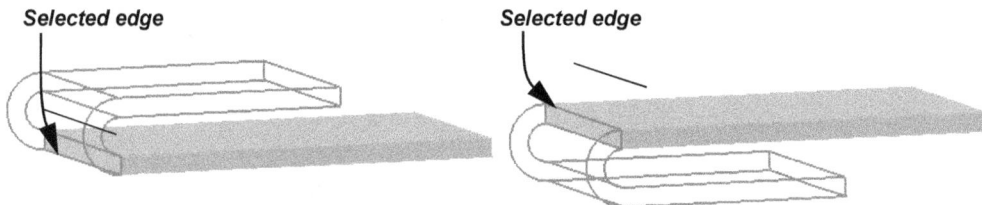

Selected edge

Selected edge

Figure 3–29

Step 2 - Select the type of swept wall feature.

Select a type of swept wall in the Swept Walls toolbar. The type of wall selected determines the shape of the profile, which is swept along the reference edge.

Flange, Hem, and Tear Drop swept walls all use pre-defined profiles. A User Flange feature is defined by a user-defined profile.

For example, if you click (Hem), the Hem Definition dialog box opens.

Step 3 - Enter parameter information.

Enter the dimensional values in the appropriate fields in the Feature Definition dialog box. A preview of how the dimensions are applied is shown on the right side of the dialog box.

By default, the bend radius is controlled by the sheetmetal parameters in the model, and the *Radius* field is inactive. You can manually enter a value by right-clicking in the *Radius* field and selecting **Formula>Deactivate**.The *Radius* field activates, and you can enter a value.

All swept wall features have a **Basic** and a **Relimited** option. When the **Relimited** option is selected, the two limit fields display enabling you to stop the swept wall at a point or plane, as shown in Figure 3–30.

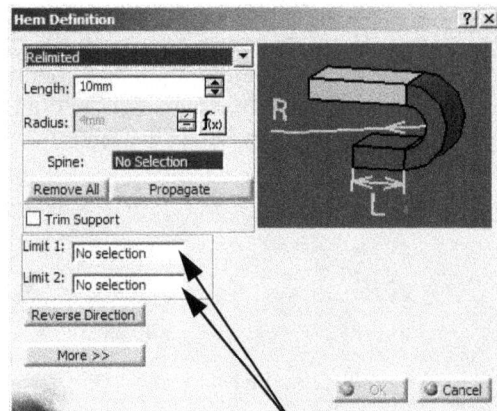

*Limiting references can be
points lying on the spine or
intersecting planes.*

Figure 3–30

Click **Propagate** to enable the swept feature to include any edges tangent to the selected spine. If you accidentally select an edge that is not required to be part of the spine, you must click **Remove All** to remove all selected edges and reselect the required edges.

User Flanges

User flanges require the selection of a sketch to define the profile. This sketch is swept along the spine to create the flange. The profile can be created before entering the User Flange operation or during the User Flange creation. If you have already created the profile, select it to update the User Defined Flange definition dialog box, as shown in Figure 3–31. If you have not created a profile, click ⬚ (Sketcher) to access the Sketcher workbench. Once the profile is complete click ⬚ (Exit Workbench) to return to the dialog box.

The profile must be tangent to the attaching wall.

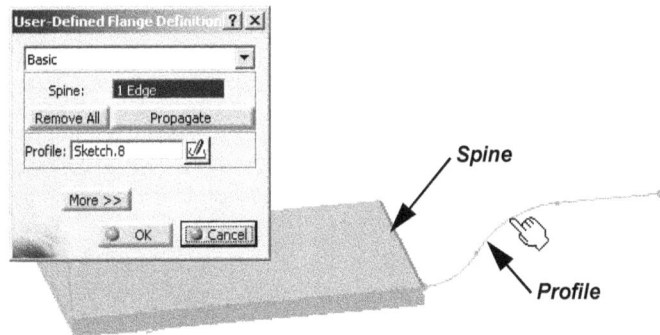

Figure 3–31

Step 4 - Complete the feature.

Click **OK** to complete the feature. A hem feature is shown in Figure 3–32.

Figure 3–32

Practice 3a

Secondary Walls

Practice Objectives

- Create a tangent wall.
- Create a wall on edge.
- Create a user-defined flange.

In this practice, you will create additional walls for the Mounting_Bracket. At the end of the practice, you will have created all of the wall and flanges required for this model, as shown in Figure 3–33.

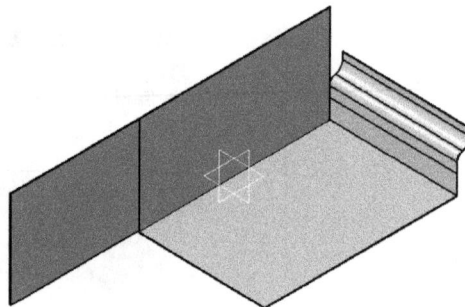

Figure 3–33

Task 1 - Open the part.

1. Open the **Ex2A_Mounting_Bracket.CATPart**.

   If you completed **Practice 2a**, open **Mounting_Bracket.CATPart** instead. The model displays as shown in Figure 3–34.

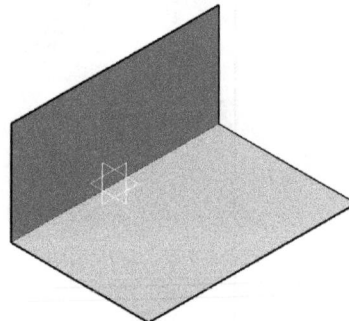

Figure 3–34

Task 2 - Create a tangent wall.

The back wall of the mounting bracket needs to be extended. To have this extension wall unbend correctly, the new profile wall will be created tangent to the back wall.

1. Select the back wall as shown in Figure 3–35 and enter the Sketcher workbench.

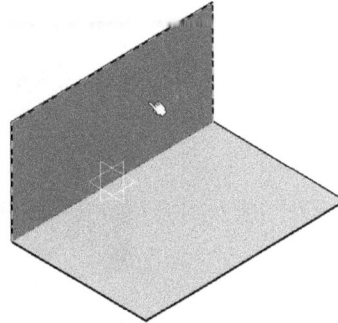

Figure 3–35

2. Create the sketch, as shown in Figure 3–36. Make the profile coincident to the side and top of the back wall. Be sure to close the sketch with a vertical line on the right side of the section.

   The bottom edge of the sketch should be **2mm** higher than the bottom edge of the vertical wall (top surface of the horizontal wall). This makes the walls look uniform when the bend is applied.

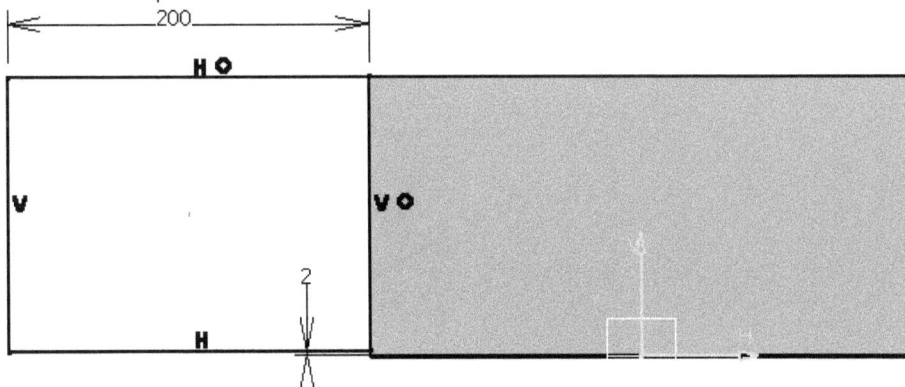

Figure 3–36

3. Exit the Sketcher workbench.

4. Highlight the sketch just created and click ![Wall icon] (Wall).

5. Select inside the *Tangent to* field and select the back wall, as shown in Figure 3–37.

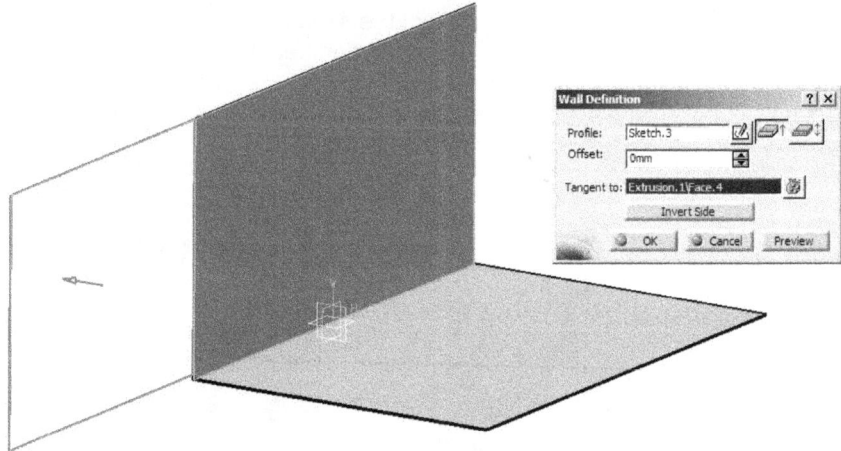

Figure 3–37

6. Click **OK** to generate the tangent wall.

Task 3 - Create a wall on edge.

1. Select the edge shown in Figure 3–38.

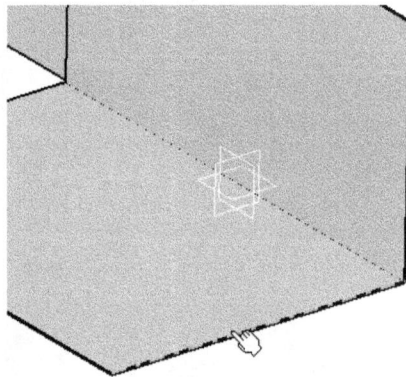

Figure 3–38

2. Click ![Wall On Edge icon] (Wall On Edge).

3. Create the wall with the following dimensions as shown in Figure 3–39:

- *Height:* **30mm**
- *Angle:* **90deg**
- *Clearance mode:* **No Clearance**
- Clear the **With Bend** option.

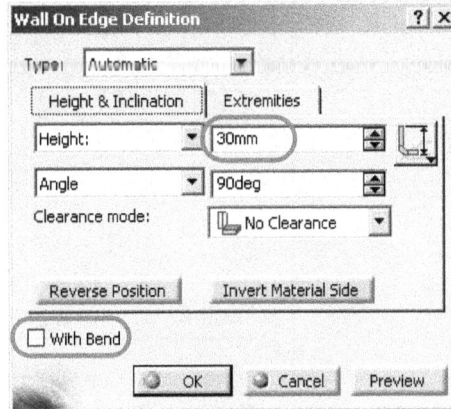

Figure 3–39

4. Ensure that the material is added outward, as shown in Figure 3–40. If the material is added in the wrong direction, click **Invert Material Side**.

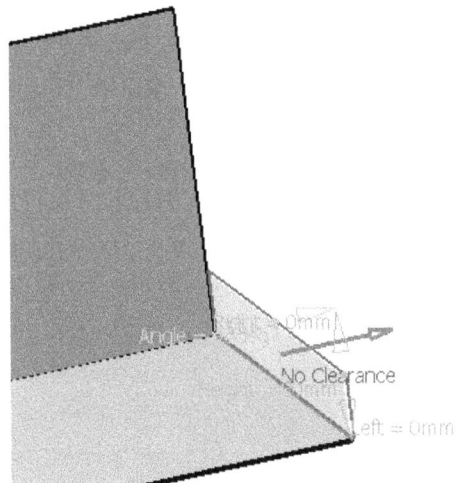

Figure 3–40

5. Click **OK** to generate the wall on edge. The wall displays as shown in Figure 3–41.

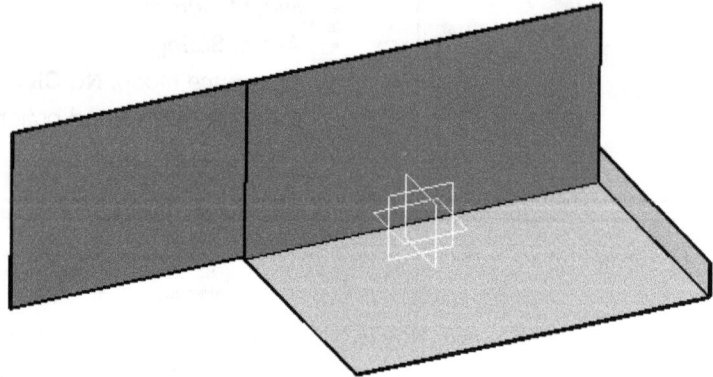

Figure 3–41

Task 4 - Create a profile for the user flange.

To create a user flange, you must first create a profile, which must be tangent to the wall to which it is attached.

1. Select the side face of the wall on edge as shown in Figure 3–42 and enter the Sketcher workbench.

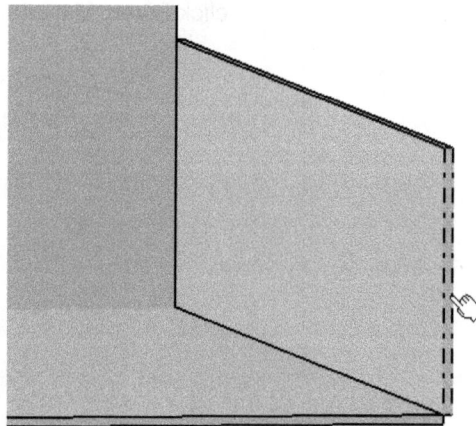

Figure 3–42

2. Create the profile as shown in Figure 3–43. Ensure that it is coincident with the outside edge of the wall.

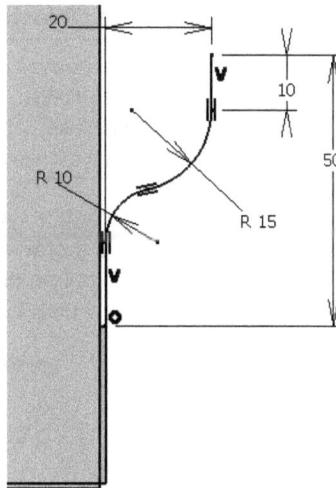

Figure 3–43

3. Exit the Sketcher workbench.

Task 5 - Create a user flange.

1. Click (User Flange).

2. Select the outside edge of the wall as the spine, and select the sketch you just created as the profile.

3. Click **OK** to generate the user flange, as shown in Figure 3–44.

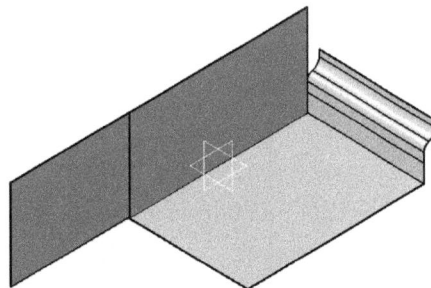

Figure 3–44

4. Save and close the file.

Practice 3b

Secondary Walls II

Practice Objectives

- Create a wall on edge.
- Create a flange.
- Create a hem.
- Create a relimited flange.

In this practice, you will build the secondary walls for the electronics bracket started in the last chapter. You will create several wall on edges and a hem. At the end of this practice, the model will display as shown in Figure 3–45.

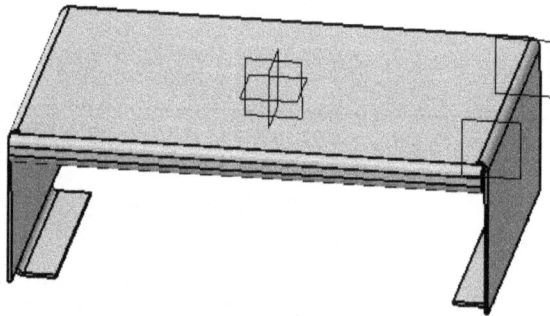

Figure 3–45

Task 1 - Open the part.

1. Open **Ex2B_Mount.CATPart**.

   If you completed **Practice 2b**, open **Mount.CATPart** instead. The model displays as shown in Figure 3–46.

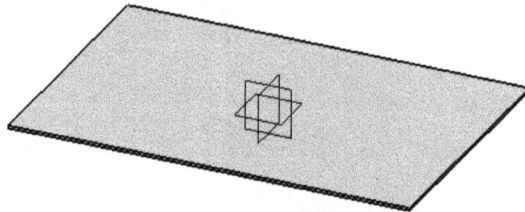

Figure 3–46

Task 2 - Create a flange.

This bracket will be mounted under equipment that might become hot. To help distance the electronics equipment from this heat, you will create a gap between the wall that is against the heated equipment and the electronic equipment.

1. Select the top edge at the bottom of the profile wall to create a flange that bends below the profile wall, as shown in Figure 3–47.

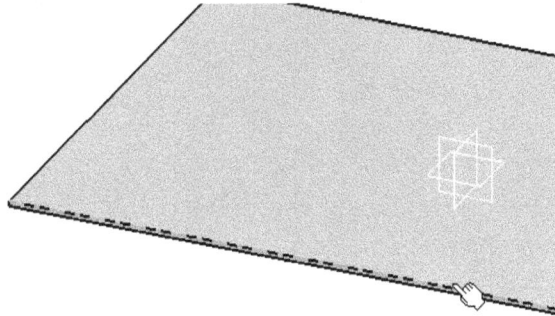

Figure 3–47

2. Click (Flange).

3. Create the flange using the following dimensions:

   - *Length:* **20mm**
   - *Angle:* **90deg**

4. Once the Flange is defined, click **OK** to finish. The flange displays as shown in Figure 3–48.

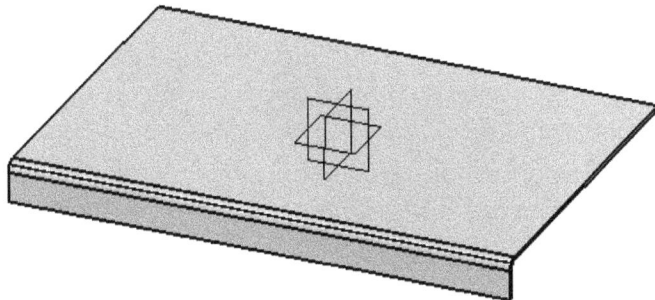

Figure 3–48

Task 3 - Create a wall on edge.

1. Highlight the edge of the flange, as shown in Figure 3–49.

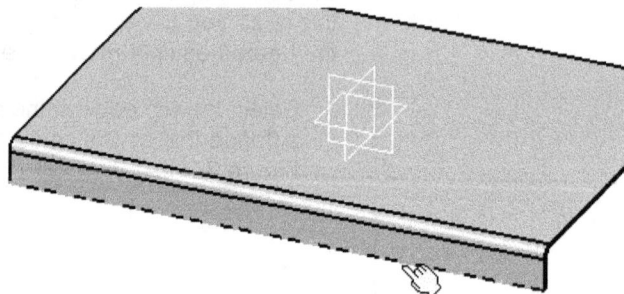

Figure 3–49

2. Click ![icon](Wall on Edge) (Wall on Edge).

3. Create the wall on edge using the following dimensions:

   - *Type:* **Automatic**
   - *Height:* **200mm**
   - *Angle:* **90deg**
   - *Clearance mode:* **No Clearance**
   - Select **With Bend**.

4. The wall should be created under the profile wall. Flip the side on which the wall is created by clicking **Reverse Position**. Add thickness in a downward direction, as shown in Figure 3–50.

*If the material is added upward, click on the arrow in the model or click **Invert Material Side**.*

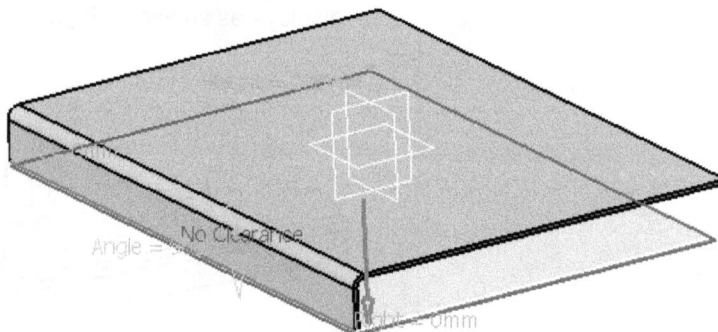

Figure 3–50

5. Click **OK** to generate the wall, as shown in Figure 3–51.

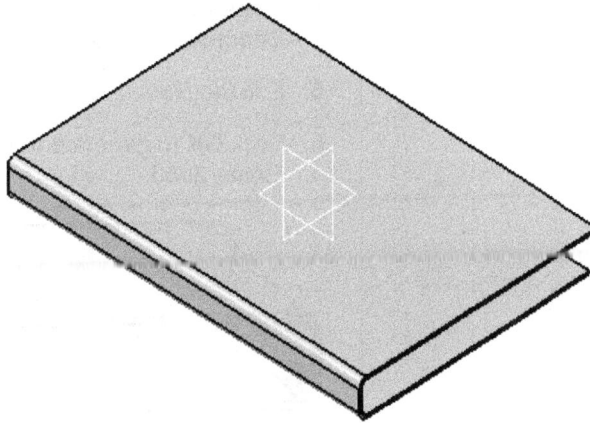

Figure 3–51

Task 4 - Create a hem.

1. Create a hem at the end of the wall on edge created in Task 3, ensuring that the hem bends under the wall. To do so, select the top edge of the wall on edge, as shown in Figure 3–52.

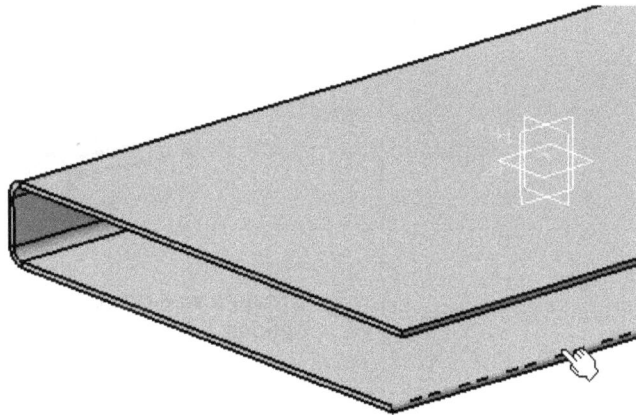

Figure 3–52

2. Click (Hem).

3. Edit the hem *Length* to **10mm**.

4. In the *Radius* field, right-click and select **Formula> Deactivate** so you can use a custom radius.

5. Edit the *Radius* to **1mm**.

6. Click **OK** to generate the hem. It displays as shown in Figure 3–53.

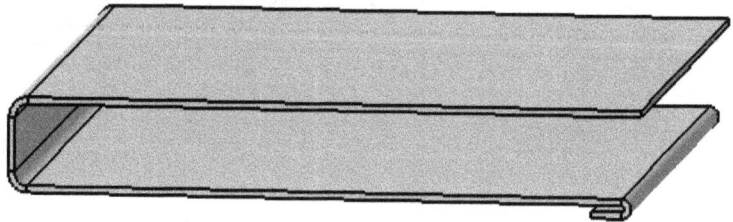

Figure 3–53

Task 5 - Create two wall on edges.

---

1. Create one side of the bracket by selecting the bottom edge shown in Figure 3–54.

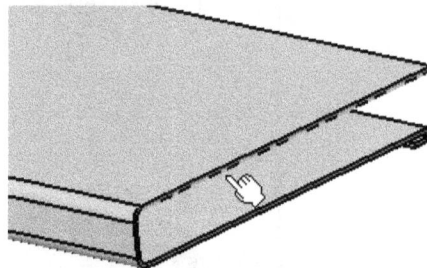

Figure 3–54

2. Create a wall on edge using the following dimensions and options:

   • *Type:* **Automatic**
   • *Height:* **100mm**
   • *Angle:* **90deg**
   • *Clearance mode:* **Monodirectional**
   • *Clearance value:* **1mm**
   • Select **With Bend**.

3. Select the *Extremities* tab.

4. Apply an offset at the front of the wall of **-5mm**. Ensure that the material is added outward, as shown in Figure 3–55.

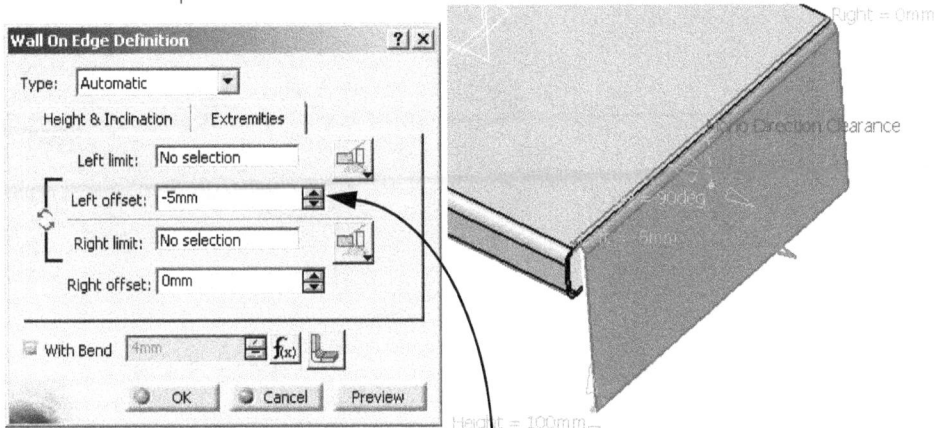

Ensure wall is offset -5mm from front edge

Figure 3–55

5. Click **OK** to create the wall, as shown in Figure 3–56.

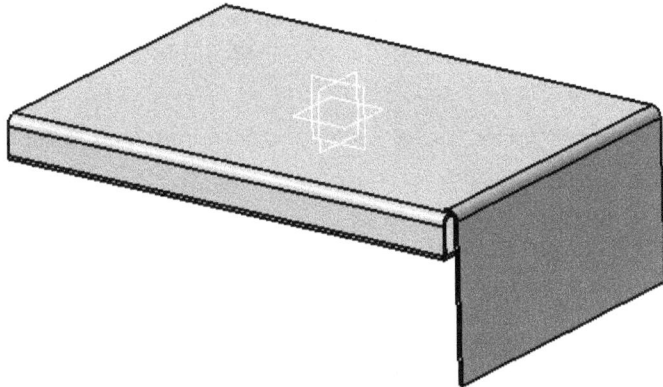

Figure 3–56

6. Create another wall on edge on the other side of the part wall, using the same dimensions. Set the *Left offset* to **0mm** and the *Right offset* to **-5mm**. Enable the **With Bend** option. The model displays as shown in Figure 3–57.

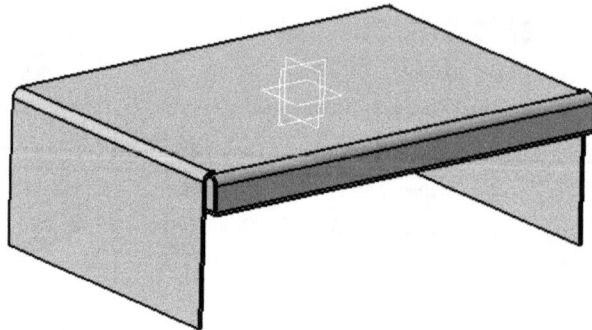

Figure 3–57

Task 6 - Create reference geometry.

In this task, you will create reference geometry that will be used to relimit flanges. These flanges will be used as the tabs to seat the equipment. The geometry used to relimit the flange must intersect the feature. Points could also be used for this purpose; however, because tabs are going to be created on either side of the bracket, creating two reference planes instead will use less features.

1. Select the front face of the bracket, as shown in Figure 3–58.

Figure 3–58

2. Click (Plane) in the Reference Elements toolbar, as shown in Figure 3–59.

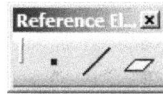

Figure 3–59

Design Considerations

By default, this toolbar is at the bottom right side and might be hidden from display. Drag the hidden toolbars to a floating position if you cannot find it, or type **c:plane** in the Power Input line, as shown in Figure 3–60. This method accesses the Plane Definition dialog box without having to find the icon.

Figure 3–60

3. Create a reference plane that is offset **25mm** from the front face. Ensure that the plane is created toward the center of the model. If it is being created in the wrong direction, click **Reverse Direction**.

4. Create a second reference plane offset from the back face **41mm**, as shown in Figure 3–61.

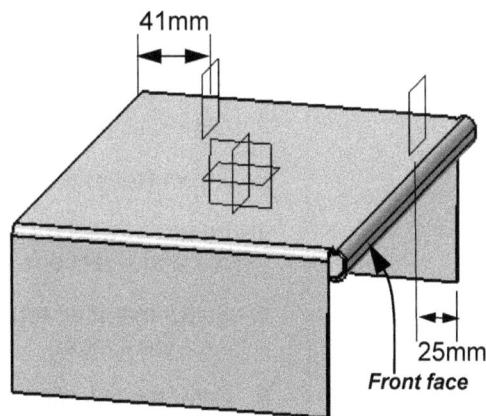

Figure 3–61

5. Ensure that the PartBody is active by right-clicking on it and selecting **Define in Work Object**, as shown in Figure 3–62.

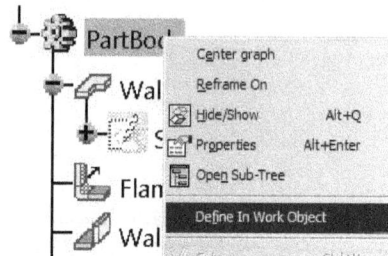

Figure 3–62

Task 7 - Create relimited flanges.

1. Select the outside edge of the side wall, as shown in Figure 3–63.

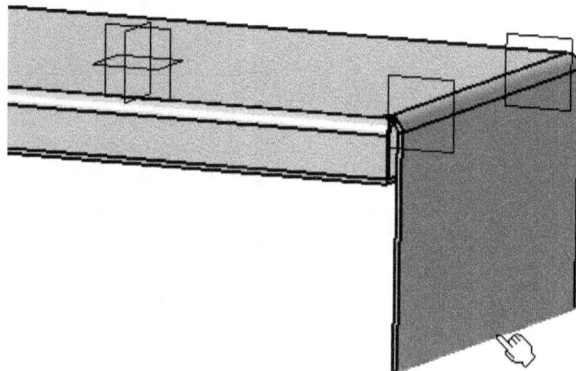

Figure 3–63

2. Click (Flange).

3. Select **Relimited** in the menu.

4. Select inside the *Limit 1* field in the Flange Definition dialog box and select one of the reference planes created in Task 6.

5. Select the other reference plane created in Task 6 to be Limit 2 for the flange.

6. Enter the following dimensions for the flange:

   • *Length:* **20mm**
   • *Angle:* **90deg**

*What would the tabs look like if they had been created with the **Wall on Edge** tool?*

7. Create a second relimited flange on the other side of the model, using the same limiting planes and dimensions.

8. Hide the Geometrical Set. The final model is shown in Figure 3–64.

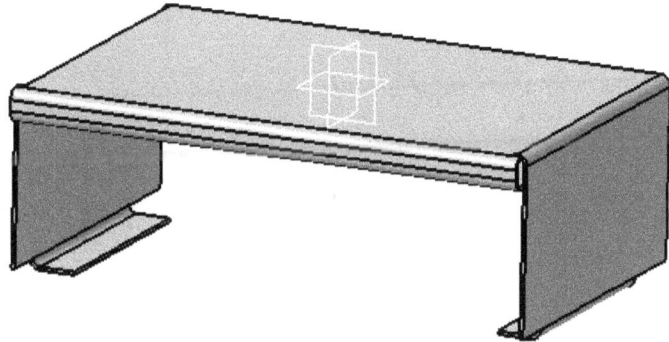

Figure 3–64

9. Save and close the file.

Practice 3c | Secondary Walls III

Practice Objectives

- Define Sheet Metal Parameters.
- Create an extruded wall.
- Create a wall on edge (Automatic).
- Create a wall on edge (Sketch based).
- Create a hem.

In this practice, you will create primary and secondary walls. At the end of the practice, the completed model will display as shown in Figure 3–65.

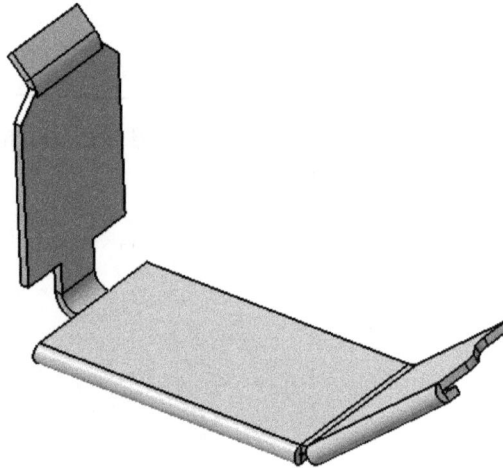

Figure 3–65

Task 1 - Open a part model.

1. Open **StaplerSpring.CATPart**. The model does not contain any visible geometry. An isolated surface is contained in **Geometrical Set.1** and is currently hidden.

Task 2 - Define sheet metal parameters.

In this task, you will define the sheet metal parameters. All sheet metal operations are unavailable until parameters have been defined.

1. Click ![icon](Sheet Metal Parameters).

2. Select the *Parameters* tab and enter **0.5** in the *Thickness* field and **1** in the *Default Bend Radius* field.

3. Click **OK** to close the Sheet Metal Parameters dialog box. The sheet metal operations are now available.

Task 3 - Create the profile for an extruded wall.

In this task, you will create the profile for an extruded wall in the Sketcher workbench.

1. Highlight the YZ plane and click . Create the line shown in Figure 3–66.

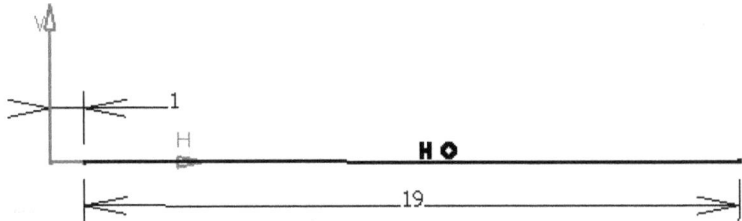

Figure 3–66

2. Click ![icon](Exit Workbench) to return to the Generative Sheetmetal Design workbench.

Task 4 - Create an extruded wall.

The sketched profile created in the previous task will be used to create the first wall of the model.

1. Highlight the sketch, if required, and click [image] (Extrusion).

2. Enter a length value of **10mm**.

You might need to enter
-10mm for the length
value to get the same
result.

3. Ensure that the material direction is upward.

4. Click **Preview** and ensure that the model displays as shown in Figure 3–67.

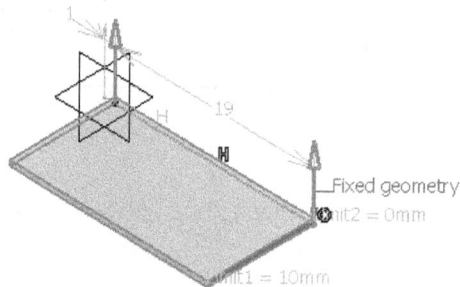

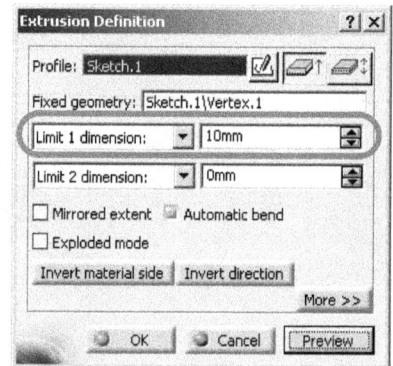

Figure 3–67

5. Click **OK**.

Task 5 - Create the profile for a wall on edge.

In this task, you will create the profile for a sketch based wall on edge in the Sketcher workbench.

1. Highlight the ZX plane and click [image] (Sketch).

2. Create the profile shown in Figure 3–68. Constrain the bottom edge of the profile with the top face of the extruded wall. Ensure that the profile is closed.

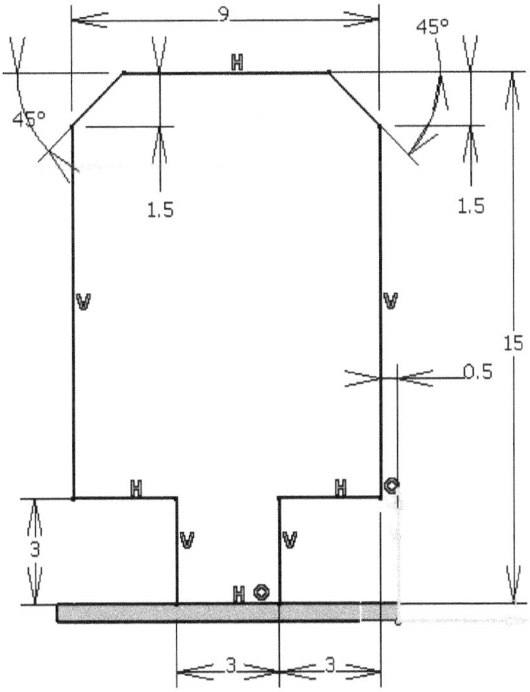

Figure 3–68

3. Click ⬆ (Exit Workbench) to return to the Generative Sheetmetal Design workbench.

Task 6 - Create a wall on edge. (Sketch based)

In this task, the profile created in the previous task will be used to create a sketch based wall on edge.

1. Click 🔲 (Wall On Edge). The Wall On Edge Definition dialog box opens.

2. Select **Sketched Based** in the Type drop-down list.

3. Select the profile in the display or specification tree.

4. Select the edge as shown in Figure 3–69. Ensure that the material direction is outward.

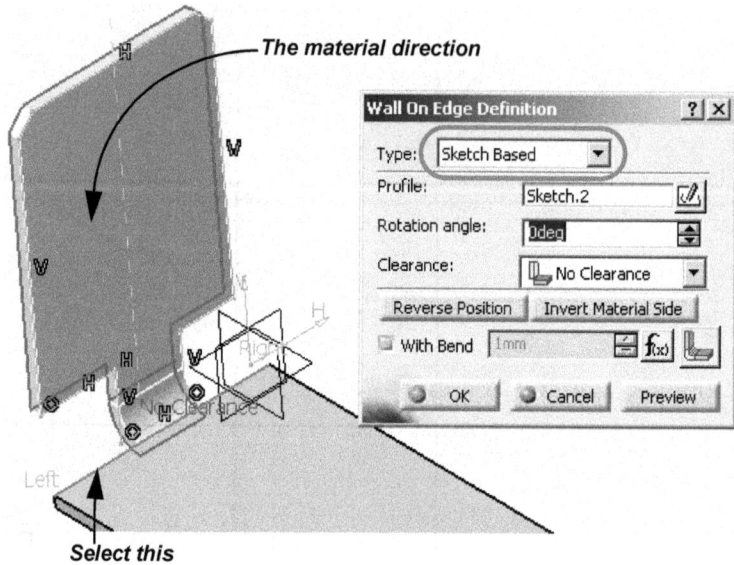

Figure 3–69

5. Click **OK** to complete the feature.

Task 7 - Create a wall on edge (Automatic).

In this task, you will create a wall on edge using the **Automatic** option. The wall will be limited by a surface element.

1. Show **Geometrical Set.1** to display the surface. The model displays as shown in Figure 3–70.

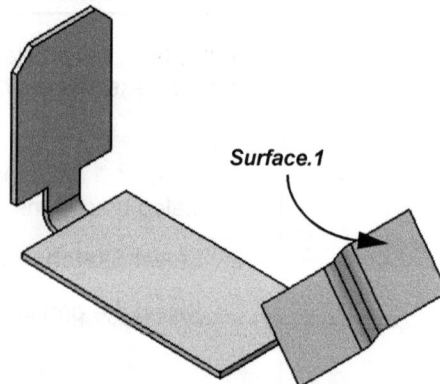

Figure 3–70

---

2. Click 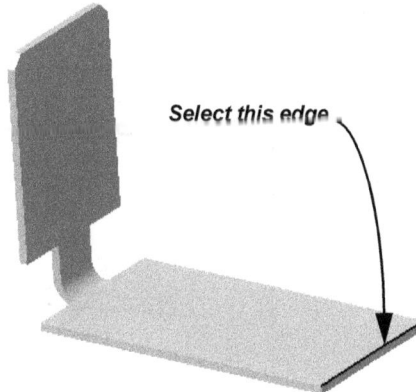 (Wall On Edge) and select **Automatic** in the Type drop-down list.

3. Select the edge shown in Figure 3–71.

Select this edge

Figure 3–71

4. Use the following dimensions and options as shown in Figure 3–72:

- *Height & Inclination:* **Up To Plane/Surface**
- Select **Surface.1** from the specification tree as the height reference
- *Angle:* **142deg**

*If you select **Surface.1** from the model, you might select a sub-element and not the entire surface. This can lead to unexpected results.*

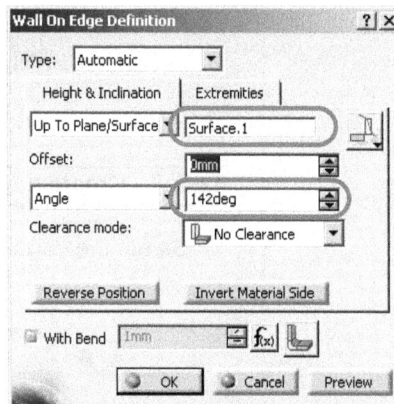

Figure 3–72

5. Ensure the material is added outward, as shown in Figure 3–73. If the material is added in the wrong direction, click **Invert Material Side**.

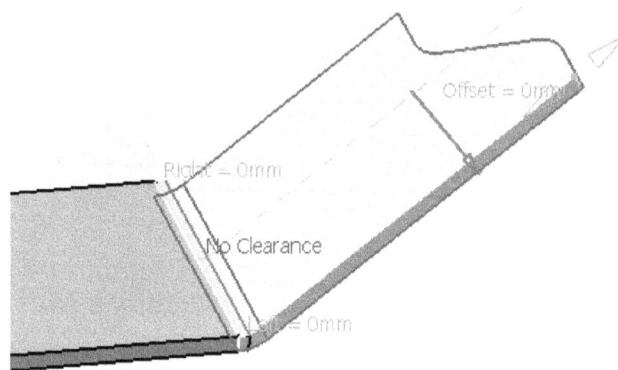

Figure 3–73

6. Click **OK** to generate the wall on edge.

7. Hide **Geometrical Set.1**. The model displays as shown in Figure 3–74.

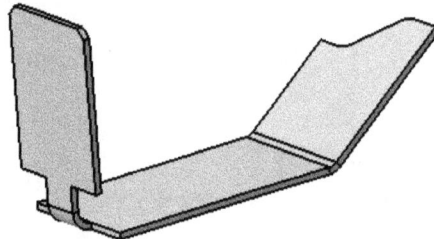

Figure 3–74

Task 8 - Create a wall on edge (Automatic).

1. Select the edge shown in Figure 3–75

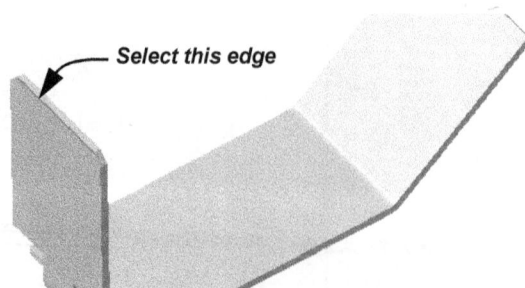

Figure 3–75

2. Click ![icon] (Wall On Edge). The Wall On Edge Definition dialog box opens.

3. Create a wall on edge using the following parameters as shown in Figure 3–76:

    - *Type:* **Automatic**
    - *Height:* **2mm**
    - *Angle:* **136deg**

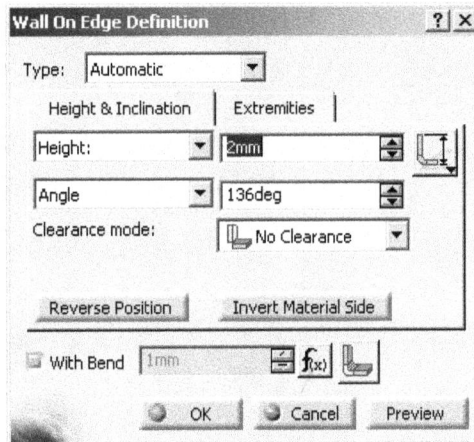

Figure 3–76

4. Click **OK** to generate the wall on edge. The wall displays as shown in Figure 3–77.

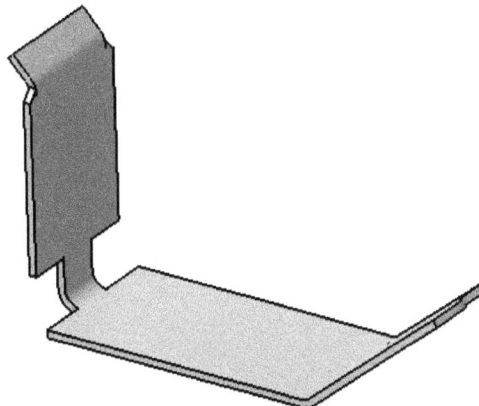

Figure 3–77

Task 9 - Create a hem.

1. Click ![icon] (Hem) in the **Swept Walls** flyout menu of Walls toolbar.

2. Edit the *Length* to **1mm**.

3. Right-click in the *Radius* field and select **Formula> Deactivate**.

4. Edit the *Radius* to **0.1mm**.

5. Select the edge shown in Figure 3–78.

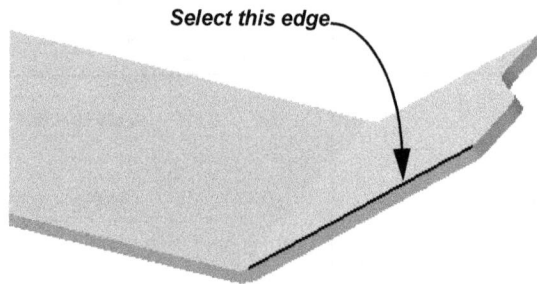

Select this edge

Figure 3–78

The Hem Definition dialog box opens as shown in Figure 3–79.

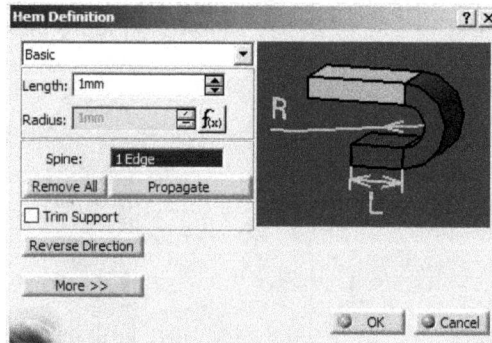

Figure 3–79

6. Click **OK** to generate the hem. The model displays as shown in Figure 3–80.

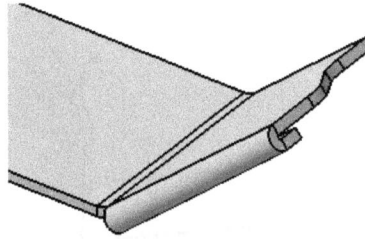

Figure 3–80

7. Click 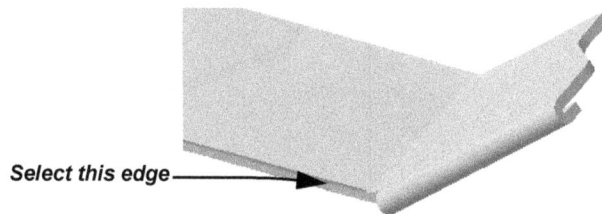 (Hem) in the **Swept Walls** flyout menu in Walls toolbar.

8. Edit the *Length* to **1mm**.

9. Right-click in the *Radius* field and select **Formula> Deactivate**.

10. Edit the *Radius* to **0.1mm**.

11. Select the edge shown in Figure 3–81.

Select this edge

Figure 3–81

12. Complete the feature. The model displays as shown in Figure 3–82.

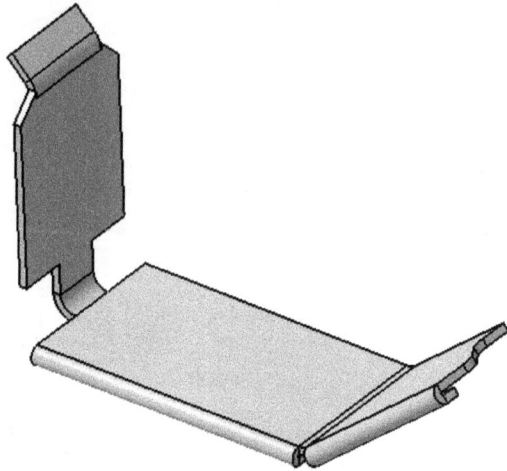

Figure 3–82

13. Flatten the part. The model displays as shown in Figure 3–83.

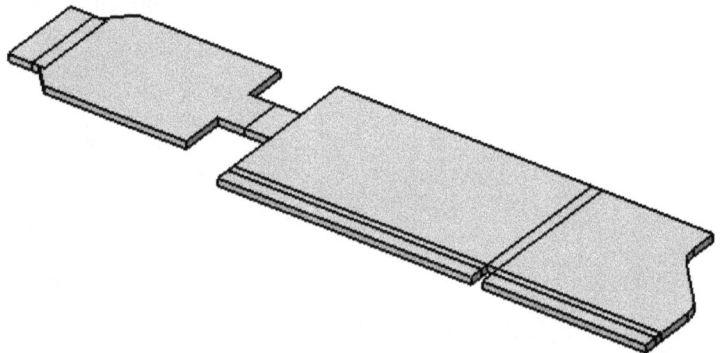

Figure 3–83

14. Save and close the file.

Bends and Unfolded View Features

Bends are used to shape the sheet metal part. In the Generative Sheetmetal workbench, bends can be applied during the creation of a wall or as a separate feature. Cylindrical bends are created between two adjoining walls while a bend from flat feature uses a sketch to define the bend line. Once bends have been created, an unfolded view of your model can be created. This unfolded view can be used to construct additional features and can be used in drawings.

Learning Objectives in this Chapter

- Add various bends to your geometry, such as Cylindrical and Conical Bends.
- Learn how to bend a model from its flat state.
- Learn how to create an Unfolded View.
- Understand how to Fold and Unfold geometry.
- Learn how to create Corner Relief.
- Use point and curve mapping to create curves and points on a folded or unfolded view.

4.1 Cylindrical Bends

Cylindrical bends are created between two adjoining walls. The bend is automatically created using the default radius, as set in the Sheet Metal parameters. Cylindrical bends can be created while creating the wall feature by selecting the **With Bend** option, or by creating a bend feature after completing the wall feature. An example of a cylindrical bend is shown in Figure 4-1.

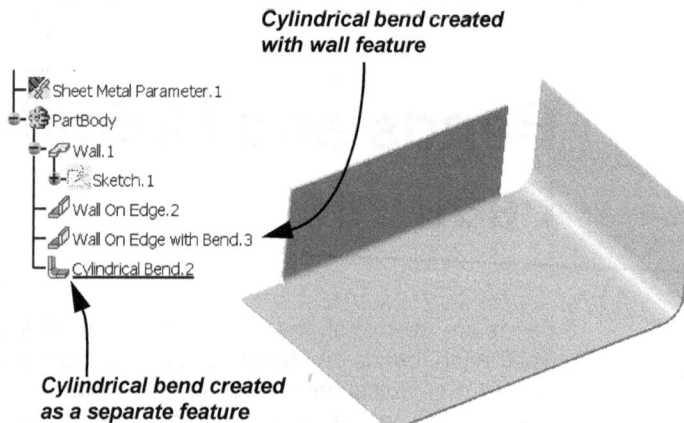

Cylindrical bend created with wall feature

Cylindrical bend created as a separate feature

Figure 4-1

General Steps

Use the following general steps to create a cylindrical bend:

1. Activate the Bend tool.
2. Select the reference walls.
3. Override parameters, if required.
4. Complete the feature.

Step 1 - Activate the Bend tool.

Click (Bend) to open the Bend Definition dialog box.

Step 2 - Select the reference walls.

Select the two adjoining walls between which the bend is created. Arrows display on the model to indicate the direction of the bend, as shown in Figure 4–2.

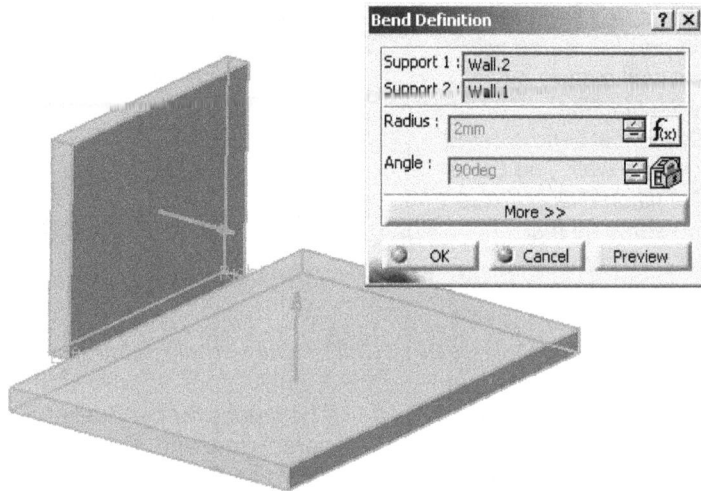

Figure 4–2

Step 3 - Override parameters, if required.

All parameter information for a bend is already defined. The angle of the wall was defined when the wall was created, and it cannot be modified from inside the Bend Definition dialog box. The default radius and bend relief are defined in the Sheet Metal Parameters dialog box. Both radius and bend relief can be overridden as required.

To override the default radius, right-click and select **Formula> Deactivate**. The *Radius* field displays enabling the radius to be edited.

The bend relief can also be overridden on an individual basis. To override the default bend relief, click **More** to expand the Bend Definition dialog box, as shown in Figure 4–3. Select the appropriate bend extremity tab and use the drop-down list on the graphical icon to select a different bend relief.

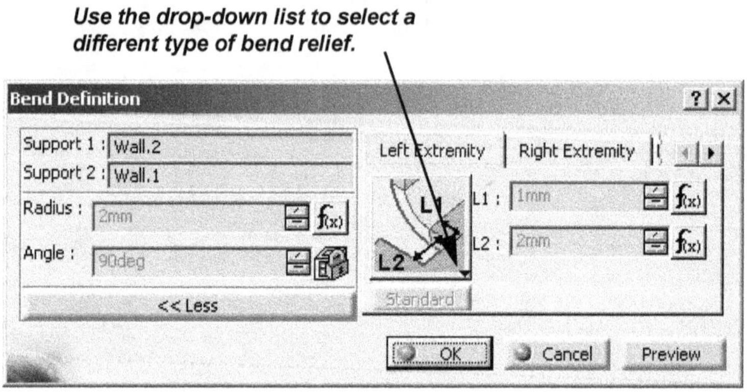

You can override the radius and bend relief on bends created with the wall feature by redefining the Cylindrical bend created with the wall. The Bend Definition dialog box is the same as that created separately.

Use the drop-down list to select a different type of bend relief.

Figure 4–3

The values for bend relief are also based on the Sheet Metal parameters and can be overridden by right-clicking and selecting **Formula>Deactivate**, as shown in Figure 4–4. Once the formula is deactivated, you can edit the field.

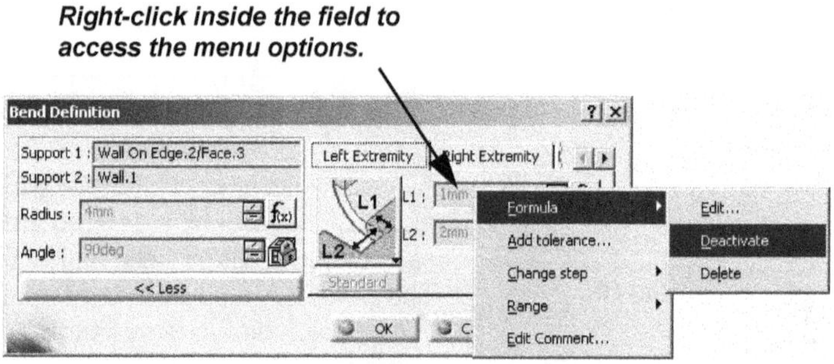

Radius and bend relief can be returned to the definitions in the Sheet Metal Parameters at any time by right-clicking and selecting Formula> Activate.

Right-click inside the field to access the menu options.

Figure 4–4

Step 4 - Complete the feature.

Click **OK** to complete the Cylindrical Bend creation, as shown in Figure 4–5.

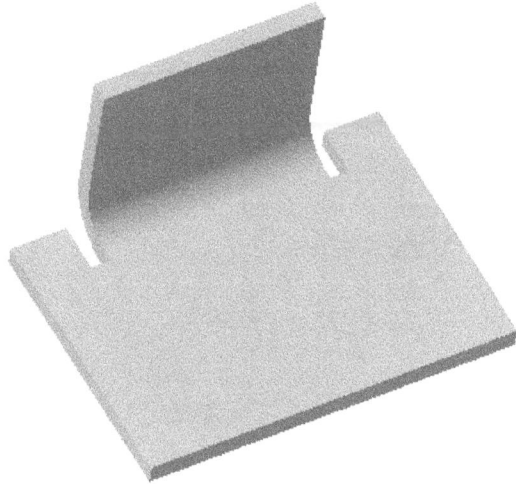

Figure 4–5

4.2 Conical Bends

Conical bends, like cylindrical bends, are created between two adjoining walls. However, a conical bend might have a different radius value at each end of the bend feature. Unlike cylindrical bends, conical bends cannot be created using the **With Bend** option during wall creation. An example of a conical bend is shown in Figure 4–6.

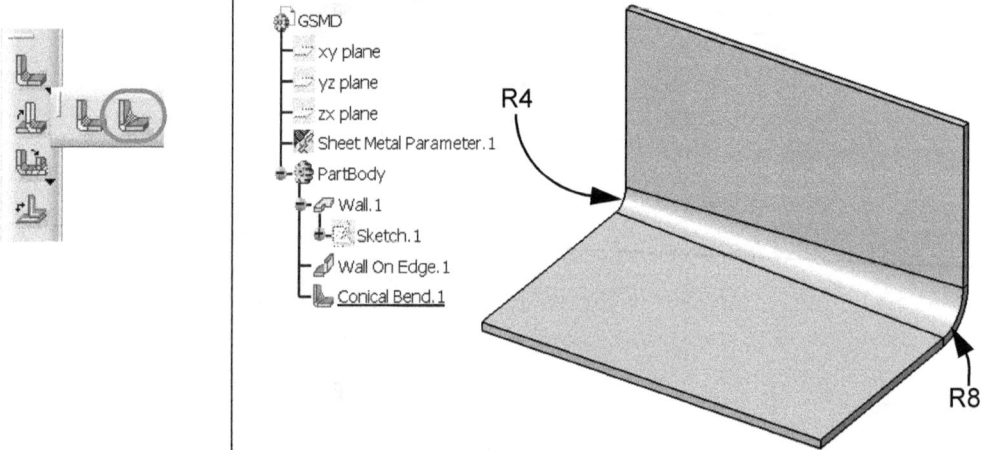

Figure 4–6

The creation of a conical bend feature is identical to that of a cylindrical bend feature. However, with a conical bend both the left and right bend radii must be specified in the Bend Definition dialog box, as shown in Figure 4–7.

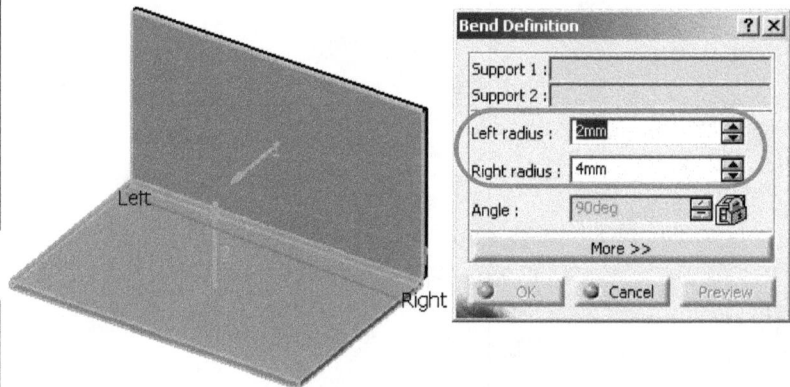

Figure 4–7

4.3 Bend From Flat

Bends can also be created on a singular wall by creating a bend line. An example of a bend from flat feature is shown in Figure 4–8.

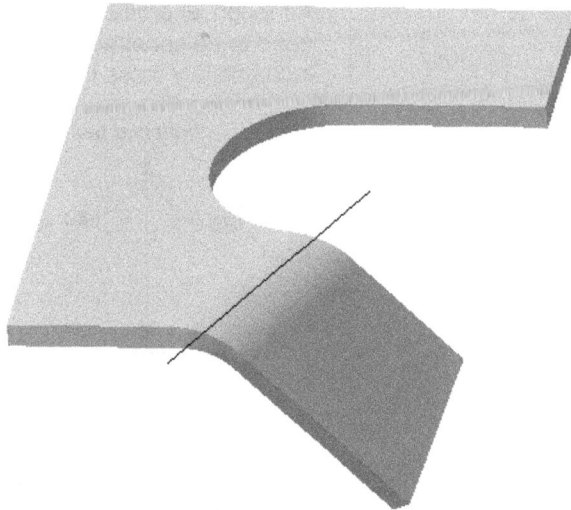

Figure 4–8

General Steps

Use the following general steps to create a bend from flat:

1. Create bend line(s).
2. Activate the **Bend From Flat** tool.
3. Define the line extrapolation.
4. Change the fixed point, if required.
5. Complete the feature.

Step 1 - Create bend line(s).

Bend lines are created in Sketcher using the wall to be bent as the sketch support. The sketch must only contain straight lines. You can create multiple bend lines in one operation by creating more than one bend line in the sketch, as shown in Figure 4–9. Although all profiles should be fully constrained, the lines do not need to be constrained to the wall; they can overlap or incompletely cross the wall.

Sketched bend lines

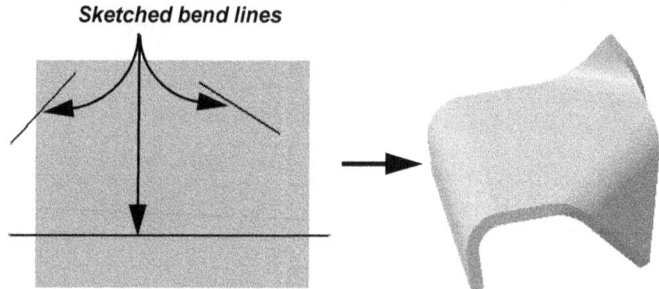

Figure 4–9

There cannot be any intersection of bend lines, both in the same sketch or between existing sketched bend lines. If an intersection occurs, an update error box opens as shown in Figure 4–10, when you attempt to complete the Bend from Flat feature.

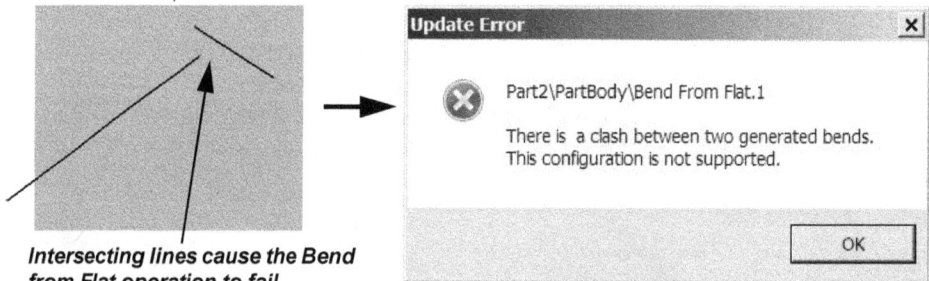

Intersecting lines cause the Bend from Flat operation to fail.

Figure 4–10

Step 2 - Activate the Bend From Flat tool.

Click (Bend From Flat) to open the Bend From Flat Definition dialog box. Select the sketch containing the bend line(s); the radius of the bends is automatically populated with the default values in the Sheet Metal Parameters dialog box, as shown in Figure 4–11.

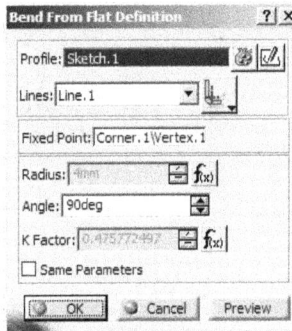

Figure 4–11

Step 3 - Define the line extrapolation.

Use the line extrapolation options as shown in Figure 4–12, to define how the sketched line affects the location of the bend.

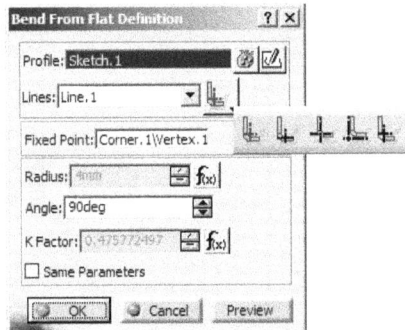

Figure 4–12

The following options are available for line extrapolation:

Option	Description	Image
(Axis)	The sketched line corresponds to the axis of the bend.	
(BTL Base Feature (Bend Tangent Line Base Feature))	The sketched line corresponds to the limit of the bend radius closest to the fixed wall.	
(IML (Inner Mold Line))	The sketched line corresponds to the intersection of the inner surface of the bend and the wall.	
(OML (Outer Mold Line))	The sketched line corresponds to the intersection of the bend support and a plane normal to the wall and normal to the OML.	
(BTL Support (Bend Tangent Line Support))	The sketched line corresponds to the limit of the bend radius closest to the side of the wall that is going to be bent.	

If you have multiple bend lines, you can toggle between them using the **Line** menu, as shown in Figure 4–13. Each line can have a different line extrapolation option, Radius, KFactor, and Angle.

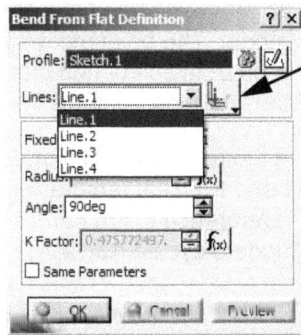

Change line extrapolation option using this flyout.

Radius, Angle, and KFactor can be different for each line.

Figure 4–13

Step 4 - Change the fixed point, if required.

If the Bend from Flat feature is created on the first wall of the model, it affects the way the model is folded and unfolded. A point is created on the wall to indicate the fixed point. It does not move when the wall is folded and unfolded.

Depending on where the point is, the wall bends and unbends differently. For example, the upper left side of Figure 4–14 shows the fixed point at the end of the wall. When the wall is bent, the model displays as shown on the upper right side. If the fixed point is moved to the center of the wall, as shown in the bottom left image of Figure 4–14, the model unfolds as shown at the bottom right side.

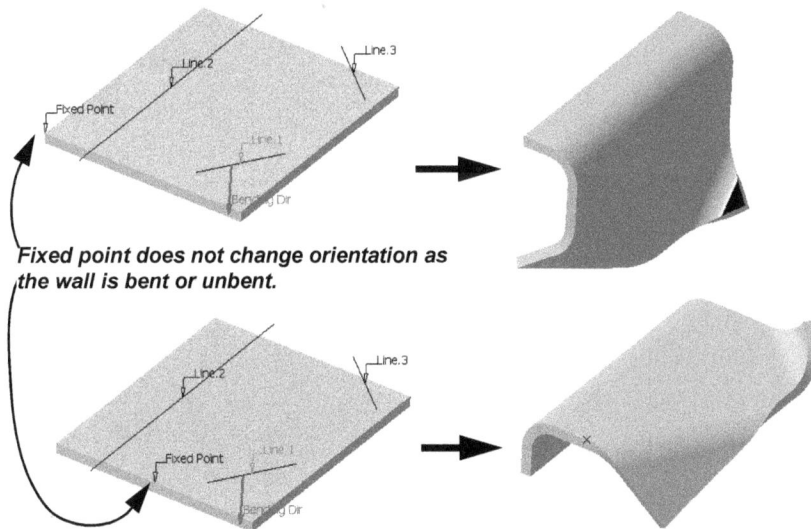

Fixed point does not change orientation as the wall is bent or unbent.

Figure 4–14

To move the fixed point, select another point or vertex on the model. The point moves to the selected location. It indicates the area between bends that remains fixed and its exact position between the bends is irrelevant.

Be sure to select a vertex from the model before you preview the bend from flat feature. Selecting the vertex after preview creates a reference to the bend from flat feature and therefore causes an update cycle error.

Step 5 - Complete the feature.

Click **OK** to complete the bend from flat feature, as shown in Figure 4–15.

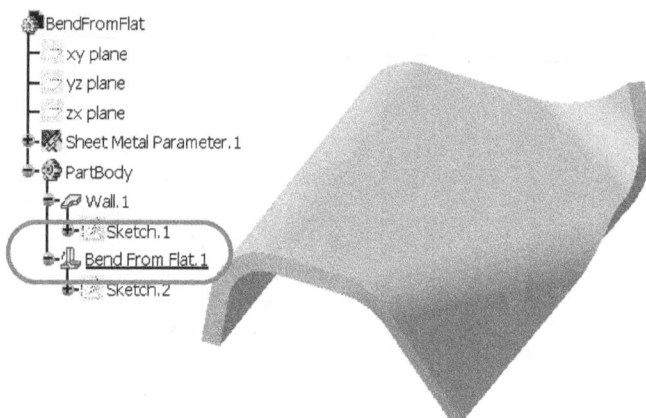

Figure 4–15

4.4 Unfolded View

Once bends have been created in the model, an unfolded view can be created. Unfolded views are required to manufacture the product. They can be documented in a drawing, and dimensioned to determine the size of metal sheet required to create the final product. Unfolded views can also be used to create additional features, such as corner relief and features that encompass more than one wall. An example is shown in Figure 4–16.

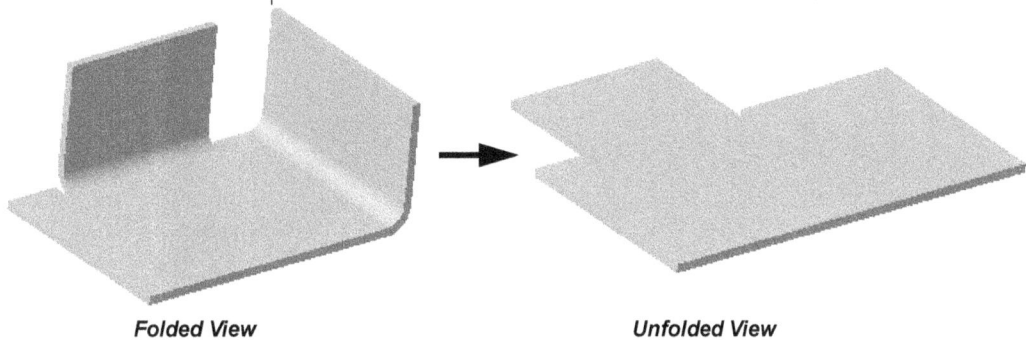

Folded View   *Unfolded View*

Figure 4–16

General Steps

Use the following general steps to create an unfolded view:

1. Unfold the model.
2. Use a multi-viewer, if required.
3. Fold the model.

Step 1 - Unfold the model.

Once all of the bends have been created, click [icon] (Fold/
Unfold). The model unfolds using the first wall (or first sketched
entity) as the fixed wall for the unfold reference as shown in
Figure 4–17.

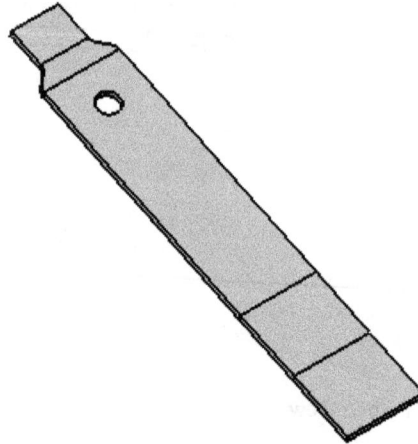

Figure 4–17

Step 2 - Use a multi-viewer, if required.

Both the folded and unfolded view can be displayed at the same

time using the multi-viewer. When [icon] (Multi Viewer) is clicked,
a new window opens so that both the folded and unfolded views
of the model are shown. Select **Window>Tile Horizontal or
Window>Tile Vertical** in the menu bar to display both views, as
shown in Figure 4–18. Toggle between the windows to work in
both views.

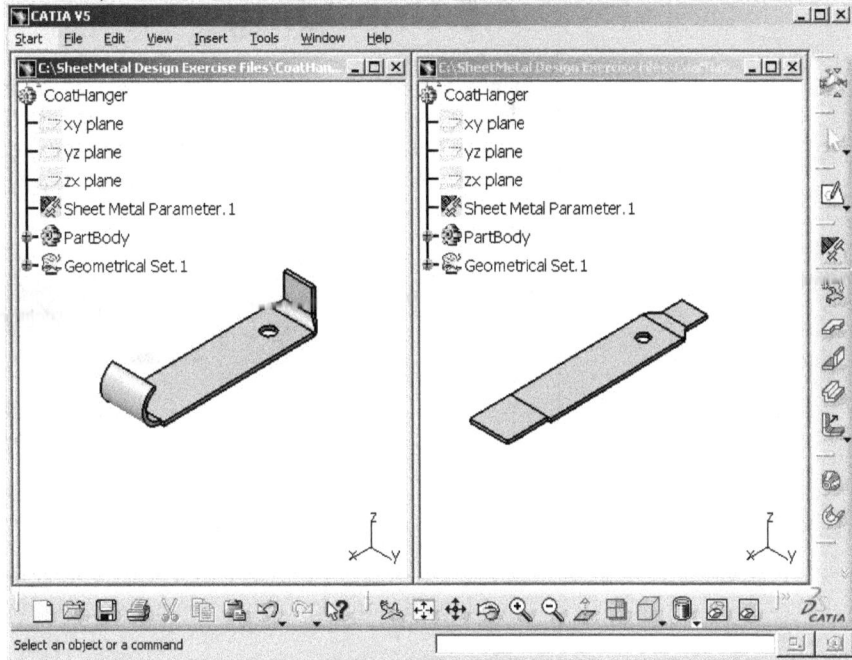

Figure 4–18

To exit Multi-viewer mode, close the view that does not have "Current" in brackets and maximize the other view. Closing the window that is current closes the entire model.

Step 3 - Fold the model.

Click (Fold/Unfold) again to return to the folded view as shown in Figure 4–19.

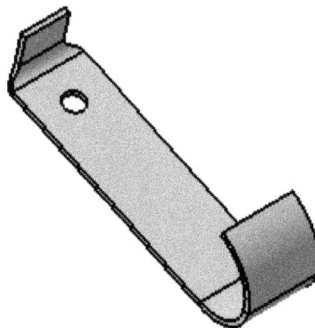

Figure 4–19

4.5 Unfolding

Unfolding enables you to flatten specific bends on the model. This is useful when working in a complex model so that you can flatten only the required geometry. Unfolding can also be used to perform a bendback operation, as shown in Figure 4–20.

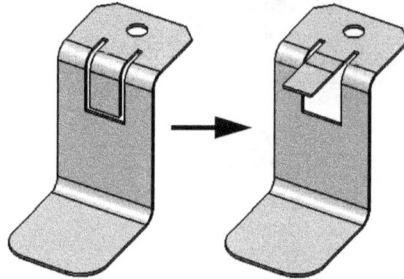

Figure 4–20

Additionally, you can use these feature to keep specified face(s) unfolded according to your design requirements.

General Steps

Use the following general steps to create an unfolded view:

1. Start the unfolding operation.
2. Define the unfolding reference geometry.
3. Complete the feature.

Step 1 - Start the unfolding operation.

To start the unfolding process, there must be at least one bend in the model. After creating a bend, click 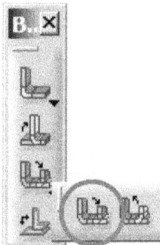 (Unfolding) in the Bending toolbar. The Unfolding Definition dialog box opens as shown in Figure 4–21.

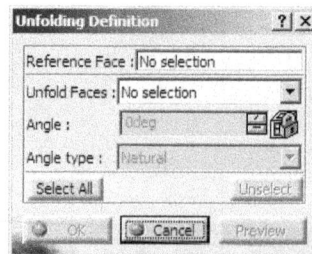

Figure 4–21

Step 2 - Define the unfolding reference geometry.

Two parameters must be specified to complete the unfolding operation:

- **Reference Face:** The wall that remains fixed during the unfold operation.

- **Unfolded Faces:** The bend faces that are unfolded. Select as many faces as required by your design intent.

An example is shown in Figure 4–22.

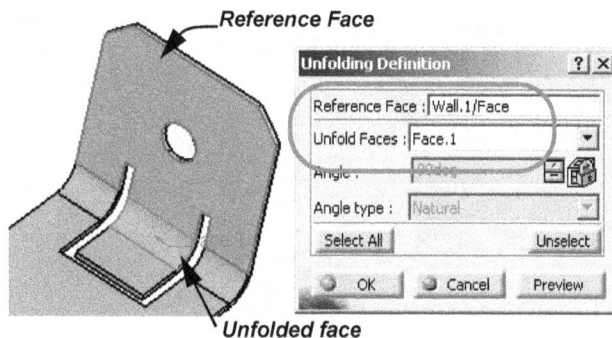

Figure 4–22

Step 3 - Complete the feature.

Click **OK** to complete the Unfolding, as shown in Figure 4–23.

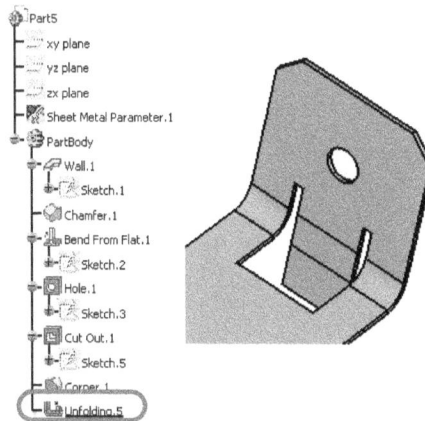

Figure 4–23

4.6 Folding

A folding operation re-forms a bend that has been unfolded. You can apply this feature only if an unfolding feature is present. An example is shown in Figure 4–24.

This feature has a very specific application. When developing a formed model from a flat, it is not possible to create geometry similar to that shown in Figure 4–24. In this example where the tab and base wall share the same bend axis, the tab can be unfolded and then returned to its new 45° angle using a Folding feature.

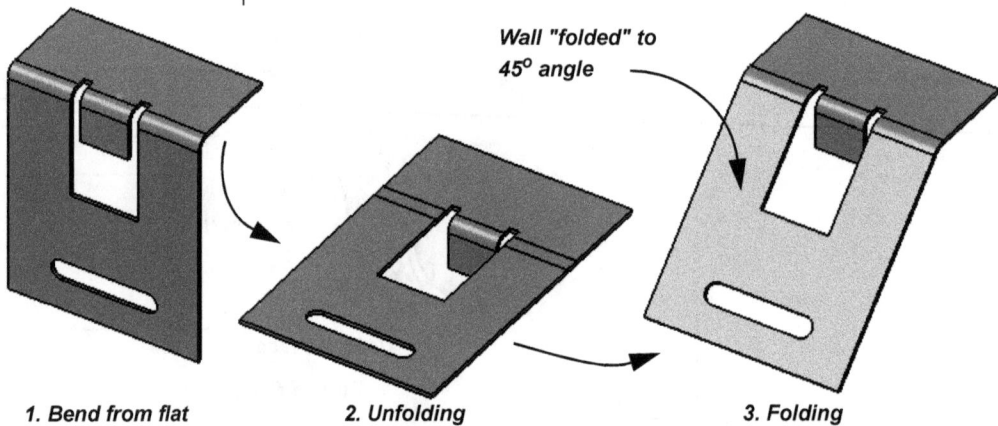

Wall "folded" to 45° angle

1. Bend from flat   2. Unfolding   3. Folding

Figure 4–24

A Bend from Flat feature could not create this geometry, however, an alternative to using the unfold - fold sequence would be to develop the tab using the **Wall on Edge** tool.

General Steps

Use the following general steps to create an unfolded view:

1. Start the folding operation.
2. Define the folding reference geometry.
3. Define the angle type.
4. Complete the feature.

Step 1 - Start the folding operation.

Click 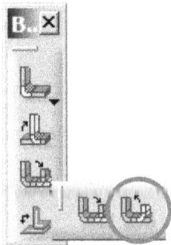 (Folding) in the Bending toolbar (in the Folding flyout).
The Folding Definition dialog box opens as shown in
Figure 4–25.

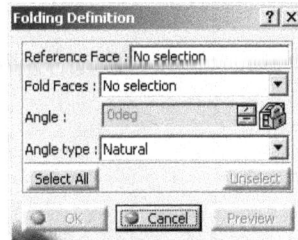

Figure 4–25

Step 2 - Define the folding reference geometry.

Two references are required to define the folding feature:

- **Reference Face:** The wall that remain fixed during the fold operation.

- **Fold Faces:** The unfolded faces that are going to be folded. Select as many faces as required by your design intent. Bend faces that have not been unfolded cannot be selected.

An example is shown in Figure 4–26.

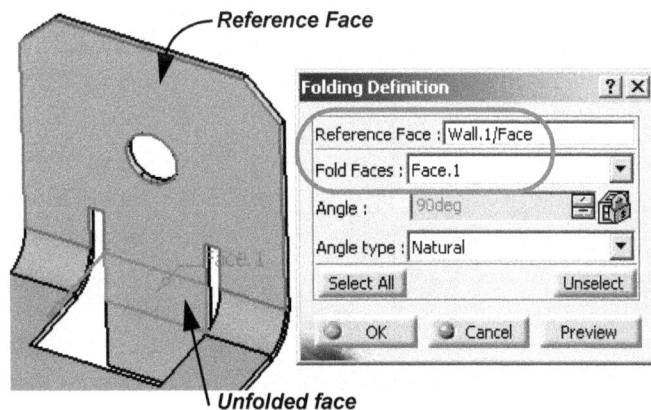

Figure 4–26

Step 3 - Define the angle type.

There are three different Angle types in the Folding Definition dialog box as shown in Figure 4–27.

• Natural

• Defined

• Spring back

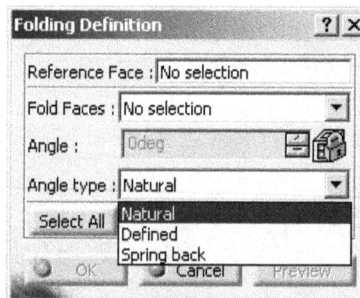

Figure 4–27

Natural

When the **Natural** option is selected, it folds the unfolded faces to their original position.

Defined

When the **Defined** option is selected, the *Angle* field becomes available and enables you to enter an angular value for folding the face, as shown in Figure 4–28. This enables you to fold the face(s) with an specified angle. The fold angle is measured from the unfolded position.

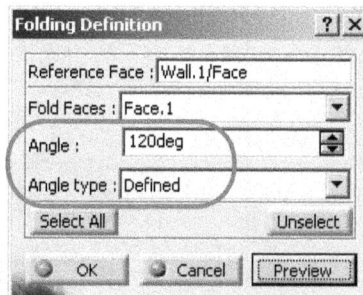

Figure 4–28

An example is shown in Figure 4–29.

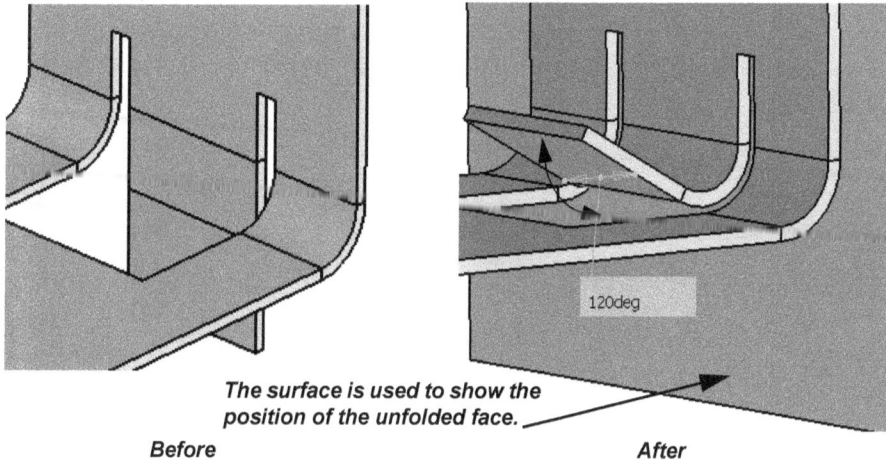

The surface is used to show the
position of the unfolded face.

Before   After

Figure 4–29

Spring back

Similar to the **Defined** option, **Spring back** enables you to
specify an angular value for folding the face. In this case, the fold
angle is measured from the original folded position of the wall
(before the unfold operation). An example is shown in
Figure 4–30.

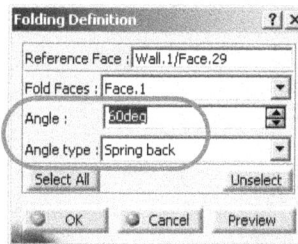

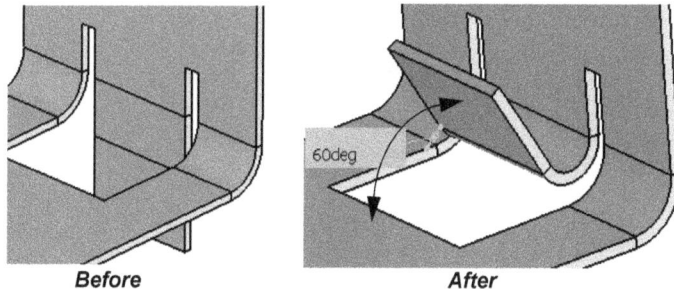

Before   After

Figure 4–30

Step 4 - Complete the feature.

Click **OK** to complete the Folding operation. A folding feature with Natural angle type is shown in Figure 4–31.

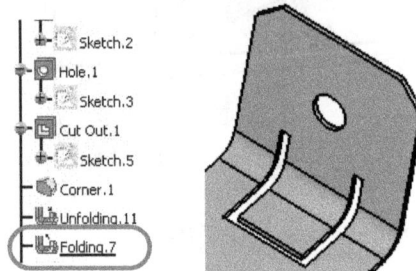

Figure 4–31

4.7 Creating Corner Relief

Corner relief is applied at the corner of intersecting walls to avoid deformation of the walls when bending. Circular and square corner reliefs can be applied to a model in the folded or unfolded view. However, user-defined corner relief can only be applied to the model in the unfolded view. The different types of corner relief are shown in Figure 4–32. The user-defined relief uses a sketched profile to define its shape.

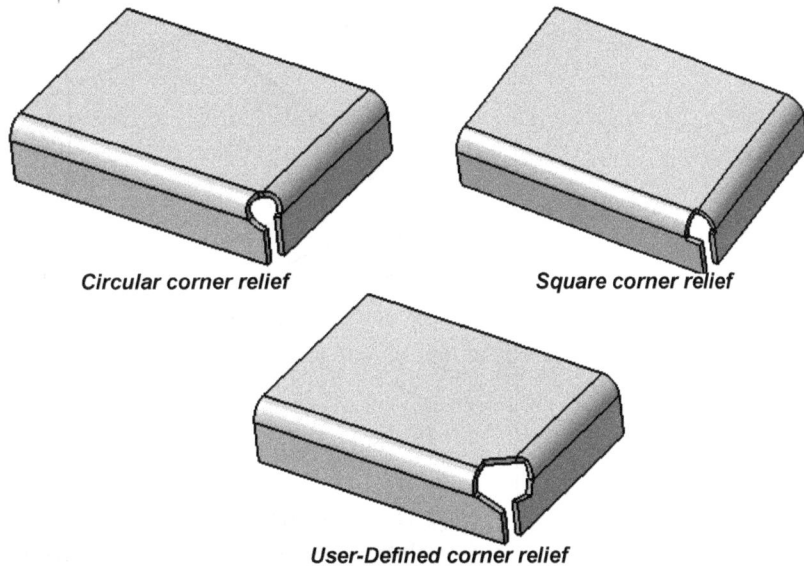

Circular corner relief   *Square corner relief*

User-Defined corner relief

Figure 4–32

General Steps

Use the following general steps to create corner relief:

1. (Optional) Unfold the model and sketch a cutting profile.
2. Activate the **Corner Relief** tool.
3. Select supports for the corner relief.
4. Complete the feature.

Step 1 - (Optional) Unfold the model and sketch a cutting profile.

This step is required if a user-defined relief is being created. The model shown in Figure 4–33 requires a user-defined relief to be applied at the corner. A user-defined corner relief can only be created in the unfolded view. To unfold the model, click

(Fold/ Unfold).

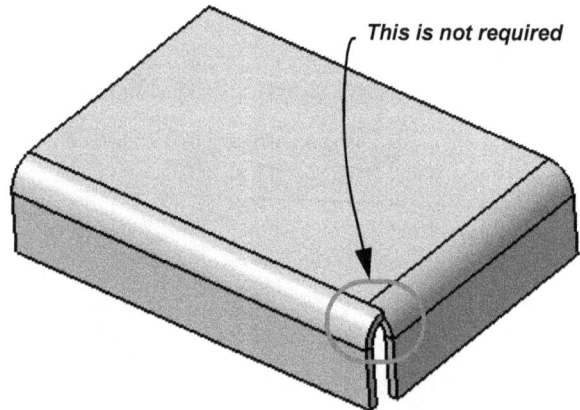

This is not required

Figure 4–33

Click (Sketch) and select a planar surface as a support. Sketch the relief cutout profile, as shown in Figure 4–34.

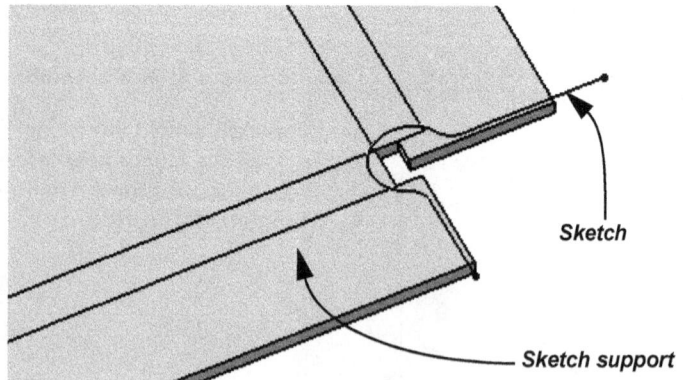

Sketch

Sketch support

Figure 4–34

Step 2 - Activate the Corner Relief tool.

Click  (Corner Relief) to create a corner relief. The Corner Relief Definition dialog box opens as shown in Figure 4–35. Select the corner relief type in the Type drop-down list.

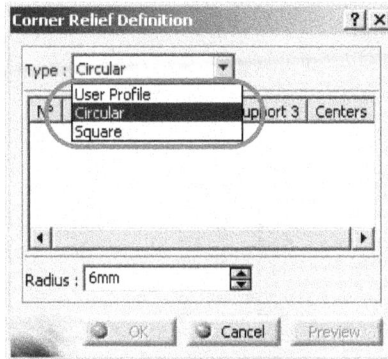

Figure 4–35

Step 3 - Select supports for the corner relief.

Circular and Square Reliefs

Select the supports on which the corner relief is to be created. Two walls are selected on the model shown in Figure 4–36.

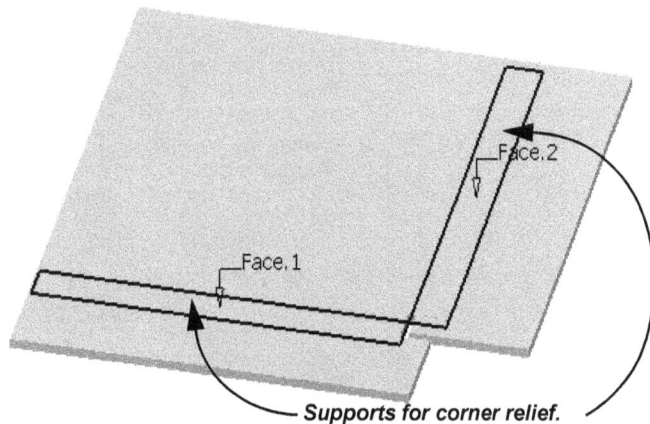

Figure 4–36

To create a corner relief on all bend features of the part, right-click on the list of supports in the Corner Relief Definition dialog box and select **Select All**, as shown in Figure 4–37.

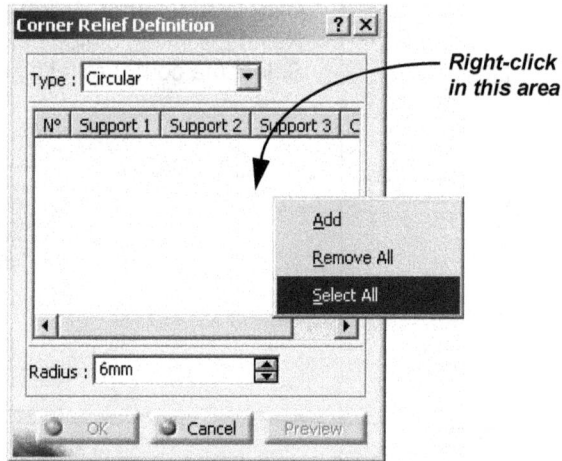

Figure 4–37

Enter the radius or length of the circular or square relief cutout.

The center of the relief cutout is located, by default, at the intersection of the two support bend axes. To redefine the cutout center, in the Corner Relief Definition dialog box, select the corner relief that you want to modify, right-click and select **Add Center** to select an existing center point or **Create Center** to define a new point, as shown in Figure 4–38.

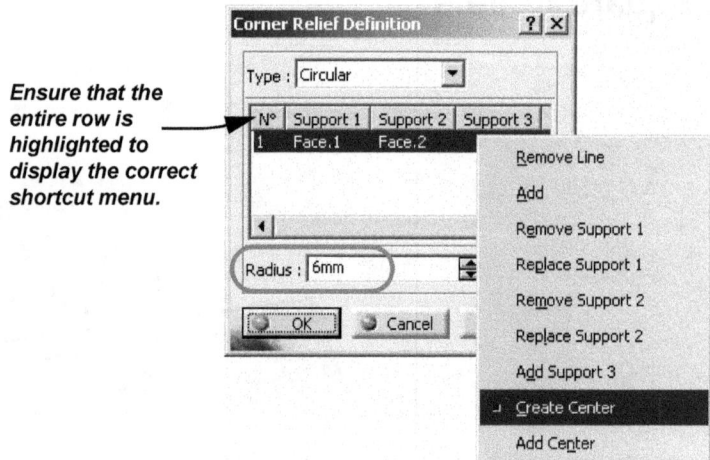

Figure 4–38

User-Defined Corner Relief

Select **User Profile** in the Type drop-down list, as shown in Figure 4–39 and select the relief profile sketch in the model or specification tree. To create a new cutout profile, click (Sketch) to enter the Sketcher workbench. Only one user-defined relief can be created at a time.

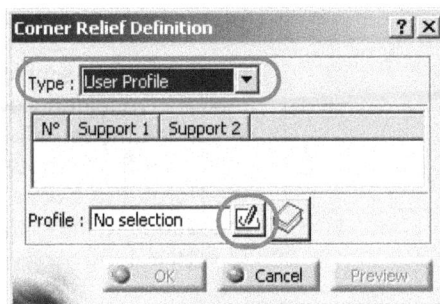

Figure 4–39

Step 4 - Complete the feature.

Once all references have been defined, click **OK** to complete the feature. If required, click (Fold/Unfold) to return to the folded view. The unfolded view must be activated to edit a user-defined corner relief.

4.8 Point and Curve Mapping

Point and curve mapping is used to create curves and points on a folded or unfolded view that were created in the other view. This is useful when creating company logos on both the folded and unfolded views, when creating stamps on bend areas, and when creating cutouts to eliminate overlapping material.

For example, a simple company logo is created on a sheet metal model in unfolded view, as shown at the top of Figure 4–40. When the model is folded, the sketch constraining the logo does not fold with the model, as shown at the bottom left side. When the **Point and Curve Mapping** tool is applied, the sketch is mapped onto the folded model as shown at the bottom right side of Figure 4–40.

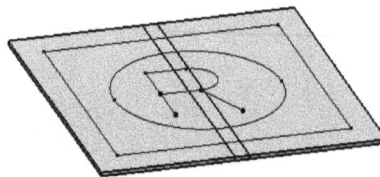

Sketch is created on an unfolded view

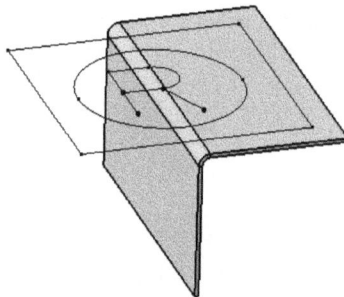

Sketch does not fold with the rest of the model

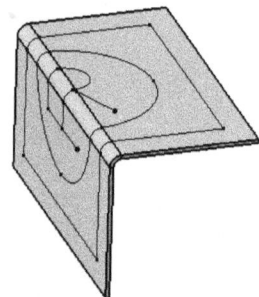

Point and curve mapping creates a folded version of the sketch

Figure 4–40

Another use of curve mapping is shown in Figure 4–41. The two profiles are created on a sheet metal model in the unfolded view, and the curves are mapped to have the surface shape. The mapped curves are then used to create a surface stamp.

Sketch is created on unfolded view.

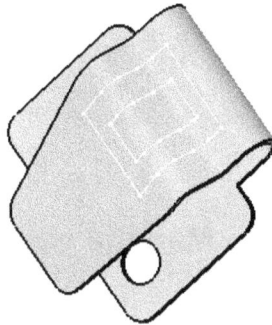

Profiles are mapped.

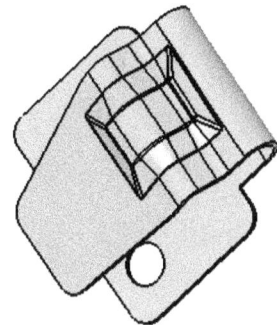

Mapped curves are used to create the surface stamp.

Figure 4–41

General Steps

Use the following general steps to map a point or curve:

1. Create wireframe geometry.
2. Map the geometry.

Step 1 - Create wireframe geometry.

Geometry to be mapped can be created using wireframe tools, such as lines and points, or by creating a sketch of the geometry. The geometry can be created in the folded or unfolded view. For example, a logo is created in the unfolded view in a sketch, as shown in Figure 4–42. The logo needs to be mapped onto a folded view.

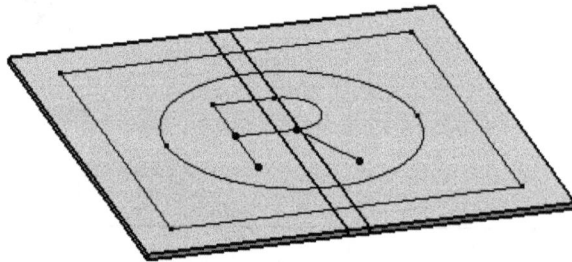

Figure 4–42

Step 2 - Map the geometry.

To map points or curves, you must be in the view in which they were created (i.e., if created in the unfolded view, you need to be in the unfolded view when activating the **Point and Curve Mapping** tool).

Select the wireframe geometry to be mapped and click

(Point or Curve Mapping). The Fold object definition dialog box opens, as shown in Figure 4–43.

Figure 4–43

Select the required mapping option in the Type drop-down list. The available mapping types are described as follows:

Mapping Type	Description
Construction element	The folded elements do not display in the unfolded drawing.
Characteristic element	The folded elements displays in the unfolded drawing by changing the standard settings in administration mode. These elements are not required for the laser process.
Marking	The folded elements are created for the laser process. The folded elements displays in the unfolded drawing by changing the standard settings in administration mode.
Engraving	The folded elements are created for the laser process. They display in the unfolded drawing by changing the standard settings in Administration mode.

Add additional elements to be mapped by clicking **Add Mode** and selecting the geometry in the specification tree or directly from the model. To remove objects from the list, click **Remove Mode** and reselect the geometry from the model or specification tree.

Click **OK** to map the selected objects. Both the folded and unfolded geometry display as shown in Figure 4–44.

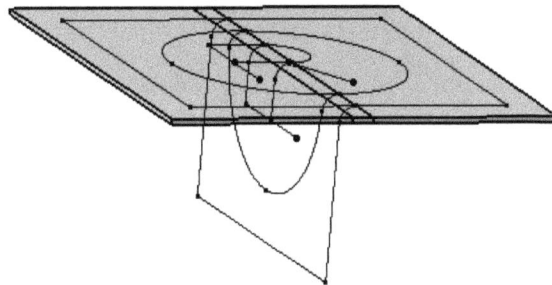

Figure 4–44

Use the **Hide/Show** tool to hide the folded or unfolded version of the geometry as required.

Practice 4a

Bend From Flat

Practice Objectives

- Create bends using Bend From Flat operation.
- Use folded and unfolded views.

In this practice, you will practice using the Bend From Flat operation. At the end of the practice, your model will look like Figure 4–45.

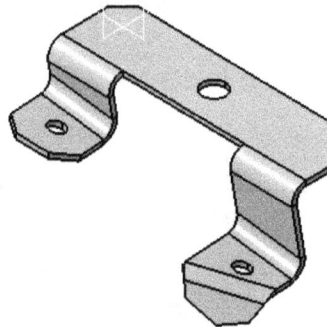

Figure 4–45

Goal

Task 1 - Open the part.

1. Open the **Bend.CATPart** file. The model displays as shown in Figure 4–46.

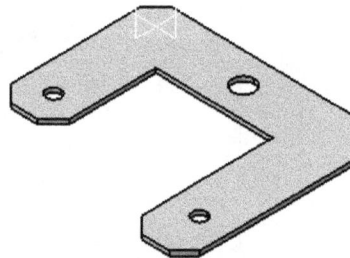

Figure 4–46

2. Review how the model was created up to this point. The holes in the model were created inside the profile wall and not as separate features.

Task 2 - Create bend profiles.

1. Select the top surface of the first wall and activate the Sketcher workbench.

2. Create the lines that represent the bend lines for the Bend From Flat operation, as shown in Figure 4–47. Create the lines in the order shown so that the line references in future steps are consistent.

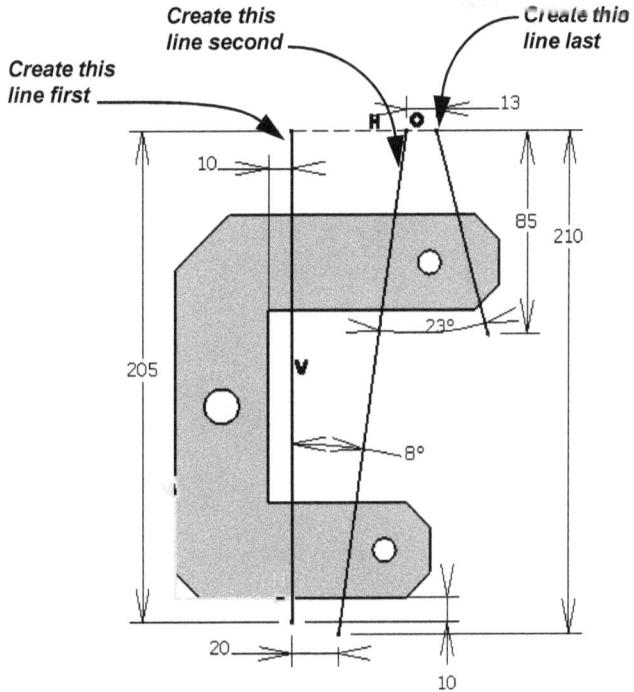

Figure 4–47

3. Exit the Sketcher workbench.

Task 3 - Create a bend from flat.

1. Click (Bend from Flat).

2. Select the sketch created in Task 2 and the system displays the bend lines on the part.

Design Considerations

Two important notes on selecting a fixed point:

- Select the fixed point as early in the creation of the feature as possible. If the fixed point is selected after preview or feature creation, an update cycle error occurs.

- Select a vertex at any location on the wall to remain fixed during bending. Its exact location on the wall is not important.

3. Ensure that a vertex similar to that shown in Figure 4–48 is selected for the fixed point.

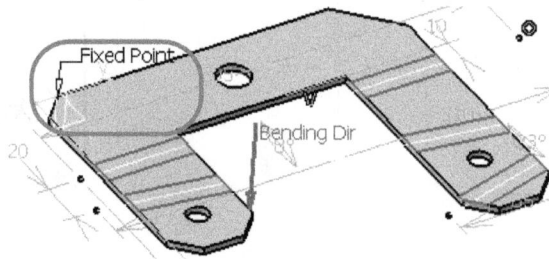

Figure 4–48

4. Change the angle on **Line.1** to **80 deg** and ensure that the bend line location is set to **Axis**.

5. Ensure that **Line.1** is the line shown in Figure 4–49. If not, use the Lines drop-down list to locate the correct line. Your lines might differ if you created them in a different order in Task 2.

6. Ensure that the bending direction for **Line.1** is pointing downward, as shown in Figure 4–49. If required, to reverse the bending direction for **Line.1**, select the Bending Dir text in the graphic.

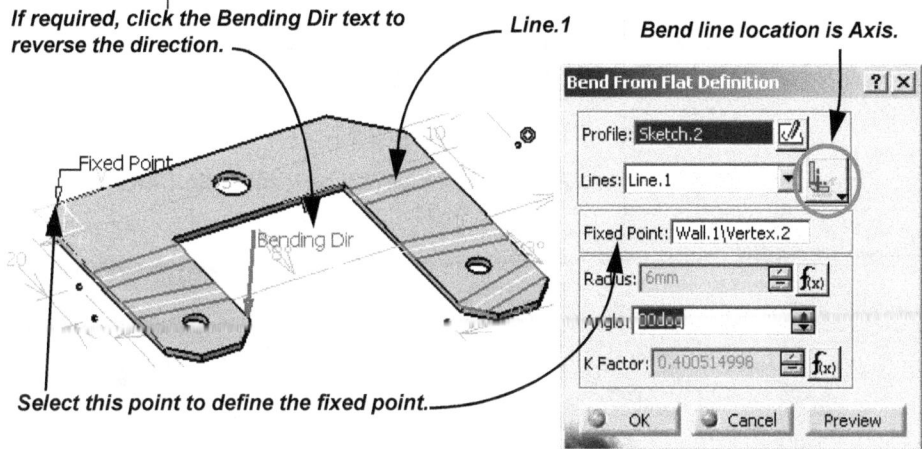

If required, click the Bending Dir text to reverse the direction.

Line.1

Bend line location is Axis.

Fixed Point

Bending Dir

Select this point to define the fixed point.

Bend From Flat Definition

Profile: Sketch.2

Lines: Line.1

Fixed Point: Wall.1\Vertex.2

Radius: 6mm

Angle: 30deg

K Factor: 0.400514998

OK   Cancel   Preview

Figure 4–49

7. Select **Line.2** in the Lines drop-down list and ensure that the line shown in Figure 4–50 is the highlighted line. If not, use the Lines drop-down list to locate the correct line.

8. Change the angle of **Line.2** to **70 deg** and ensure that the bend line location is set to **Axis**.

9. Ensure that the bending direction for **Line.2** is upward, as shown in Figure 4–50.

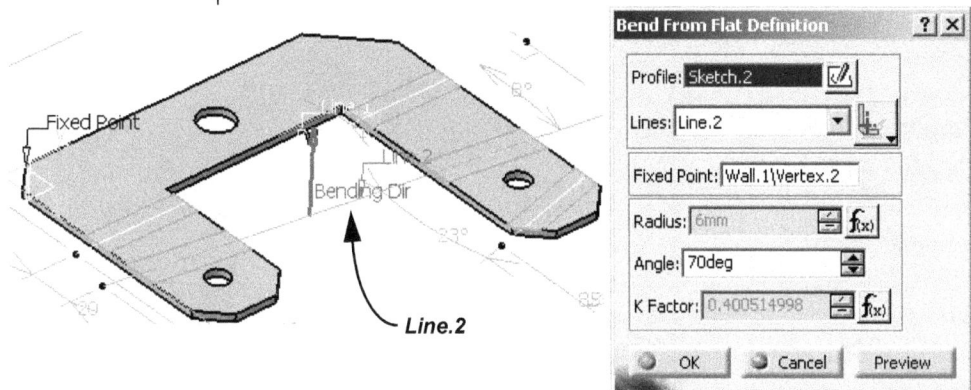

Fixed Point

Bending Dir

Line.2

Bend From Flat Definition

Profile: Sketch.2

Lines: Line.2

Fixed Point: Wall.1\Vertex.2

Radius: 6mm

Angle: 70deg

K Factor: 0.400514998

OK   Cancel   Preview

Figure 4–50

10. Select **Line.3** in the Lines drop-down list and ensure that the line shown in Figure 4–51 is the highlighted line. If not, use the Lines drop-down list to locate the correct line.

11. Change the angle to **120 deg**.

12. Change the bend line location to **OML**, as shown in Figure 4–51.

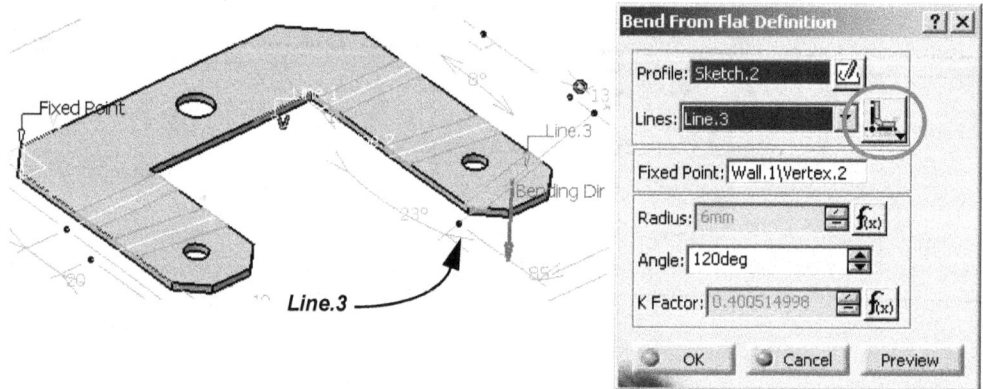

Figure 4–51

13. Ensure the bending direction is downward.

14. Click **OK** to generate the bends. The model displays as shown in Figure 4–52.

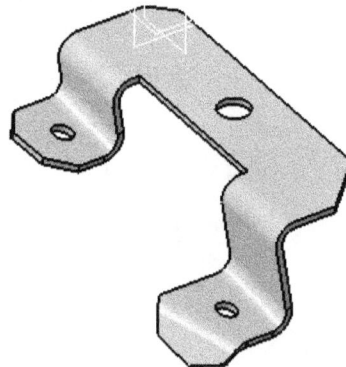

Figure 4–52

Task 4 - Change to the unfolded view.

1. Click ⬙ (Fold/Unfold). The model unfolds as shown in Figure 4–53.

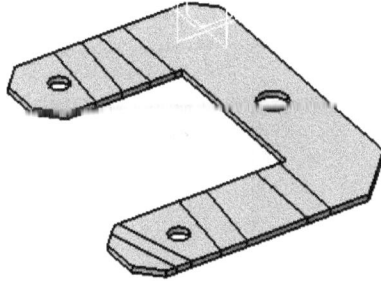

Figure 4–53

2. Click ⬙ (Fold/Unfold) again to return to the folded view.

3. Save and close the file.

Practice 4b

Bends and Corner Relief

Practice Objectives

- Create a bend.
- Create a corner relief.
- Use the multi-viewer.

In this practice, you will create the bends for the mounting bracket you have been creating in the last two chapters. You will also add a corner relief to the model. At the end of the practice, the model will display as shown in Figure 4–54.

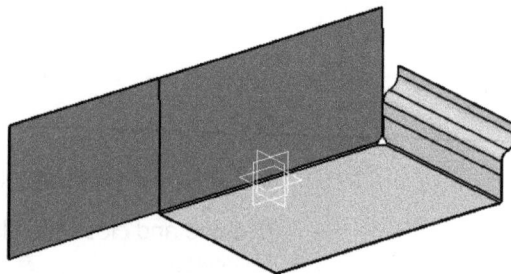

Figure 4–54

Task 1 - Open the part.

1. Open **Ex3A_Mounting_Bracket.CATPart**.

   If you completed Practice 3a, open **Mounting_Bracket.CATPart** instead. The model displays as shown in Figure 4–55.

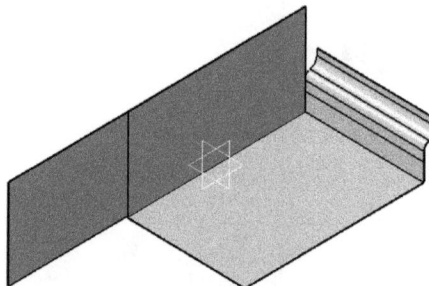

Figure 4–55

Task 2 - Create bends.

1. Click ⌐ (Bend).

2. Select the two walls shown in Figure 4–56.

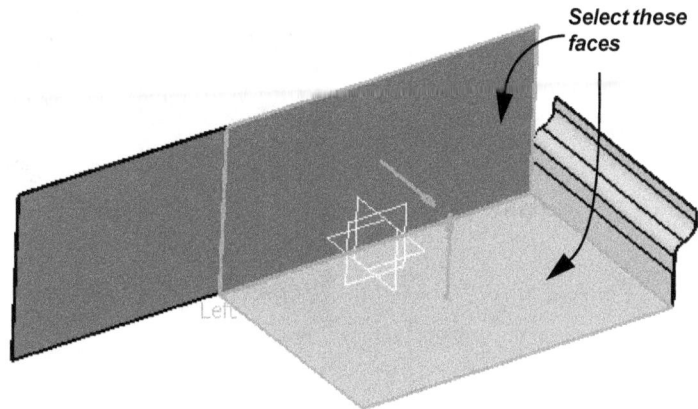

Select these faces

Figure 4–56

3. Click **OK** to generate the bend. The bend is created between the walls, as shown in Figure 4–57.

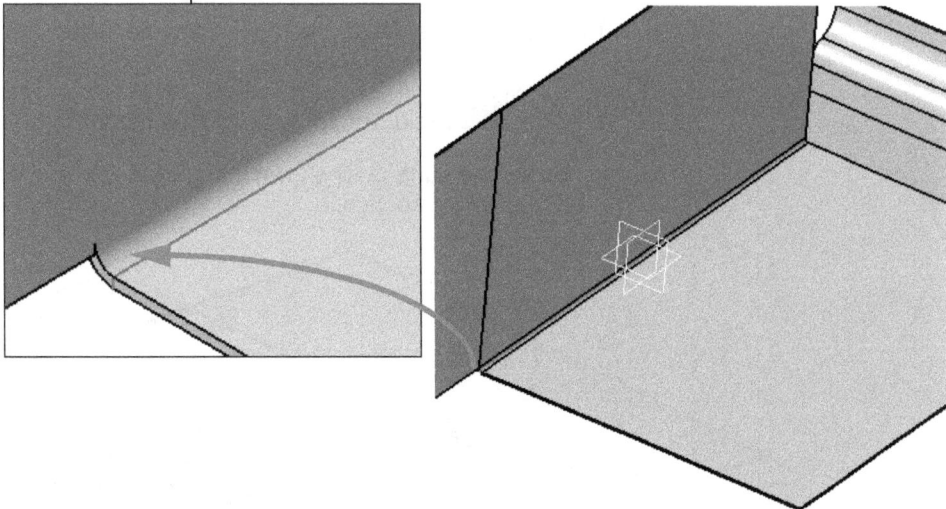

Figure 4–57

4. Create a bend between the side and bottom walls using the same technique. The model displays as shown in Figure 4–58.

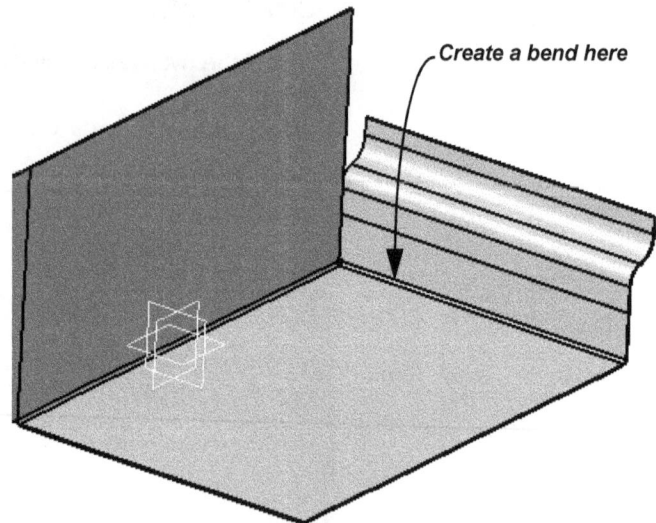

Create a bend here

Figure 4–58

Task 3 - Create a profile for a user-defined corner relief.

To create a corner relief, the model must be in the Unfolded view.

1. Click [icon] (Fold/Unfold) to unfold the model.

2. Select the surface as shown in Figure 4–59, and enter the Sketcher workbench.

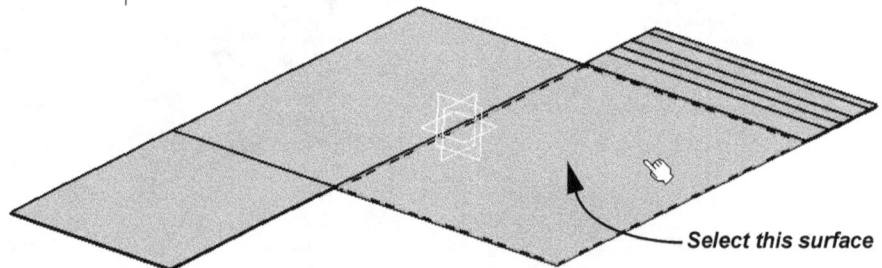

Select this surface

Figure 4–59

3. Create a sketch as shown in Figure 4–60. A close-up of the sketch is shown in Figure 4–61.

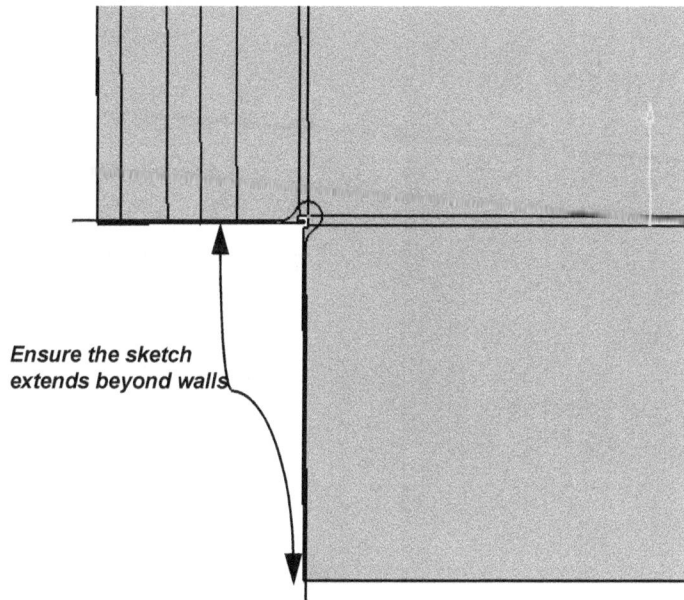

Ensure the sketch extends beyond walls

Figure 4–60

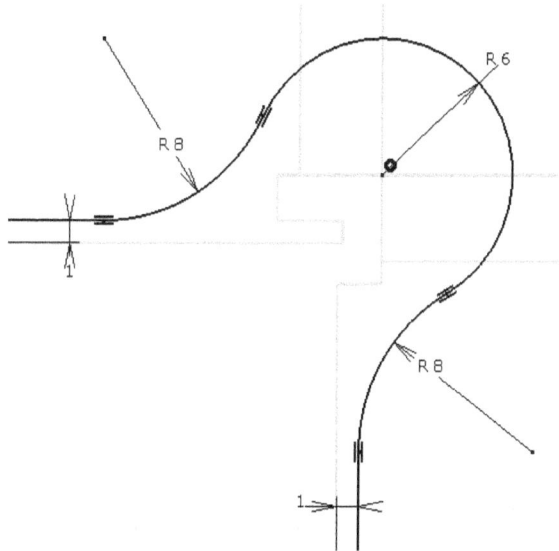

Figure 4–61

4. Exit the Sketcher workbench.

Task 4 - Create a corner relief.

1. Click [icon] (Corner Relief) and select **User Profile** in the Type drop-down list.

2. Select the two faces as supports.

3. Click in the *Profile* field and select the sketch created in Task 3 as shown in Figure 4–62.

Select these two faces

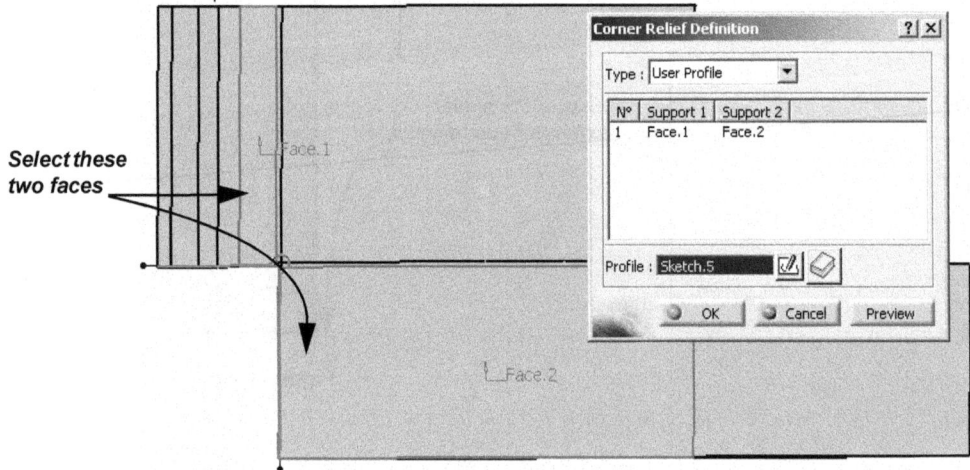

Figure 4–62

4. Click **OK** to generate the corner relief. The corner displays as shown in Figure 4–63.

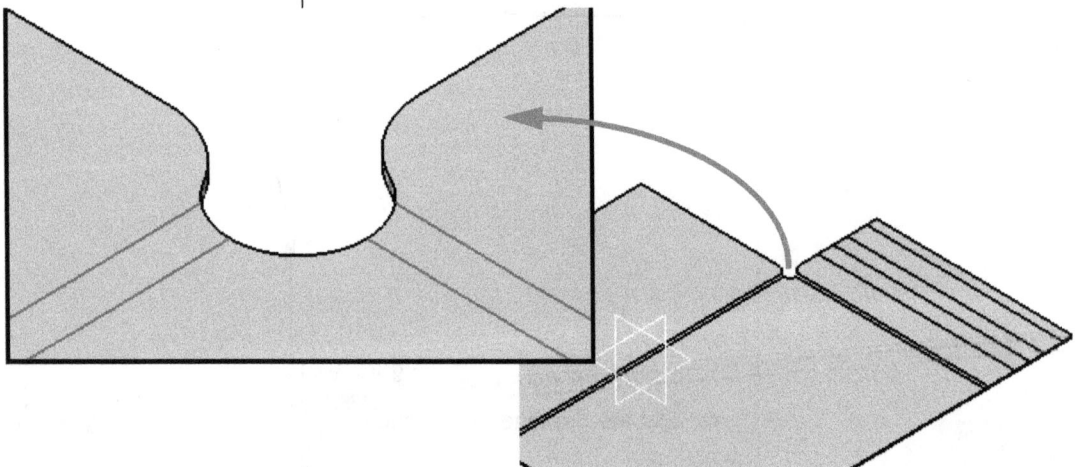

Figure 4–63

Task 5 - Use the multi-viewer.

1. Click ▦ (Multi Viewer).

2. Select **Window>Tile Horizontally**. Both the folded and unfolded views can be seen at the same time, as shown in Figure 4–64.

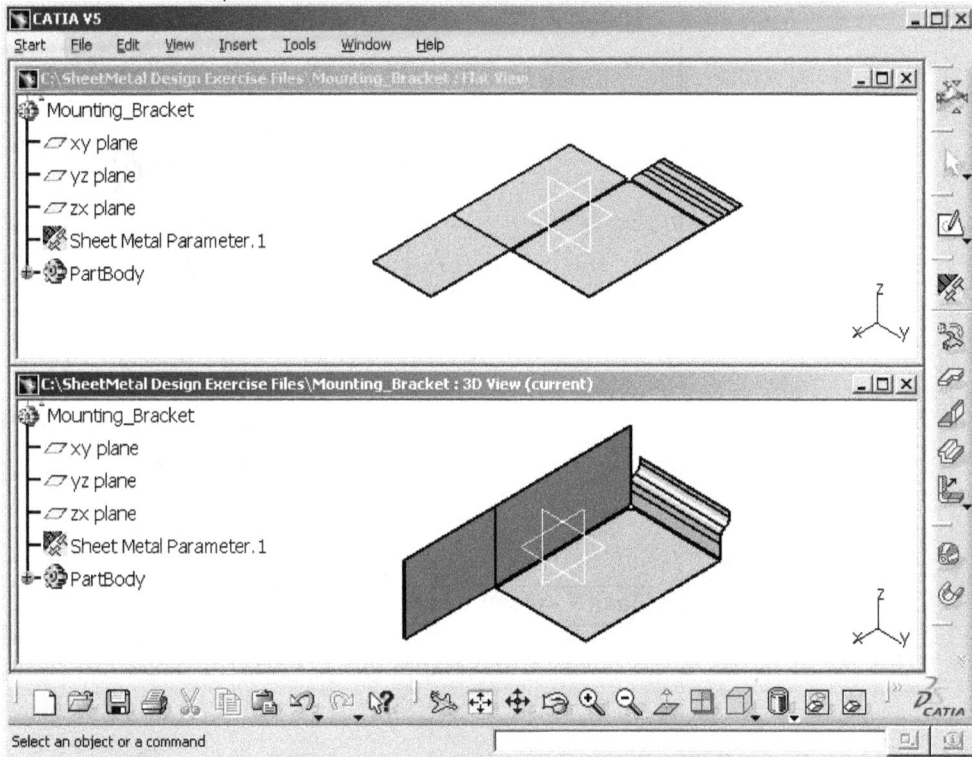

Figure 4–64

3. Save and close the file.

Practice 4c | Curve Mapping

Practice Objectives

- Create a mapped curve.
- Create a user defined pattern.

In this practice, you will map the curves and create user-defined patterns. At the end of the practice, the model will display as shown in Figure 4–65.

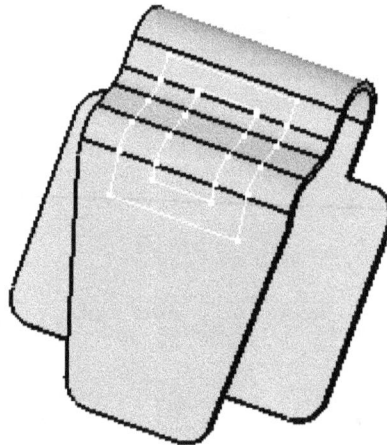

Figure 4–65

Task 1 - Open a part.

1. Open **CurveMapping.CATPart**. The model displays as shown in Figure 4–66.

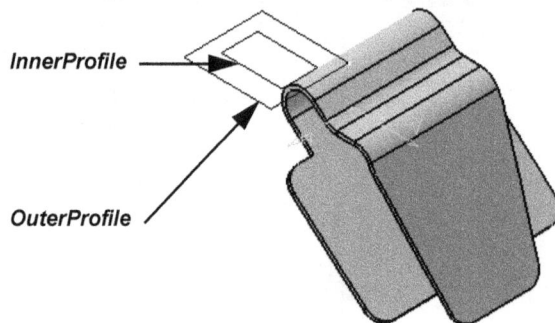

Figure 4–66

Task 2 - Unfold the part.

1. Click ⚒ (Fold/Unfold) to unfold the model

You can map a point or curve only in an unfolded view.

Task 3 - Map a curve.

1. Click ⬏ (Point or curve mapping) in the Bending toolbar. The Fold object definition dialog box opens as shown in Figure 4–67.

Figure 4–67

2. Select **OuterProfile** in the specification tree. The system displays a preview of the mapped curve as shown in Figure 4–68.

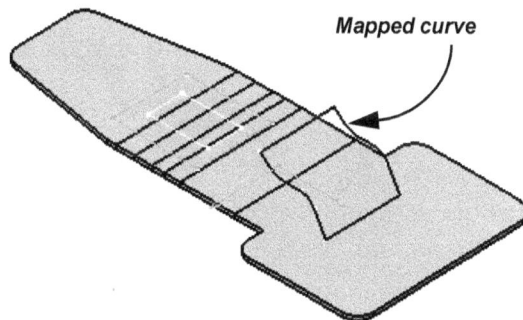

Figure 4–68

3. Click **OK**.

Design Considerations

After creating a mapped curve, it is added to a geometrical set and displays on the model. The sketch that was mapped is automatically hidden.

Task 4 - Map a second curve.

1. Click (Point or curve mapping) in the Bending toolbar.

2. Select the inner profile in the specification tree.

3. Click **OK**. The Update Error dialog box opens as shown in Figure 4–69.

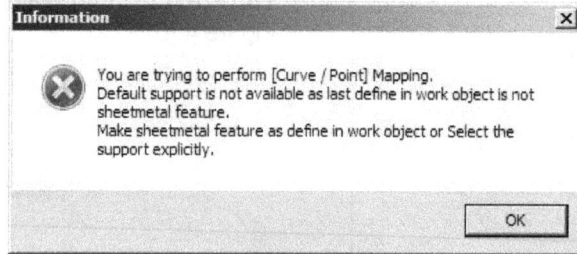

Figure 4–69

When the **Point or curve mapping** tool is used, the mapped point or curve is saved under a geometrical set, not under the part body. After every use of this tool, you need to define the work object as the part body.

4. Click **OK** to close the Update Error dialog box.

5. Close the Fold Object definition dialog box.

6. Right-click on the PartBody and select **Define In Work Object** as shown in Figure 4–70.

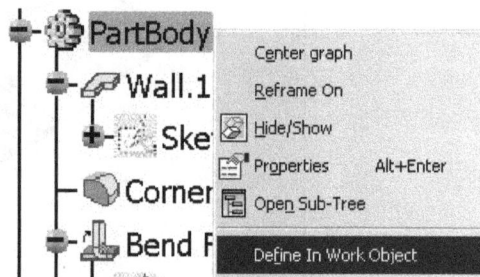

Figure 4–70

7. Click (Point or curve mapping) in the Bending toolbar and select **InnerProfile** in the display or specification tree.

8. Click **OK** to complete the feature. The model displays as shown in Figure 4–71.

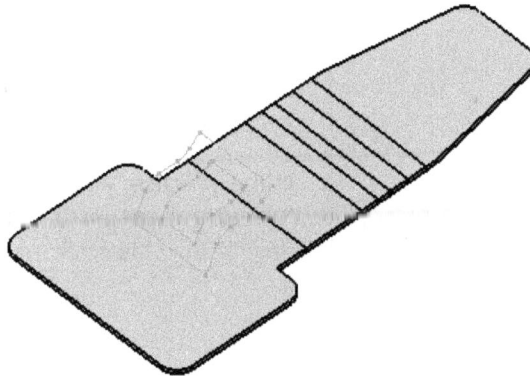

Figure 4–71

Task 5 - Unfold the part.

1. Click (Fold/Unfold) to fold the model as shown in Figure 4–72.

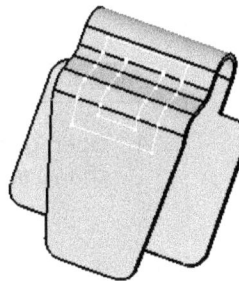

Figure 4–72

2. Save and close the file.

This part is used in a later practice where the curves are used to develop a stamp feature.

Practice 4d

Unfolding/Folding

Practice Objectives

- Create a bend from flat.
- Create an unfolding.
- Create a folding.

In this practice, you will create a bend from flat, unfolding, and folding features. At the end of the practice, the model will display as shown in Figure 4–73.

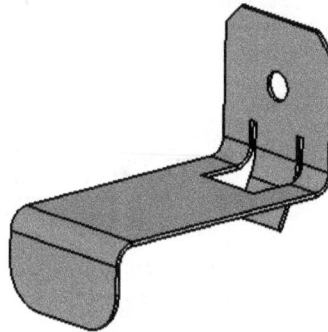

Figure 4–73

Task 1 - Open a part.

1. Open **Unfolding_Folding.CATPART**. The model displays as shown in Figure 4–74.

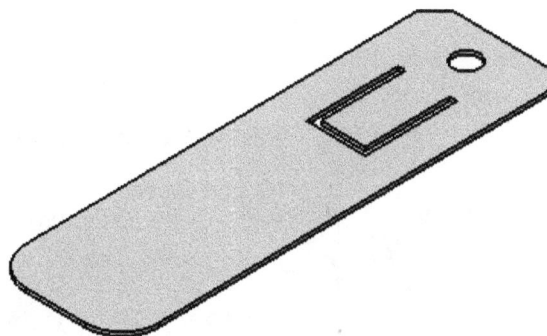

Figure 4–74

Task 2 - Create bend profiles.

1. Select the top surface of the first wall and activate the Sketcher workbench.

2. Create the profile as shown in Figure 4–75.

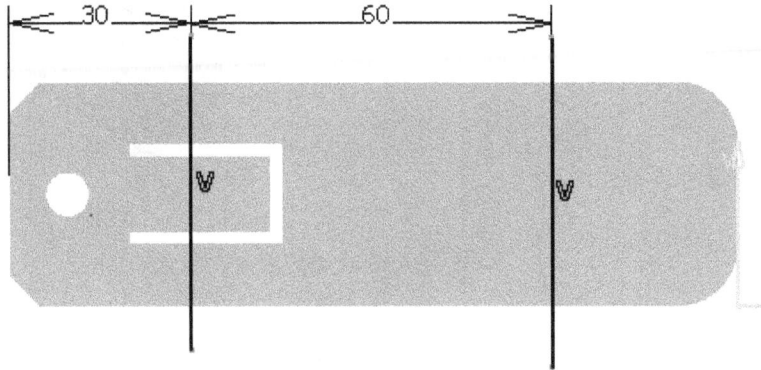

Figure 4–75

3. Exit the Sketcher workbench.

Task 3 - Create a fix point.

In this task, you will create a point element to use in the next task to specify the fixed point for the bend from flat feature. This point will define the fixed wall for flattening.

The power input line is located in the bottom right corner of the CATIA window.

1. Click ▪ (Point). If you cannot locate the icon, you can enter **c:point** in the power input line instead, as shown in Figure 4–76.

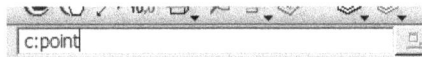

Figure 4–76

2. Select **On surface** in the Point type drop-down list and select the top face as the surface. Select a location on the surface that lies between the lines as shown in Figure 4–77. The location is approximate.

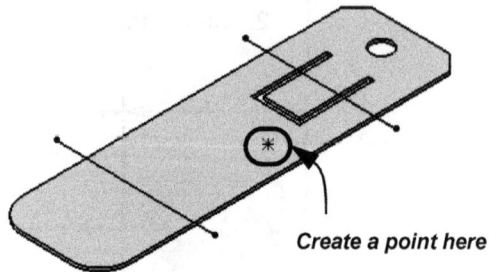

Create a point here

Figure 4–77

3. Click **OK** to create the point.

Task 4 - Create a bend from flat.

---

1. Right-click on the **PartBody** in the specification tree and select **Define In Work Object**.

2. Click (Bend from Flat).

3. Select the sketch created in Task 2.

4. Select the point just created as the Fixed Point.

5. Ensure that the angle of **Line.1** is **90 deg**.

6. Ensure that the bending direction for **Line.1** is upward, as shown in Figure 4–78.

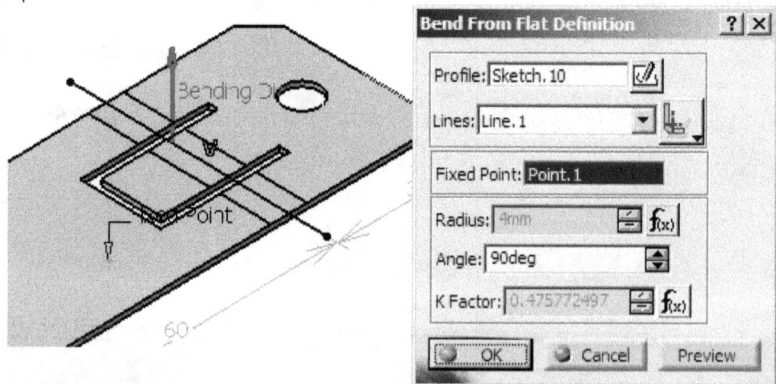

Figure 4–78

7. Select **Line.2** in the Lines drop-down list.

8. Ensure that the angle of **Line.2** is **90 deg**.

9. Ensure that the bending direction for **Line.2** is downward, as shown in Figure 4–79.

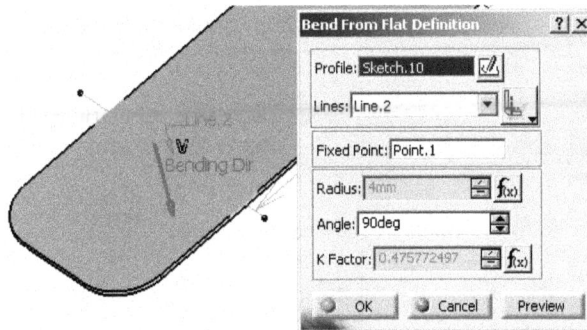

Figure 4–79

10. Click **OK** to generate the bends. The model displays as shown in Figure 4–80.

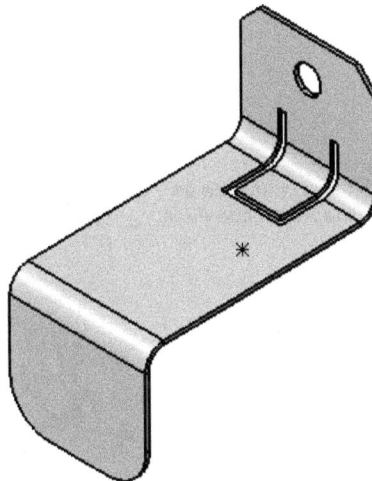

Figure 4–80

11. Hide the fixed point.

Task 5 - Perform an unfolding operation

The design intent of this model is to position the tab at a 25° angle from vertical. Since this cannot be done using a bend from flat feature, the tab must be unfolded and then folded to the correct angle. In this task, you will unfold the cutout bend face and unfold it to the flat position.

1. Click  (Unfolding). The Unfolding Definition dialog box opens as shown in Figure 4–81.

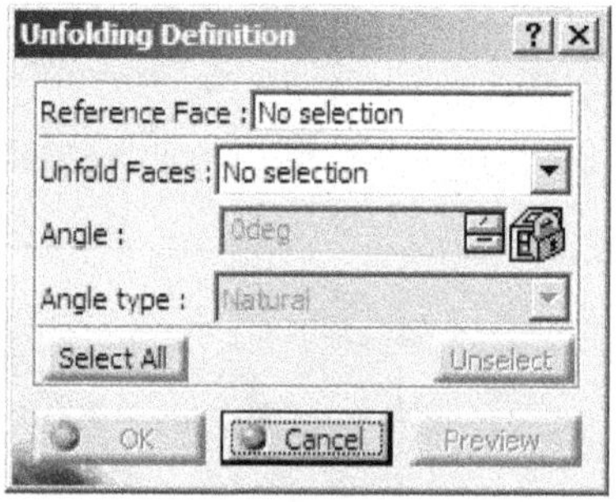

Figure 4–81

2. Select the reference face and unfolding face as shown in Figure 4–82.

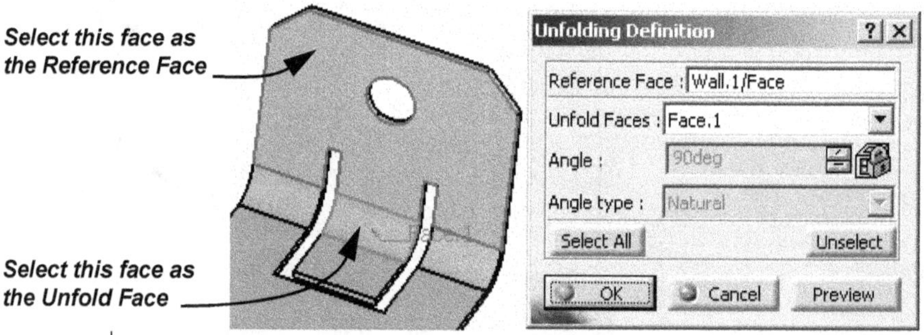

Select this face as the Reference Face

Select this face as the Unfold Face

Figure 4–82

3. Click **OK** to complete the feature. The model displays as shown in Figure 4–83.

Figure 4–83

Task 6 - Perform a folding operation.

1. Click (Folding).

2. Select the Reference Face and Fold Face, and make the following selections:

   - *Angle type:* **Defined**
   - *Angle:* **25**

   The Folding Definition dialog box opens as shown in Figure 4–84.

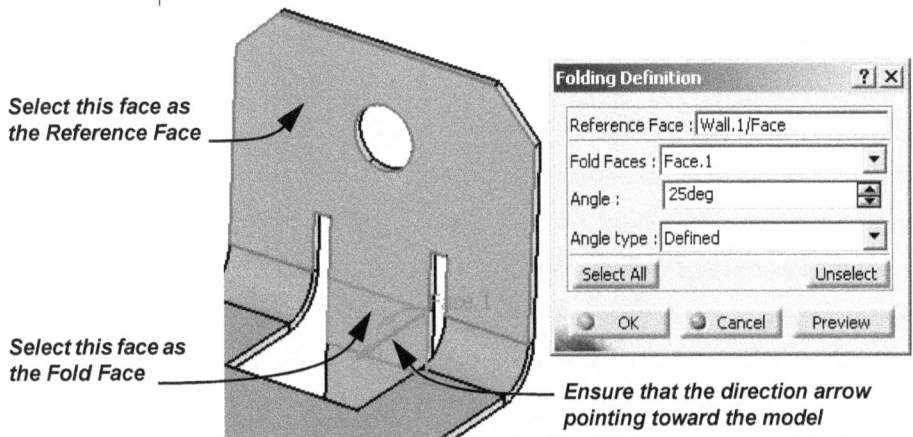

Select this face as the Reference Face

Select this face as the Fold Face

Ensure that the direction arrow pointing toward the model

Figure 4–84

3. Click **OK** to complete the feature. The model displays as shown in Figure 4–85.

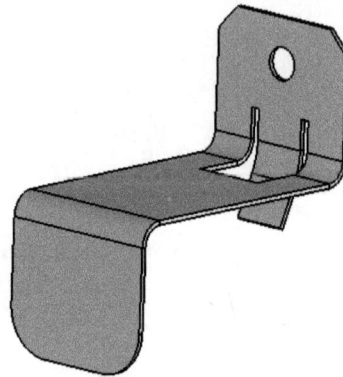

Figure 4–85

4. Save and close the file.

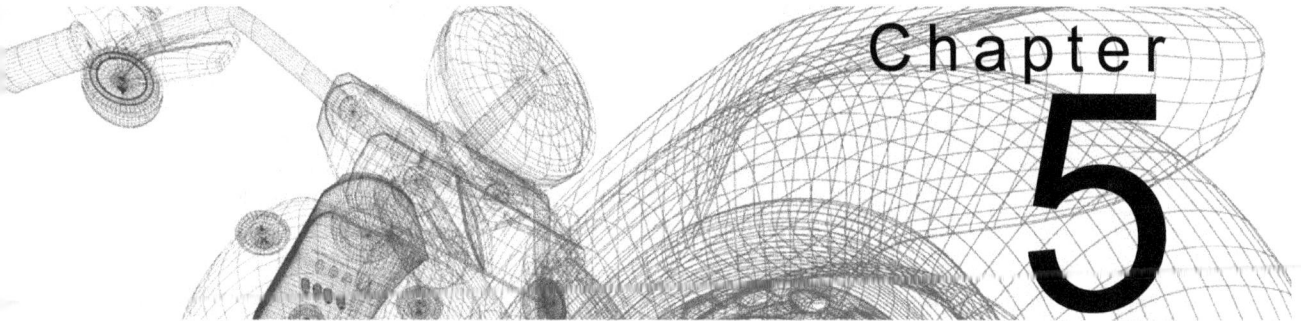

Sheet Metal Stamps

Stamps are created in a sheet metal part through a stamping and/or die process. You can use the standard stamp tools or create a user-defined stamp. CATIA enables you to create a stamp with specific geometry that can be reused on different models.

Learning Objectives in this Chapter

- Learn how to use Standard, Surface, Bead and Curve Stamps.
- Understand the Flanged Cutout.
- Use the Louver and Bridge tool.
- Create a Flanged Hole.
- Understand the Circular Stamp.
- Add a Stiffening Rib and a Dowel.
- Create a Punch with Opening Faces and use a Punch and Die.

5.1 Standard Stamps

Stamps are created in a sheet metal part using a stamping and/or die process. Stamps are created on walls, with the exception of the stiffening rib which is created on a bend. CATIA has many standard stamps as well as the ability to create your own. Figure 5–1 shows examples of the different standard stamps available.

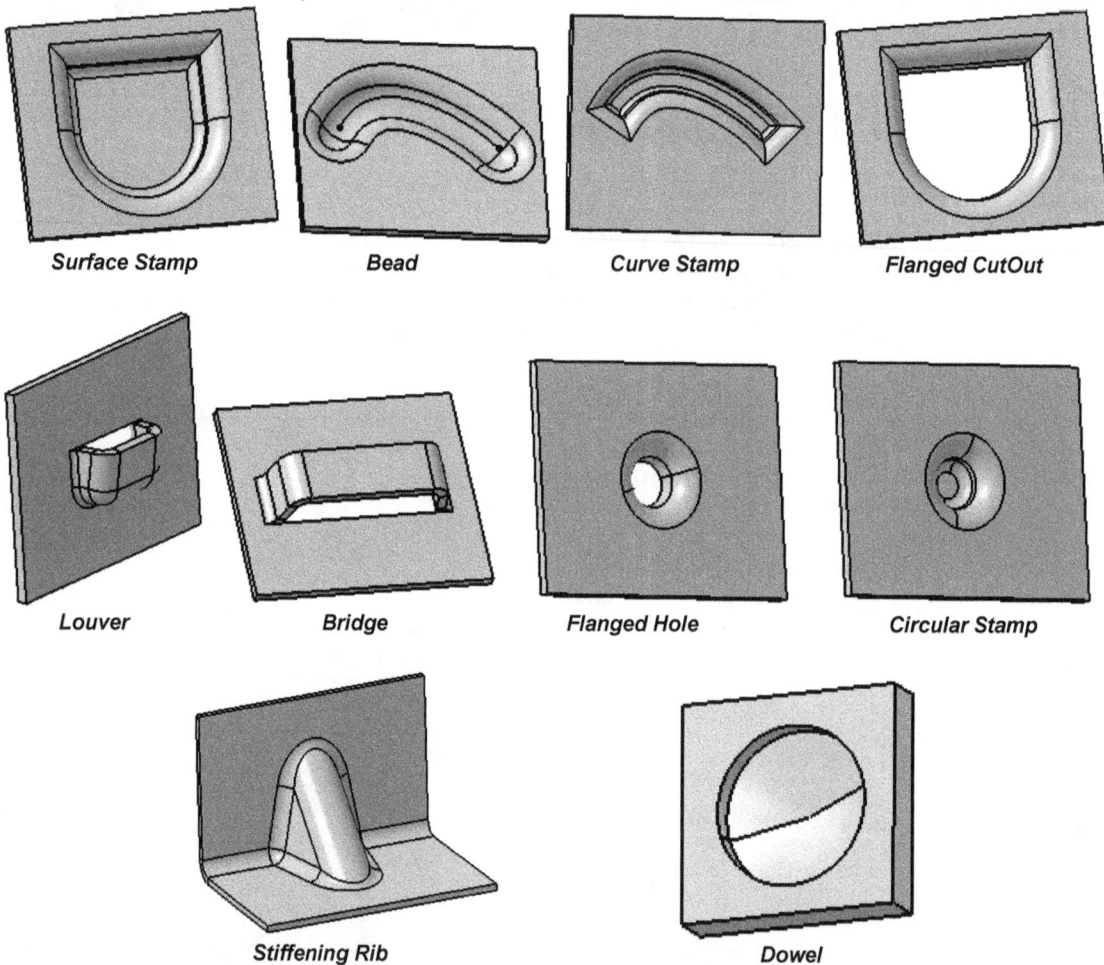

Surface Stamp   **Bead**   **Curve Stamp**   **Flanged CutOut**

Louver   **Bridge**   **Flanged Hole**   **Circular Stamp**

Stiffening Rib   **Dowel**

Figure 5–1

Locating Points

Many stamps and other sheet metal features, require a locating point to place the feature. Locating points are created by creating a reference point or adding them to the sketch. When activating feature creation, you select the locating point and the surface on which to create the feature.

The locating point does not need to lie directly on the surface that is to be stamped; it can be created on any plane. If the locating point does not lie on the selected surface, it is orthogonally projected onto the surface for placement. For example, stiffening ribs are placed on sheet metal bends. Bends are not planar; therefore, creating a point on them can be difficult because a sketch cannot be placed on a non-planar face. Instead, the point is sketched on a planar surface or reference plane, as shown in Figure 5–2.

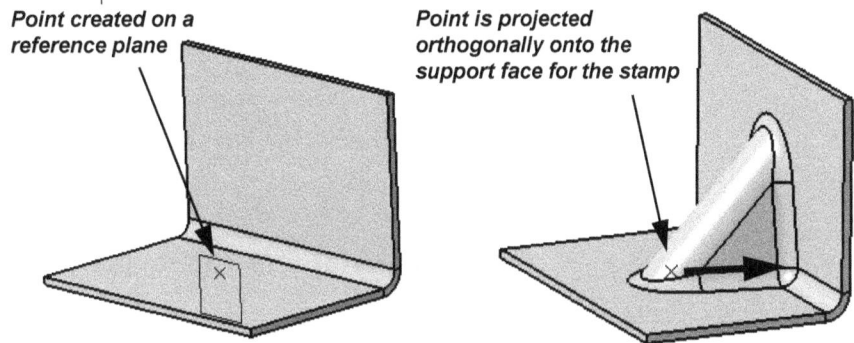

Point created on a reference plane

Point is projected orthogonally onto the support face for the stamp

Figure 5–2

If no locating point is selected when creating the stamp, the system generates one directly under the cursor when the reference surface is selected. This system-generated point can be edited after the stamp has been placed by double-clicking on the sketch associated with the stamp, as shown in Figure 5–3.

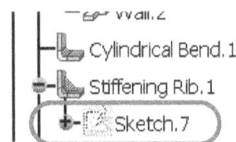

Figure 5–3

General Steps

Use the following general steps to create a standard stamp:

1. Create locating geometry.
2. Activate the required **Stamp** tool.
3. Define the stamp parameters.
4. Complete the stamp.

Step 1 - Create locating geometry.

The locating geometry varies depending on the type of stamp created. Some stamps require a point to locate the center of the feature, while others require a profile to indicate the shape and location of the geometry. For example, a locating point must first be created to create a flanged hole, as shown in Figure 5–4.

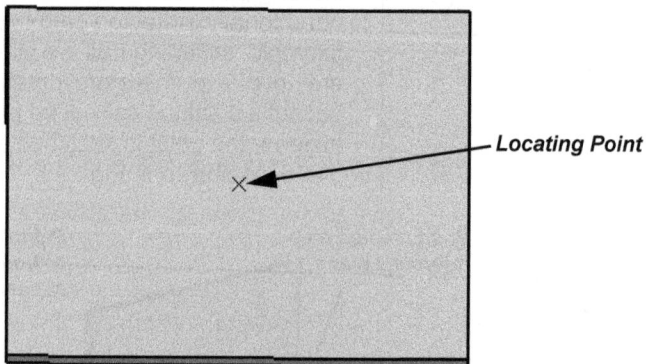

Figure 5–4

Step 2 - Activate the required Stamp tool.

Select the locating point and surface on which to place the feature. You can also select a geometry profile on which to place the feature. You then click the icon for the required stamp as shown in Figure 5–5.

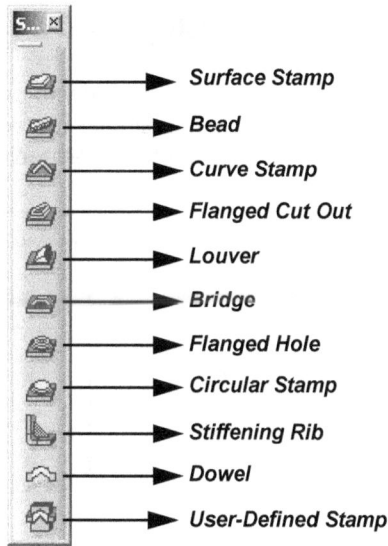

Figure 5–5

Descriptions of each of the stamps are provided in the following sections.

Step 3 - Define the stamp parameters.

The Stamp definition dialog box opens for the selected stamp. Enter the parameters for the stamp. An illustration of the stamp is shown on the right side of the dialog box to help locate the correct dimensions. The dialog box for a Flanged hole is shown in Figure 5–6.

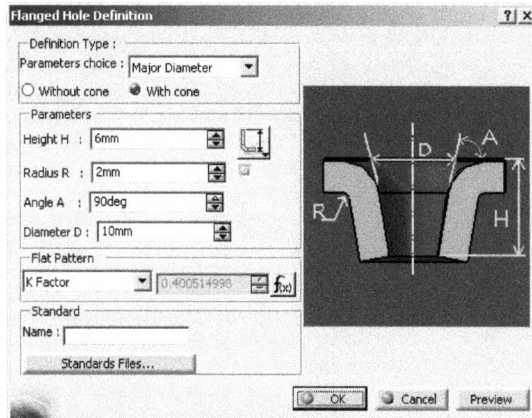

Figure 5–6

Step 4 - Complete the stamp.

Click **Preview** to preview the stamp. Once the stamp is dimensioned correctly, click **OK** to complete the feature. The completed flanged hole is shown in Figure 5–7.

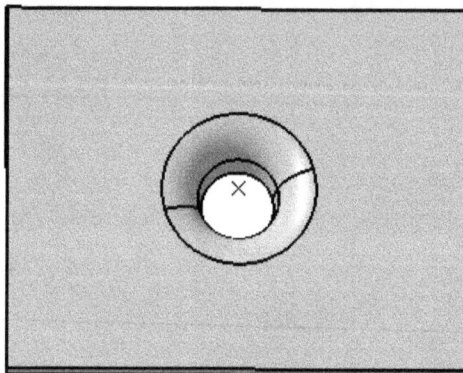

Figure 5–7

5.2 Surface Stamp

How To: Create a Surface Stamp

1. Create a profile to use as the "punch" for the stamp. The curve or sketched profile must be closed and created on the surface that is to be stamped, as shown in Figure 5–8.

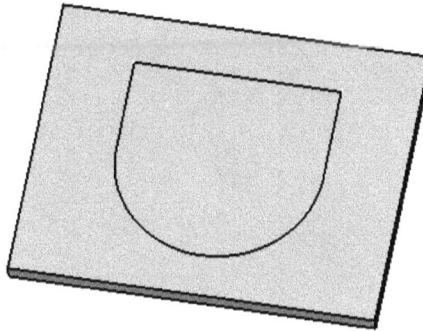

Figure 5–8

2. Select the punch profile.
3. Activate the Surface stamp operation by clicking

    (Surface Stamp).

4. Select an option in the **Parameters choice** menu. The available options are described as follows:

Option	Description
Angle	Stamps the selected profile into the part by a defined angle and height (or limiting plane). Opening edges can be defined by selecting a sketched edge. An example is shown below.

Punch & Die	Requires a profile containing two closed loops. The stamp transitions between the profiles by a defined height or limiting plane. Opening edges can be defined to create openings in the stamp, as shown below. 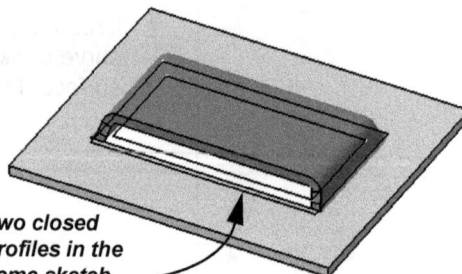 *Two closed profiles in the same sketch*
Two Profiles	Creates a stamp that transitions between two sketches to a specified depth or limiting plane. Although this option does not enable you to define opening faces, as in the **Punch & Die** option, it can accommodate more complex sketched shapes and profiles that have a different number of elements as shown below. 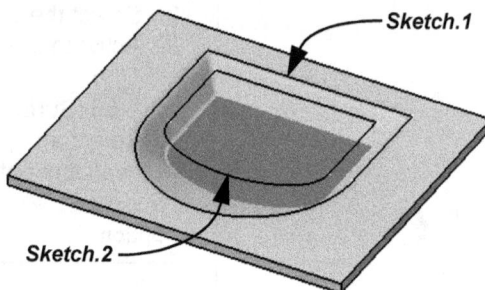 *Sketch.1* *Sketch.2*

5. Based on the type of surface stamp being created, enter the parameters required to define the feature. Use the illustration on the right side of the dialog box to help identify the parameters. An example of the Surface Stamp Definition dialog box using Angle parameters is shown in Figure 5–9.

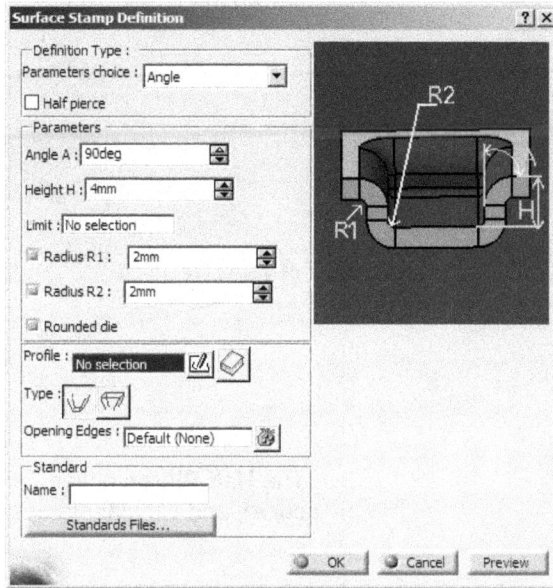

Figure 5–9

6. Click **OK** to create the stamp, as shown in Figure 5–10.

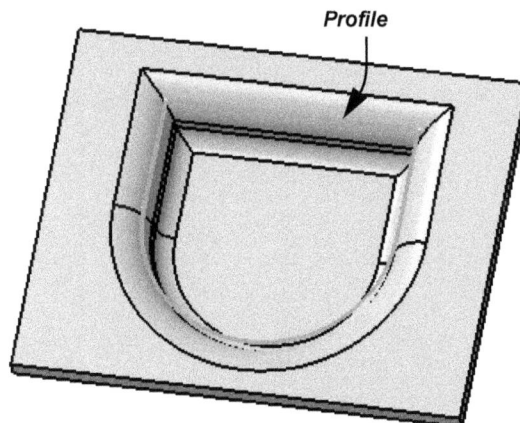

Figure 5–10

Half Pierce Option

The **Half Pierce** option can be used to push a stamp into the sheet metal wall to a maximum depth of half the wall thickness. No fillets can be applied to a half pierce stamp. An example is shown in Figure 5–11.

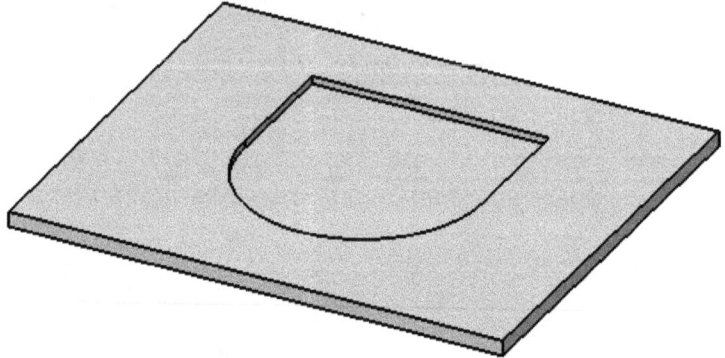

Figure 5–11

The **Half Pierce** option can be applied when creating surface, curve, and circular stamps.

5.3 Bead

How To: Create a Bead Stamp

1. Create a curve to act as a spine. The Bead stamp is created along the sketched curve. The curve (or sketched profile) must be open and created on the surface that is to be stamped, as shown in Figure 5–12.

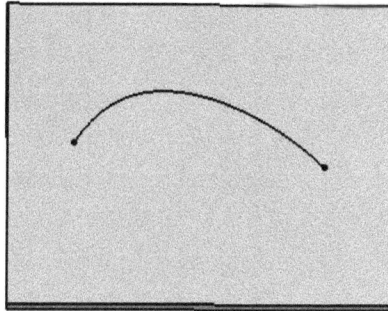

Figure 5–12

2. Select the curve to be used as the spine.

3. Activate the Bead operation by clicking (Bead).

4. Enter the parameters using the Bead Definition dialog box, as shown in Figure 5–13. Use the illustration on the right side of the dialog box to help identify the parameters.

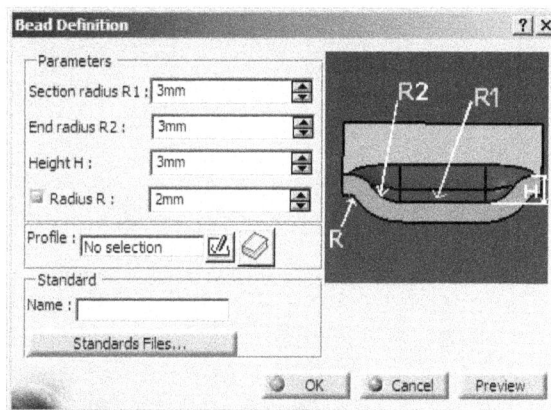

Figure 5–13

5. Click **OK** to create the stamp, as shown in Figure 5–14.

Spine

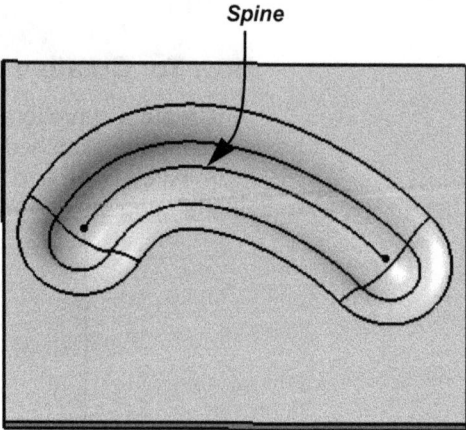

Figure 5–14

5.4 Curve Stamp

How To: Create a Curve Stamp

1. Create a spine. The profile of the stamp is moved along the spine to create the stamp. The spine must be created on the surface that is to be stamped and the curve or sketch representing the spine must be open, as shown in Figure 5–15.

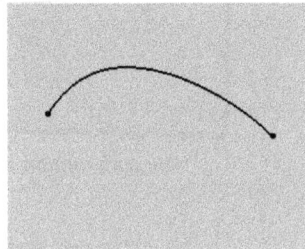

Figure 5–15

2. Select the curve to be used as the spine.

3. Activate the Curve Stamp operation by clicking (Curve Stamp).

4. Enter the parameters using the Curve Stamp Definition dialog box, as shown in Figure 5–16. Use the illustration on the right side of the dialog box to help identify the parameters.

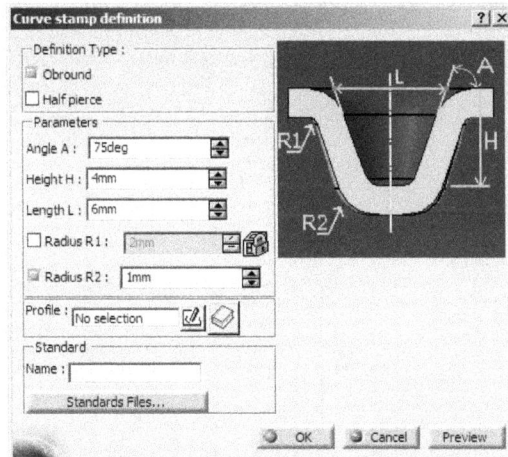

Figure 5–16

5. Use the **Obround** option to indicate the shape of the edges of the stamp. When the option is selected, the edges of the stamp are rounded. When the option is cleared, the edges are not rounded. Both options are shown in Figure 5–17.

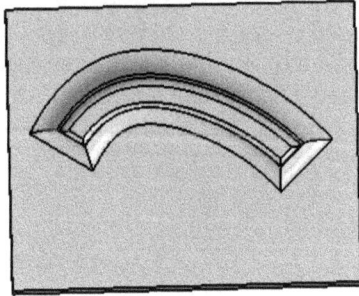

Obround option disabled   *Obround option enabled*

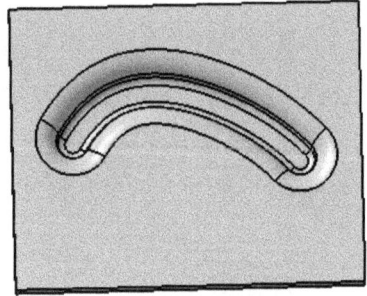

Figure 5–17

6. Use the **Half Pierce** option to push the stamp into the sheet metal wall to a maximum depth of half the wall thickness. Fillets cannot be applied to a half pierce stamp.
7. Click **OK** to create the stamp.

5.5 Flanged Cutout

How To: Create a Flanged Cutout Stamp

1. Create a profile to use as the punch for the stamp. The curve or sketched profile must be closed and created on the surface on which the stamp is to be applied, as shown in Figure 5–18.

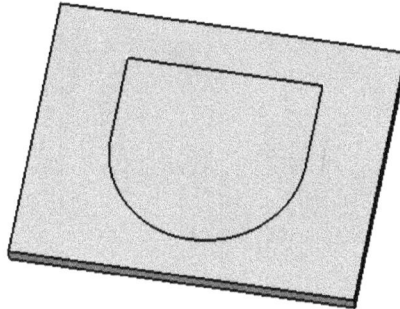

Figure 5–18

2. Select the punch profile.
3. Activate the Flanged Cutout operation by clicking

    (Flanged Cut Out).

4. Enter the parameters using the Flanged Cutout Definition dialog box, as shown in Figure 5–19. Use the preview on the right side of the dialog box to help identify the parameters.

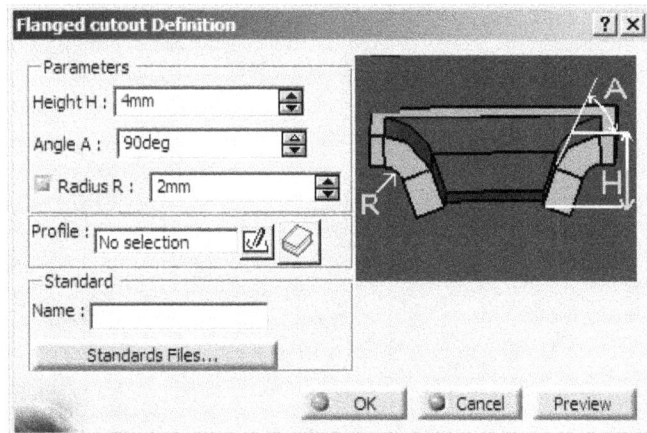

Figure 5–19

---

5. Click **OK** to create the stamp, as shown in Figure 5–20.

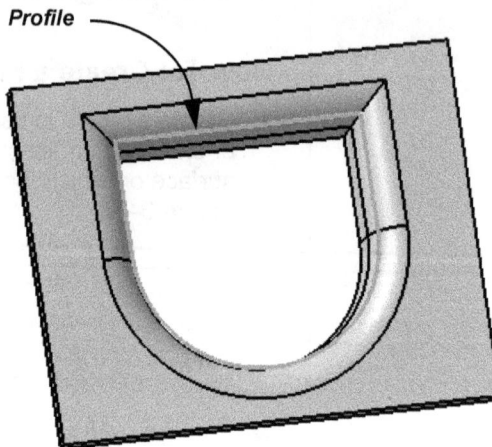

Figure 5–20

5.6 Louver

How To: Create a Louver Stamp

1. Create the Louver profile to use as the punch for the stamp. The profile for a louver must contain one line that is not tangent with any other geometry in the profile, as shown in Figure 5–21. This line is used as the opening face for the stamp. The curve or sketch representing the punch must be a closed profile and created on the wall that is to be stamped.

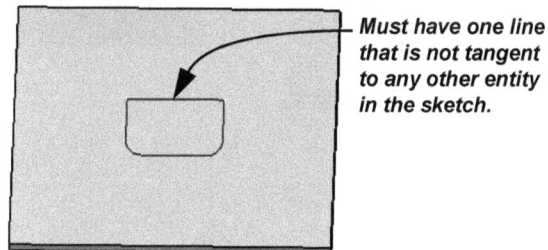

Must have one line that is not tangent to any other entity in the sketch.

Figure 5–21

2. Select the punch profile.

3. Activate the Louver operation by clicking (Louver).

4. Enter the parameters using the Louver Definition dialog box, as shown in Figure 5–22. Use the preview on the right side of the dialog box to help identify the parameters.

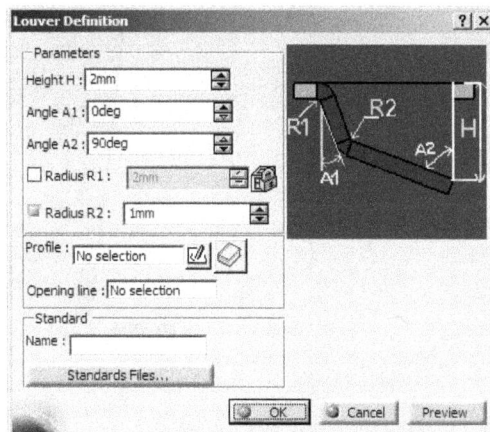

Figure 5–22

5. Activate the *Opening Line* field and select the opening line on the model, as shown in Figure 5–23. It indicates the position of the opening face of the stamp and must not be tangent to any other entity in the profile.

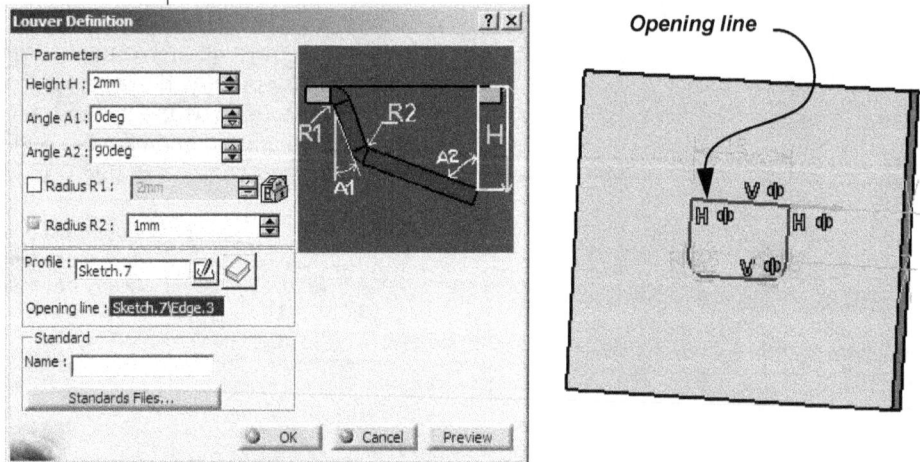

Figure 5–23

6. Click **OK** to create the stamp, as shown in How To:Figure 5–24.

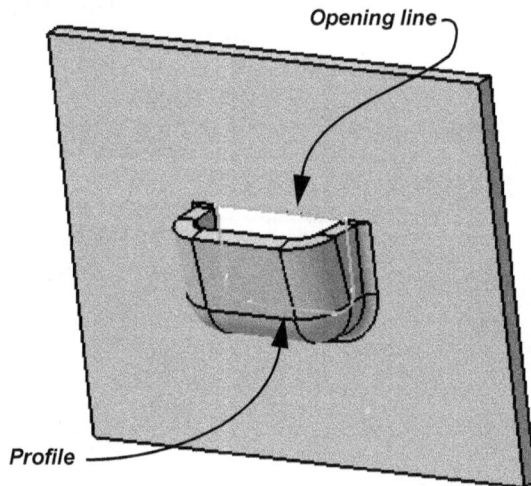

Figure 5–24

5.7 Bridge

How To: Create a Bridge Stamp

1. Create a locating point to locate the center of the bridge.
2. Select the locating point and the surface on which to create the bridge.
3. Activate the Bridge operation by clicking ![icon] (Bridge).
4. Enter the parameters using the Bridge Definition dialog box, as shown in Figure 5–25. Use the preview on the right side of the dialog box to help identify the parameters.

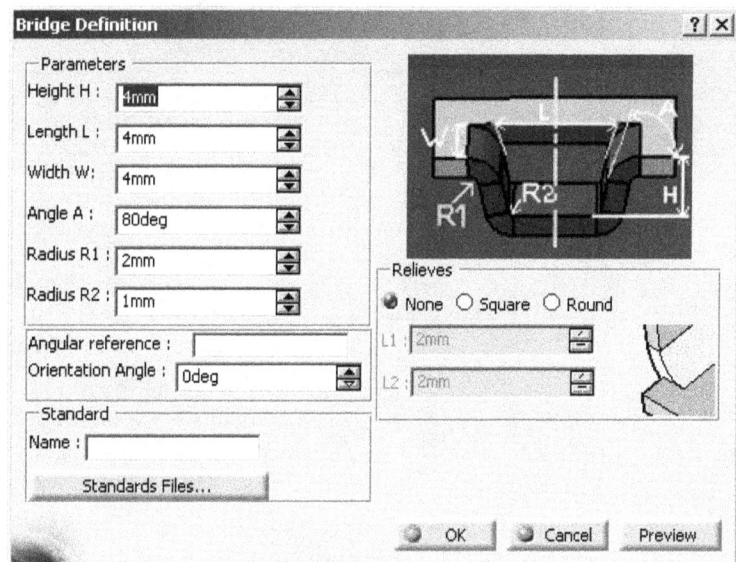

Figure 5–25

5. Select an angular reference to place the bridge. The angular reference is used to give the bridge a direction. For example, in Figure 5–26, the bottom edge of the support is selected as the angular reference at an angle of 45 degrees.

6. A round or square bend relief can also be applied to the bridge stamp. In Figure 5–26, a square relief is applied to the bridge stamp. The default relief set in the Sheet Metal Parameters is not used.

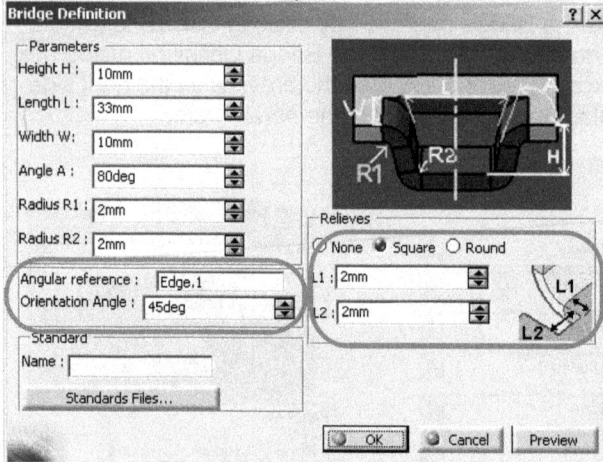

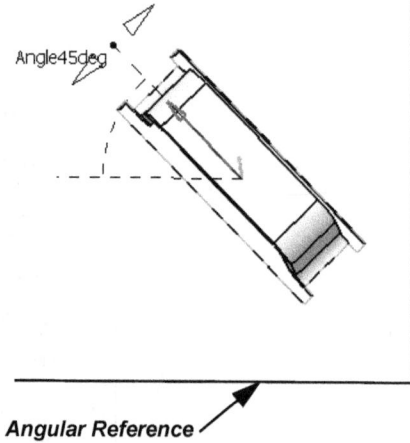

Figure 5–26

7. Click **OK** to create the stamp. Figure 5–27 shows the bridge created using the selected reference at a 45 degree angle.

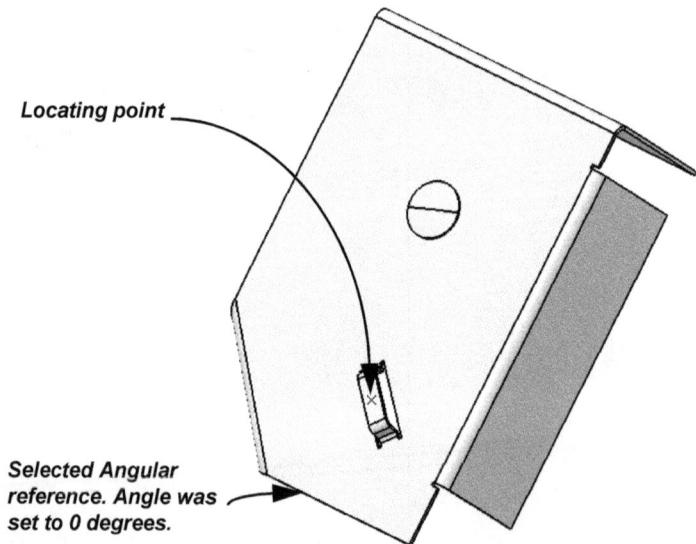

Figure 5–27

5.8 Flanged Hole

How To: Create a Flanged Hole Stamp

Before accessing the Flanged Hole stamp definition, a locating point needs to be created.

1. Create a locating point to locate the center of the feature.
2. Select the locating point and surface on which to construct the stamp.
3. Activate the Flanged Hole operation by clicking

   ▨ (Flanged Hole).
4. Specify an option in the Parameters choice drop-down list. These options determine the dimensions used to size the stamp. The available options are described as follows:

Option	Description
Major Diameter	The diameter of the stamp is controlled by the major diameter and an angle, as shown below. 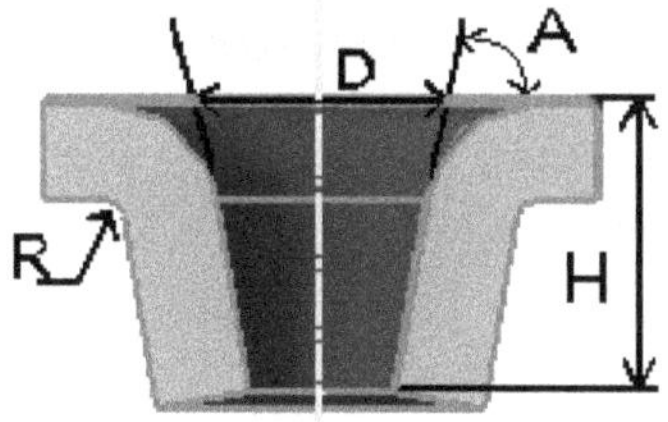
Minor Diameter	The diameter of the stamp is controlled by the minor diameter and an angle, as shown below. 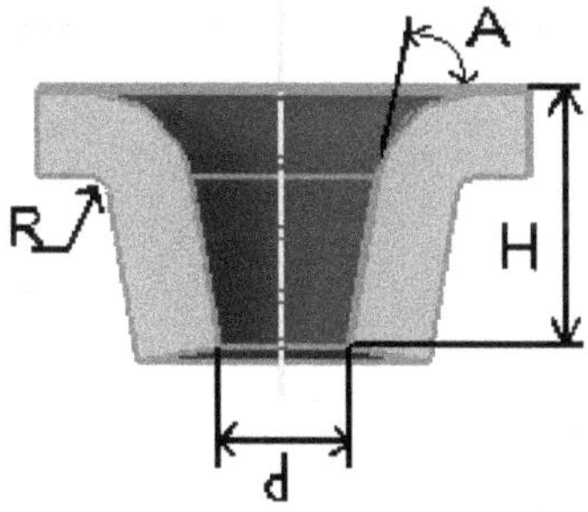

Two Diameters	The diameter of the stamp is controlled by the major and minor diameter, as shown below. 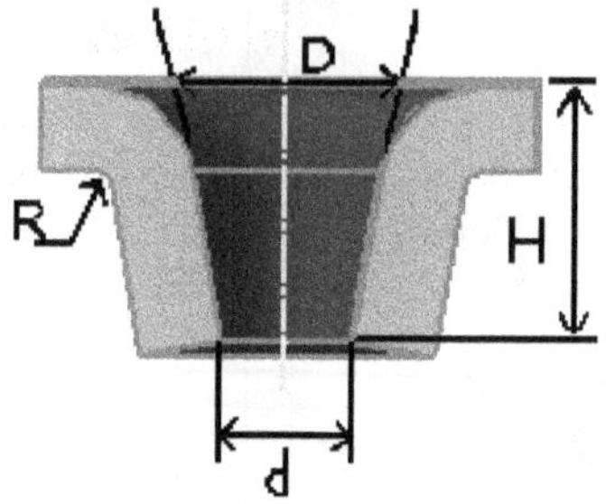

Punch & Die	The diameter of the stamp is controlled by the outer diameter and the minor diameter, as shown below. 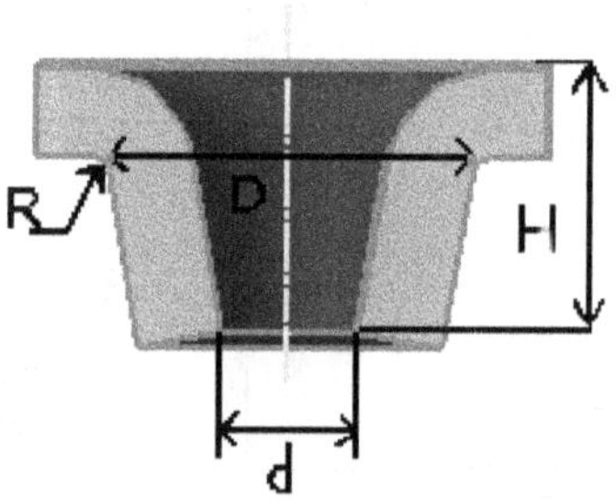

5. Enter the parameters using the Flanged Hole Definition dialog box, as shown in Figure 5–28. Use the illustration on the right side of the dialog box to help identify the parameters.

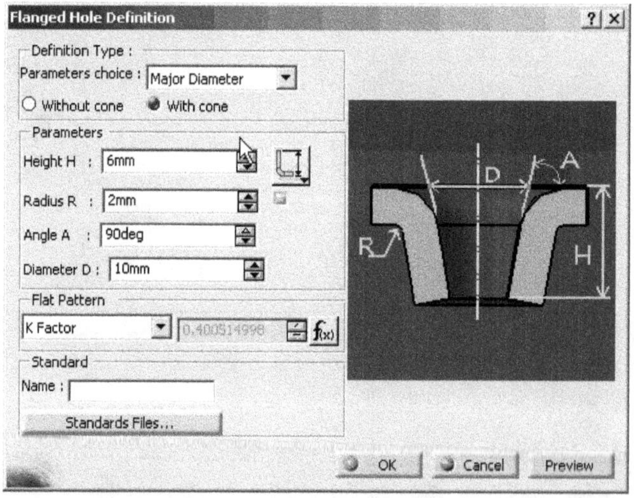

Figure 5–28

6. Click **OK** to create the stamp. The completed stamp is shown in Figure 5–29.

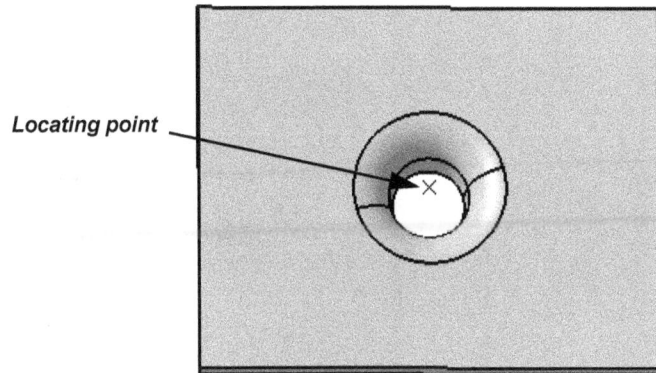

Locating point

Figure 5–29

5.9 Circular Stamp

How To: Create a Circular Stamp

1. Create a locating point to locate the center of the feature.
2. Select the locating point and the surface on which to create the stamp.
3. Activate the Circular Stamp operation by clicking

   (Circular Stamp).
4. Specify an option in the **Parameters choice** menu. These options determine the dimensions used to size the stamp. The available options are described as follows:

Option	Description
Major Diameter	The diameter of the stamp is controlled by the major diameter and an angle, as shown below. 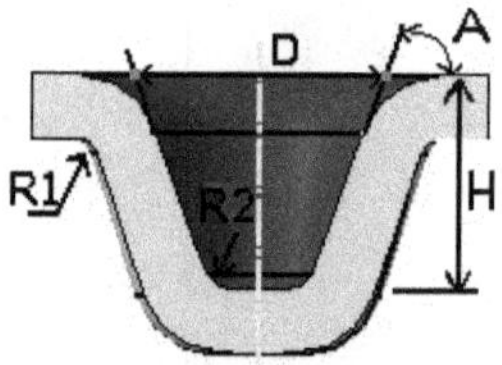
Minor Diameter	The diameter of the stamp is controlled by the minor diameter and an angle, as shown below. 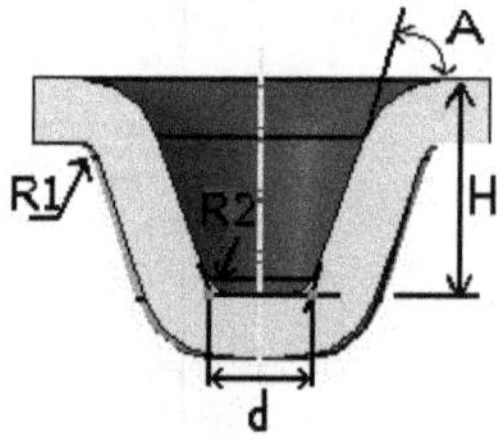
Two Diameters	The diameter of the stamp is controlled by the major and minor diameter, as shown below. 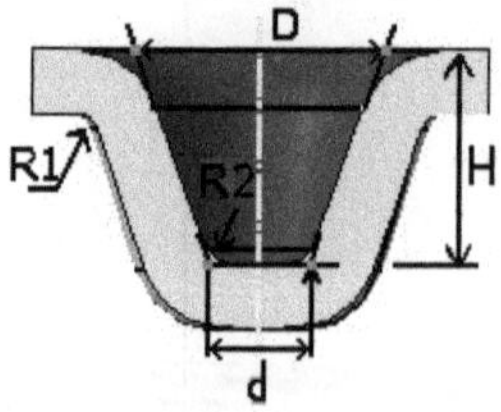

Punch & Die	The diameter of the stamp is controlled by the outer diameter and the minor diameter, as shown below.
	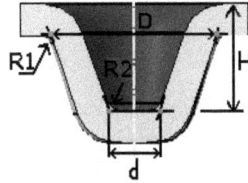

5. Enter the parameters using the Circular Stamp Definition dialog box, as shown in Figure 5–30. Use the illustration on the right side of the dialog box to help identify the parameters.

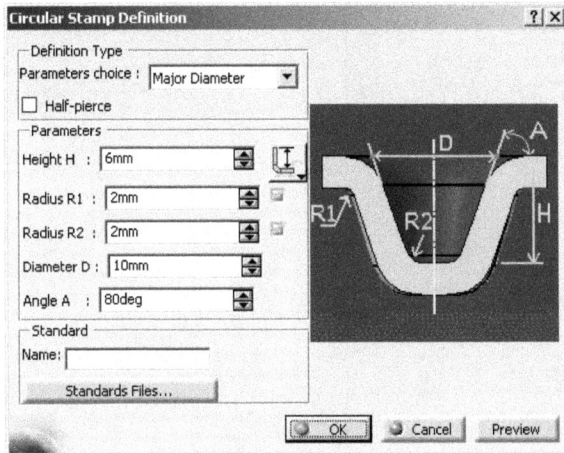

Figure 5–30

6. Use the **Half Pierce** option to push the stamp into the sheet metal wall to a maximum depth of half the wall thickness. No fillets can be applied to a half pierce stamp.

7. Click **OK** to create the stamp, as shown in Figure 5–31.

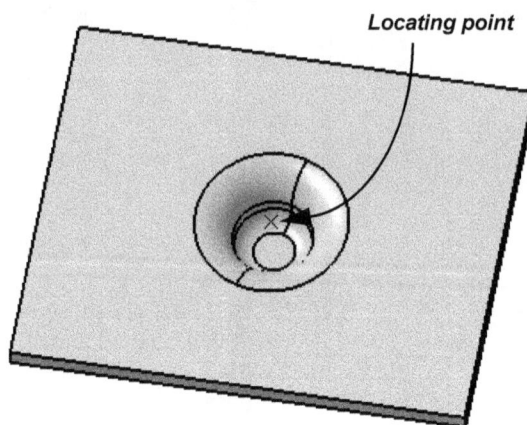

Figure 5–31

5.10 Stiffening Rib

How To: Create a Stiffening Rib Stamp

Before accessing the Stiffening Rib definition, a locating point needs to be created.

1. Create a locating point to locate the center of the feature. The point does not need to be created on the surface that is to be stamped. If the point is created on a different support, it is projected orthogonally on to the surface to be stamped, as shown in Figure 5–32.

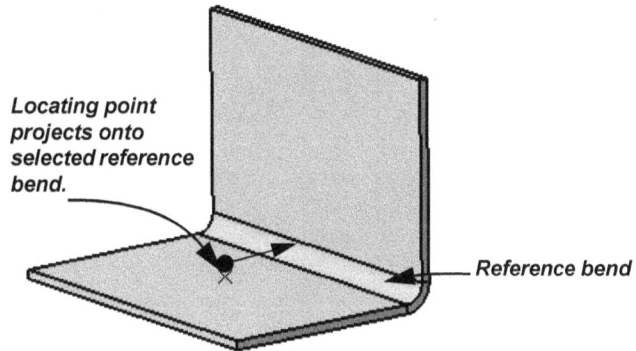

Locating point projects onto selected reference bend.

Reference bend

Figure 5–32

2. Select the locating point and the outside face of a bend on which the rib is to be created. If the inside surface is selected, the Error message shown in Figure 5–33 opens.

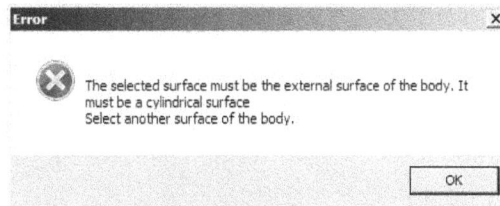

Figure 5–33

3. Activate the Stiffening Rib operation by clicking

(Stiffening Rib).

4. Enter the parameters using the Stiffening Rib Definition dialog box, as shown in Figure 5–34. Use the preview on the right side of the dialog box to help identify the parameters.

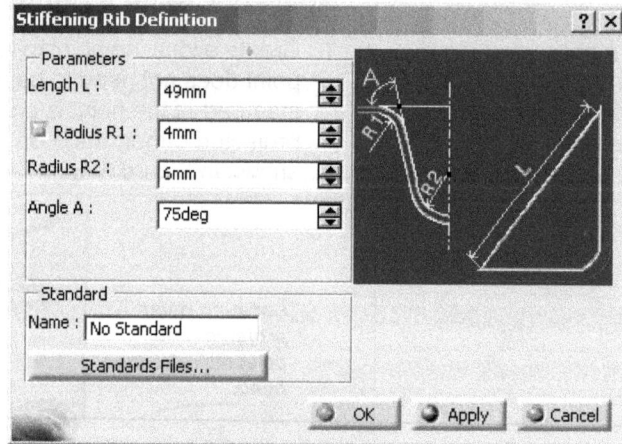

Figure 5–34

5. Click **OK** to create the stamp, as shown in Figure 5–35.

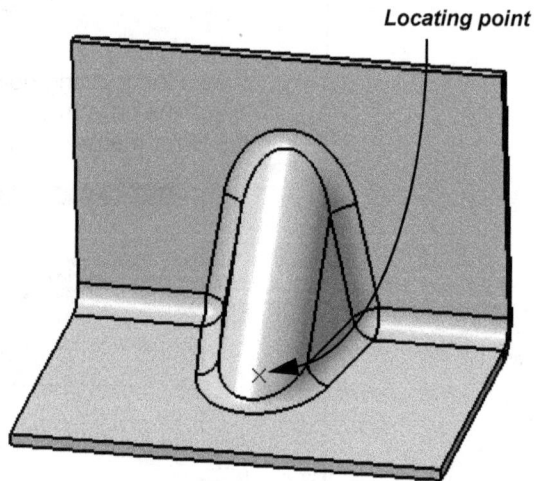

Figure 5–35

5.11 Dowel

How To: Create a Dowel Stamp

1. Click ⌂ (Dowel) and select the surface on which to create the dowel stamp.
2. Enter the diameter value in the Dowel Definition dialog box as shown in Figure 5–36.

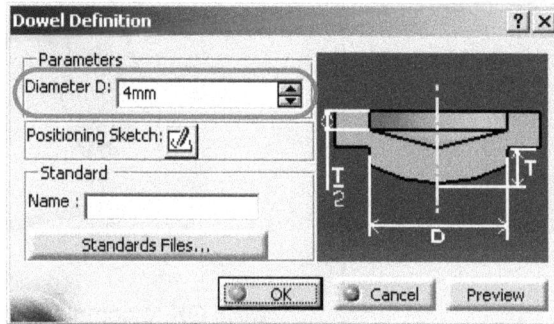

Figure 5–36

3. Click 🖉 (Sketch) to activate the Sketcher workbench and reposition the dowel stamp. The asterisk point defines the center of the stamp. Apply dimensional or geometrical constraints on the locating point, as shown in Figure 5–37.

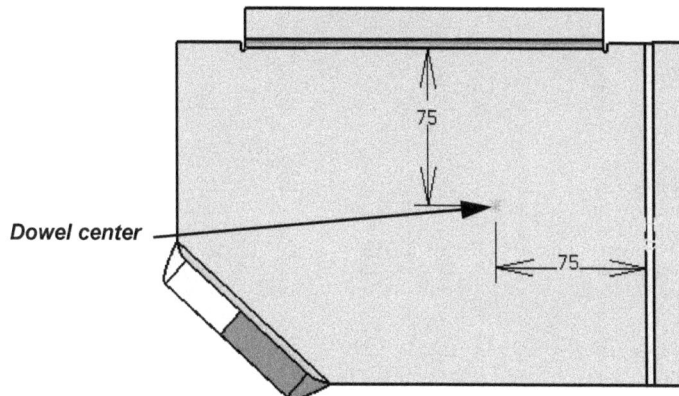

Figure 5–37

4. If required, click on the arrow to change the direction of the dowel, as shown in Figure 5–38.

Figure 5–38

5. Click **OK** to complete the creation of the dowel stamp feature.

5.12 Punch with Opening Faces

The Punch with Opening Faces user stamp requires that only a punch be defined. With this tool, opening faces can be defined, as shown in Figure 5–39. Like the Punch and Die user stamp, the punch must be defined in a separate body from the rest of the model.

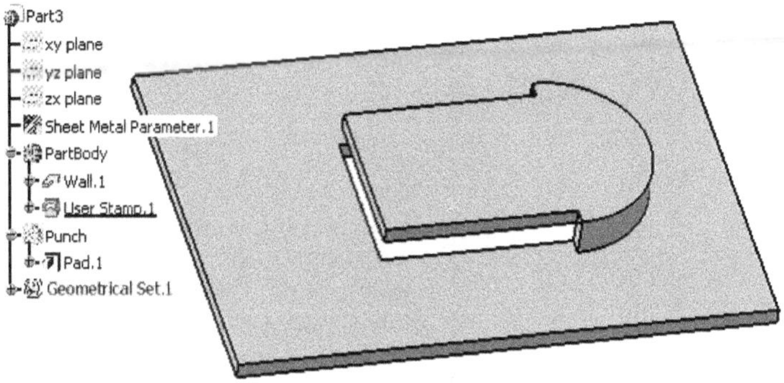

Figure 5–39

General Steps

Use the following general steps to define a Punch with Opening Faces user stamp:

1. Create the punch.
2. Activate the **User Stamp** tool.
3. Locate the stamp on the wall.
4. Select the punch body.
5. Define the opening faces.
6. Define the fillet.
7. Rotate the stamp, if required
8. Complete the feature.

Step 1 - Create the punch.

It is helpful to rename the body to help identify it in the specification tree.

The punch must be created in a separate body. Therefore, this body can exist in the sheet metal model or in a separate CATPart file. If the geometry is placed in another part model, the punch geometry is copied into the sheet metal part using a linked solid.

To create a new body in the model, select **Insert>Body**. The empty body displays at the bottom of the specification tree. The new body should be underlined, as shown in Figure 5–40. This indicates that the body is active, and all new features are created inside it. If the body is not active, select it in the specification tree, right-click and select **Define in Work Object**.

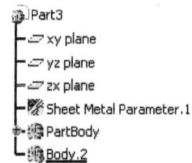

Figure 5–40

Punches must be solid features created in the Part Design workbench. To access the Part Design workbench, select **Start> Mechanical Design>Part Design**. The punch is located using the origin of the part and the punching direction is always equal to the Z-direction. An example of a punch is shown in Figure 5–41.

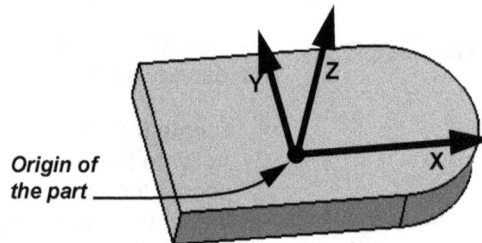

Figure 5–41

When the punch is applied, the Z-direction is oriented normal to the selected surface, as shown in Figure 5–42. Therefore, you must always create the punch geometry in the positive Z-direction to obtain predictable results.

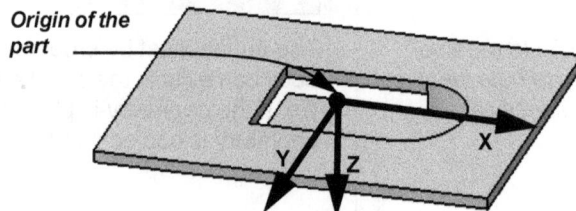

Figure 5–42

Step 2 - Activate the User Stamp tool.

Return to the body containing the Sheet metal features by
selecting it in the specification tree, right-clicking and selecting
Define in Work Object. Return to the Generative Sheetmetal
Design workbench by selecting **Start>Mechanical Design>
Generative Sheetmetal Design**.

Click (User Stamp) and, in the User-Defined Stamp
Definition dialog box, select **Punch** in the Type drop-down list, as
shown in Figure 5–43.

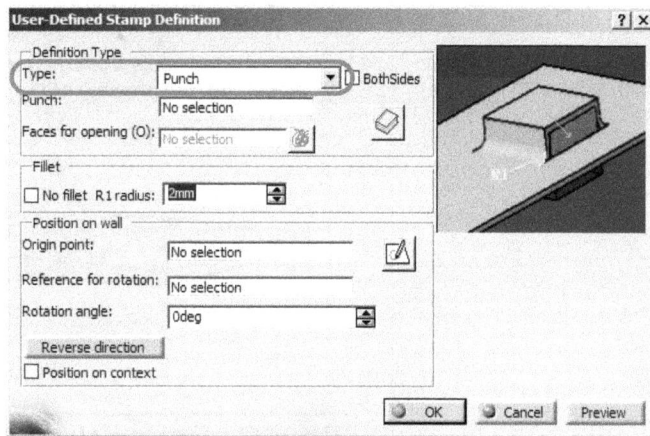

Figure 5–43

Step 3 - Locate the stamp on the wall.

Click and select the face on which to create the user stamp.
In the Sketcher environment, create a sketched point to locate
the origin of the user stamp. Once the point has been created
and constrained, exit the Sketcher environment to return to the
User-Defined Stamp Definition.

Step 4 - Select the punch body.

Select in the *Punch* field and select the body that contains the punch. The user-defined Stamp Definition dialog box populates with the selected body and a preview of the stamp displays on the model.

Step 5 - Define the opening faces.

Activate the *Faces for Opening (O)* field and select the surfaces on the model to remove from the stamp. The selected surfaces are shown in Figure 5–44.

Select open faces from the punch
model, not the preview of the stamp.

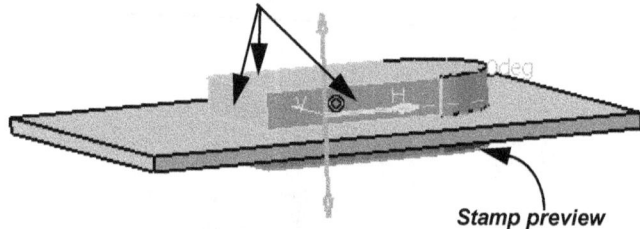

Stamp preview

Figure 5–44

Step 6 - Define the fillet.

By default, a fillet is applied to the edge of the stamp. Enter the radius of the fillet using the *R1 radius* field or select the **No Fillet** option if you do not want to include a fillet.

Step 7 - Rotate the stamp, if required.

You can change the orientation of the stamp by selecting a reference for rotation and entering an angle in the *Rotation Angle* field.

Step 8 - Complete the feature.

Once the stamp has been defined, click **OK** to complete it.

5.13 Punch and Die

Punch and die features can be used when no standard stamp fits the requirements of the design. These features enable you to customize the stamp. Punch and dies must be created in separate bodies from each other and other features in the model. These bodies can be used in other sheet metal models by copying the punch and die bodies into the required models. For example, Figure 5–45 shows a cross-section of a stamp created using punch and die features.

The specification tree has a separate body for the punch and for the die. This type of stamp enables the part to have a variable wall thickness.

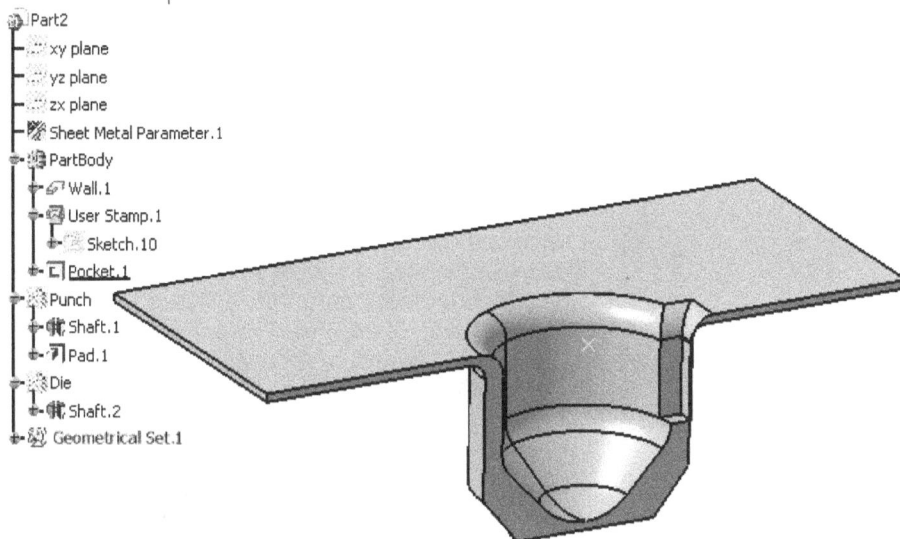

Figure 5–45

General Steps

Use the following general steps to define a punch and die user stamp:

1. Create a punch feature.
2. Create a die feature.
3. Activate the **User Stamp** tool.
4. Locate the stamp on the wall.
5. Select punch and die bodies.
6. Define the fillet of the stamp.
7. Rotate the stamp, if required.
8. Complete the feature.

Step 1 - Create a punch feature.

It is helpful to rename the body to help identify it in the specification tree.

The punch must be created in a separate body. Therefore, this body can exist in the sheet metal model or in a separate CATPart file. If the geometry is placed in another part model, the punch geometry is copied into the sheet metal part using a linked solid.

To create a new body in the model, select **Insert>Body**. The empty body displays at the bottom of the specification tree. The new body should be underlined, as shown in Figure 5–46. This indicates that the body is active, and all new features are created inside this body. If the body is not active, select it in the specification tree, right-click and select **Define in Work Object**.

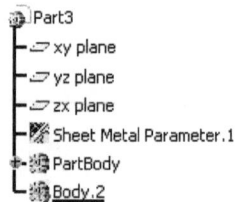

Part3
— xy plane
— yz plane
— zx plane
— Sheet Metal Parameter.1
— PartBody
— Body.2

Figure 5–46

Punches must be solid features that are created in the Part Design workbench. To access the Part Design workbench, select **Start>Mechanical Design>Part Design**. The punch is located using the origin of the part. The punching direction is always equal to the Z-direction. An example of a punch is shown in Figure 5–47.

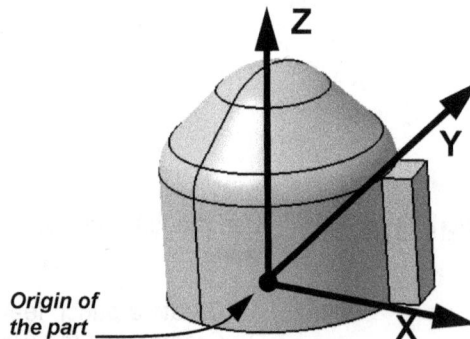

Origin of the part

Figure 5–47

When the punch is applied, the Z-direction is oriented normal to the selected surface, as shown in Figure 5–48. Therefore, you must always create the punch geometry in the positive Z-direction to obtain predictable results.

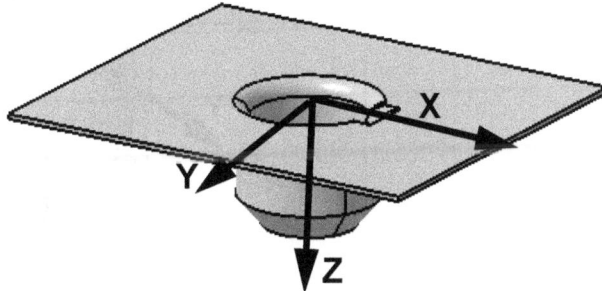

Figure 5–48

Step 2 - Create a die feature.

It is helpful to rename the body to identify it in the specification tree

The die must also be created in a separate body, and must be a solid feature that is created in the Part Design workbench. The die geometry can exist in the sheet metal model or a separate CATPart model.

The die is located using the origin of the part, and the punching direction is always equal to the positive Z-direction. An example of the cross-section of a die is shown in Figure 5–49.

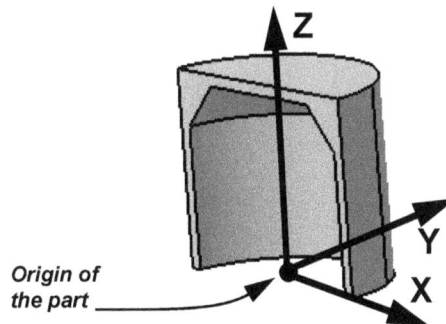

Figure 5–49

When the die is applied, its Z-direction is always oriented to be normal to the selected surface. Figure 5–50 shows a user stamp cross-section.

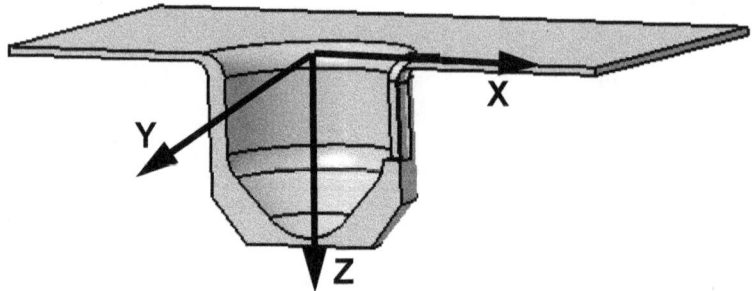

Figure 5–50

Step 3 - Activate the User Stamp tool.

Return to the body containing the sheet metal features by selecting it in the specification tree, right-clicking and selecting **Define in Work Object**. Return to the Generative Sheetmetal workbench by selecting **Start>Mechanical Design>Generative Sheetmetal Design**.

Expand the Stamping flyout in the Cutting/Stamping toolbar and click ▨ (User Stamp). In the User-Defined Stamp Definition dialog box, select **Punch and Die** in the Type drop-down list.

Step 4 - Locate the stamp on the wall.

Click ▨ and select the face on which to create the user stamp. In the Sketcher environment, create a sketched point to locate the origin of the user stamp. Once the point has been created and constrained, exit the Sketcher environment to return to the User-Defined Stamp Definition.

Step 5 - Select punch and die bodies.

Select in the *Punch* field and select the body that contains the punch and then select the body that contains the die. The user-defined Stamp Definition dialog box populates with the selected bodies, as shown in Figure 5–51. A preview of the stamp also displays on the model.

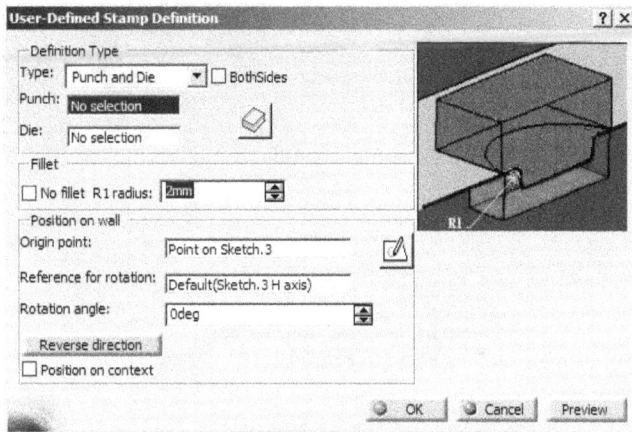

Figure 5–51

Step 6 - Define the fillet of the stamp.

By default a fillet is applied to the edge of the stamp. Enter the radius of the fillet using the *R1 radius* field or select the **No Fillet** option if you do not want to include a fillet. An example of a stamp with and without a fillet is shown in Figure 5–52.

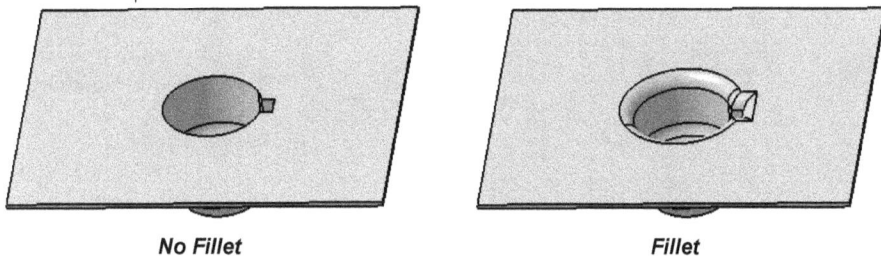

No Fillet   *Fillet*

Figure 5–52

Step 7 - Rotate the stamp, if required.

You can change the orientation of the stamp by selecting a reference for rotation and entering an angle. For example, the bottom edge of the wall is selected as the rotation reference in Figure 5–53.

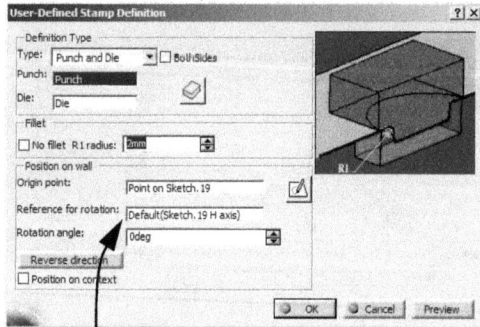

Select in this field, and select a reference for rotation

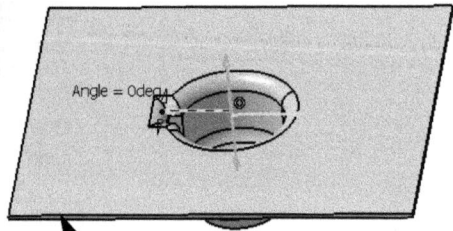

Selected rotational reference

Figure 5–53

Once the reference is selected, enter the angle of revolution. Figure 5–54 shows the stamp rotated by 45 degrees.

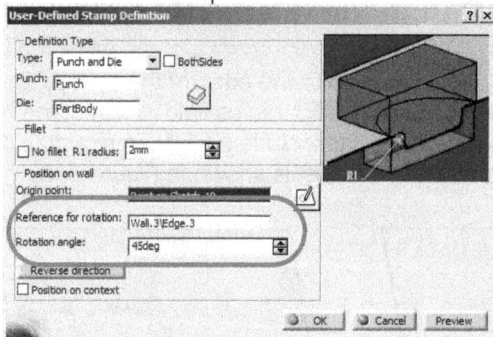

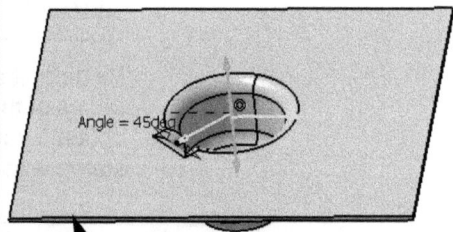

Reference for Rotation

Figure 5–54

Step 8 - Complete the feature.

Once the stamp has been defined, click **OK** to complete it.

Practice 5a

Standard Stamps

Practice Objectives

- Create a Louver.
- Create a Surface Stamp.
- Create a Flanged Hole.

In this practice, you will create louvers for the side of the bracket. These louvers will be powercopied to the other side of the bracket in a later practice. You will also create a surface stamp for the front of the bracket, and a flanged hole that will be patterned in a later practice. At the end of the practice, the model will display as shown in Figure 5–55.

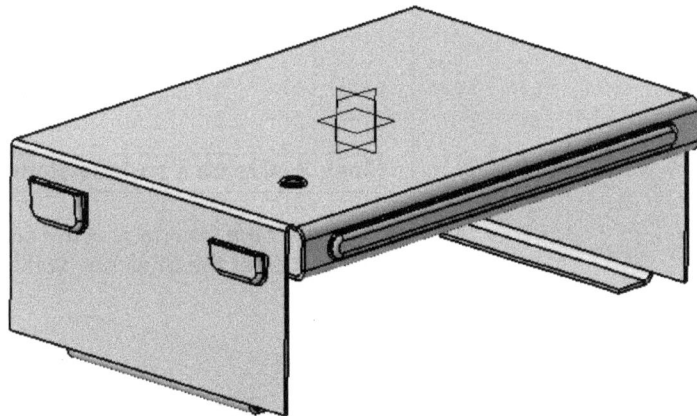

Figure 5–55

Goal

Task 1 - Open the part.

1. Open **Ex5A_Mount.CATPart**.

   If you completed **Practice 3b** open **Mount.CATPart** instead. The model displays as shown in Figure 5–56.

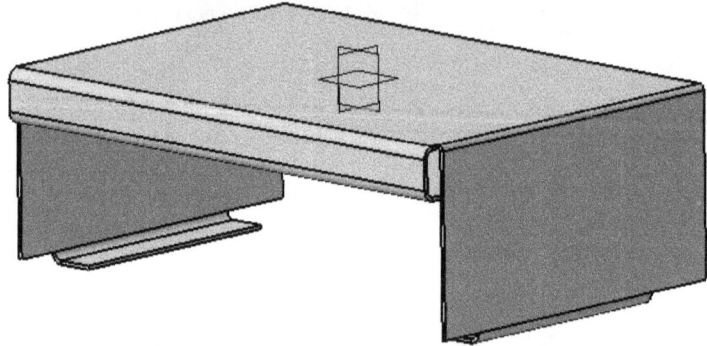

Figure 5–56

Task 2 - Create a surface stamp profile.

1. Select the front face of the bracket, as shown in Figure 5–57, and enter the Sketcher workbench.

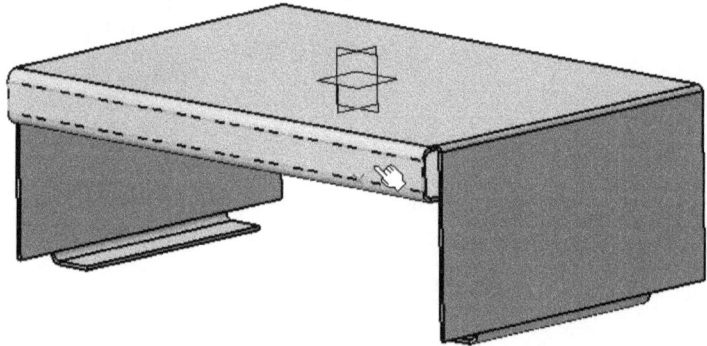

Figure 5–57

2. Create a sketch that is centered vertically and horizontally on the front face, as shown in Figure 5–58.

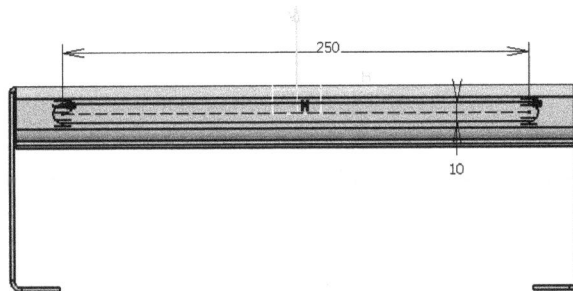

Figure 5–58

3. Exit the Sketcher workbench.

4. Rename the sketch as **Surface_Stamp_Profile**.

Task 3 - Create a surface stamp.

---

1. Select the **Surface_Stamp_Profile** sketch and click

    (Surface Stamp).

2. The stamp should protrude from the bracket, as shown in Figure 5–59. Change the direction of stamp creation by clicking on the orange arrow.

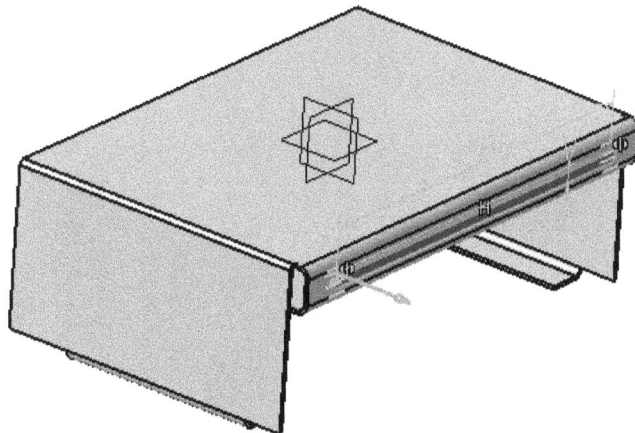

Figure 5–59

3. Enter the following parameters for the Surface Stamp:

- ***Angle A:* 75deg**
- *Height H:* **4mm**
- *Radius R1:* **1mm**
- *Radius R2:* **1mm**

4. Click **OK** to create the surface stamp. The model displays as shown in Figure 5–60.

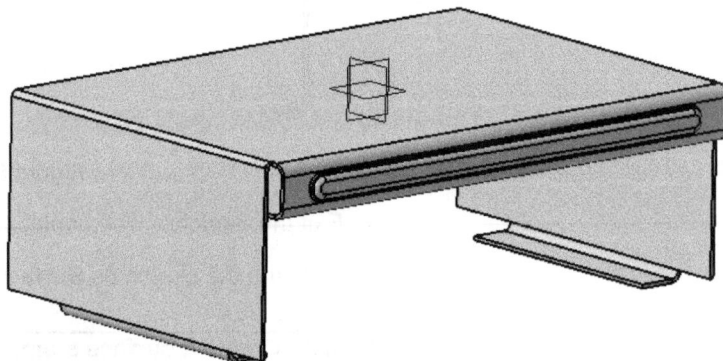

Figure 5–60

Task 4 - Create profiles for louvers.

1. Select the surface shown in Figure 5–61 and enter the Sketcher workbench.

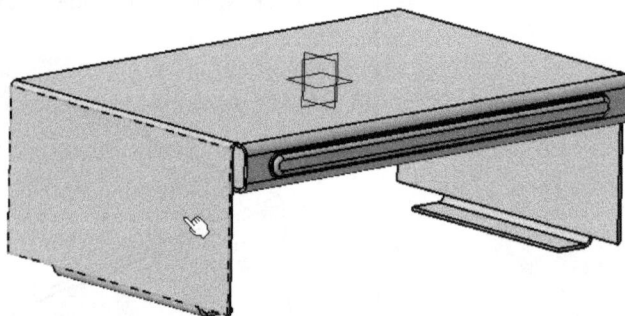

Figure 5–61

The sketch is used as a powercopy in a later practice.

2. Create the sketch, as shown in Figure 5–62. To keep track of references, create the Horizontal reference dimension before you create the Vertical reference dimension. Be sure to create the dimensions as shown in Figure 5–62.

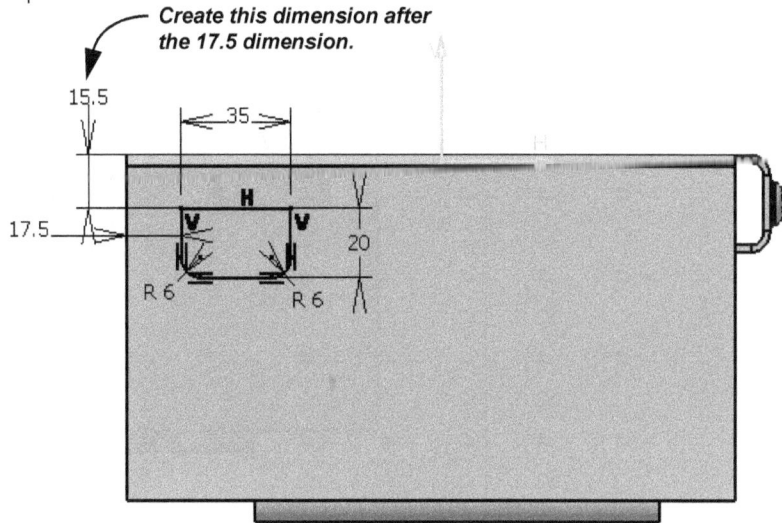

Figure 5–62

3. Exit the Sketcher workbench.

4. Select the sketch, right-click and select **Copy**.

5. Select the surface as shown in Figure 5–63, right-click and select **Paste**.

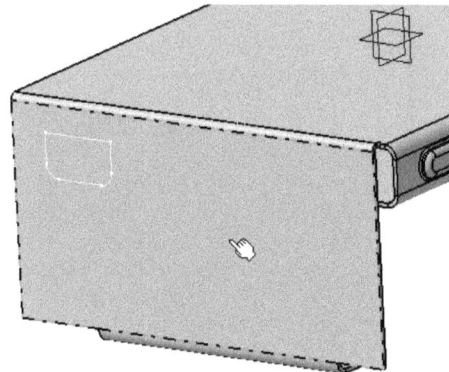

Figure 5–63

6. Double-click on the new sketch in the specification tree to edit it. Delete the horizontal reference dimension and recreate it, as shown in Figure 5–64.

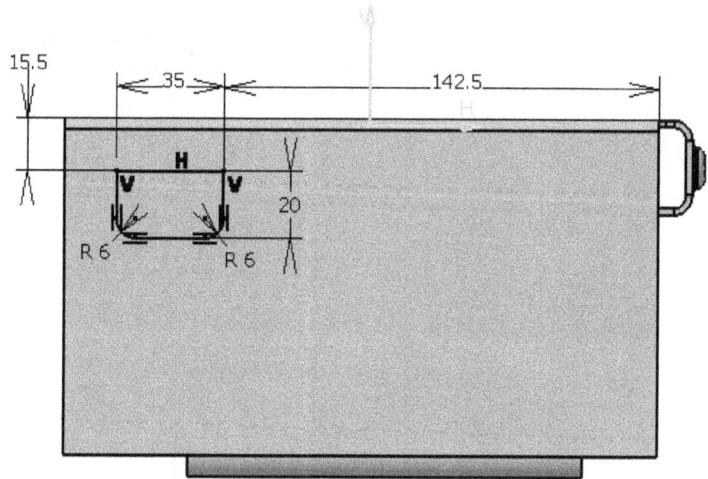

Figure 5–64

7. Change the dimensions of the sketch, as shown in Figure 5–65.

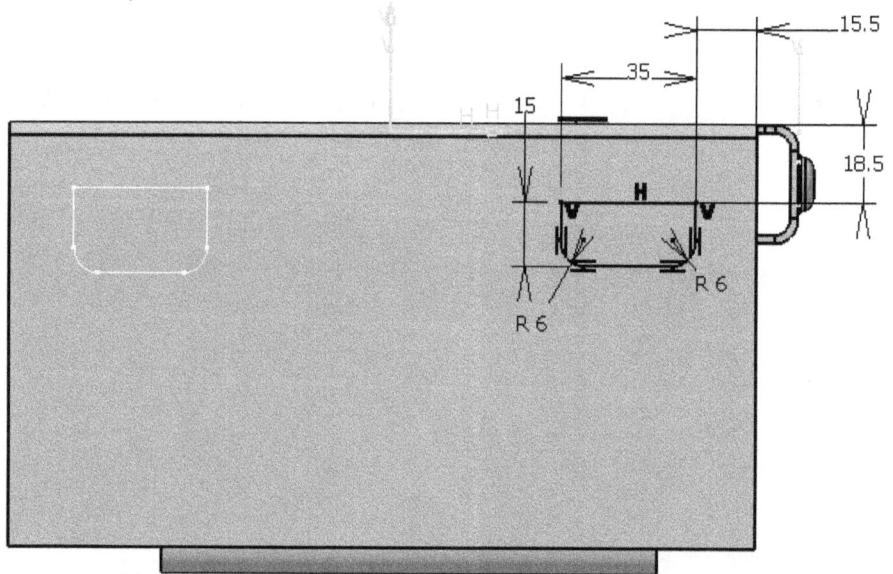

Figure 5–65

8. Exit the Sketcher workbench.

Task 5 - Create louvers.

1. Select the first sketched profile created in Task 4.

2. Click ![Louver icon] (Louver).

3. Create the Louver using the following dimensions:

   - *Height H:* **4mm**
   - *Angle A1:* **10deg**
   - *Angle A2:* **85deg**
   - *Radius R1:* **1mm**
   - *Radius R2:* **1mm**

4. Select inside the *Opening Line* field.

5. Select the top line of the profile to act as the open surface for the louver, as shown in Figure 5–66.

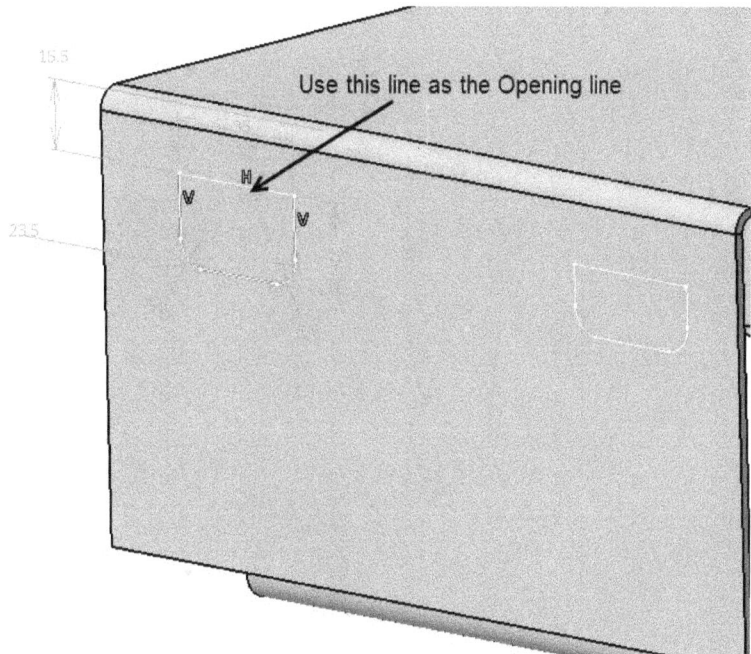

Use this line as the Opening line

Figure 5–66

6. Click **OK** to complete the feature. The model displays as shown in Figure 5–67.

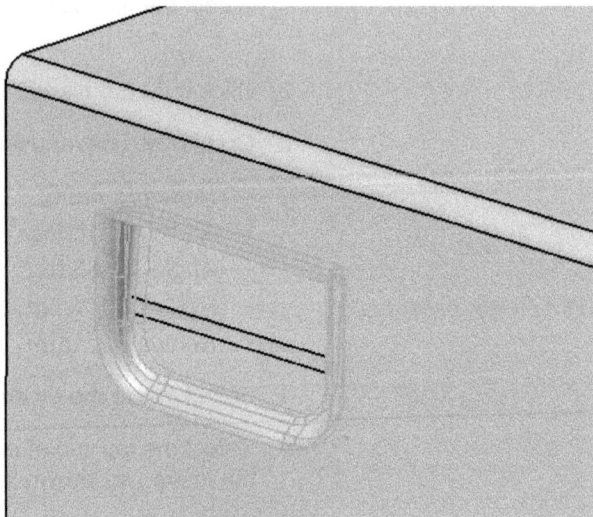

Figure 5–67

7. The Louver was created in the wrong direction. Double click **Louver.1** in the specification tree.

8. Select the orange arrow to change the direction.

9. Click **OK** to complete the feature and click on the screen. The model displays as shown in Figure 5–68.

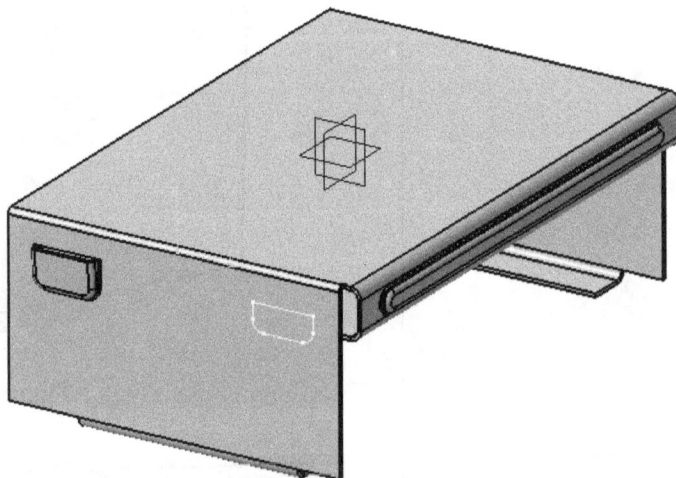

Figure 5–68

10. Use the other profile created in Task 4 - to create a second louver.

11. Create the second louver using the following dimensions:

- *Height H:* **3mm**
- *Angle A1:* **10deg**
- *Angle A2:* **85deg**
- *Radius R1:* **1mm**
- *Radius R2:* **1mm**

The model displays as shown in Figure 5–69.

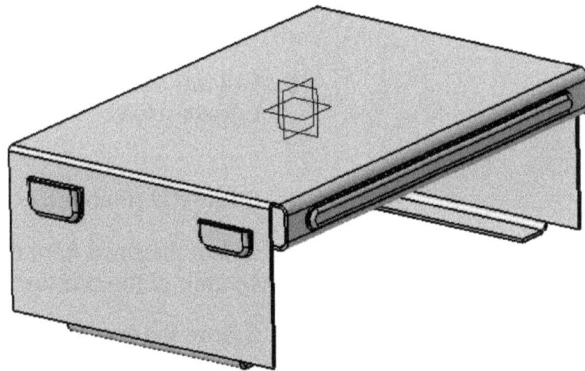

Figure 5–69

Task 6 - Create a flanged hole.

1. Select the top surface of the bracket, as shown in Figure 5–70, and enter the Sketcher workbench.

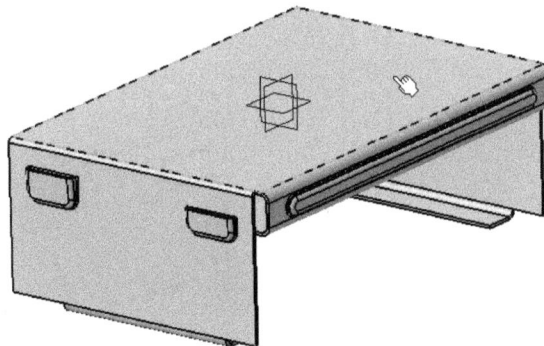

Figure 5–70

2. Create a point, as shown in Figure 5–71.

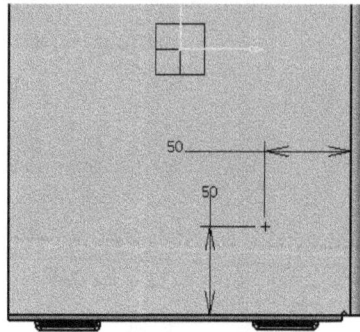

Figure 5–71

3. Exit the Sketcher workbench. Rename the sketch to **Locate_Hole**.

4. Click ⌨ (Flanged Hole).

5. Select the point from the **Locate_Hole** sketch and the top surface of the bracket.

6. Create the flanged hole using the following dimensions:

   - *Height H:* **3mm**
   - *Radius R:* **1mm**
   - *Angle A:* **80deg**
   - *Diameter D:* **10mm**

7. Ensure the flanged hole is created facing upward, as shown in Figure 5–72.

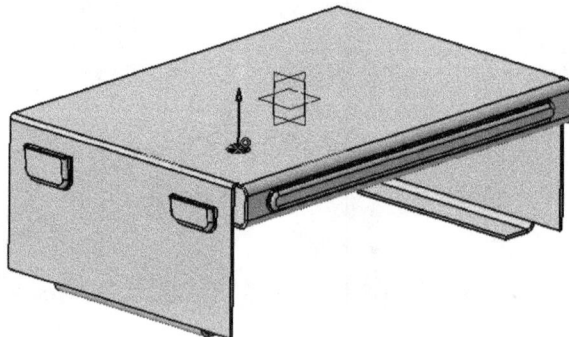

Figure 5–72

8. Click **OK** to generate the feature.

9. Hide the **Locate_Hole** sketch. The model displays as shown in Figure 5–73.

You will pattern this flanged hole in a later practice.

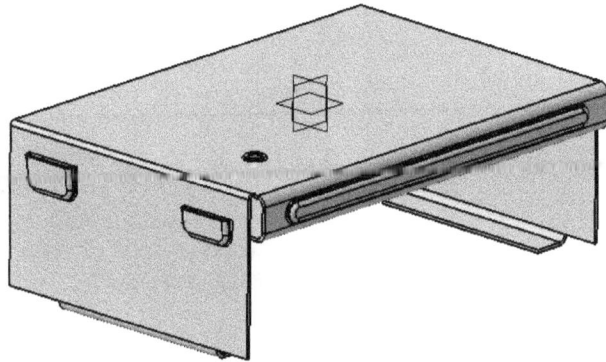

Figure 5–73

10. Save and close the file.

Practice 5b

Standard and User-Defined Stamps

Practice Objectives

- Create a Stiffening rib and a circular stamp.
- Create a Punch, a Die, and a User-defined Stamp.

In this practice, you will add two stiffening ribs, a circular stamp, and a user-defined stamp to a mounting bracket. The circular stamp will be patterned using a User-Defined pattern in a later practice. At the end of the practice, the model will display as shown in Figure 5–74.

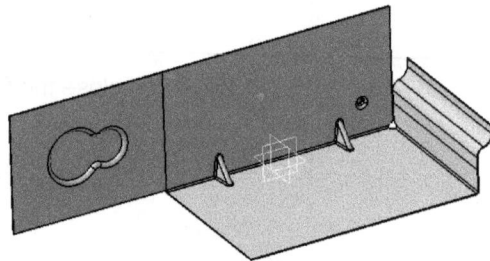

Figure 5–74

Task 1 - Open the part.

1. Open **Ex5B_Mounting_Bracket.CATPart**.

   If you completed **Practice 4b**, open **Mounting_Bracket.CATPart** instead. The model displays as shown in Figure 5–75.

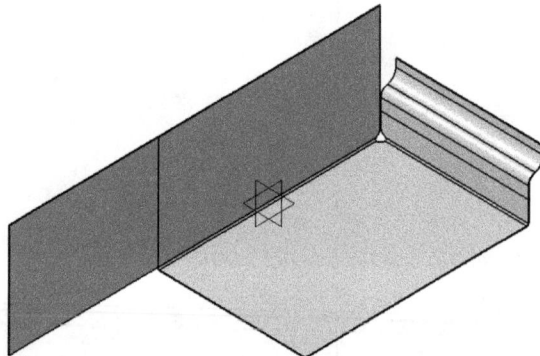

Figure 5–75

Task 2 - Create a punch.

1. Open the file **Punch.CATPart**. The model displays as shown in Figure 5–76. This file contains the geometry you will use for the punch. It has been defined about the part origin and is oriented so that its height is in the Z-direction, as required.

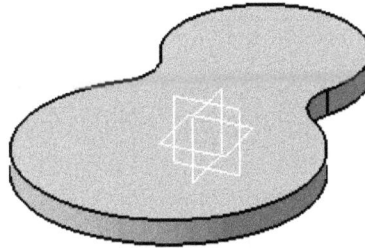

Figure 5–76

2. Select the PartBody, right-click and select **Copy**.

3. Return to the **Mounting_Bracket** model, select the top item in the specification tree, right-click and select **Paste**, as shown in Figure 5–77.

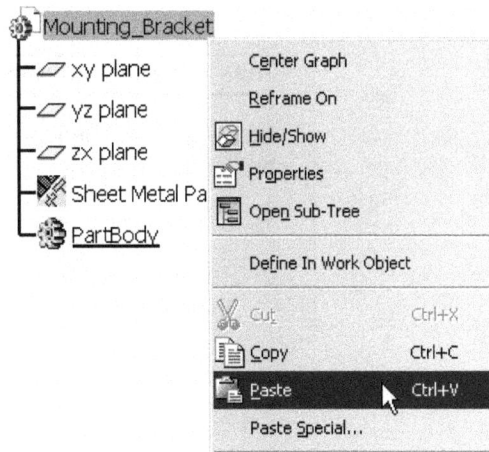

Figure 5–77

4. Rename the body by selecting it in the specification tree, right-clicking and selecting **Properties**, as shown in Figure 5–78.

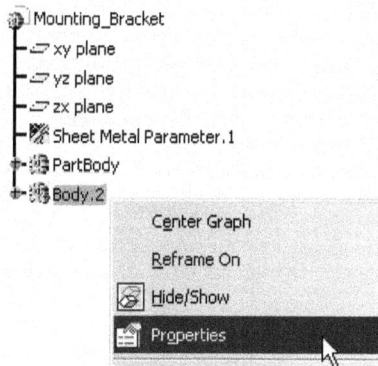

Figure 5–78

5. Change the feature name to **Punch** in the *Feature Properties* tab.

6. Click **OK** to close the Properties dialog box.

7. Close the **Punch.CATPart** file.

Task 3 - Create another body.

Both the punch and the die used in the user-defined stamp must be defined in separate bodies inside the part file.

1. Create a new body by selecting **Insert>Body**.

2. Rename the body as **Die**. The specification tree opens as shown in Figure 5–79.

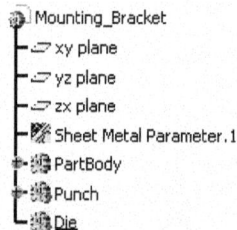

Figure 5–79

Task 4 - Create the die.

1. For clarity, hide the sheet metal model by selecting the PartBody, right-clicking and selecting **Hide/Show**.

2. Ensure that the Die body is active by selecting it, right-clicking and selecting **Define in Work Object**. The Die body should be underlined in the specification tree.

3. Select **Start>Mechanical Design>Part Design** to access the Part Design workbench. A Warning message opens indicating that the features created in Part design workbench cannot be unfolded, as shown in Figure 5–80.

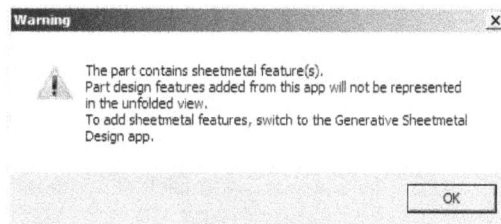

Figure 5–80

4. Click **OK**.

5. Select the XY plane and enter the Sketcher workbench.

6. Create the rectangular profile for the die so that it is symmetric about the origin, as shown in Figure 5–81.

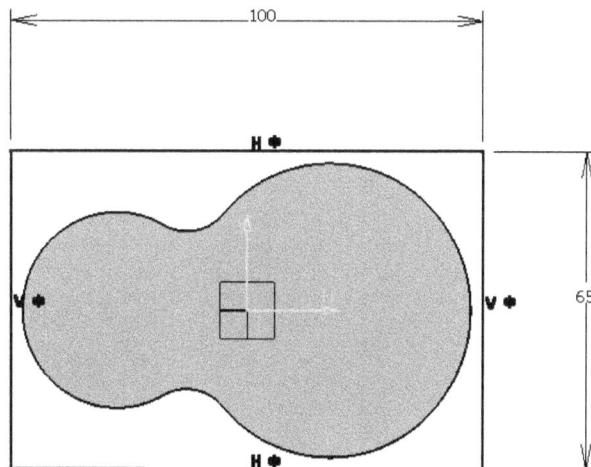

Figure 5–81

7. Exit the Sketcher workbench.

8. Highlight the profile for the die and click [icon] (Pad).

9. Create a pad with a **7mm** height, as shown in Figure 5–82.

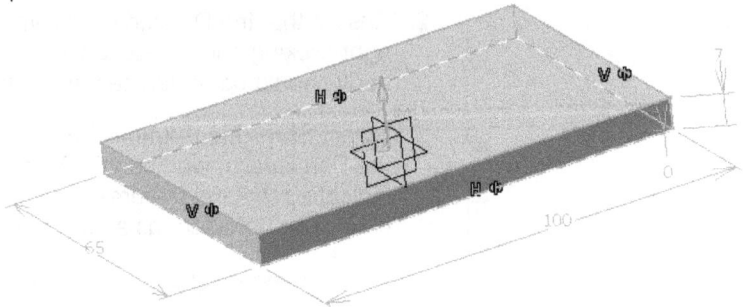

Figure 5–82

10. Select the bottom face of the pad, as shown in Figure 5–83, and click [icon] (Shell).

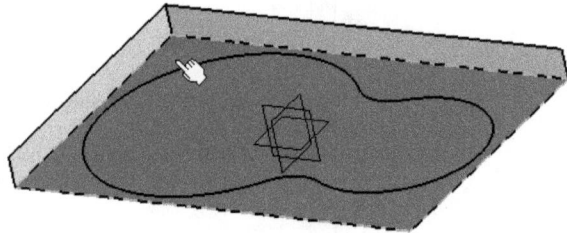

Figure 5–83

11. Shell the die with a **1mm** default outside thickness, as shown in Figure 5–84.

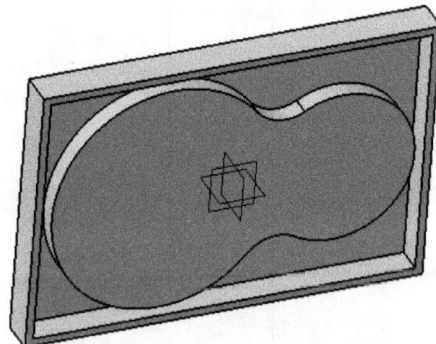

Figure 5–84

Task 5 - Create a locating point for the user stamp.

To locate the user stamp correctly, you will create a locating point. This point acts as the origin for the stamp when it is being placed.

1. Activate the Generative Sheetmetal Design workbench.

2. Select the **PartBody** in the specification tree, right-click and select **Hide/Show** to display the sheet metal model.

3. Activate the PartBody by right-clicking on it and selecting **Define in Work Object**. The PartBody is underlined in the specification tree, as shown in Figure 5–85.

Figure 5–85

4. Click ⬛ (User Stamp).

5. Click ⬛ and select the face shown in Figure 5–86 to enter the Sketcher workbench and create the origin point.

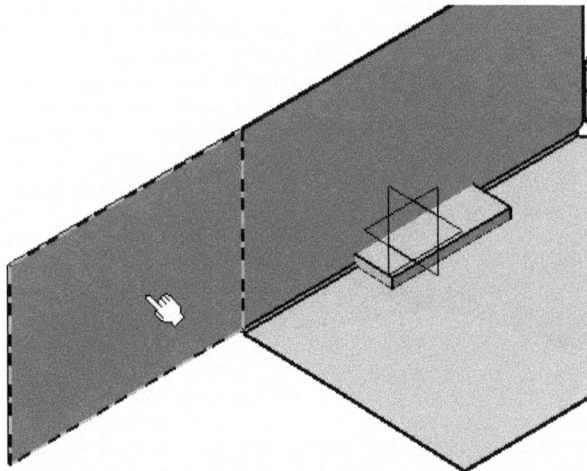

Figure 5–86

6. Dimension the point as shown in Figure 5–87.

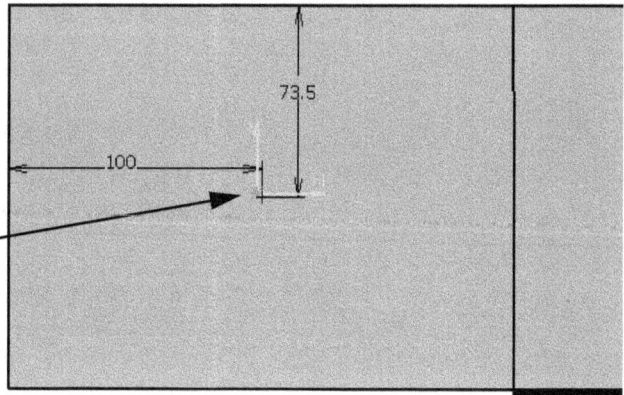

Use dimensions to locate the point. The point is not located at the origin of the sketch.

Figure 5–87

7. Exit the Sketcher workbench.

8. Select **Punch and Die** in the Type drop-down list, as shown in Figure 5–88.

9. Select in the *Punch* field in the User-Defined Stamp Definition dialog box and select the Punch body in the specification tree.

10. The *Die* field automatically activates. Select the Die body in the specification tree. The user-defined Stamp Definition dialog box updates and a preview of the punch displays on the model, as shown in Figure 5–88.

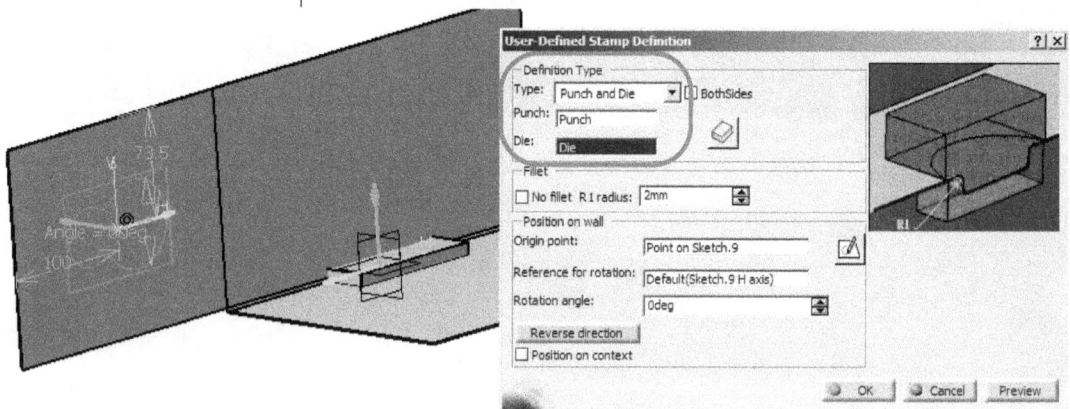

Figure 5–88

11. Rotate the punch and die 180 degrees by selecting in the *Reference for rotation* field and selecting the Top edge of the tangent wall as the reference, as shown in Figure 5–89.

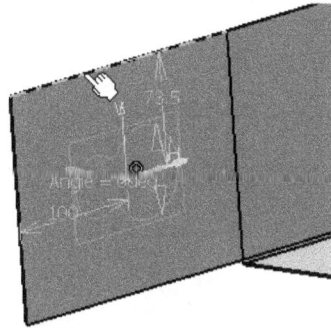

Figure 5–89

12. If required, enter **180** in the *Rotation Angle* field so your model looks as shown in Figure 5-100.

13. Click **Preview** and the stamp rotates 180 degrees.

14. Click **OK** to complete the stamp. The model displays as shown in Figure 5–90.

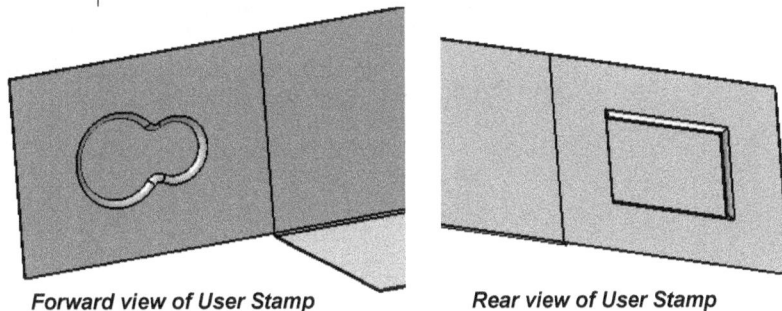

Forward view of User Stamp   *Rear view of User Stamp*

Figure 5–90

Task 6 - Create locating points for the stiffening ribs.

You must first create a locating point to place a stiffening rib. This point can be created on any plane and will be projected orthogonally onto the bend to which the rib is applied. In this practice, you will create two stiffening ribs. Although these ribs cannot be created at the same time, you can create the points in the same sketch.

1. Select the ZX plane and enter the Sketcher workbench.

2. Create two points as shown in Figure 5–91.

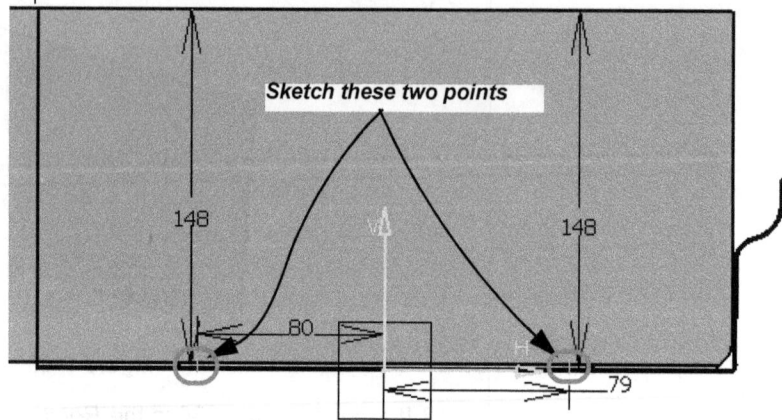

Figure 5–91

3. Exit the Sketcher workbench.

4. Rename the sketch as **Locate_Ribs**.

Task 7 - Create the stiffening ribs.

1. Highlight one of the locating points and the outside surface of the bend, as shown in Figure 5–92.

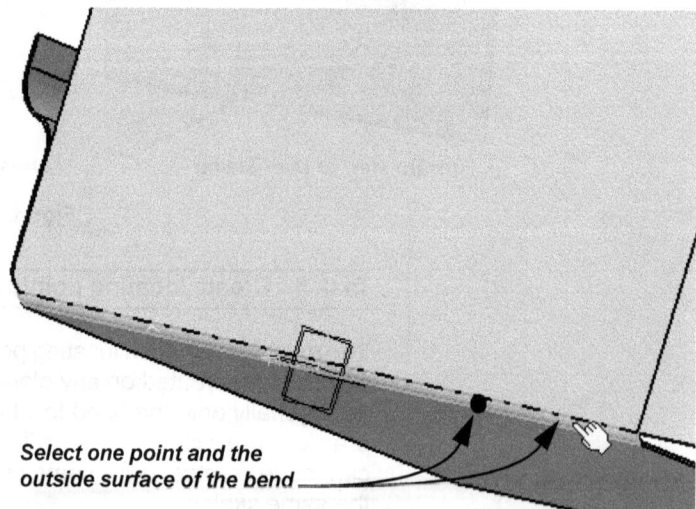

Figure 5–92

2. Click ![icon](Stiffening Rib) (Stiffening Rib).

3. Enter the following parameters for the rib:

    - *Length L:* **40mm**
    - *Radius R1:* **2mm**
    - *Radius R2:* **2mm**
    - *Angle A:* **80deg**

4. Click **OK** to generate the rib.

5. Create a second rib using the other locating point and the same bend as the references.

6. Use the parameters that were used for the previous rib.

7. Hide the **Locate_Ribs** sketch. The model displays as shown in Figure 5–93.

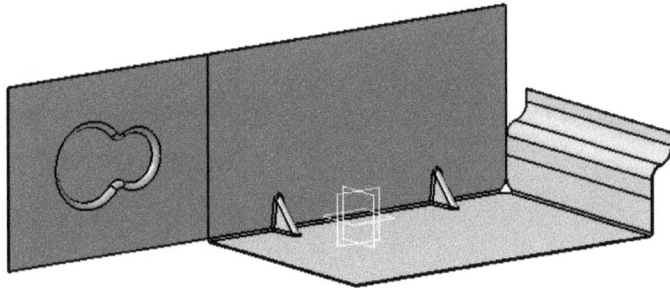

Figure 5–93

Task 8 - Create a circular stamp.

In this task, you will create a circular stamp, which will be patterned in a later practice.

1. Select the wall shown in Figure 5–94 and enter the Sketcher workbench.

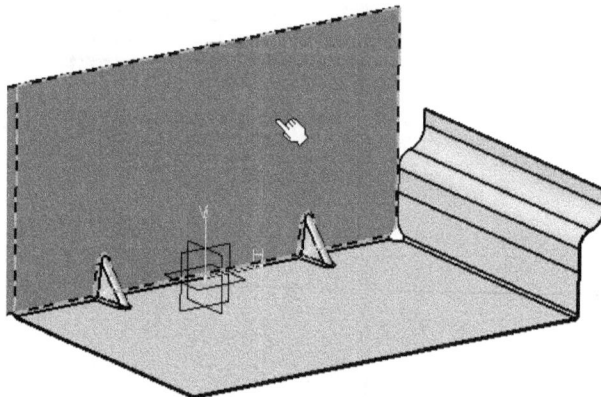

Figure 5–94

2. Create a locating point, as shown in Figure 5–95.

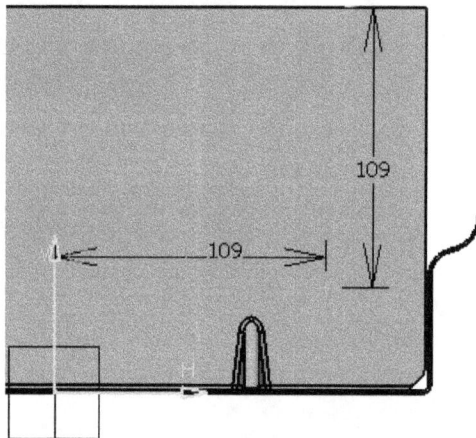

Figure 5–95

3. Exit the Sketcher workbench.

4. Rename the sketch as **Locate_Circular_Stamp**.

5. Highlight the locating point and the back wall, as shown in Figure 5–96.

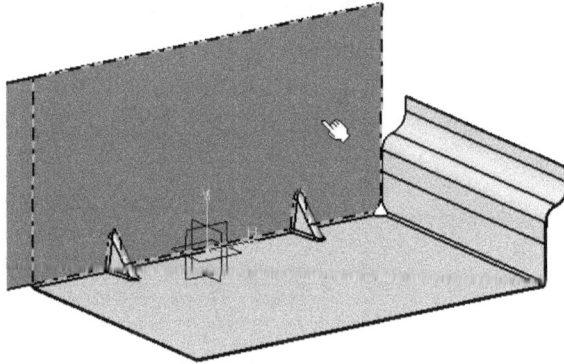

Figure 5–96

6. Click ![icon](Circular Stamp).

7. Create a circular stamp using the following dimensions:

   - *Height H:* **7mm**
   - *Radius R1:* **2mm**
   - *Radius R2:* **1mm**
   - *Diameter D:* **10mm**
   - *Angle A:* **84deg**

8. Set the direction arrow to point out the back of the part.

9. Click **OK** to complete the circular stamp.

10. Hide the **Locate_Circular_Stamp** sketch. The model displays as shown in Figure 5–97.

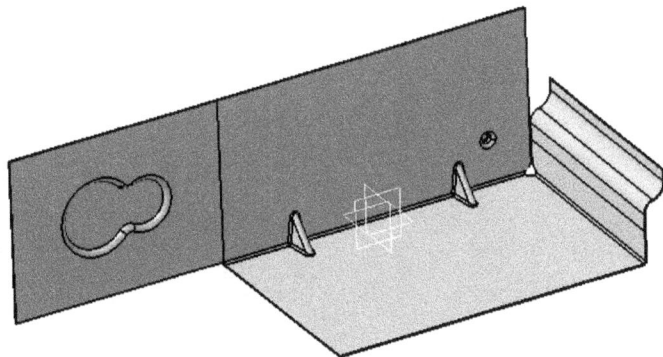

Figure 5–97

11. Save and close the file.

Practice 5c

Two Profiles Surface Stamp

Practice Objective

- Create a Surface stamp.

In this practice, you will create a surface stamp with two mapped curves.

Task 1 - Open the part.

1. Open the **Ex5c_CurveMapping.CATPart**.

    If you completed **Practice 4c**, open **CurveMapping.CATPart** instead. The model displays as shown in Figure 5–98.

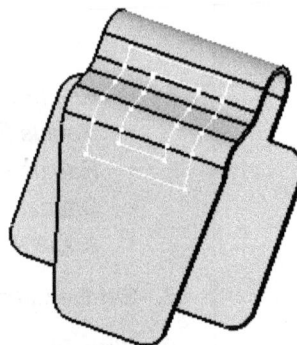

Figure 5–98

2. Examine the features of the model. The part consists of a primary wall and bend from flat features. Two sketched curves have also been mapped to the formed part.

Task 2 - Create a surface stamp.

In this task, you will create a surface stamp using the mapped curves.

1. Click (Surface Stamp) in the **Stamping** flyout menu of Cutting/Stamping toolbar.

2. Expand the **Geometrical Set.1** branch in the specification tree and select **Folded curve.1** and **Folded curve.2**, as shown in Figure 5–99.

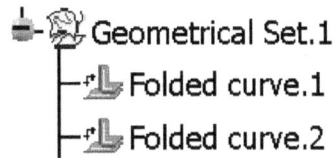

Figure 5–99

3. Specify the following parameters:

- *Parameters choice:* **Two profiles**
- *Height:* **0.2mm**
- *Radius R1:* **0.075mm**
- *Radius R2:* **0.075mm**
- Enable the **Rounded die** option.

The Surface Stamp Definition dialog box opens as shown in Figure 5–100.

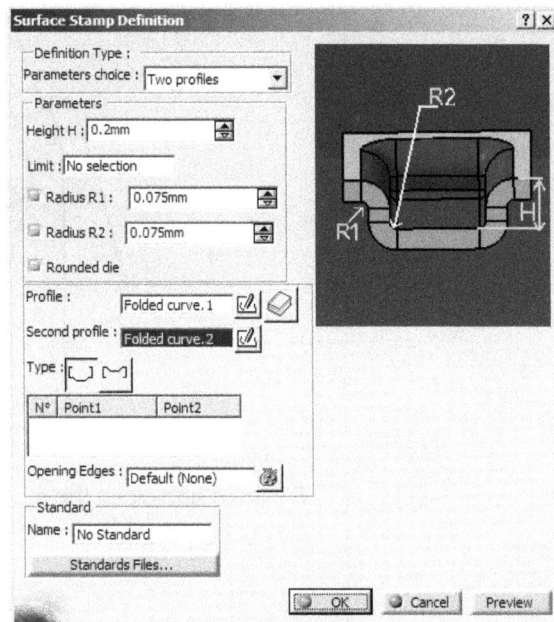

Figure 5–100

A preview of the feature displays as shown in Figure 5–101.

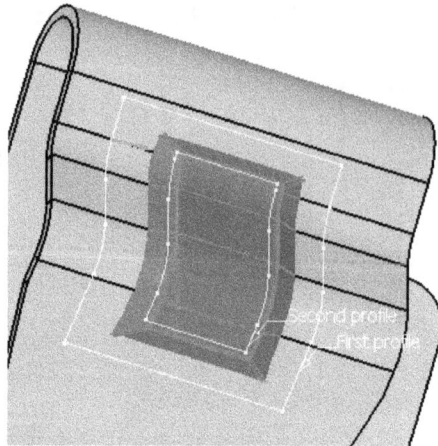

Figure 5–101

4. Click **OK** to complete the feature. The model displays as shown in Figure 5–102.

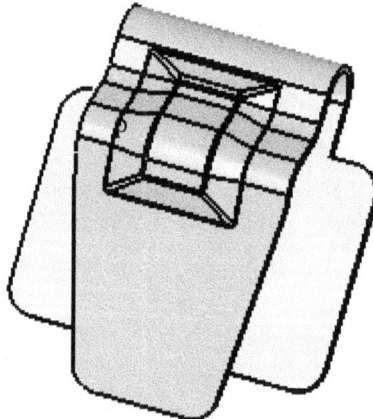

Figure 5–102

5. Save and close the model.

Sheet Metal Features

Sheet metal features, such as corners, chamfers, cuts, and holes, can be created using methods that are similar to the Part Design workbench.

Learning Objectives in this Chapter

- Learn how to create Corner, Sheet Metal Cutouts, Circular Cutouts, and Holes.
- Understand how to add Chamfers.

6.1 Corners

A corner is the equivalent to a fillet in the Part Design workbench. In sheet metal parts corners are used to remove sharp edges and help maintain material strength and thickness. An example of a corner is shown in Figure 6–1.

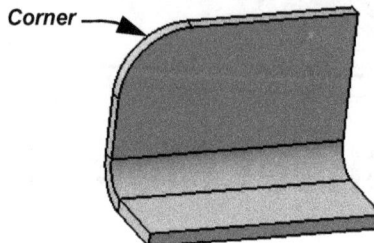

Corner

Figure 6–1

General Steps

Use the following general steps to create a corner:

1. Activate the **Corner** tool.
2. Select edges to corner.
3. Enter a radius for the corner.
4. Complete the feature.

Step 1 - Activate the Corner tool.

To create a corner, click  (Corner). The Corner dialog box opens as shown in Figure 6–2.

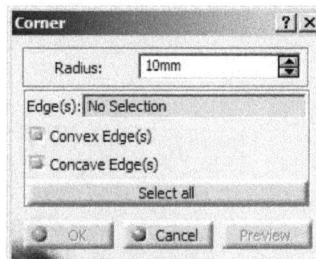

Figure 6–2

Step 2 - Select edges to corner.

Corners can be applied to any sharp edge that does not intersect two walls, as shown in Figure 6–3.

Select the edge belonging to a sharp corner.

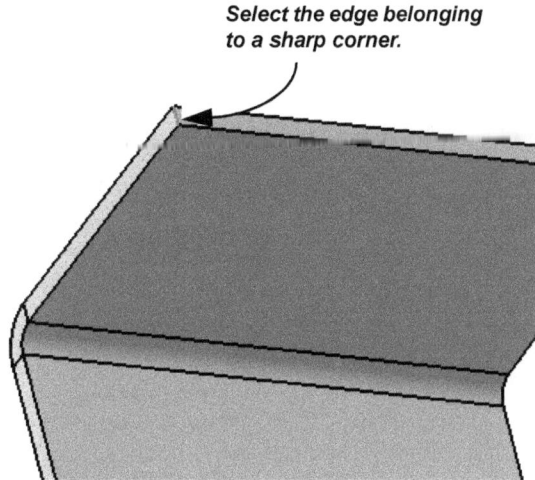

Figure 6–3

*You can clear the selected edge by clicking on it. If you want to reset the selection, click **Cancel selection**.*

Edges can be manually selected one by one, or all at once by clicking **Select all**. The type of edges that are selected can be controlled using the **Convex Edge(s)** or **Concave Edge(s)** option. Figure 6–4 shows an example with both concave and convex corners; the concave corner is identified.

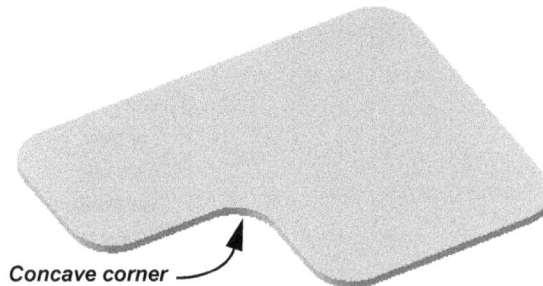

Concave corner

Figure 6–4

Step 3 - Enter a radius for the corner.

Enter the corner radius in the *Radius* field, as shown in Figure 6–5. A preview of the corners updates on the model.

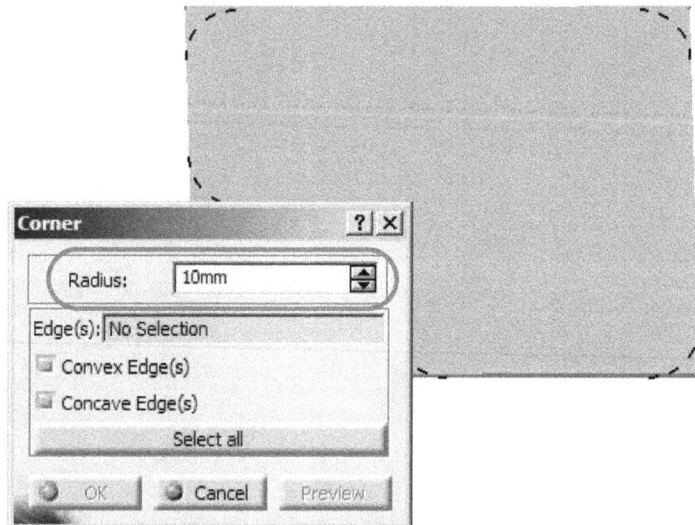

Figure 6–5

Step 4 - Complete the feature.

To complete the corner, click **OK**. The model updates as shown in Figure 6–6.

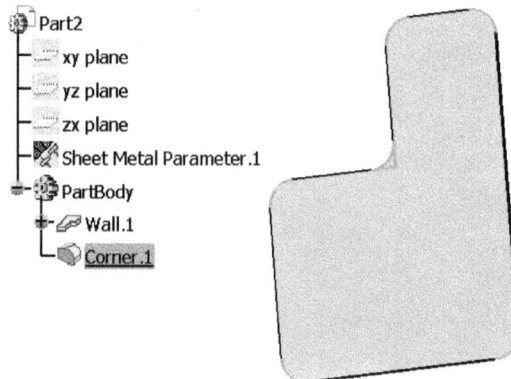

Figure 6–6

6.2 Chamfers

Chamfers in the Generative Sheetmetal Design workbench are the same as those created in the Part Design workbench. Like corners, chamfers can be applied to sharp corners. An example of a chamfer is shown in Figure 6–7.

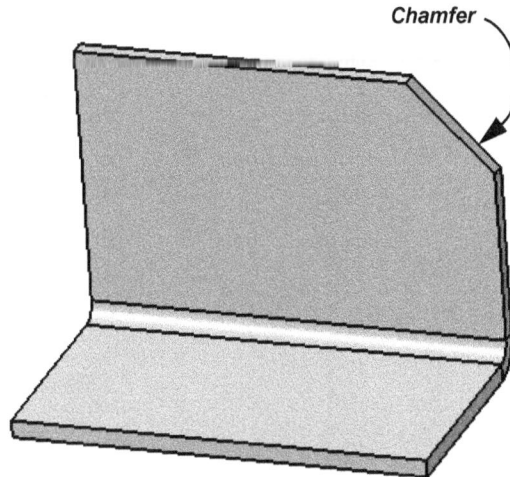

Chamfer

Figure 6–7

General Steps

Use the following general steps to create a chamfer:

1. Activate the **Chamfer** tool.
2. Select the edges to chamfer.
3. Select method of propagation.
4. Dimension the chamfer.

5. Complete the feature.

Step 1 - Activate the Chamfer tool.

Click  (Chamfer) to open the Chamfer dialog box, as shown in Figure 6–8.

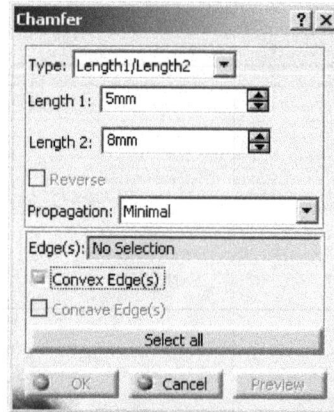

Figure 6–8

Step 2 - Select the edges to chamfer.

As with corners, chamfers can be applied to any sharp edge that does not intersect two walls. Edges can be manually selected one by one, or all at once by clicking **Select all**. The type of edges that are selected can be controlled using the **Convex Edge(s)** or **Concave Edge(s)** option.

You can clear the selected edge by clicking on it. If you want to reset the selection, click **Cancel selection**.

Step 3 - Select method of propagation.

By default, the system automatically continues to chamfer the adjacent edges that are tangent to the selected edge. This process is known as propagation. The Chamfer dialog box provides two options for controlling propagation, which are described as follows:

Propagation	Image	Description
Minimal		Disables propagation and only the selected edge is chamfered.
Tangency		The chamfer continues along adjacent edges of the selected edge until a non-tangency condition is encountered.

Step 4 - Dimension the chamfer.

Chamfers can be dimensioned using one of two methods: **Length1/Length2** or **Length/Angle**. Select the dimensioning scheme in the Type drop-down list, as shown in Figure 6–9, and enter the dimensional values. A preview of the chamfer displays on the model.

Use the Reverse option to change the side of the edge used by the dimensional fields.

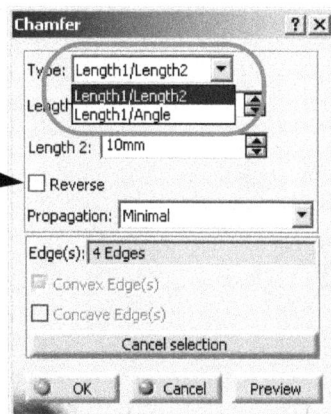

Figure 6–9

Step 5 - Complete the feature.

To complete the chamfer, click **OK**. The model updates as shown in Figure 6–10.

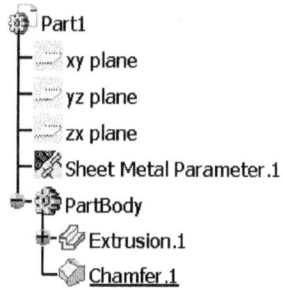

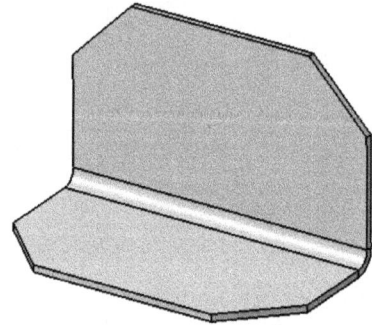

Figure 6–10

6.3 Sheet Metal Cutouts

A sheet metal cutout is similar to a pocket in the Part Design workbench. It is used to remove material from the model. Cuts can be created in the folded or unfolded view. Creating the cut in the unfolded view enables you to create a cut whose profile consists of more than one wall, as shown in Figure 6–11.

Figure 6–11

General Steps

Use the following general steps to create a sheet metal cut:

1. Create the cut profile.
2. Activate the cut feature.
3. Define the cut.

4. Complete the feature.

Step 1 - Create the cut profile.

Create the profile for the cut in the Sketcher workbench. The profile can be created in the unfolded or folded view. Profiles can be opened or closed. Open profiles remove the material on one side of the profile to the end of the material, as shown in Figure 6–12.

Open profile removes material on one side to the end of the material. Profile does not need to be coincident with the ends of the model; the system trims/extends the profile as required.

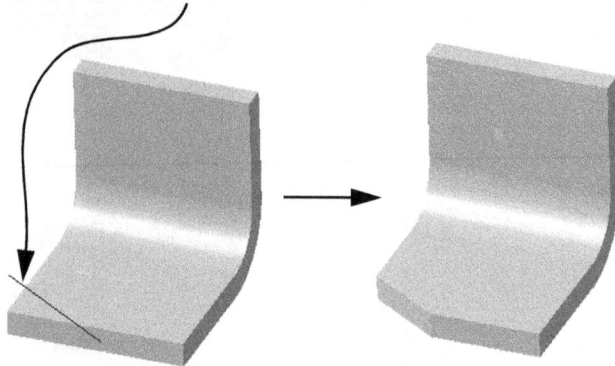

Figure 6–12

Step 2 - Activate the cut feature.

It is important to create the cutout in the correct view. Figure 6–13 uses the same profile in both images. The cutout on the left side is created in the folded view and the cutout on the right side is created in the unfolded view.

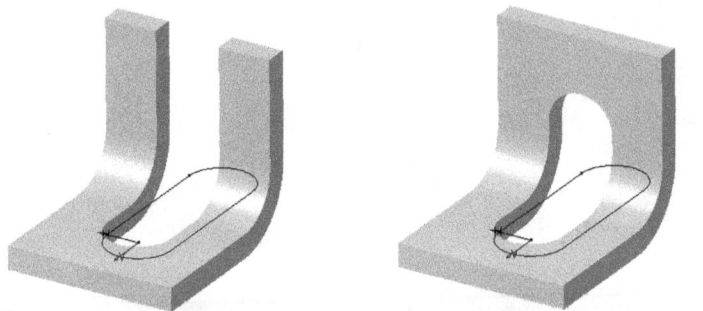

Cutout created in Folded view   *Cutout created in Unfolded view*

Figure 6–13

To create a cutout, select the profile from the model or specification tree and click 🔲 (Cutout). The Cutout definition dialog box opens as shown in Figure 6–14.

Figure 6–14

There are two types of cutout features that can be created by selecting one of the following options in the Type drop-down list:

- **Sheetmetal standard:** this feature uses dimension or up to depth options to define the limit of the cutout.

- **Sheetmetal pocket:** this feature can only be defined with a dimension depth.

Step 3 - Define the cut.

Select the depth option in the Type drop-down list. The depth options available for a sheet metal cutout are described as follows:

Option	Description
Dimension	Depth of cutout must be entered.
Up to Next	Sketch is extruded to the next surface that intersects the entire sketch.
Up to Last	Sketch is extruded through the entire model.

Click **Reverse Side** to change the material side being removed (inside or outside of the profile). Click **Reverse Direction** to change the direction in which the cut is created.

Cutouts can also cut material in two directions. Click **More** to expand the Cutout definition dialog box, and change the Start Limit as required. Depth options for the *Start limit* are the same as those for the *End limit*. Figure 6–15 shows a profile created on the middle wall. The cut can remove material from all three walls if required.

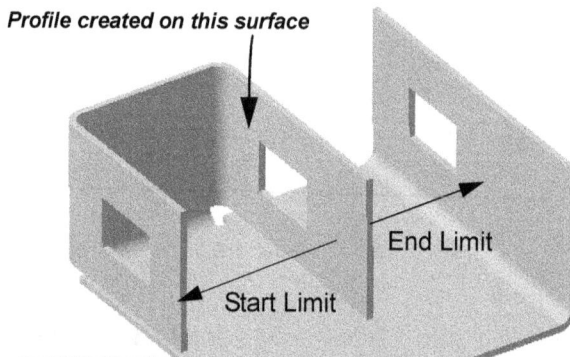

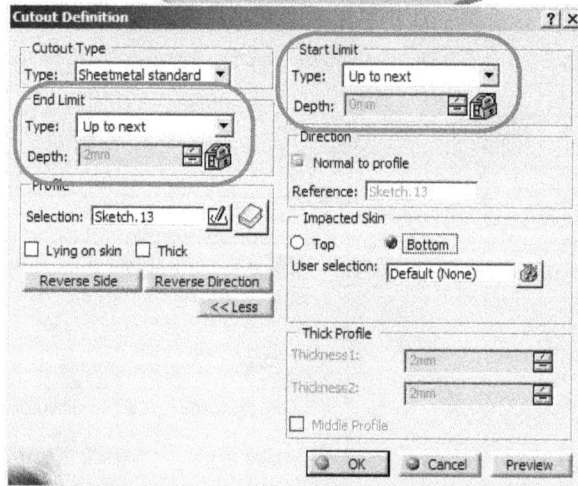

Figure 6–15

Step 4 - Complete the feature.

Once all elements of the cutout have been defined, click **OK** to complete the feature. The model updates as shown in Figure 6–16.

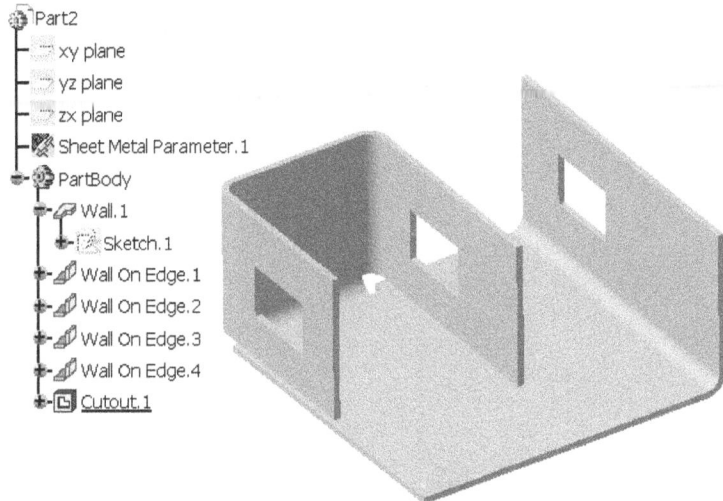

Figure 6–16

Note that you can use an open sketch to create the cutout. In the Cutout Definition dialog box, enable the **Thick** option and select or sketch an open profile.

You can enter a *Thickness* value for either or both sides of the open sketch, as shown in Figure 6–17.

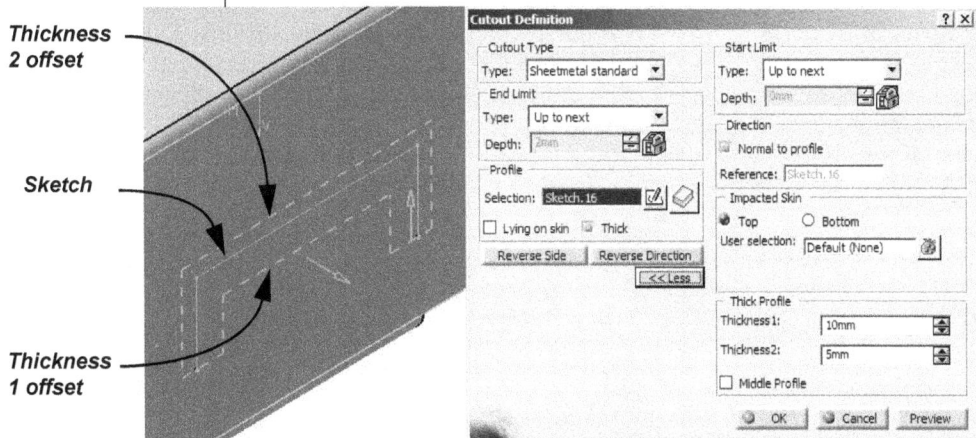

Figure 6–17

6.4 Circular Cutouts

Like cutouts, circular cutouts remove material from the model. The profile of a circular cutout is always circular, as shown in Figure 6–18.

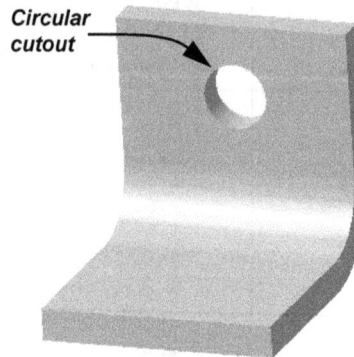

Circular cutout

Figure 6–18

General Steps

Use the following general steps to create a circular cut out:

1. Create a locating point.
2. Activate the **Circular Cutout** tool.
3. Define the circular cutout feature.
4. Complete the feature.

Step 1 - Create a locating point.

If no point is created, the circular cutout is placed directly under the cursor when you select the surface.

To locate the circular cutout correctly, a point should be sketched or created before accessing the **Circular Cutout** tool. Several points can be created in the same sketch. In the example shown in Figure 6–19, holes of the same diameter are created centered around each point.

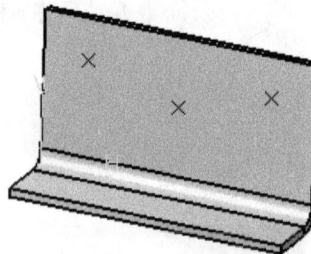

Figure 6–19

Step 2 - Activate the Circular Cutout tool.

Circular cutouts can be created in either the folded or unfolded view. To activate the **Circular Cutout** tool, highlight the locating point(s) and click (Circular Cutout). Select the surface on which to create the circular cutout(s).

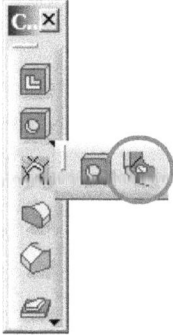

Step 3 - Define the circular cutout feature.

When defining a Circular Cutout feature, only the Diameter parameter can be modified. The depth of the cutout always extends to completely cut the support wall.

Enter the diameter of the Circular Cutout in the *Diameter* field. A preview displays on the model, as shown in Figure 6–20.

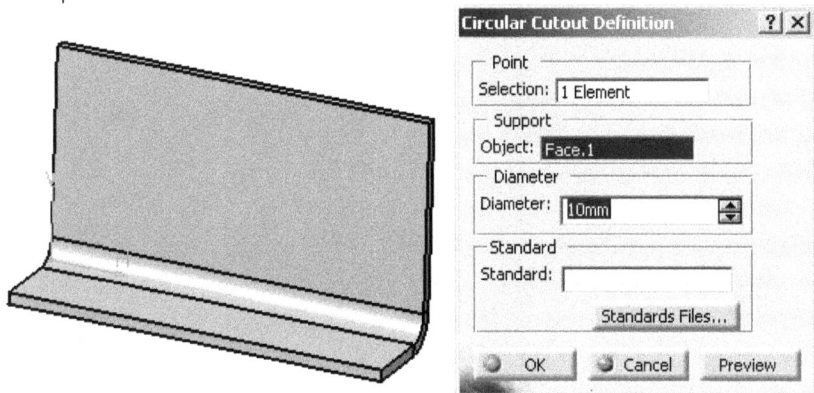

Figure 6–20

Step 4 - Complete the feature.

Once all elements in the circular cutout have been defined, click **OK** to complete the feature. The model updates as shown in Figure 6–21.

Locating point(s) for the circular cutout can be edited by double-clicking on the sketch.

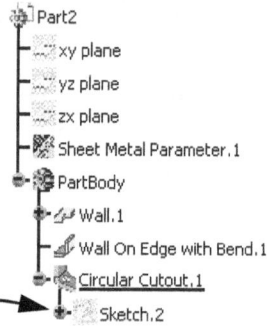

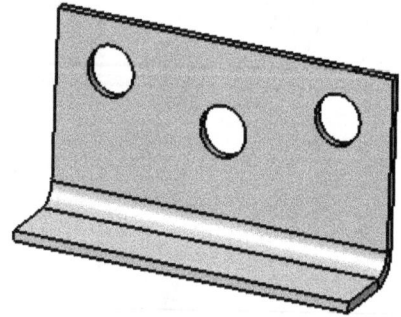

Part2
— xy plane
— yz plane
— zx plane
— Sheet Metal Parameter.1
— PartBody
— Wall.1
— Wall On Edge with Bend.1
— Circular Cutout.1
— Sketch.2

Figure 6–21

6.5 Holes

The **Hole** tool can also be used to create cutouts with a circular profile. The **Circular Cutout** tool is more limited than the **Hole** tool, because it can only create straight cutouts through the sheet without any geometry control except for the diameter. The **Hole** tool is the same as the one in the Part Design workbench and provides all **Hole** options.

Holes in Generative Sheetmetal Design have two limitations compared to Circular Cutouts, which are present in Part Design as well:

- Holes can only be placed on planar surfaces.

- Holes must be created one at a time: a single Hole feature cannot use multiple locating points. To create multiple holes in a single feature, consider using the **Circular Cutout** tool.

General Steps

Use the following general steps to create a hole:

1. Create a locating point, if required.
2. Activate the **Hole** tool.
3. Define the hole feature.
4. Complete the feature.

If no point is created, the hole is placed directly under the cursor when you select the surface.

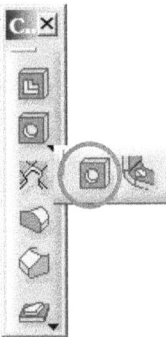

Step 1 - Create a locating point, if required.

If required, a locating point sketch can be created before the hole feature is created. This facilitates the creation of the hole feature.

Step 2 - Activate the Hole tool.

Holes can be placed on a planar or bend surface; however, holes cannot be placed at a transition location between a wall and a bend. Holes can be created in either the folded or unfolded view.

To activate the **Hole** tool, select the locating point and a face while pressing <Ctrl>. Then click (Hole).

Step 3 - Define the hole feature.

In the Hole Definition box you can change any of the following properties of the hole:

- Diameter

- Depth options

- Bottom properties

- Hole direction

- Hole type

- Thread/Tap definition

- Deformation

An example of a hole is shown in Figure 6–22. It uses the **Up to Last** depth option so that it extends from the placement surface through the part.

Click *(Sketch) to enter the Sketcher workbench.*

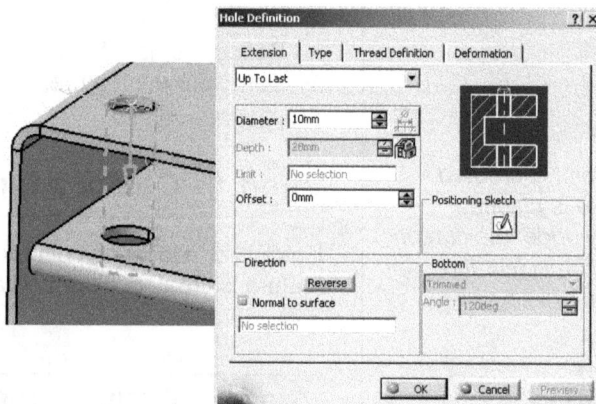

Figure 6–22

Step 4 - If no point is created, the hole is placed directly under the cursor when you select the surface.

Once all elements on the Hole are correct, complete the feature as shown in Figure 6–23.

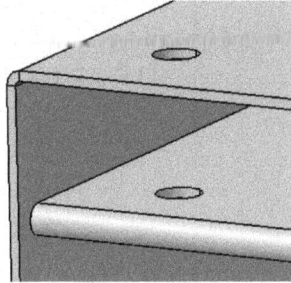

Figure 6–23

Practice 6a

Sheet Metal Features I

Practice Objectives

- Create a cut.
- Create a cut in the unfolded view.
- Create a cut using a mapped curve.
- Create a hole feature.
- Create chamfers and corners.

In this practice, you will add cuts, holes, chamfers, and corners to the mounting bracket. The final model displays as shown in Figure 6–24.

Figure 6–24

Task 1 - Open the part.

The model you will use in this practice is the same as the mounting bracket model used in previous practices. However, it includes some reference geometry required to complete the practices for this chapter and the next chapter.

1. Open **Mounting_Bracket_2.CATPart** file. The model displays as shown in Figure 6–25.

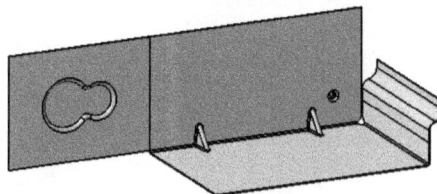

Figure 6–25

Task 2 - Create a cutout feature.

In this task, you will create a sheet metal cutout feature. To save time, the profile for the cutout has already been created for you.

1. Show the **CutOut_Profile** sketch from the specification tree (located in the **Reference_Geometry** Geometrical Set), as shown in Figure 6–26.

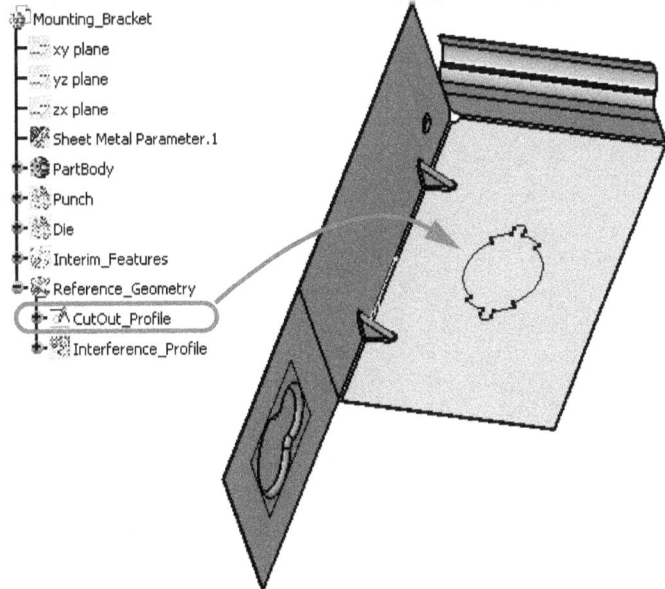

Figure 6–26

2. Highlight the sketch and click (Cutout).

3. Select **Up to next** in the *End Limit* Type drop-down list and create the cutout, as shown in Figure 6–27. Ensure that the cut is created inside the profile. If the arrow faces outward, click **Reverse Side**. Ensure that the cut is created downward through the material. Click **Reverse Direction** if the arrow is pointing in the other direction.

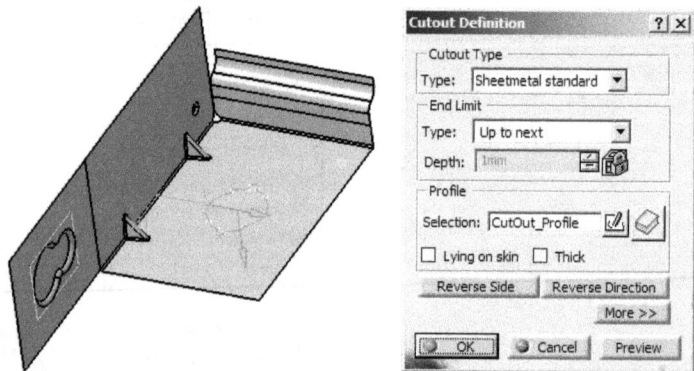

Figure 6–27

4. Click **OK** to generate the cut.

Task 3 - Create a cutout in the unfolded view.

The profile for the required cut must be created over two walls and a bend. Therefore, the profile must be created in the unfolded view.

1. Click ▨ (Fold/Unfold).

2. Select the surface shown in Figure 6–28 and enter the Sketcher workbench.

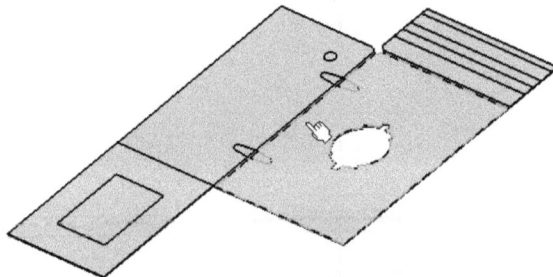

Figure 6–28

3. Create the rectangular sketch shown in Figure 6–29.

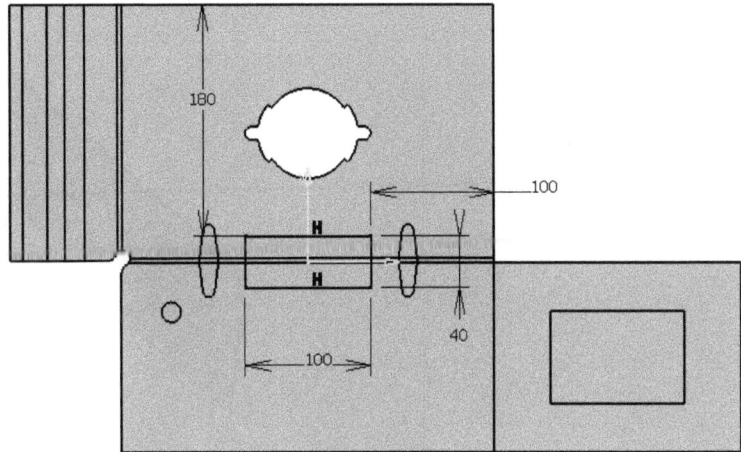

Figure 6–29

4. Exit the Sketcher workbench.

5. Highlight the sketch and click ⬜ (Cutout).

6. Create the cutout shown in Figure 6–30.

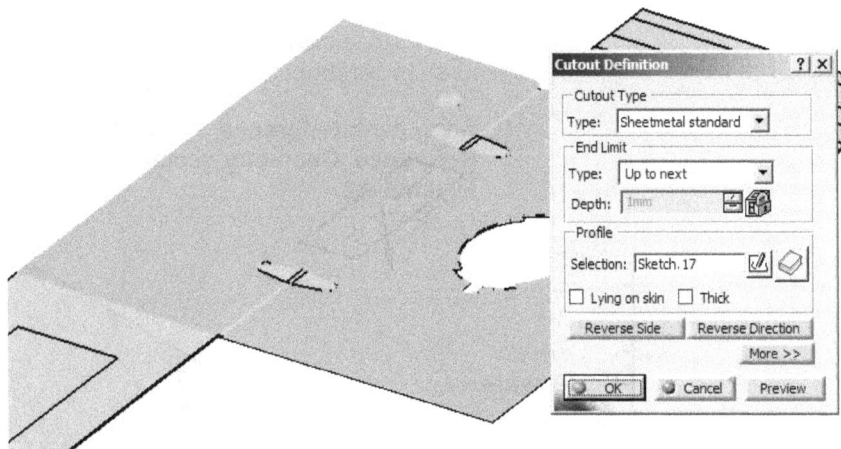

Figure 6–30

7. Click **OK** to complete the feature.

8. Return to the folded view. The model displays as shown in Figure 6–31.

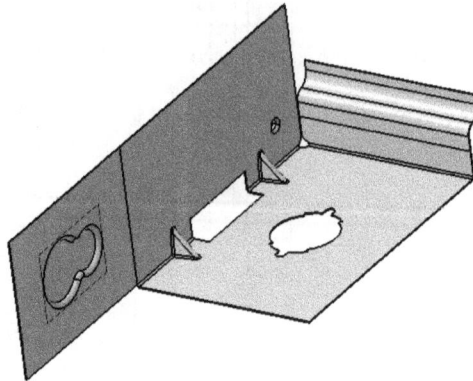

Figure 6–31

Task 4 - Create a cutout from a mapped profile.

Another component will intersect with this bracket when it is assembled into the final product. Using the Generative Shape Design workbench, another designer has projected the outline of the profile; this profile needs to be removed from the model to prevent interference. For the purposes of demonstration, you will map the profile onto the unfolded view to create a cutout feature. However, since the profile is not created over two walls, it is not required to perform the extra mapping step.

1. Show the **Interference_Profile** located in the **Reference_Geometry** geometrical set, as shown in Figure 6–32.

Figure 6–32

2. Highlight the **Interference_Profile** and click (Point or Curve Mapping).

3. Click **OK** to map the curves to the Unfolded view, as shown in Figure 6–33.

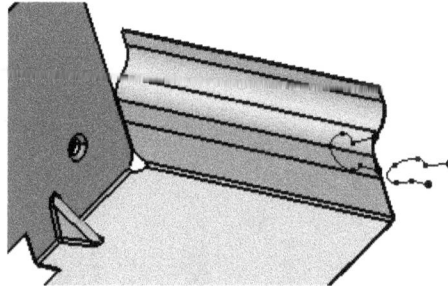

Figure 6–33

4. Click (Fold/Unfold).

5. Define PartBody to be the work object.

6. Highlight the Unfolded Curve and click (Cutout).

7. Ensure that the cutting area is inside the profile, as shown in Figure 6–34. Click **Reverse Side** to change the direction of the arrow.

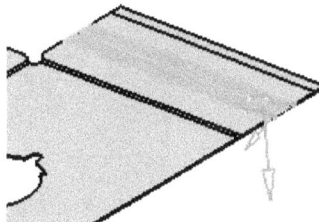

Figure 6–34

8. Select **Up to next** in the *End Limit* Type drop-down list.

9. Click **OK** to create the cut.

10. Return to the folded view.

Task 5 - Create a hole feature.

1. Select the support shown in Figure 6–35 and enter the Sketcher workbench.

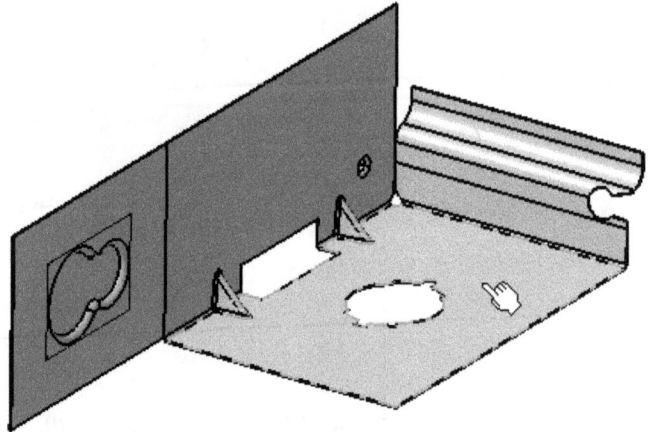

Figure 6–35

2. Create the point shown in Figure 6–36.

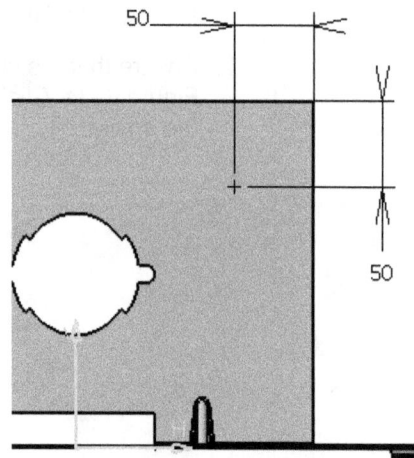

Figure 6–36

3. Exit the Sketcher workbench.

4. Select the point and support as shown in Figure 6–37.

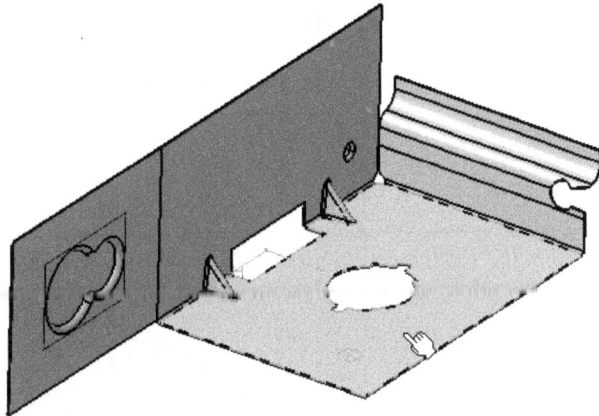

Figure 6–37

5. Click ▣ (Hole) to create a Hole feature. The hole is centered on the sketched point.

6. Select **Up to Next** from the menu and enter a diameter of **10 mm**.

7. Click **OK** to generate the hole. If required, hide the sketch of the point. The model displays as shown in Figure 6–38.

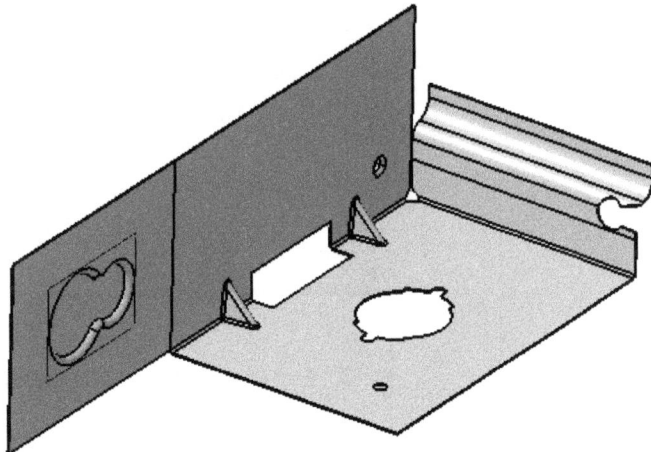

Figure 6–38

Task 6 - Create multiple holes in one operation.

1. Select the support shown in Figure 6–39 and enter the Sketcher workbench.

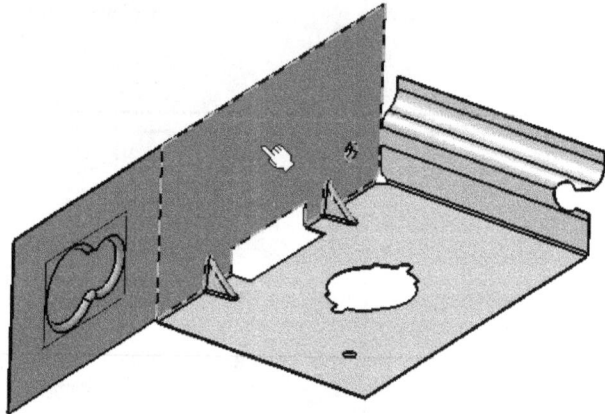

Figure 6–39

2. Create the points shown in Figure 6–40.

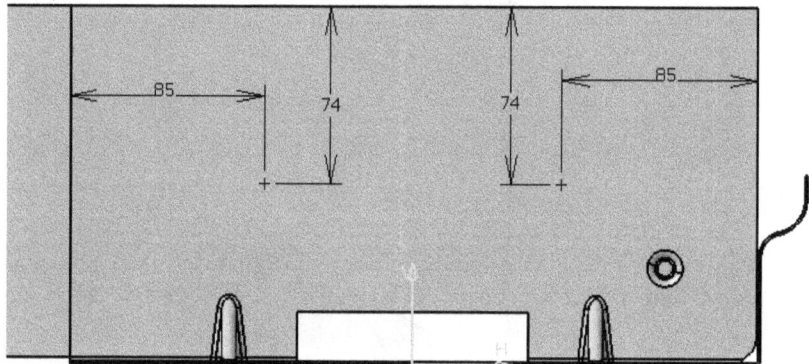

Figure 6–40

3. Exit the Sketcher workbench.

4. Click [icon] (Circular Cutout). Select the points and the back surface, as shown in Figure 6–41.

5. Create the holes with a **50mm** diameter.

6. Click **OK** to generate the holes. The model displays as shown in Figure 6–41.

Select the points created in Step 2 and the back surface

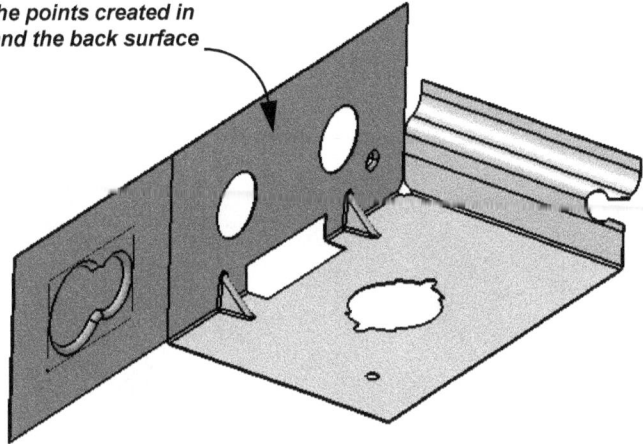

Figure 6–41

Task 7 - Create a chamfer feature.

1. Click (Chamfer).

2. Select the short, vertical edge shown in Figure 6–42.

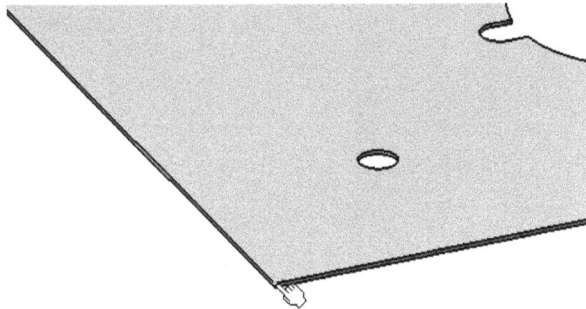

Figure 6–42

3. Enter the following values:

   • *Type:* **Length1/Length2**
   • *Length 1:* **50mm**
   • *Length 2:* **50mm**

4. Click **OK** to create the chamfer. The model displays as shown in Figure 6–43.

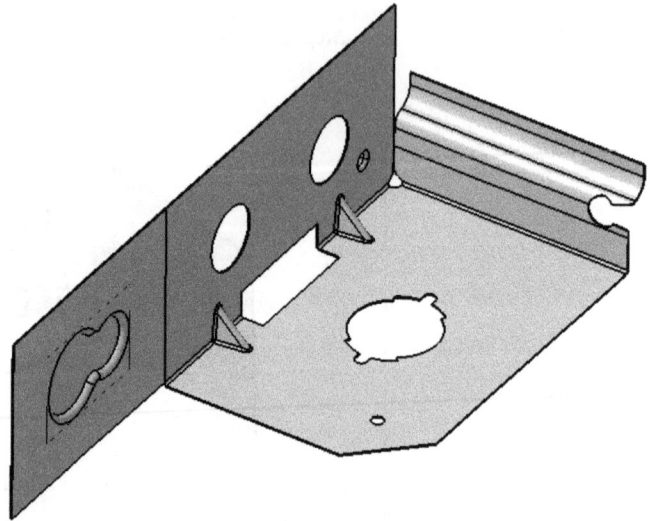

Figure 6–43

Task 8 - Create corners on the model.

1. Click (Corner).

2. Select the two edges shown in Figure 6–44.

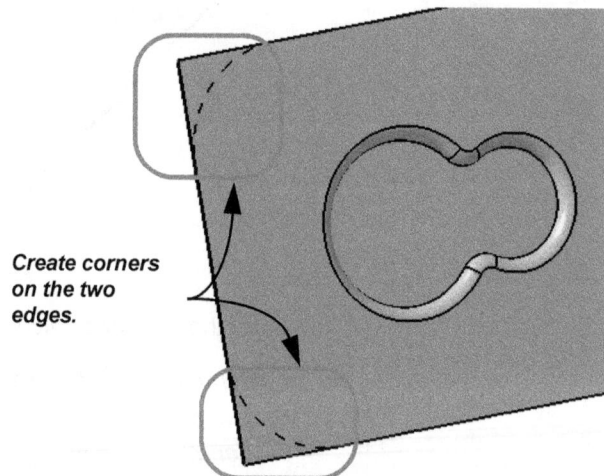

Create corners on the two edges.

Figure 6–44

3. Enter a *Radius* of **40mm**.

4. Click **OK** to create the corners.

5. Create another corner using a **100mm** *Radius*, as shown in Figure 6–45.

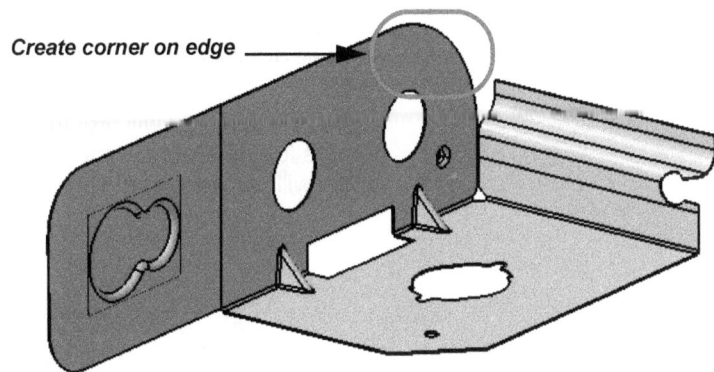

Figure 6–45

6. Save and close the file.

Practice 6b | Sheet Metal Features II

Practice Objectives

- Create a cut.
- Create a circular cutout.
- Create corners.
- Create chamfers.

In this practice, you will create cuts, holes, chamfers, and corners for the Mount model. At the end of this practice, the model will display as shown in Figure 6–46.

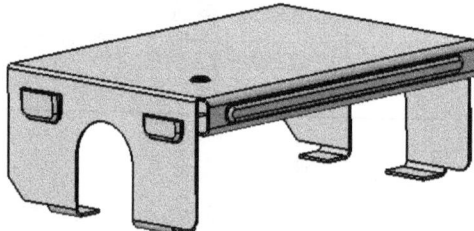

Figure 6–46

Task 1 - Open the part.

1. Open **Ex6B_Mount.CATPart**.

   If you completed **Practice 5a**, open **Mount.CATPart** instead. The model displays as shown in Figure 6–47.

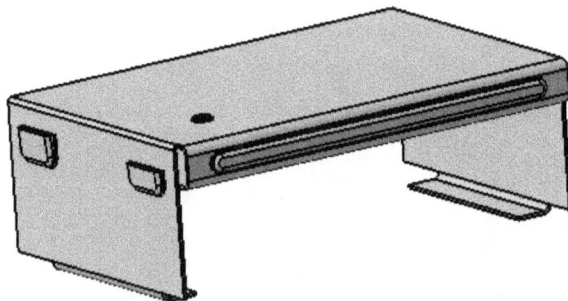

Figure 6–47

Task 2 - Create a cut.

This model requires a cut that runs through the entire length of the model. To create the cut using one feature, it can be created in folded view using the **Up to Last** option.

1. Select the surface shown in Figure 6–48 and enter the Sketcher workbench.

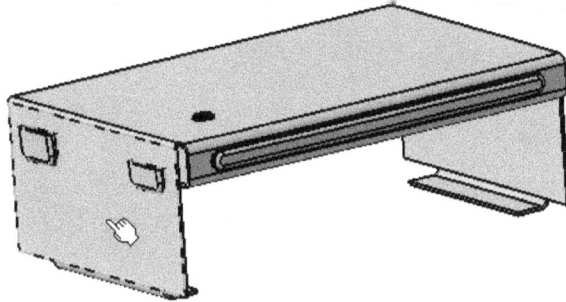

Figure 6–48

2. Create the sketch as shown in Figure 6–49. Make the profile symmetric about the YZ plane. The length of the profile is not important as long as it extends completely past the model.

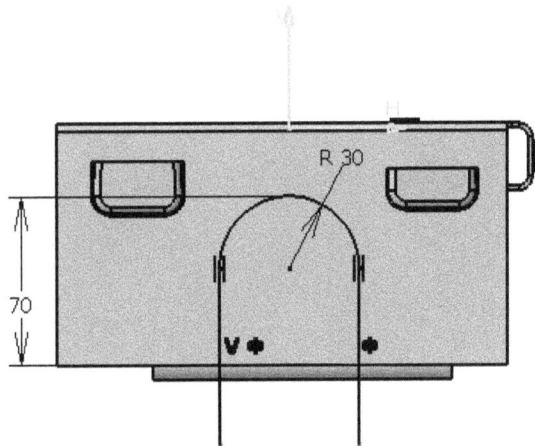

Ensure that the profile extends past the end of the model.

Figure 6–49

3. Exit the Sketcher workbench.

4. Highlight the sketch and click ⬚ (Cutout).

5. Select **Up to last** in the Type drop-down list.

6. Create the cutout as shown in Figure 6–50. Ensure that the cut is created inside the profile. If the arrow faces outward, click **Reverse Side**. Ensure that the cut is created toward the other side wall; click **Reverse Direction** if the arrow is pointing in the other direction.

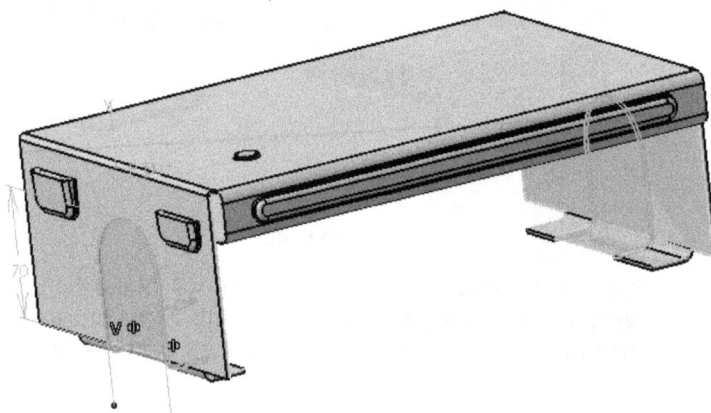

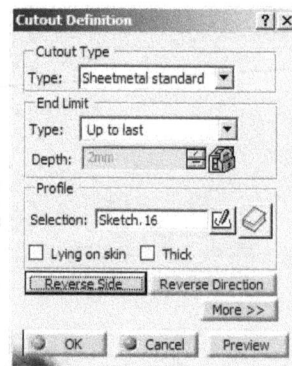

Figure 6–50

7. Click **OK** to complete the feature. The model displays as shown in Figure 6–51.

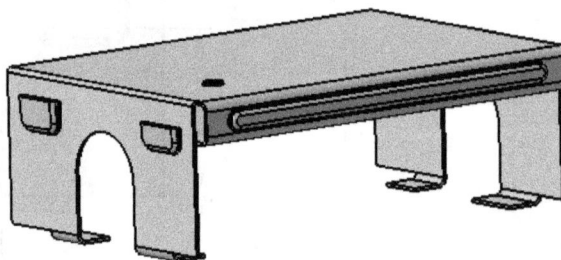

Figure 6–51

Task 3 - Create a circular cutout.

A circular cutout will be created on the bottom support directly in line with the flanged hole. Instead of creating another locating point, the locating point for the Flanged hole can be reused.

1. Show and select the **Locate_Hole** sketch and click

   (Circular Cutout).

2. Select in the *Support object* field and select the surface shown in Figure 6–52.

3. Enter **10** in the *Diameter* field.

4. Click **OK** to create the circular cutout. The model displays as shown in Figure 6–52.

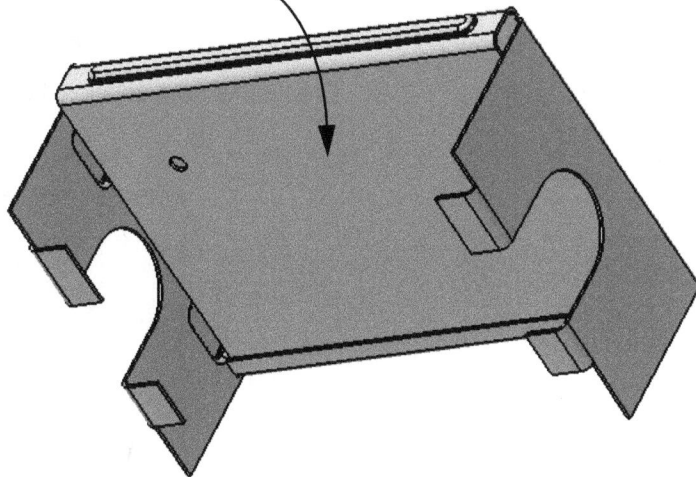

Select this surface

Figure 6–52

Task 4 - Redefine the hole.

In this task, you will redefine the hole sketch to add three additional locating points. CATIA will automatically add additional holes at these new points.

1. Double-click on the **Locate_Hole** sketch in the specification tree, as shown in Figure 6–53.

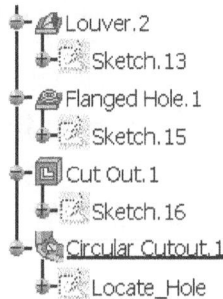

Figure 6–53

2. Create the three additional points, as shown in Figure 6–54.

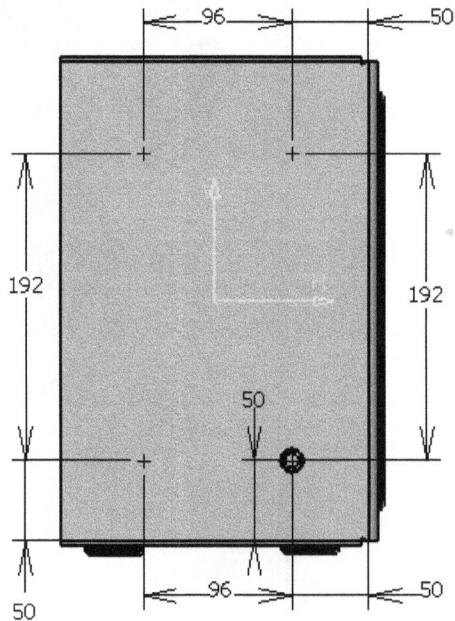

Figure 6–54

3. Exit the Sketcher workbench. Holes are automatically generated at the new points, as shown in Figure 6–55.

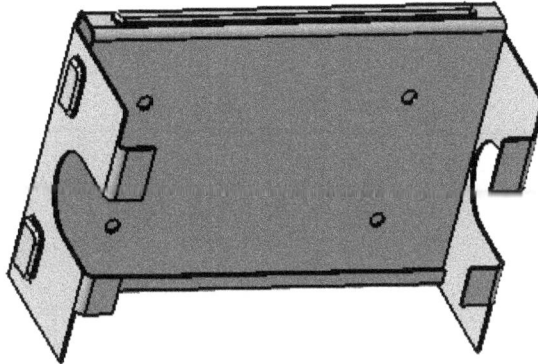

Figure 6–55

Task 5 - Create chamfers.

1. Click (Chamfer) and create two chamfers using the **Length1/Angle** option, as shown in Figure 6–56.

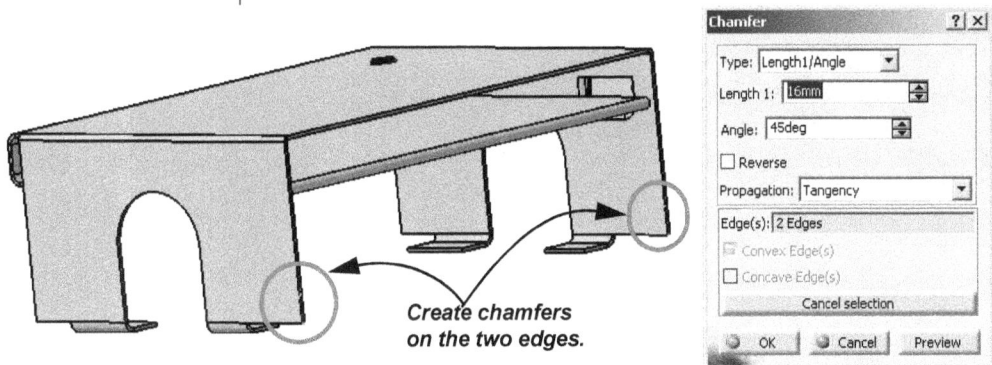

Create chamfers
on the two edges.

Figure 6–56

Task 6 - Create corners.

1. Click (Corner).

2. Create the corners using a **10mm** radius, as shown in Figure 6–57.

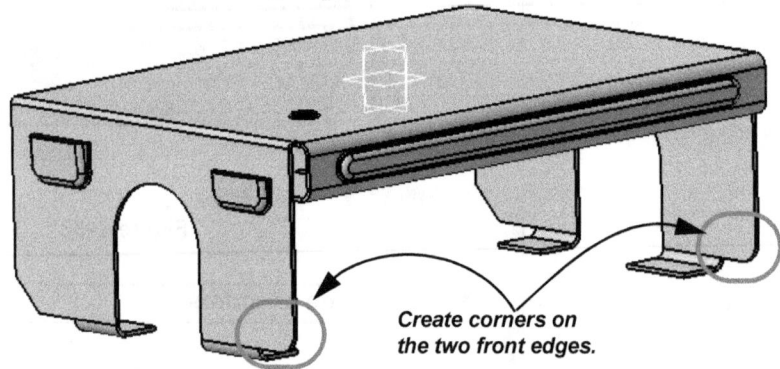

Create corners on the two front edges.

Figure 6–57

3. Hide the XY, YZ, and ZX planes.

4. Save and close the file.

Feature Duplication

Patterns are quick way of duplicating geometry to be used in several models. With patterned features, the patterned instances update to the new dimensions when any dimensional change occurs to the original feature. You can also create user-defined patterns when a less uniform pattern is required.

Learning Objectives in this Chapter

- Learn how to Mirror geometry.
- Learn how to use Isometries.
- Understand Patterning, including User Patterns.
- Learn how to Create a PowerCopy.
- Learn to Instantiate a PowerCopy.

7.1 Mirroring

The **Mirror** tool is used to duplicate an existing part or feature with respect to a mirroring plane. By default, the Mirror function duplicates the entire sheet metal part, although individual features can be selected. The resulting mirrored geometry is added to the specification tree in the form of a Mirror feature.

Hole, wall, wall on edge, cutout, flange, stamp and existing mirror features can be duplicated using the **Mirror** tool. When mirroring individual elements, the resulting element must lie on an existing solid part of the model; for instance, a mirrored hole that lies in empty space produces an error.

General Steps

Use the following general steps to mirror a sheet metal feature:

1. Activate the **Mirror** tool.
2. Select the Mirroring plane.
3. Select optional elements.
4. Complete the feature.

Step 1 - Activate the Mirror tool.

Click ▯▯ (Mirror) in the Transformations toolbar. The Mirror Definition dialog box opens as shown in Figure 7–1.

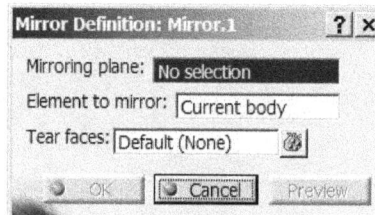

Figure 7–1

Step 2 - Select the Mirroring plane.

Select a planar reference to define the mirroring plane. This reference can be a face of the model or reference plane. Remember to consider parent/child relationships and downstream compatibility when selecting a mirroring plane.

By default, the mirror function mirrors the entire sheet metal part, as shown in Figure 7–2.

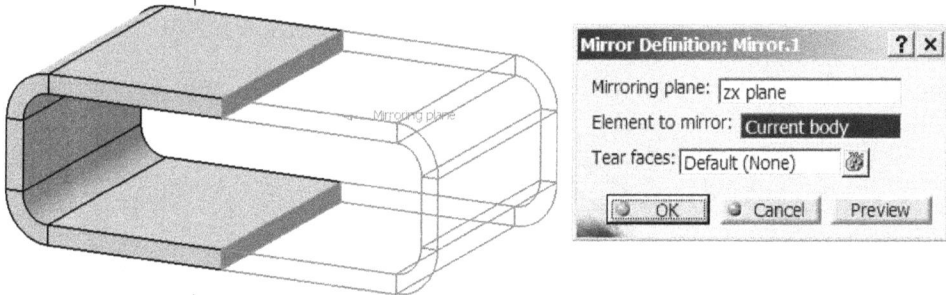

Figure 7–2

Step 3 - Select optional elements.

Element to Mirror

To specify an individual element to mirror, select the *Element to mirror* field and select it in the specification tree or model display as shown in Figure 7–3. Right-click on the *Element to mirror* field and select **Clear Selection** to reset the selection and mirror the entire model.

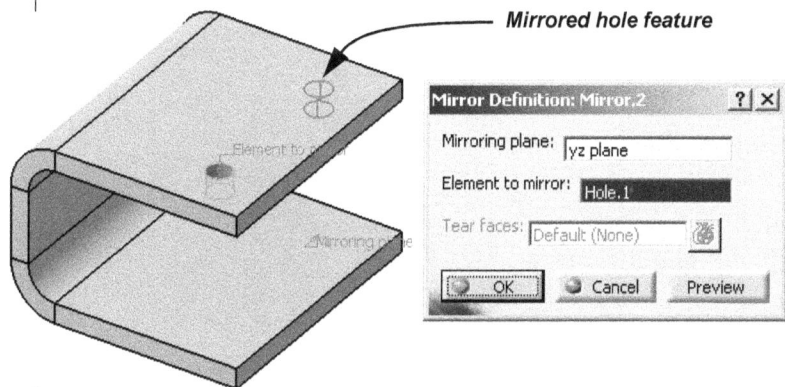

Figure 7–3

Tear Faces

If the **Mirror** tool produces closed geometry, as shown in Figure 7–4, a Tear face must be selected. Similar to a tear wire, the Tear face defines where the model separates when unfolded.

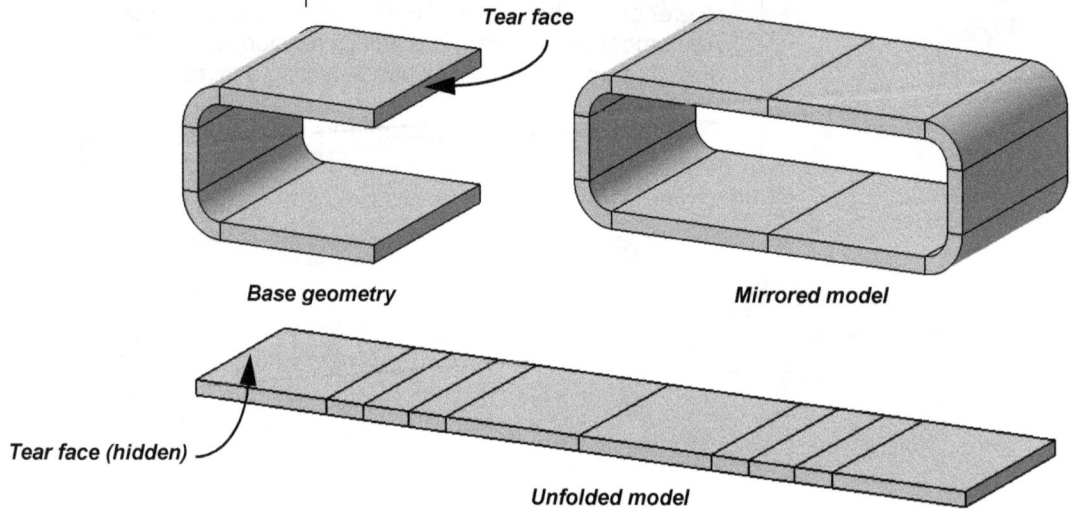

Base geometry   Mirrored model

Unfolded model

Figure 7–4

Step 4 - Complete the feature.

Click **OK** to complete the feature. The duplicate geometry is placed in the specification tree as a Mirror feature.

7.2 Isometries

Isometries change the orientation and position of the part bodies. The isometries toolbar is shown in Figure 7–5.

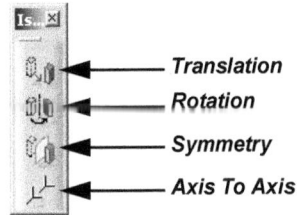

Figure 7–5

Translate, Rotate, Symmetry and Axis to Axis operations are identical to those in the Part Design workbench. This section reviews these operations.

Translate

A Translate operation moves or translates a part body. To perform a Translate operation, click ![icon] (Translation). The Translate Definition dialog box opens as shown in Figure 7–6.

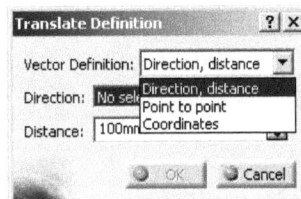

Figure 7–6

In the *Direction* field, you can right-click to access the X, Y, Z options.

Rotate

The Rotate operation enables you to rotate a part body around an axis. To perform a Rotate operation, click (Rotatation). The Rotate Definition dialog box opens, as shown in Figure 7–7, enabling you to define a rotational axis or line and enter an angular value.

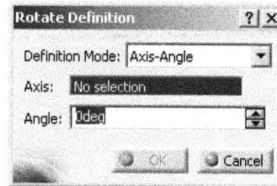

Figure 7–7

Symmetry

The Symmetry operation creates a mirrored copy of a part body about a point, line, or plane. To perform a Symmetry operation, click (Symmetry). The Symmetry Definition dialog box opens, as shown in Figure 7–8.

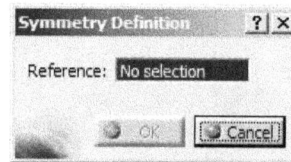

Figure 7–8

Axis to Axis

The Axis To Axis operation moves a part body using two axis systems. Click (Axis to Axis) to open the Axis To Axis Definition dialog box, as shown in Figure 7–9. The body shown in Figure 7–9 is moved to the target axis system.

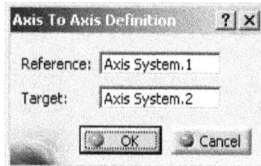

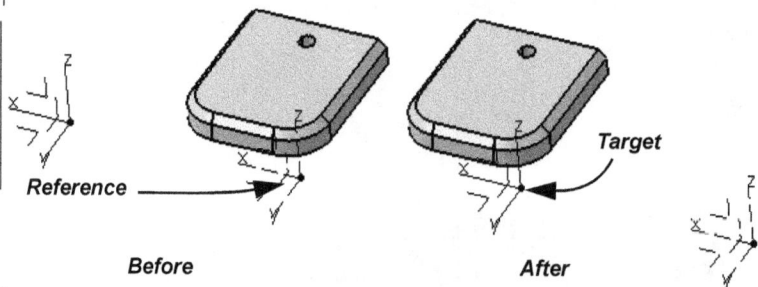

Figure 7–9

7.3 Patterning

Rectangular and circular patterns were discussed in the Introduction to Modeling course.

Patterns are used to quickly duplicate geometry. Once the initial feature(s) is created, several instances of the same geometry can be patterned by a specified dimensional increment. The pattern can be created as a rectangular or a circular pattern. If any dimension change occurs to the original feature, the instances update to the new dimensions. In the Generative Sheetmetal design workbench, cutouts, holes, and stamps (excluding stiffening ribs) can be patterned.

Patterns can be created in the folded or the unfolded view. To pattern across more then one wall, you must pattern in the unfolded view. Once created, the model can return to the folded view and the pattern remains in the correct position. Figure 7-10 shows a pattern created in the unfolded view so that it can be created on more than one wall. The same pattern would fail if attempted in the folded view.

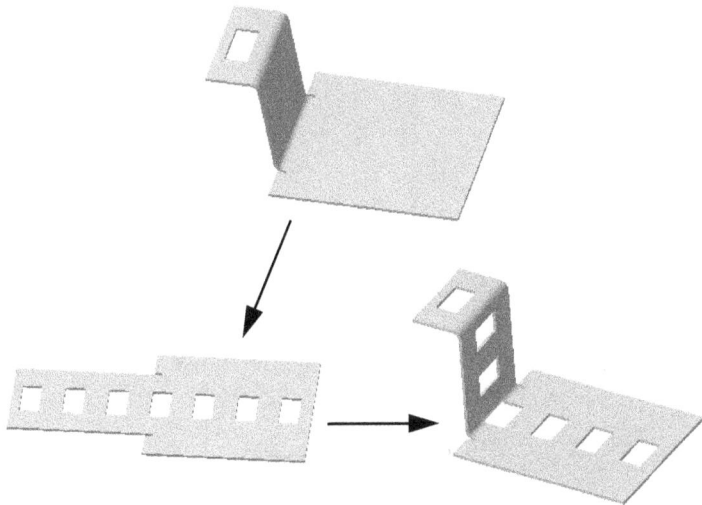

Figure 7–10

Rectangular Patterns

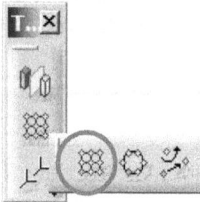

Rectangular patterns duplicate sheet metal features in one or two linear directions.

How To: Create a Rectangular Pattern

1. Select the feature to be patterned and click [icon] (Rectangular Pattern). The Rectangular Pattern Definition dialog box opens as shown in Figure 7–11.

Figure 7–11

2. Select the first reference direction by selecting an element, typically an edge, that is in the correct direction.
3. Define parameters for the first direction. Rectangular patterns can be defined by selecting one of the following combinations.

Combination	Description
Instance(s) & Spacing	Define the pattern by the number of instances and the spacing between them.
Instance(s) & Length	The spacing between the instances is calculated by dividing the total length by the number of instances.
Spacing & Length	The number of instances is calculated by dividing the total length by the spacing between the instances. The calculated value for the number of instances is always rounded up.
Instance(s) & Unequal spacing	Different distance values can be defined between different instances enabling an irregular placement of features.

After selecting the parameter type, the dialog box updates accordingly. Figure 7–12 shows a pattern and the corresponding dialog box.

Select to reverse the direction of the pattern.

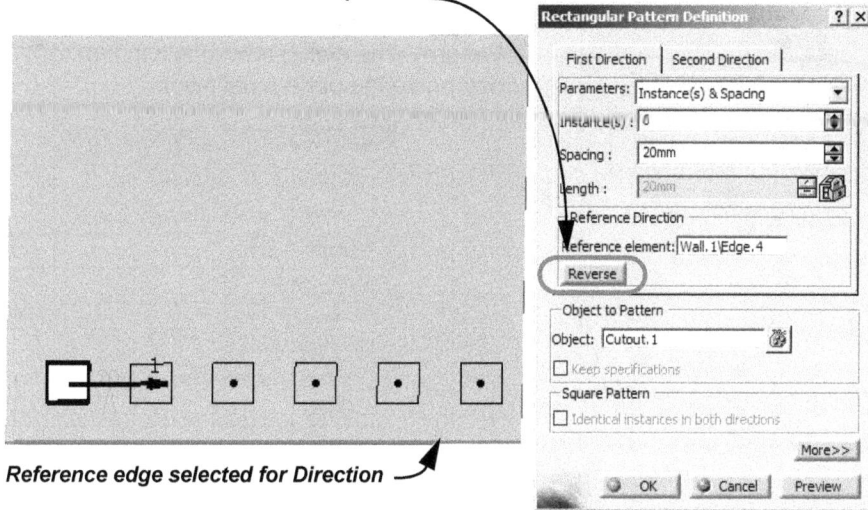

Reference edge selected for Direction

Figure 7–12

4. Define a second direction, if required, in the *Second Direction* tab. Select in the *Reference Element* field and select a reference on the model in the correct direction.
5. Define parameters for the second direction. Parameters used to define the second direction do not need to be the same as those used to define the first direction.

To re-display the instance, select the position marker again.

6. Remove any unwanted instances in the pattern by clicking the red dot in the center of the instance (position marker). The instance is toggled off, as shown in Figure 7–13.

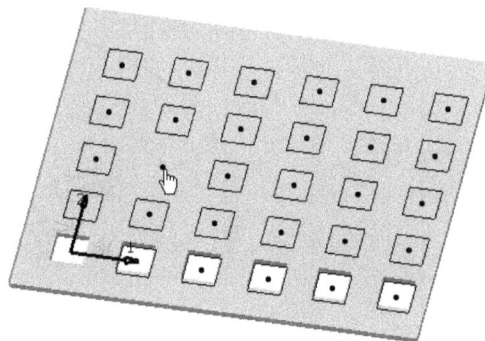

Figure 7–13

7. Click **OK** to complete the feature.

Circular Patterns

Circular patterns duplicate sheet metal features axially and radially.

How To: Create a Circular Pattern

1. Select the feature to be patterned and click 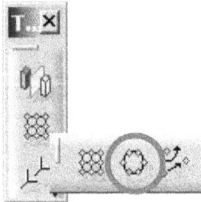 (Circular Pattern). The dialog box shown in Figure 7–14 is used to determine the pattern definition.

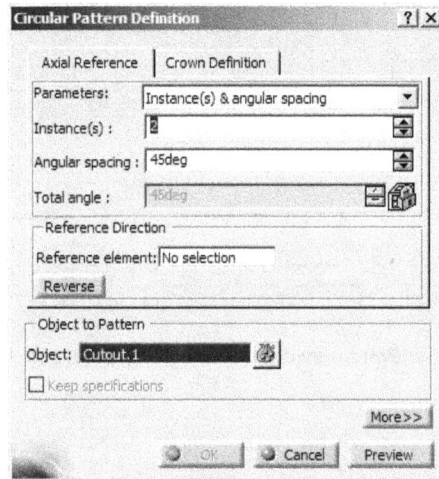

Figure 7–14

2. Select a reference about which to rotate. The reference can be any planar face or edge. If a planar face is selected, the rotation axis would be normal to the selected face. For example, the cutout shown in Figure 7–15 needs to be patterned. The surface is selected as the reference; therefore, the axis of revolution for the pattern is normal to the selected surface.

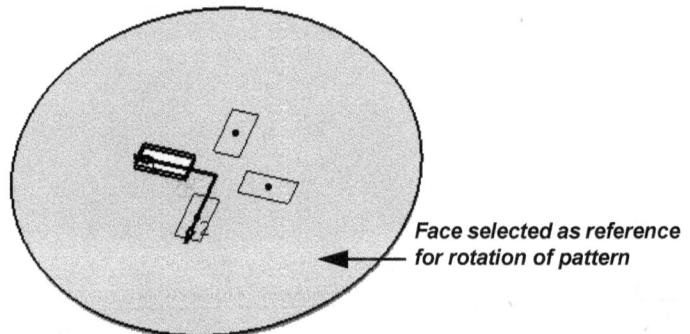

Face selected as reference for rotation of pattern

Figure 7–15

3. Define parameters for axial direction. The axial direction can be defined by selecting one of the following combinations.

Combination	Description
Instance(s) & Angular Spacing	Define the pattern by the number of instances and the spacing between them.
Instance(s) & Total Angle	The spacing between the instances is calculated by dividing the total angle by the number of instances.
Angular Spacing & Total Angle	The number of instances is calculated by dividing the total angle by the angular spacing between instances. The calculated value for the number of instances is always rounded up.
Complete Crown	The angular spacing between instances is calculated by dividing the complete crown (360°) by the number of instances.
Instance(s) & Unequal Angular Spacing	Different angular values can be defined between different instances enabling an irregular placement of features.

4. If required, define a radial direction of the pattern in the *Crown Definition* tab. The following gives a description of the possible combinations when defining the pattern radially.

Combination	Description
Circle(s) & Circle Spacing	The additional pattern rows are defined by entering the number of circles (including the original) and spacing between rows.
Circle(s) & Crown Thickness	The additional pattern rows are defined by entering the number of circles (including the original) and the distance to the last row.
Circle Spacing & Crown Thickness	The number of additional pattern rows is calculated by dividing the distance to the last row by the spacing between the rows. The calculated value is rounded up.

5. Remove any unwanted instances in the pattern by clicking the position marker in the center of the instance. To re-display the instance, click the position marker again.

6. Click **OK** to complete the feature. Figure 7–16 shows a feature that was patterned both axially and radially.

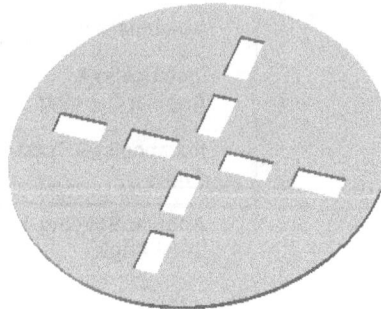

Figure 7–16

While creating patterns, the patterns should located in the model.

You can pattern the following features:

- cutouts

- flanges

- holes

- walls

- mirrors

- walls on edges

- stamps (except stiffening ribs)

- stamps without fillet (radius=0)

7.4 User Patterns

User patterns are often required when the pattern is not uniform. Although you can toggle off instances in a circular or rectangular pattern, it is often simpler to create a user pattern that only includes the required instances. As with the other pattern types, user patterns can pattern cutouts, holes and stamps (excluding stiffening ribs). User patterns can be created in the folded or unfolded view.

General Steps

Use the following general steps to create a user pattern:

1. Create location points.
2. Start the creation of the user pattern.
3. Change the position of the anchor, if required.
4. Remove instances and validate the pattern.

Step 1 - Create location points.

Start the creation of the pattern by specifying positions to place the instances. These positions are marked by points. The points must be in the same body as the feature you are patterning. Since you cannot pattern features outside of the current body, you must create points inside the Sketcher workbench.

Step 2 - Start the creation of the user pattern.

Select features for a user pattern, as you would for the other types of patterns. Click ![icon](User Pattern) to open the User Pattern Definition dialog box, as shown in Figure 7–17.

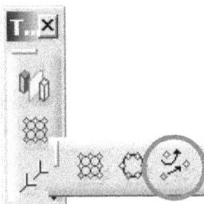

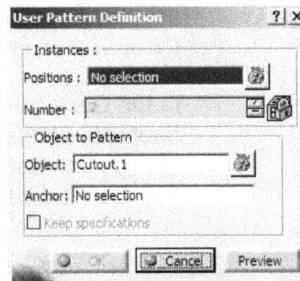

Figure 7–17

Step 3 - Change the position of the anchor, if required.

The anchor is the point on each instance where the position marker is located. By default, CATIA uses the center of gravity (center of the feature) of each instance. If this position is not correct, you can change it by changing the anchor location. To change the anchor location, click in the *Anchor* field and select a point on an instance to act as the new anchor. The anchor in the left graphic of Figure 7–18 is kept as the center of gravity, while the anchor in the right graphic of Figure 7–18 is set to the top of the feature.

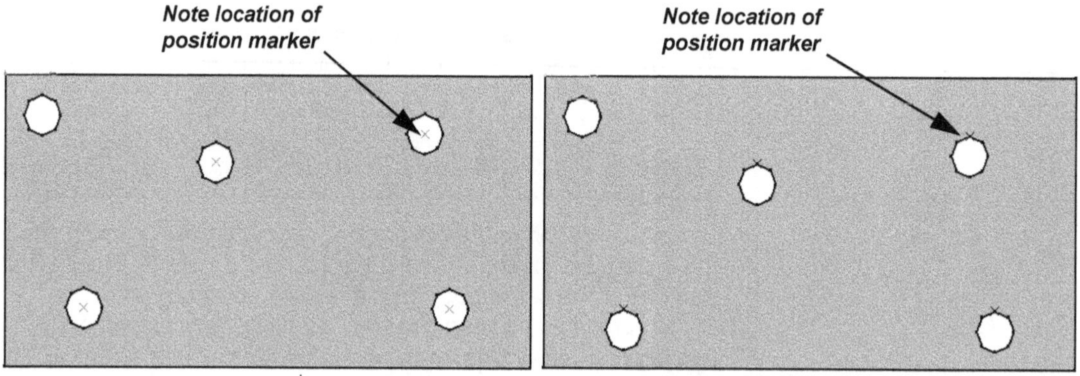

Note location of position marker

Note location of position marker

Figure 7–18

Step 4 - Remove instances and validate the pattern.

As with other types of patterns, you can remove instances from the pattern by selecting the position marker (anchor) of the instance while in the User Pattern Definition dialog box. Select the position marker again to return the instance to the display. Once you complete the pattern, click **OK**.

In the Generative Sheetmetal Design workbench, you can only duplicate flanges, cutouts, holes, walls, walls on edges, mirrors, stamps (except stiffening ribs), stamps without fillet (radius=0), and Generative Sheetmetal Design patterns.

7.5 Create a PowerCopy

PowerCopies are useful when a feature, or group of features, are required in several models. Rather than recreate the features in each model, you create them once and use PowerCopy to copy the original feature(s) into another model. Unlike the **Paste** option, you can also control the referencing features and dimensions while placing the feature.

Carefully consider which references to select when you create features for a PowerCopy. Consider the following tips:

- When creating sketches, try to constrain the sketch to edges and faces and not to reference planes. This technique makes placing the PowerCopy easier since the reference planes might not exist.

- Avoid constraining features that you plan to use in a PowerCopy with respect to the horizontal-vertical (HV) absolute axis. This is because the origin and orientation of the absolute axis cannot be controlled; therefore, the results of placing the PowerCopy are unreliable.

- Avoid using projections and intersections in a sketch that you plan to use in a PowerCopy.

- Ensure that your sketch is ISO-constrained, (i.e., the sketched entities are green) so that the results of the PowerCopy are as expected.

General Steps

Use the following general steps to create a PowerCopy:

1. Start the creation of the PowerCopy.
2. Add features to the PowerCopy.
3. Rename the features.
4. Set variable parameters, if required.
5. Set an icon or preview for the PowerCopy.
6. Complete the PowerCopy.

Step 1 - Start the creation of the PowerCopy.

Once all of the features for the PowerCopy have been created, save the model.

Select **Insert>Knowledge Templates>PowerCopy**, to open the Powercopy Definition dialog box, as shown in Figure 7–19.

You cannot create a PowerCopy in a model with unsaved changes.

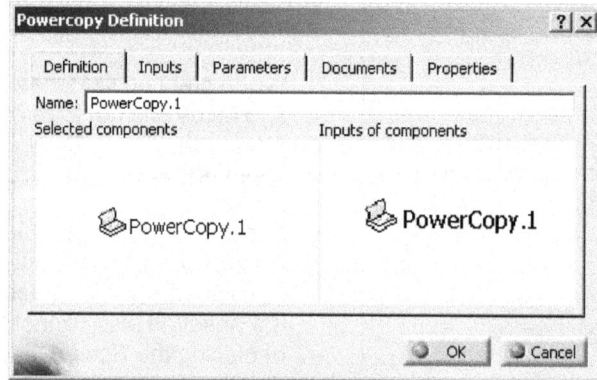

Figure 7–19

Enter a descriptive name (so you can easily identify it later) for the PowerCopy and press <Enter>.

Step 2 - Add features to the PowerCopy.

Select the *Definition* tab to begin adding features to the PowerCopy.

If you accidentally select a feature you do not want in the PowerCopy, select the feature again in the specification tree to remove it.

A PowerCopy can contain a variety of features, such as geometric features, formulas, and constraints. To add a feature to a PowerCopy, select it in the specification tree. Once selected, the feature displays in the *Components* area of the Powercopy Definition dialog box. Any references used when the features were created are listed in the *Inputs of components* area, as shown in Figure 7–20.

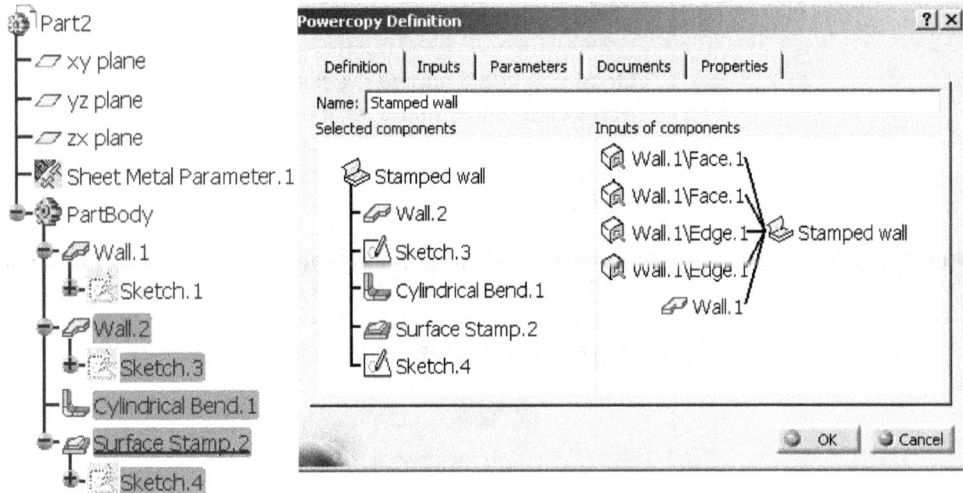

Figure 7–20

These references are used as inputs when the PowerCopy is placed in another model.

Avoid adding a large number of features to the PowerCopy when possible. Keeping the number of features to a minimum avoids making the PowerCopy complicated and avoids problems that could occur when placing the PowerCopy later.

Step 3 - Rename the features.

Once you finish adding the features to the PowerCopy, enter a more descriptive name for the features. This makes placing the PowerCopy easier. It is a good idea to leave the parameter inputs with their default names. This saves time when placing the PowerCopy.

To rename an input, select the *Inputs* tab. Select the feature in the Input window and enter a new name in the *Name* field at the bottom of the dialog box. The original name of the feature remains in brackets, as shown in Figure 7–21.

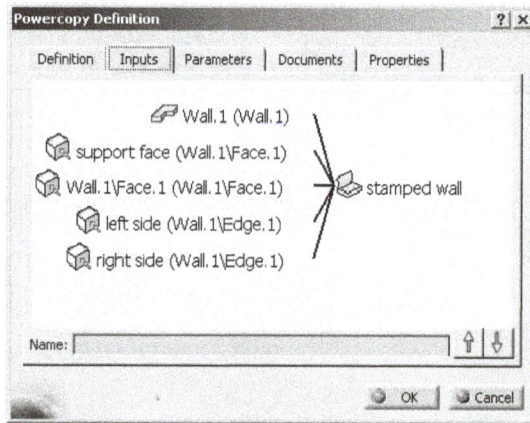

Figure 7–21

Step 4 - Set variable parameters, if required.

Select the *Parameters* tab to define which parameter values you want to be variable when placing the PowerCopy feature. A variable parameter enables you to change its value to suit the model in which it is placed.

To create a modifiable parameter, select the parameter and select the **Published** option. When the *Name* field displays, enter a more descriptive name for the feature. This new name is now used when the PowerCopy is placed in the new model.

For example, the parameter selected in Figure 7–22 is published. Therefore, this parameter is now variable.

The rest of the values associated with the PowerCopy are not published; therefore, their values are not modifiable during placement.

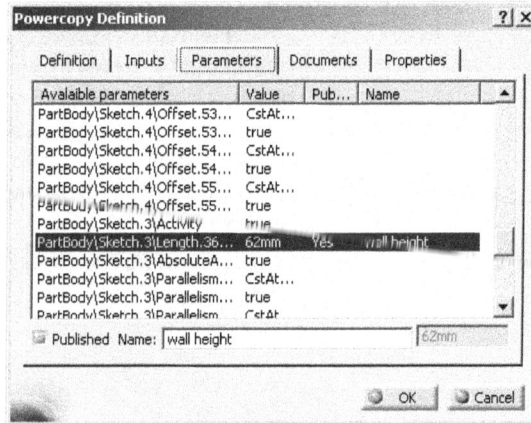

Figure 7–22

Step 5 - Set an icon or preview for the PowerCopy.

Select the *Properties* tab to select an icon to identify the

PowerCopy in the specification tree. Click ⌐ to expand a list of commonly selected icons, as shown in Figure 7–23.

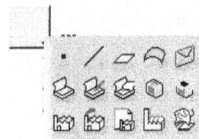

Figure 7–23

The *Properties* tab with an icon selected is shown in Figure 7–24.

You can also browse through all of the icons loaded in your CATIA session by clicking ....

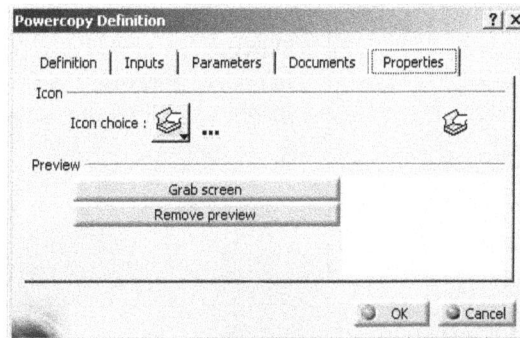

Figure 7–24

Preview

The *Properties* tab also enables you to create a preview that is stored with the PowerCopy Definition. To create a preview, set up the model display the way you want it to appear in the preview. Select **View>Specifications** or **View>Compass** to clear the display of the specification tree and compass if required. Then click **Grab screen** to take a screen shot to use as the preview, as shown in Figure 7–25.

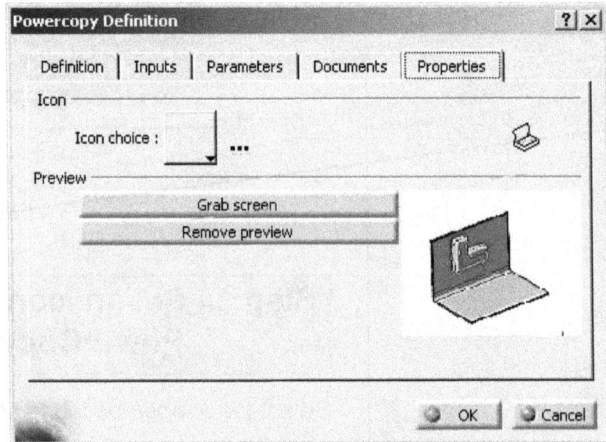

Figure 7–25

To remove the preview click **Remove preview**.

Step 6 - Complete the PowerCopy.

Once you have completed the PowerCopy Definition, click **OK** to exit the dialog box.

Modifying the PowerCopy

To make modifications to the PowerCopy, modify the features that have been added to the PowerCopy. The next time the PowerCopy is instantiated, the modified features are used. Previous instantiations of the PowerCopy do not update. There is no link between the PowerCopy source model and the model in which the PowerCopy was instantiated.

7.6 Instantiate a PowerCopy

Once a PowerCopy has been created it is ready to use in other models. Any variable parameters that were created can be modified to suit the new model.

General Steps

Use the following steps to instantiate the PowerCopy.

1. Select the PowerCopy to be instantiated.
2. Place the PowerCopy.
3. Change parameters and complete instantiation.

Step 1 - Select the PowerCopy to be instantiated.

The document containing the PowerCopy must be closed (i.e., not in session) when it is being inserted into another document.

Select **Insert>Instantiate From Document** in the target model (where you are placing the PowerCopy).

Navigate to the document containing the PowerCopy in the File Selection dialog box and click **Open** to begin inserting the object.

PowerCopies can also be inserted into the document in which they were created by selecting the PowerCopy in the specification tree, right-clicking and selecting **PowerCopy.x Object>Instantiate...**, as shown in Figure 7–26.

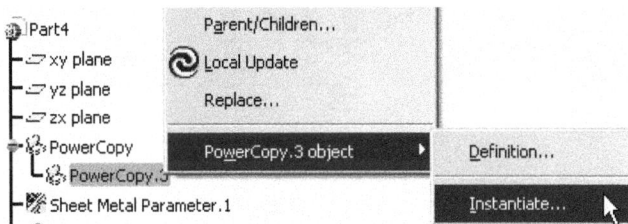

Figure 7–26

Step 2 - Place the PowerCopy.

Once you select a document to open, the Insert Object dialog box opens. Select the correct PowerCopy in the Reference drop-down list if more then one exists in the source document.

If the name of the reference in the target model is the same as in the source model, you can place references by clicking **Use identical name**. CATIA automatically places the reference by matching the reference name in the PowerCopy to the reference name in the new model. For example, if the parameters were left at the default names, click **Use identical name** to populate the parameters with the values in the current model.

Once all parameters with names matching those in the new model are entered, the Insert Object dialog box opens as shown in Figure 7–27. Because **Wall.1** was an input in the PowerCopy and the first feature in the model is **Wall.1**, the input is identified on the model.

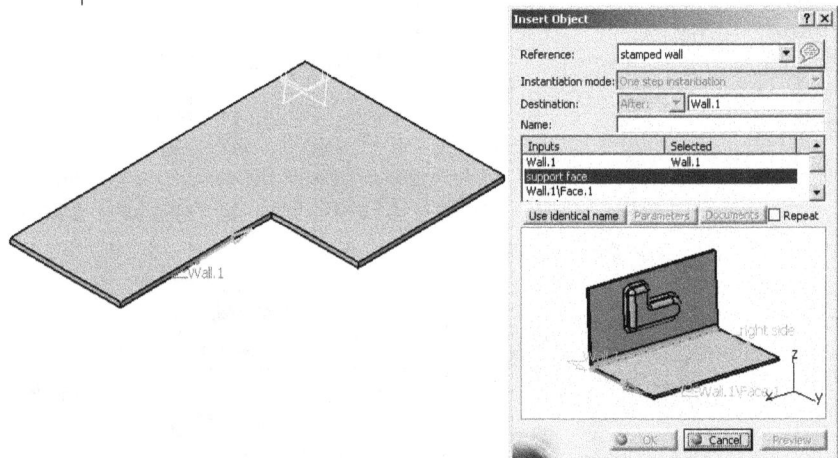

Figure 7–27

Inputs not found in the new model still need to be referenced. When CATIA highlights a reference in the Inputs column of the dialog box, you must select the corresponding feature in the new model. Each time a new reference is selected, CATIA highlights the next input reference and waits for you to select a new reference in the active model. While selecting the references, ensure that the arrow in the main window matches the direction of the arrow in the preview window.

Once all references are selected, the object can be placed.

A profile wall with the stamped wall inserted onto the back edge is shown in Figure 7–28. The references indicated on the model are selected to correspond to the references listed as inputs in the dialog box.

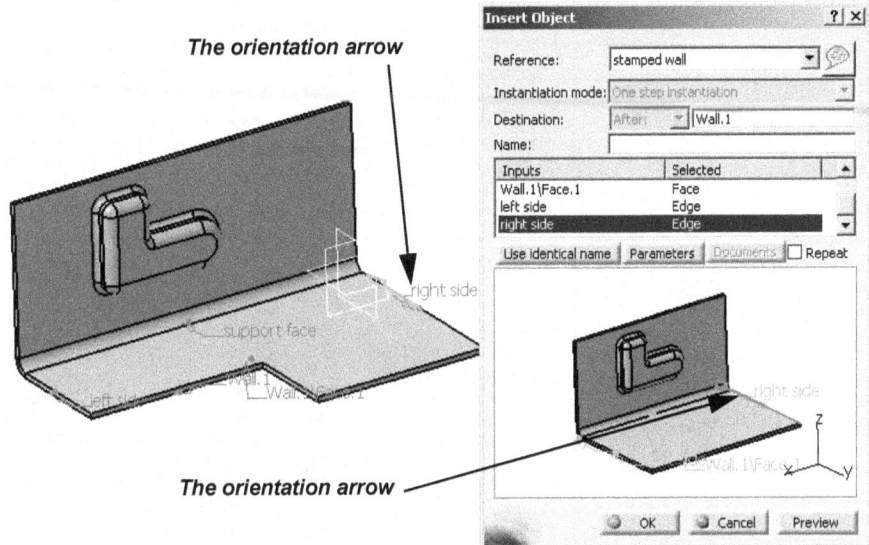

The orientation arrow

The orientation arrow

Figure 7–28

Step 3 - Change parameters and complete instantiation.

Once instantiated, each feature of a PowerCopy becomes a separate feature and is no longer linked to the original PowerCopy.

If any parameters have been published with the PowerCopy, **Parameters** is available. Select it to open the Parameters dialog box. Any modifiable parameters are listed with the default values, as shown in Figure 7–29.

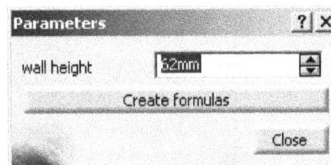

Figure 7–29

Once the PowerCopy is placed correctly in the model, click **OK** to complete the instantiation.

Practice 7a

Patterns I

Practice Objectives

- Create a circular pattern.
- Create a user-defined pattern.

In this practice, you will complete the mounting bracket model you have been building throughout this course. You will use the circular and user-defined pattern options to create duplicate holes and circular stamps. At the end of this practice, the mounting bracket will display as shown in Figure 7–30.

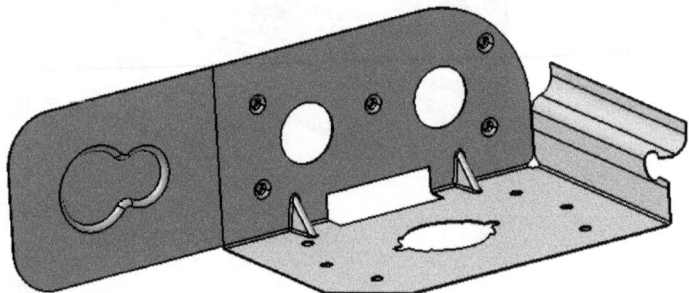

Figure 7–30

Task 1 - Open the part.

1. Open **Ex7A_Mounting_Bracket_2.CATPart**.

   If you completed **Practice 6a**, open **Mounting_Bracket_2.CATPart** instead. The model displays as shown in Figure 7–31.

Figure 7–31

Task 2 - Create reference geometry for the circular pattern.

In this task, you will create the reference geometry required to create a circular pattern of the hole on the first wall. The hole will be patterned around the cut feature in the center of the wall. To pattern about this point, an axis is required. Therefore, you will create a line to act as the axis for the circular pattern.

1. Ensure that the Reference_Geometry Geometrical Set is active by selecting it in the specification tree, right-clicking and selecting **Define in Work Object**.

2. Create a reference point that is located in the center of the cut feature on the first wall by clicking ▪ (Point). If you cannot locate the icon, enter **c:point** in the Power Input line instead, as shown in Figure 7–32.

Figure 7–32

3. Create a point at coordinate (0, 100, 0).

4. Click **OK** to generate the point. The point is created in the center of the first wall, as shown in Figure 7–33.

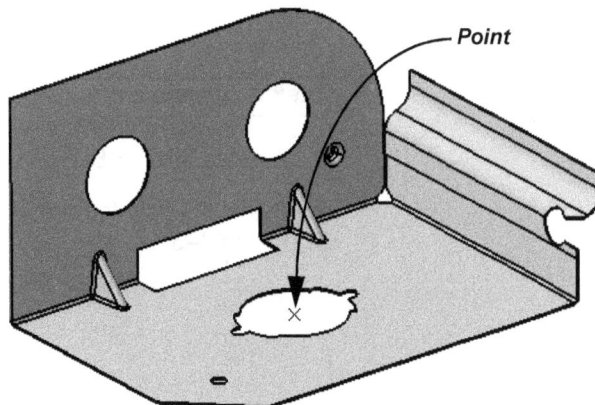

Figure 7–33

5. Create a line to act as the axis for the circular pattern by clicking (Line). If you cannot locate the icon, enter **c:Line** in the Power input line instead.

The start and end length are not important because the line length is arbitrary. The line only needs to be in the correct orientation to pattern about.

6. Create a line using the following conditions:

   • *Line type:* **Point-Direction**
   • *Point:* **(Select the point just created)**
   • *Direction:* **Select the XY plane**.
   • *Start:* **0mm**
   • *End:* **20mm**

7. Click **OK** to generate the line. The line displays as shown in Figure 7–34.

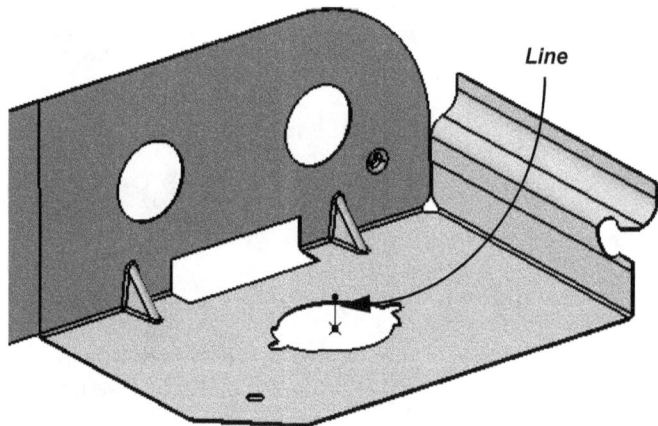

Figure 7–34

Task 3 - Create a circular pattern.

1. Activate the PartBody.

2. Select the hole feature in the first wall, as shown in Figure 7–35.

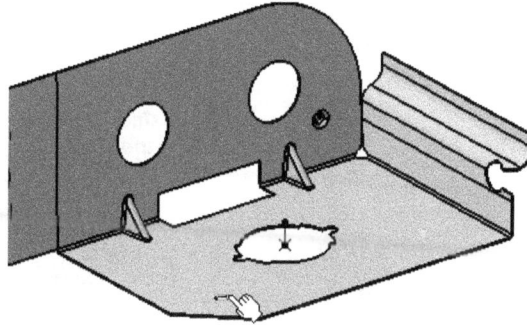

Figure 7–35

3. Click ⬡ (Circular Pattern).

4. Select **Complete Crown** in the Parameters drop-down list.

5. Enter **12** in the *Instances* field.

6. Select inside the *Reference element* field and select the line created in the last task. A preview of the pattern displays on the model, as shown in Figure 7–36.

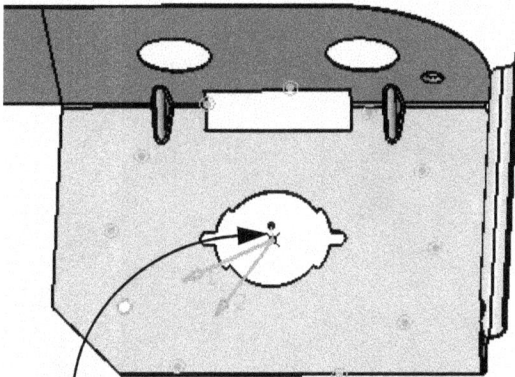

Select line for reference element

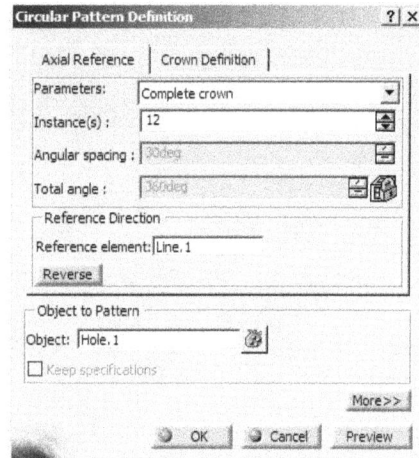

Figure 7–36

Any line or cylindrical surface can be used to define the Reference Direction. In this case, a line is created to demonstrate how to drive a circular pattern when no cylindrical surface is available.

7. Toggle the display of the six holes off, as shown in Figure 7–37, by clicking the position maker in the center of the instance.

Select position marker to toggle off the instance

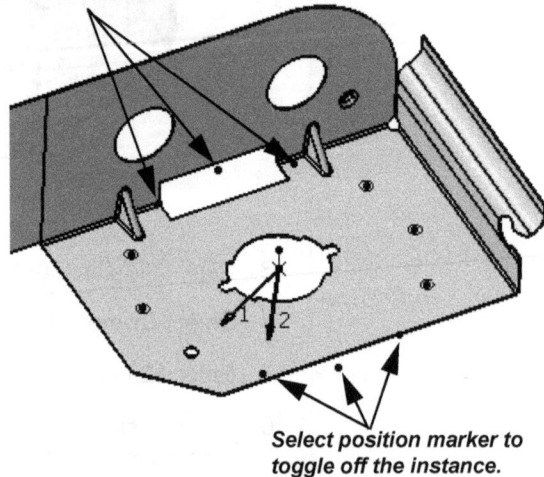

Select position marker to toggle off the instance.

Figure 7–37

8. Click **OK** to create the pattern. The model displays as shown in Figure 7–38.

Figure 7–38

Task 4 - Create reference points for a user pattern.

1. Select the wall shown in Figure 7–39, and enter the Sketcher workbench.

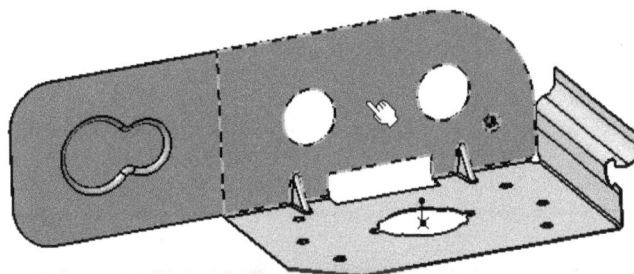

Figure 7–39

2. Create four points as shown in Figure 7–40.

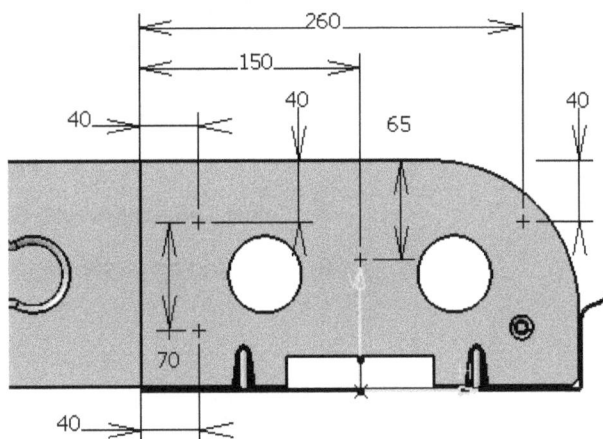

Figure 7–40

3. Exit the Sketcher workbench.

Task 5 - Create the user pattern.

1. Select the circular stamp, as shown in Figure 7–41.

Figure 7–41

2. Click ![icon](User Pattern) and select the points created in the previous task.

3. Click **OK** to create the pattern. The model displays as shown in Figure 7–42.

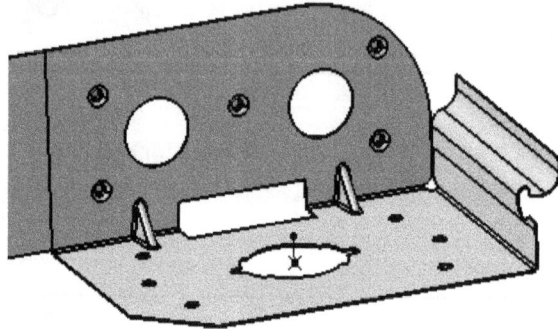

Figure 7–42

4. Select **Tools>Hide>All Geometrical Sets**.

5. Save and close the file.

Practice 7b

Patterns II

Practice Objectives

- Create a hole.
- Create a user-defined pattern.
- Create a cutout.
- Create a rectangular pattern.

In this practice, you will use rectangular and user-defined patterns to duplicate holes and cutouts. At the end of this practice, the model will display as shown in Figure 7–43.

Figure 7–43

Task 1 - Open the part.

1. Open **Ex7B_CurveMapping.CATPart**.

   If you completed Practice 5c, open **Cuve mapping.CATPart** instead. The model displays as shown in Figure 7–44.

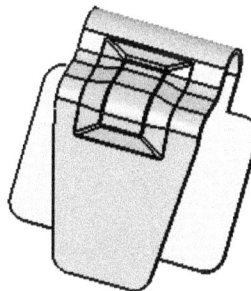

Figure 7–44

Task 2 - Flatten the part.

1. Click (Fold/Unfold) to unfold the model.

Task 3 - Create the location points for holes.

In this task, you will create the position points. These points will be used in the next task to create a hole, and then to duplicate this hole with a user-defined pattern.

1. Highlight the surface shown in Figure 7–45, and click

   ✏️ (Sketch) to enter the Sketcher workbench.

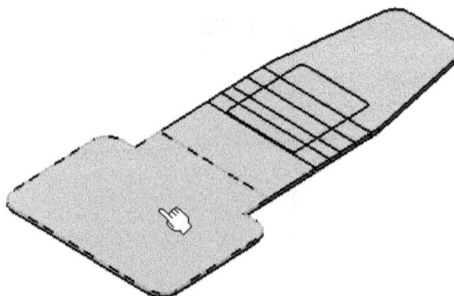

Figure 7–45

2. Sketch three points as shown in Figure 7–46.

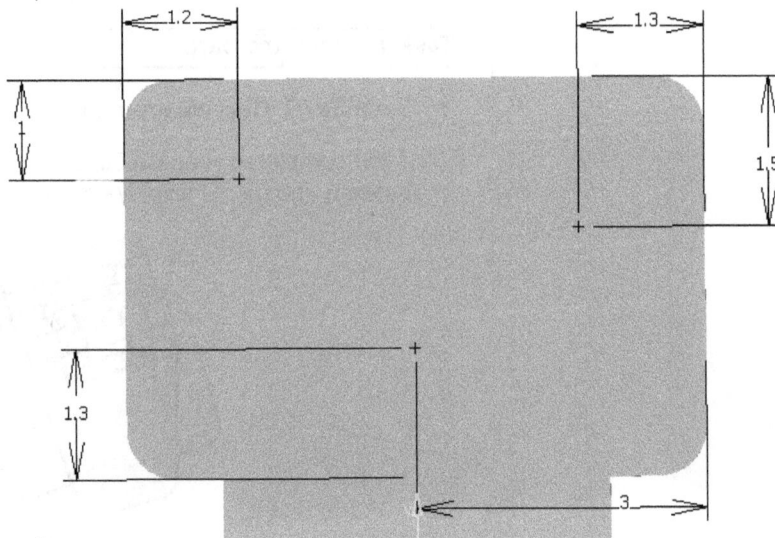

Figure 7–46

3. Click ⬆️ (Exit workbench) to exit from the Sketcher workbench.

Task 4 - Create a hole.

1. Select the point and the surface as shown in Figure 7–47.

2. Click ⬚ (Hole) in the Cutting/Stamping toolbar.

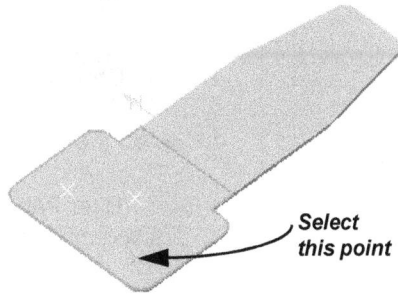

Select this point

Figure 7–47

3. The Hole definition dialog box opens as shown in Figure 7–48. Make the following selections in the *Extension* tab.

    *   *Extension type:* **Up To Next**
    *   *Diameter:* **1mm**

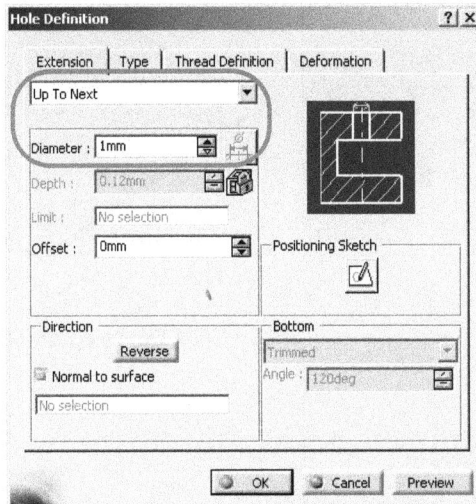

Figure 7–48

4. Select the *Type* tab and define a Countersunk hole with the following parameters:

   - *Mode:* **Depth & Angle**
   - *Depth:* **0.05mm**
   - *Angle:* **90deg**

5. Click **OK** to complete the feature.

Task 5 - Create holes with a user-defined pattern.

---

1. Select the hole from the display or specification tree and click

   (User Pattern) in the **Pattern** flyout menu of the Transformations toolbar.

2. Select the sketch in which the position points are created as shown in Figure 7–49.

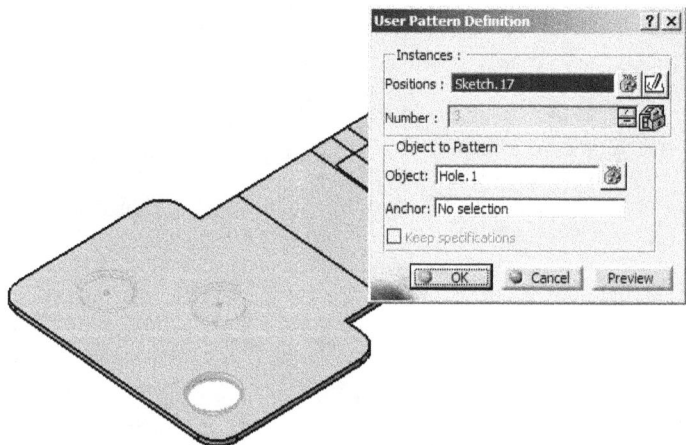

Figure 7–49

3. Click **OK** to complete the feature.

Task 6 - Create a profile for a cutout

In this task, you will create a profile to be used to create a cutout. This cutout will be duplicated using a rectangular pattern.

1. Highlight the surface shown in Figure 7–50, and click ✍️ (Sketch) to enter the Sketcher workbench.

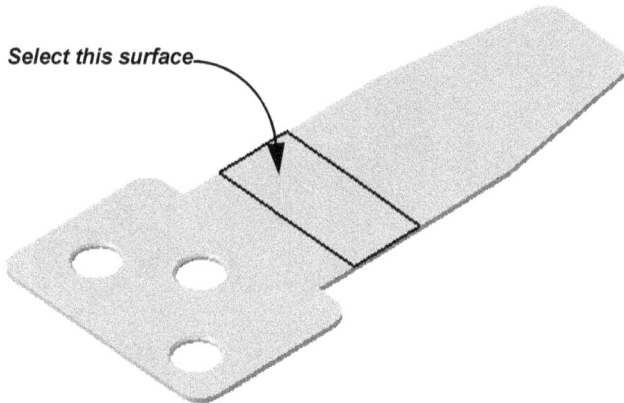

Select this surface

Figure 7–50

2. Create the profile shown in Figure 7–51.

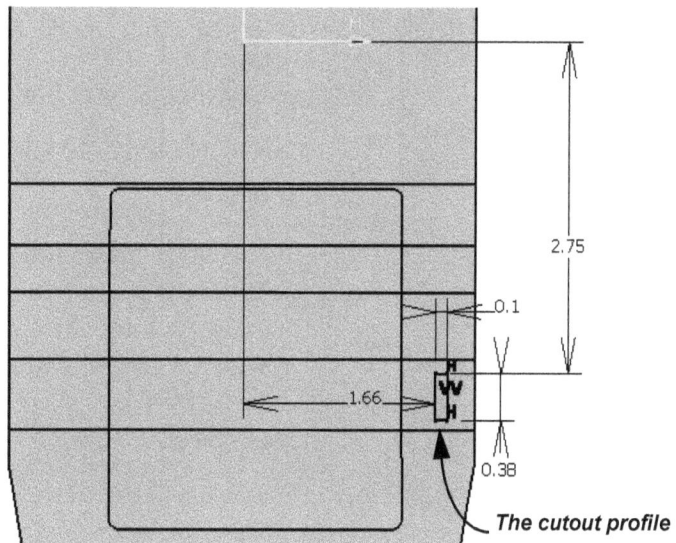

2.75

0.1

1.66

0.38

The cutout profile

Figure 7–51

Task 7 - Create a cutout.

1. Highlight the sketch you created in the previous task and create a cutout feature using the **Up to next** depth option.

2. Click **OK** to complete the feature. The model displays as shown in Figure 7–52.

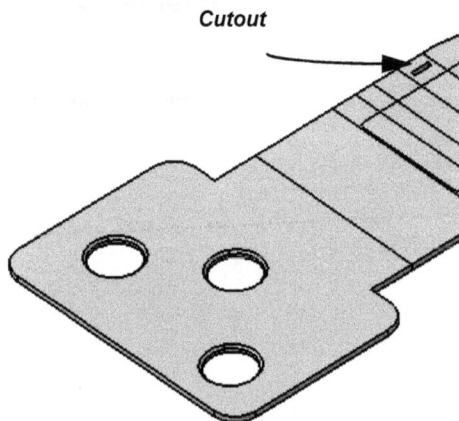

Cutout

Figure 7–52

Task 8 - Create a rectangular pattern

1. Highlight **Cut Out.1** in the display or specification tree and click [⊞] (Rectangular Pattern) in the Pattern toolbar.

2. Specify the following parameters for the pattern:

* First Direction

    * *Parameters:* **Instance(s) & Spacing**
    * *Instance(s):* **2**
    * *Spacing:* **3.4mm**
    * *Reference element:* Select the edge shown in Figure 7–53.

* Second Direction

    * *Parameters:* **Instance(s) & Spacing**
    * *Instance(s):* **2**
    * *Spacing:* **1.5mm**
    * Reference element: Select the edge shown in Figure 7–53.

*Reference element
for first direction*

*Reference element
for second direction*

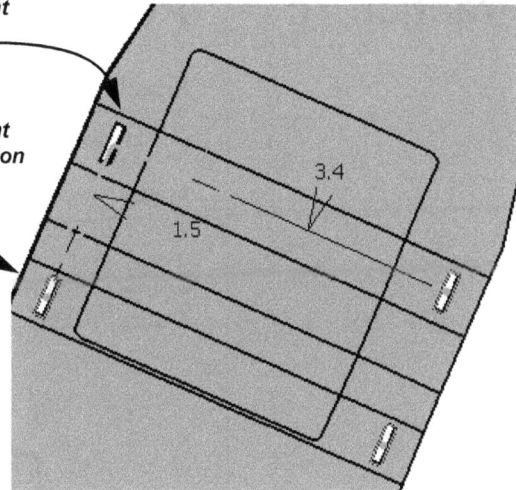

3.4

1.5

Figure 7–53

3. Click **OK** to complete the feature.

Task 9 - Fold the model.

1. Click (Fold/Unfold) to fold the model. The model displays as shown in Figure 7–54.

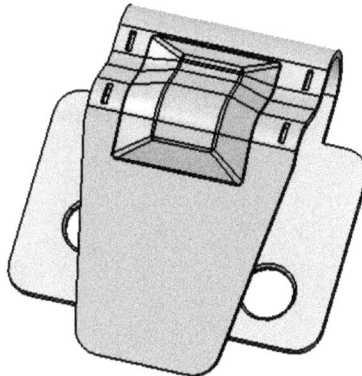

Figure 7–54

2. Save and close the file.

Practice 7c | PowerCopy

Practice Objective

*   Instantiate a PowerCopy.

In this practice, you will instantiate a surface stamp to a model and modify the profile of a surface stamp using PowerCopy. The model and the PowerCopy are already created for this practice. At the end of the practice, the model will display as shown in Figure 7–55.

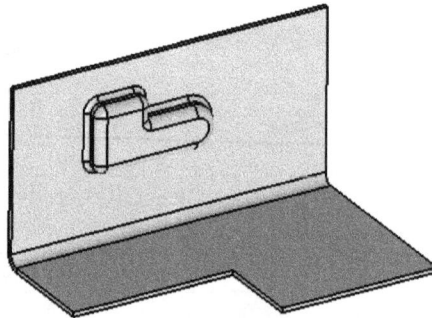

Figure 7–55

Task 1 - Investigate the PowerCopy model.

In this task, you will open a part that contains a surface stamp that has been powercopied.

1. Open **Power.CATPart**. The model displays as shown in Figure 7–56.

Figure 7–56

2. Expand the PartBody. The model consists of two walls joined by a bend. A surface stamp has been applied to one of the walls.

3. Expand the PowerCopy branch of the tree and double-click on **stamped wall**. The Powercopy Definition dialog box opens as shown in Figure 7–57. The PowerCopy references the stamp feature and its sketch. To place the PowerCopy, the required references are a placement face and two edges used to position the sketch for the stamp.

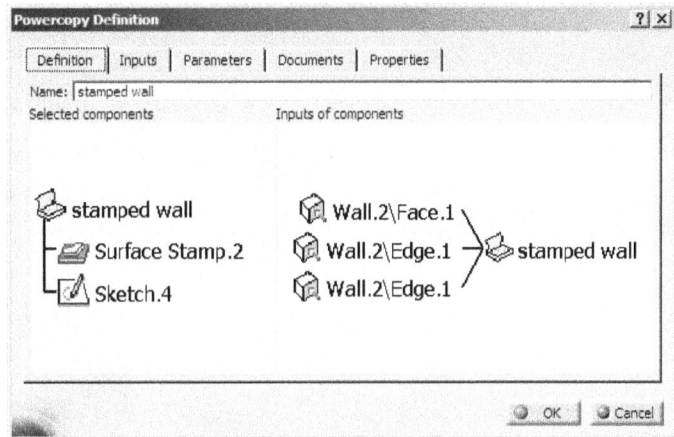

Figure 7–57

4. Close the Powercopy Definition dialog box.

Task 2 - Open the model.

1. Open **FirstWalls.CATPart**. The model displays as shown in Figure 7–58.

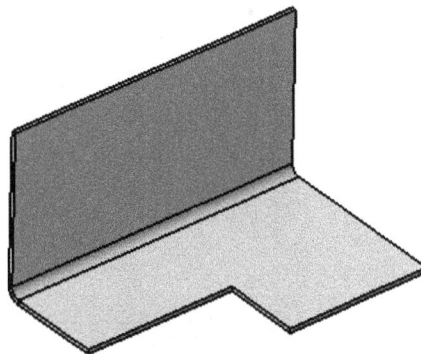

Figure 7–58

2. Select **Window>Tile Horizontally** so that both models display.

3. Ensure that **FirstWalls.CATPart** is the active window.

Task 3 - Instantiate the PowerCopy.

1. Select **Insert>Instantiate From Selection** and select the **Stamped Wall PowerCopy** from Power.CATPart. The Insert Object dialog box opens as shown in Figure 7–59.

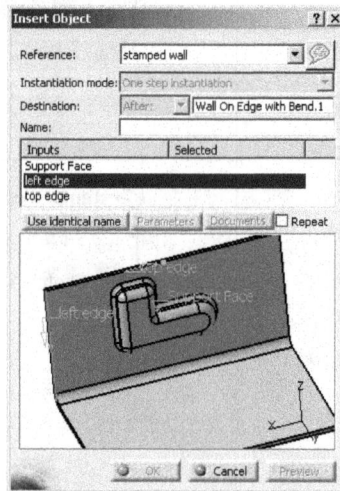

Figure 7–59

2. Move the cursor so that it is in the preview window. Use the mouse to rotate, pan, and zoom the preview. One reference is highlighted in the window and the highlighting indicates that the system is waiting for input on this reference

3. Select the face to specify as the Support Face, as shown in Figure 7–60.

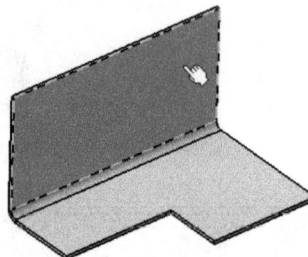

Figure 7–60

4. Ensure that the orientation arrow on the model matches the one in the preview window. If required, change the direction by clicking on the arrow as shown in Figure 7–61.

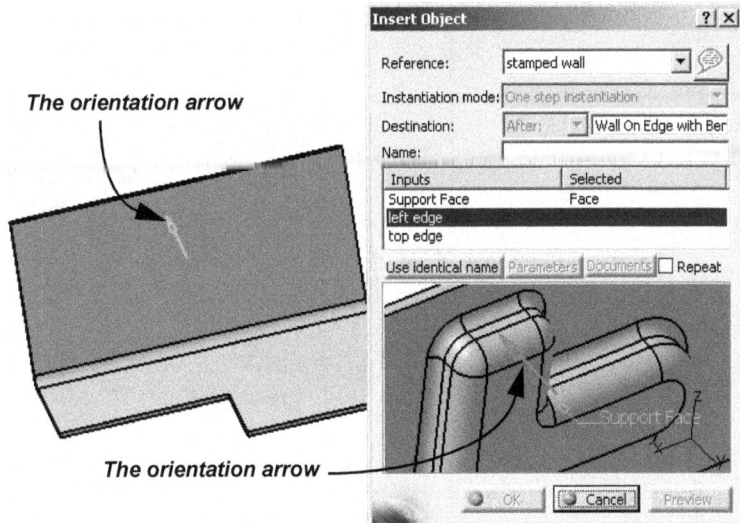

The orientation arrow

The orientation arrow

Figure 7–61

5. The system now requires input for the left edge references. Select the left edge of the model as shown in Figure 7–62. If required, change the direction of orientation arrow.

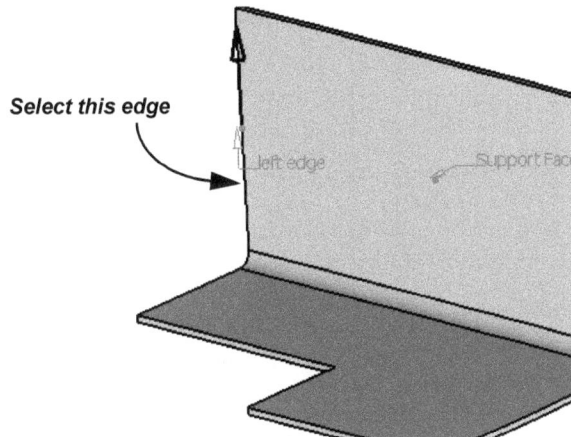

Select this edge

Figure 7–62

6. Select the top edge of the model, as shown in Figure 7–63. If required, change the direction of orientation arrow.

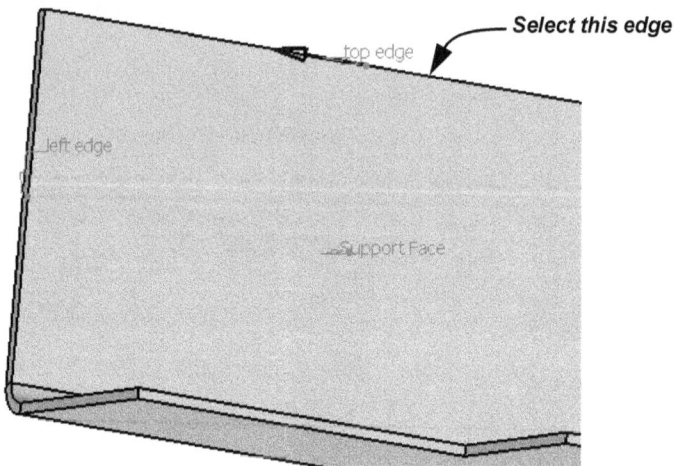

Figure 7–63

7. Click **Preview**. The preview displays as shown in Figure 7–64.

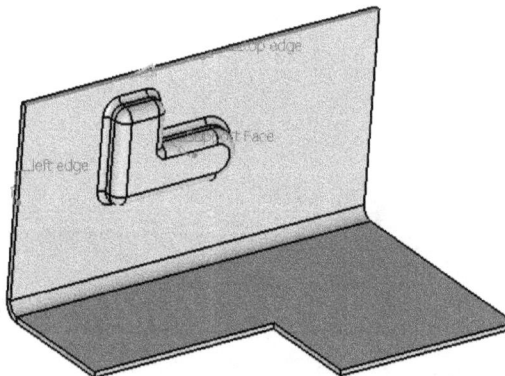

Figure 7–64

8. Click **Parameters**. The Parameters dialog box opens as shown in Figure 7–65.

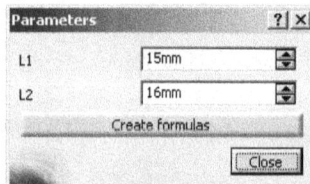

Figure 7–65

The Parameters L1 and L2 are created in the PowerCopy to modify the profile of the surface stamp as shown in Figure 7–66.

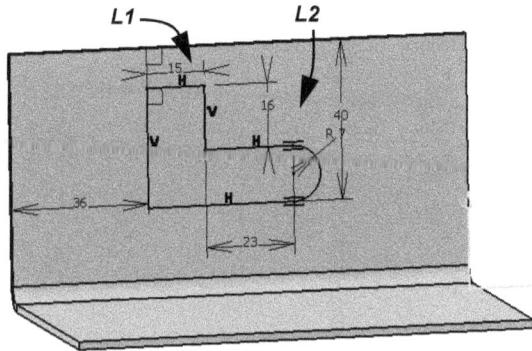

Figure 7–66

9. Enter the following values in the Parameters dialog box.

    • *L1:* **20mm**
    • *L2:* **10mm**

10. Click **Close** in the Parameters dialog box, and click **OK** to complete the feature. The model displays as shown in Figure 7–67.

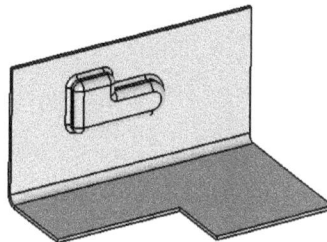

Figure 7–67

11. Expand the specification tree and review the features that have been added to the model, as shown in Figure 7–68. This feature can be modified at any time. There is no link created between the PowerCopy and the instantiated model.

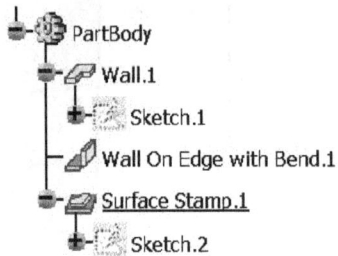

Figure 7–68

12. Save and close the files.

Practice 7d

Patterns and PowerCopies

Practice Objectives

- Create a rectangular pattern.
- Create a PowerCopy.
- Instantiate a PowerCopy.

In this practice, you will create the final features for a Mount model. You will create two PowerCopies for the two louvers created in the side of the model. You will then instantiate the PowerCopies in the same model in which they were created, to create the louvers for the other side of the model. You also create a rectangular pattern to complete the mounting holes. At the end of the practice, the model will display as shown in Figure 7–69.

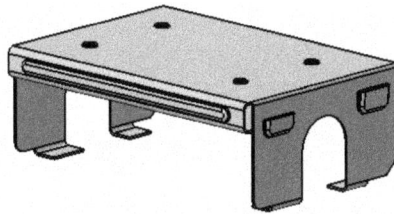

Figure 7–69

Task 1 - Open the model.

1. Open **Ex7D_Mount.CATPart**.

   If you completed Practice 6b, open **Mount.CATPart** instead. The model displays as shown in Figure 7–70.

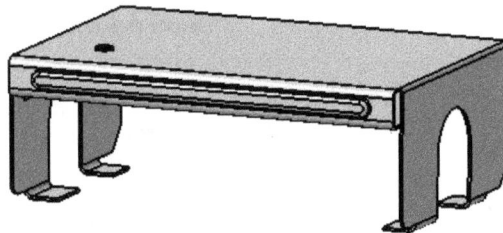

Figure 7–70

Task 2 - Create a rectangular pattern.

The Flanged hole on the top of mount must be patterned to line up with the holes on the wall underneath.

1. Select the **Flanged Hole.1** in the specification tree or display, as shown in Figure 7–71.

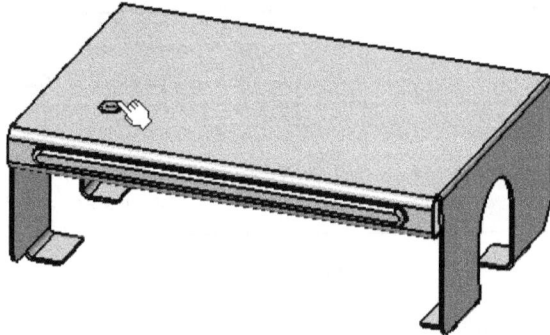

Figure 7–71

2. Click ▦ (Rectangular Pattern) in the Transformations toolbar.

3. Enter the following parameters:

   - *Parameters:* **Instance(s) & Spacing**
   - *Instance(s):* **2**
   - *Spacing:* **96mm**

4. Select inside the *Reference element* field and select the edge shown in Figure 7–72.

Select this edge

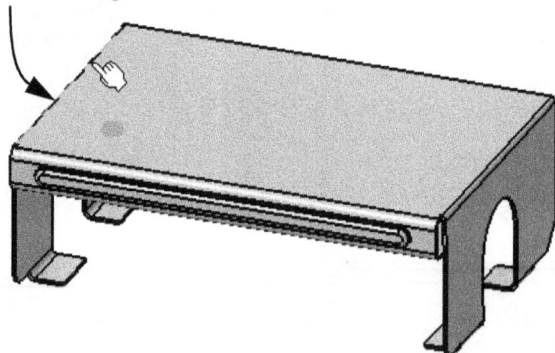

Figure 7–72

5. Ensure that the pattern is created in the correct direction, as shown in Figure 7–73. Click **Reverse** to change direction if required.

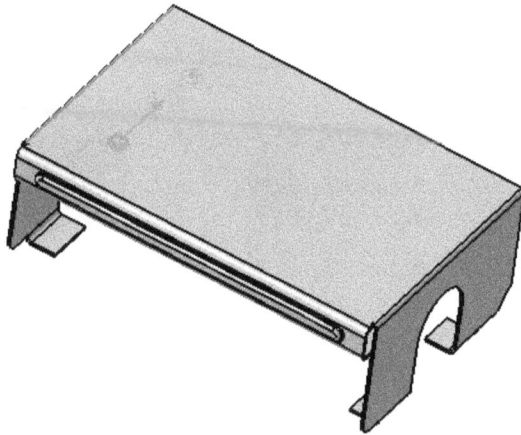

Figure 7–73

6. Select the *Second Direction* tab and enter the following parameters:

   - *Parameters:* **Instance(s) & Spacing**
   - *Instance(s):* **2**
   - *Spacing:* **192**

7. Select inside the *Reference element* field and select the edge shown in Figure 7–74.

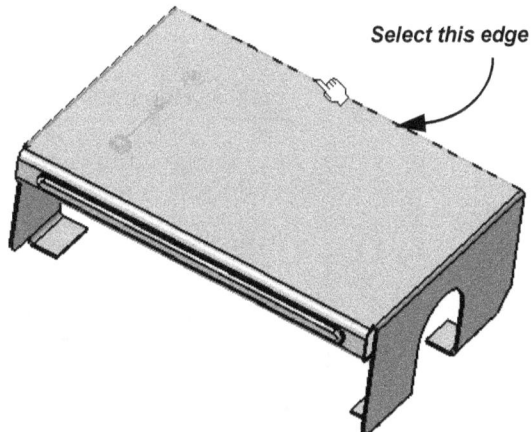

Figure 7–74

8. Ensure that the pattern is created in the correct direction, as shown in Figure 7–75. Click **Reverse** to change direction if required.

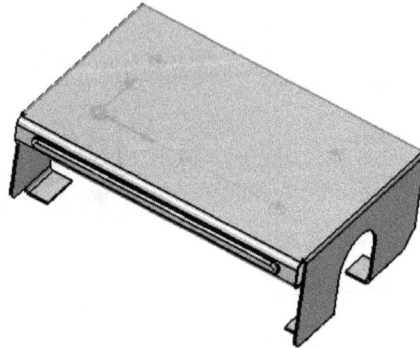

Figure 7–75

9. Click **OK** to generate the pattern. The model displays as shown in Figure 7–76.

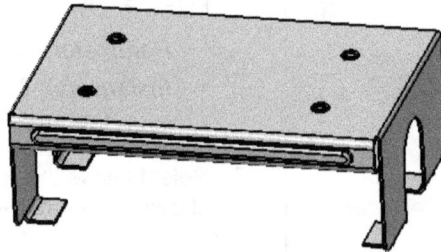

Figure 7–76

Task 3 - Rename the louvers.

1. Rename **Louver.1** as **Louver_big** and **Louver.2** as **Louver_small**.

2. Click on the screen to ensure that no features are selected.

Task 4 - Create a PowerCopy.

In this task, you will create a PowerCopy for the big louver. The PowerCopy is then instantiated in the same model to create one more louver on the opposite side of the model. A PowerCopy is used in this situation, rather then a pattern, because the references need to be changed to correctly position and orient the duplicated louver.

1. Select **Insert>Knowledge Templates>PowerCopy**. Enter **Louver_big** in the *Name* field.

2. Select the features **Louver_big** and the sketch used to create Louver_big in the specification tree. The PowerCopy definition dialog box updates to display the selected features, as shown in Figure 7–77.

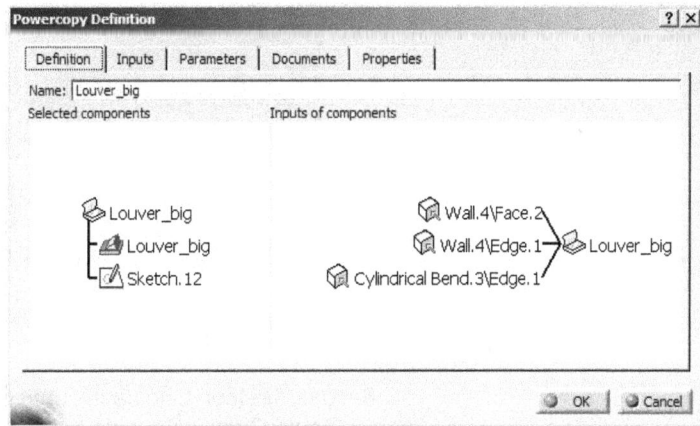

Figure 7–77

3. Select the *Inputs* tab.

4. Select the first **Wall.4\Face.2(Wall.4\Face.2)** input.

5. Change the name of the input to **support face** in the *Name* field, as shown in Figure 7–78.

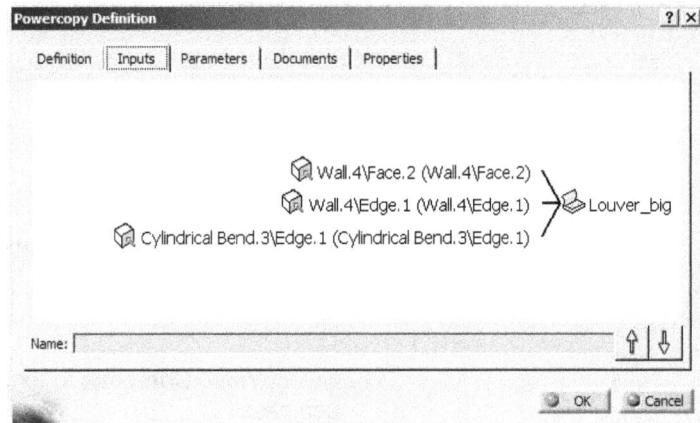

Figure 7–78

6. Change the names of the other inputs, as shown in Figure 7–78.

   Depending on how you dimension the Louvers, the inputs might not be in the same order. When an input name is changed, it updates on the model. Verify that the correct name has been entered for the reference, as shown in Figure 7–79.

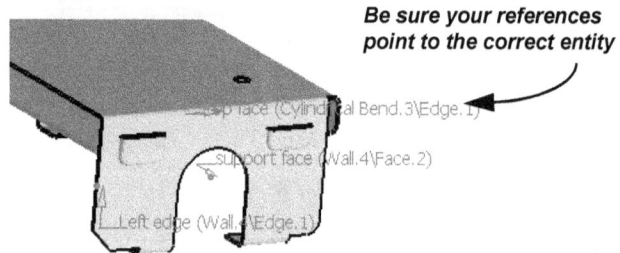

Be sure your references point to the correct entity

Figure 7–79

7. Select the *Properties* tab.

8. Use the Icon Choice flyout to change the icon for the PowerCopy, as shown in Figure 7–80.

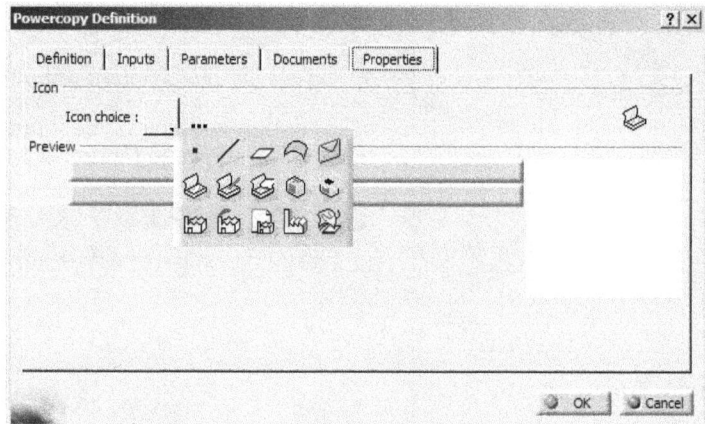

Figure 7–80

9. Select **View>Specifications** to toggle off the display of the specification tree.

10. Select **View>Compass** to toggle off the display of the compass.

11. Rotate the model so that the louver displays clearer, as shown in Figure 7–81.

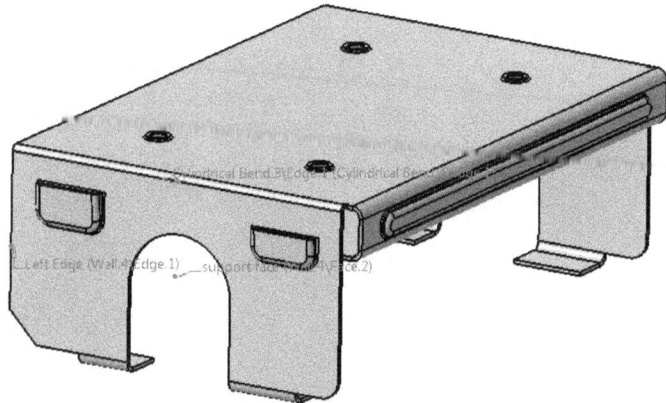

Figure 7–81

12. Click **Grab screen** in the PowerCopy Definition dialog box. An image of the screen is taken, as shown in Figure 7–82.

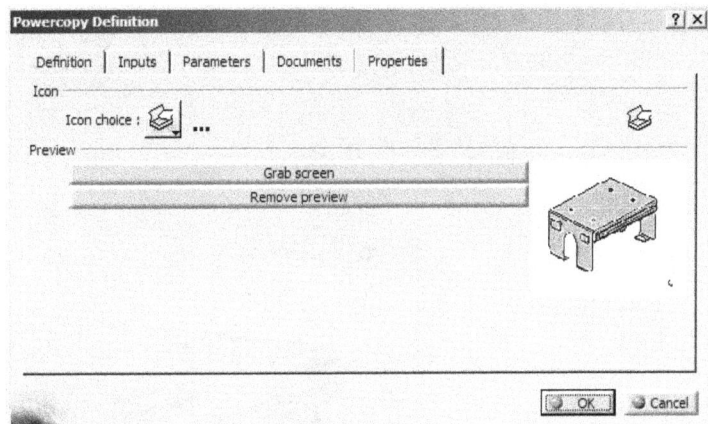

Figure 7–82

13. Click **OK** to create the PowerCopy.

14. Toggle the display of the specification tree and compass back on.

Task 5 - Instantiate the PowerCopy.

1. Select the PowerCopy in the specification tree, right-click and select **louver_big object>Instantiate**.

2. Move the cursor so that it is in the preview window. Use the mouse to rotate, pan, and zoom the preview. One reference is highlighted in the window and the highlighting indicates that the system is waiting for input on this reference as shown in Figure 7–83.

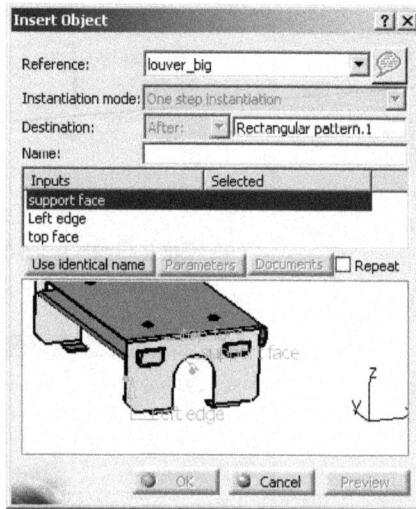

Figure 7–83

3. Select the surface shown in Figure 7–84 for the support face.

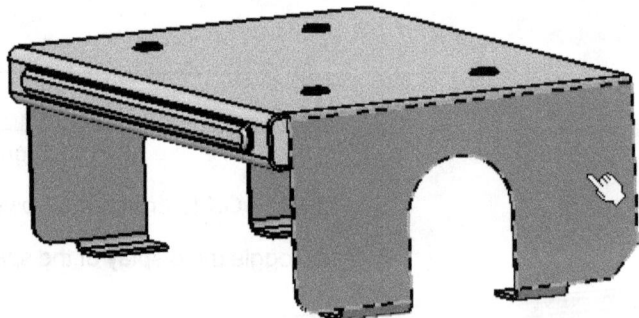

Figure 7–84

In the previous practice, while instantiating the PowerCopy in the model, the orientation arrows matched the ones in the preview window. This is because the source and target orientation were the same. In this practice, the louvers are instantiated on the other side of the model. Therefore, the orientations of the surface stamps are symmetrical to the original surface stamps. While selecting the references, ensure that the orientation arrow in the main window is in the opposite direction to the orientation arrow in the preview window.

4. If required, change the direction for the support face by clicking on the arrow, as shown in Figure 7–85.

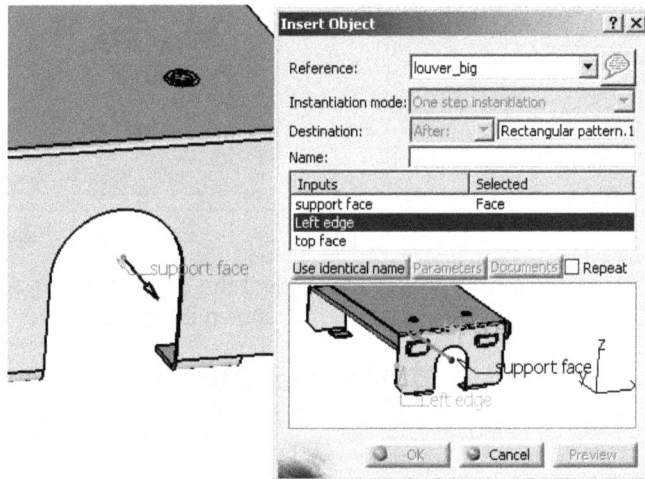

Figure 7–85

The reference might not be called out in the same order in your PowerCopy. Ensure you are selecting the right reference for the highlighted parameter.

5. Select the edge as shown in Figure 7–86. Ensure that the orientation arrows are pointing the opposite direction.

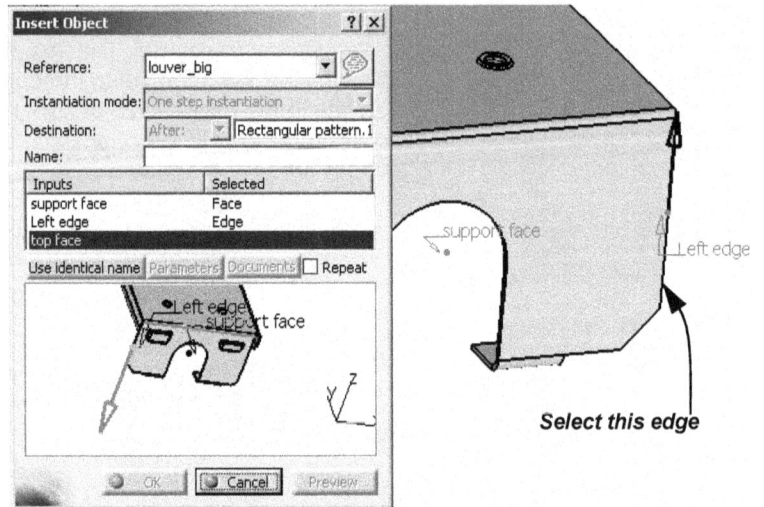

Figure 7–86

6. Select the edge shown in Figure 7–87 and orient the arrows as shown in Figure 7–87.

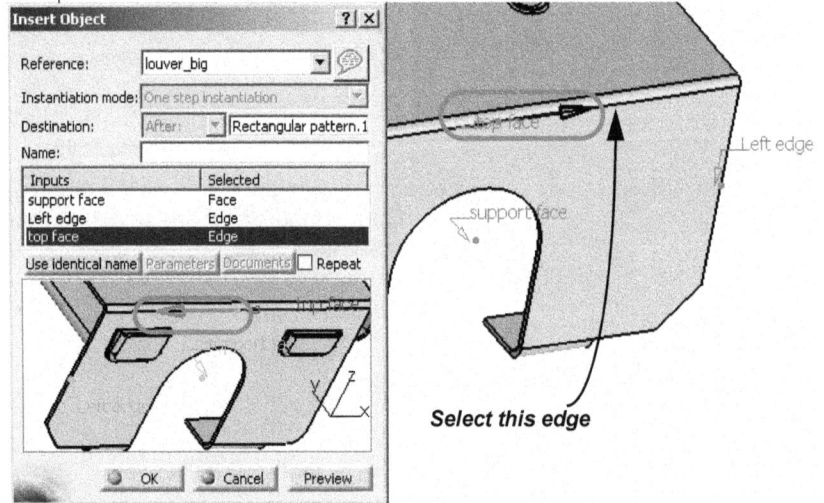

Figure 7–87

7. Click **Preview** to view the louver.

8. Click **OK** to create the new louver. The model displays as shown in Figure 7–88.

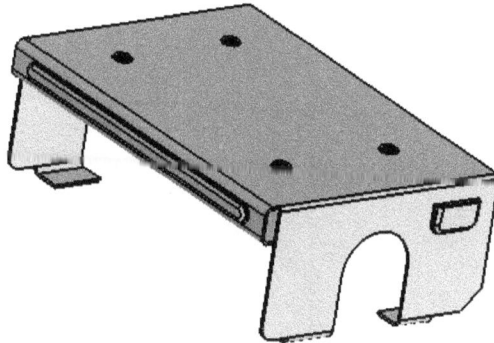

Figure 7–88

Task 6 - Create a PowerCopy.

In this task, you will create a PowerCopy for the small louver. The PowerCopy is then instantiated in the same model to create one more small louver on the opposite side of the model. The completed model displays as shown in Figure 7–89.

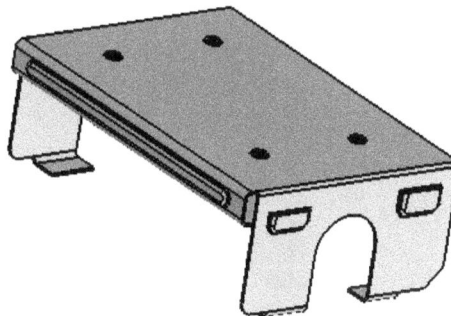

Figure 7–89

1. Create the PowerCopy for the small louver.

2. Instantiate the PowerCopy.

3. Save and close the file.

Part Conversion

Solid models, such as those created in the Part Design workbench, can be converted into a sheet metal part using the **Recognize** tool. This chapter discusses the methods available to check that the model has converted correctly. Once the model has converted, you can make changes to it.

Learning Objectives in this Chapter

- Understand part conversion.
- Learn how to check for overlap.

8.1 Part Conversion

Solid models, such as those created in the Part Design workbench, can be converted into a sheet metal part. The Generative Sheet Metal Design workbench also provides tools to check a model before it goes into production.

To convert a model to sheet metal, it must have uniform thickness. Models that do not have uniform thickness do not fully convert. For example, Figure 8–1 shows what a model with non-uniform thickness would look like when converted to sheet metal. The additional wall, which was not the same thickness as the reference wall, is no longer displayed in the model.

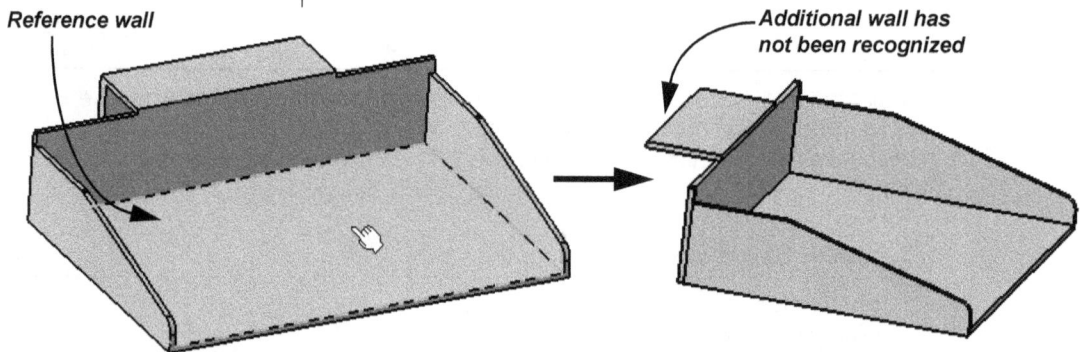

Figure 8–1

General Steps

Use the following general steps to convert a solid model to a sheet metal model

1. Activate the **Recognize** tool.
2. Specify internal profiles.
3. Complete the conversion.

Step 1 - Activate the Recognize tool.

Click ![icon] (Recognize) and select a reference wall, as shown in Figure 8–2. The reference wall acts as the first wall in the sheet metal model. When unfolding the model, the reference wall remains fixed. The thickness of the reference defines the default thickness for the model. Any wall that is not of this thickness is not included in the final sheet metal model.

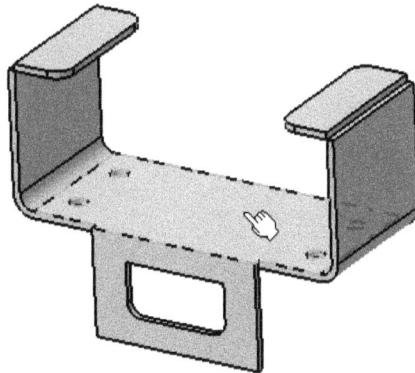

Figure 8–2

The Recognize Definition dialog box opens as shown in Figure 8–3. The selected surface is recognized as the reference face.

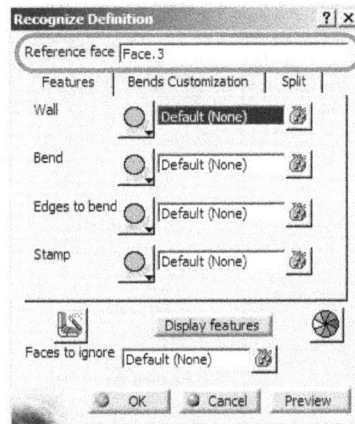

Figure 8–3

Step 2 - Specify internal profiles.

Select options in the Recognize Definition dialog box to control the types of elements that are recognized. Recognition mode settings can be specified for each feature type, using the individual recognition icon in the Recognize Definition dialog box. Walls, bends, and stamps are recognized automatically when the

⊙ (Full Recognition) option is enabled as shown in Figure 8–4.

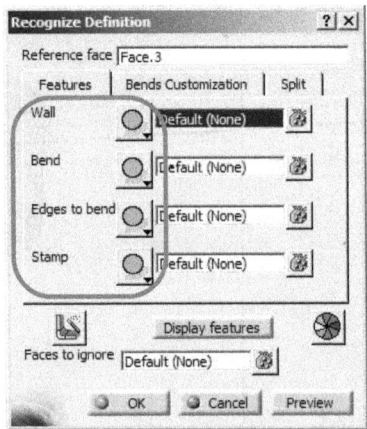

Figure 8–4

The different recognition modes are described as follows:

Mode	Description
Wall, Bend and Stamp	
⊙ (Full Recognition)	Select this option to automatically recognize all features of the selected type.
⊙ (Partial Recognition)	Select this option to recognize the features manually.
⊙ (No Recognition)	Select this option to not recognize any features of a given type. Available only for bends and stamps.
Edges to bend	
⊙ (Automatic Bends)	Select this option to automatically add bends to selected edges.

(No automatic bends)	Select this option to toggle off any edges automatically selected for bends.

Compulsory walls can also be selected to resolve wall ambiguity. Without selecting a compulsory wall, a gap is created between any walls that connect on a sharp corner. An example is shown in Figure 8–5.

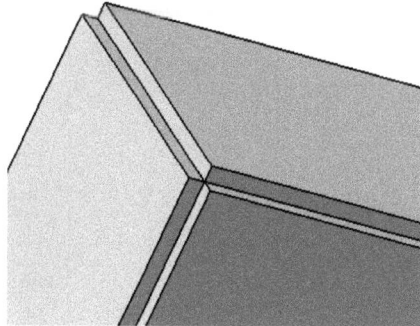

Figure 8–5

By defining a compulsory wall, the system uses it as a limiting element for adjacent walls. For example, Figure 8–6 shows a simplified box; by selecting the outside face of one wall and the inside face of the other, overlapping is avoided when the walls are generated.

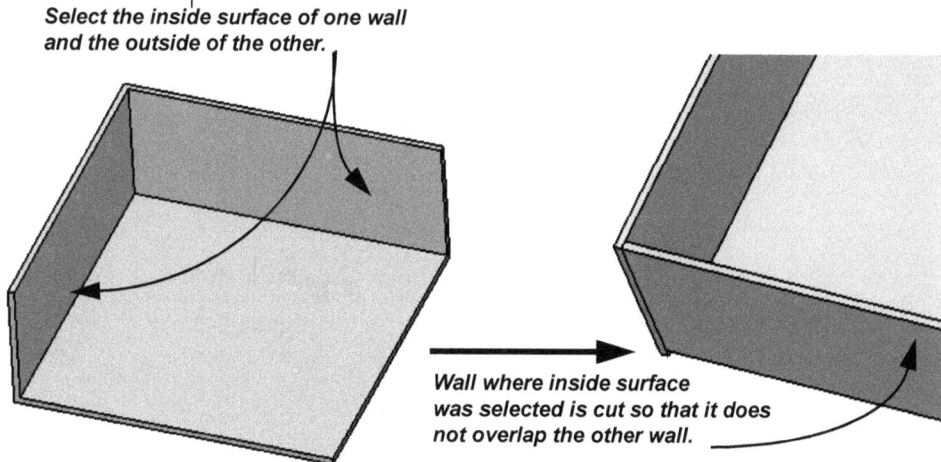

Select the inside surface of one wall and the outside of the other.

Wall where inside surface was selected is cut so that it does not overlap the other wall.

Figure 8–6

To define compulsory walls, activate the *Faces to keep* field and select the surfaces to keep. To prevent a wall from being recognized, activate the *Faces to ignore* field and select the surfaces to remove as shown in Figure 8–7.

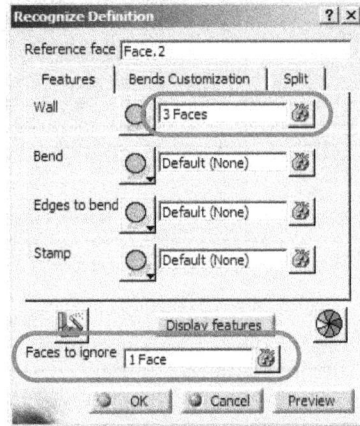

Figure 8–7

Step 3 - Complete the conversion.

Click **Display features** to preview the selection. Use the

 (Color Selector) tool to set the colors used to display the various features, as shown in Figure 8–8.

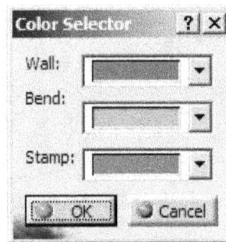

Figure 8–8

Click **OK** to complete the conversion. The sheet metal features are generated in the model, as shown in Figure 8–9. A Recognize feature is placed in the specification tree. The model can now be folded and unfolded as if it were initially created in the Generative Sheet Metal Design workbench.

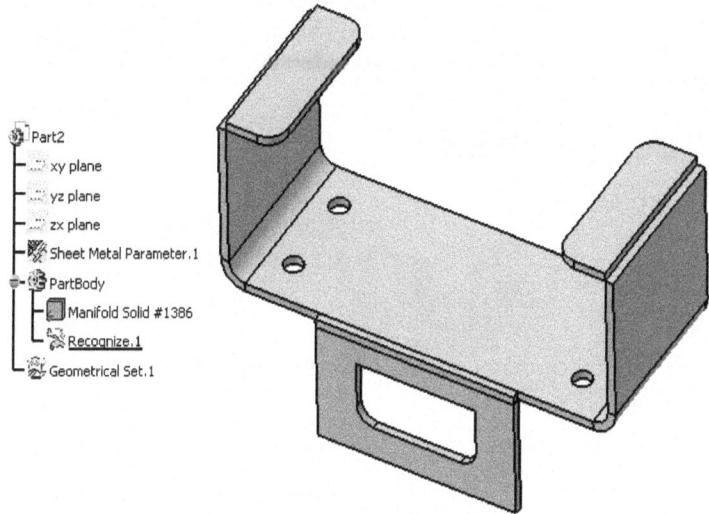

Part2
— xy plane
— yz plane
— zx plane
— Sheet Metal Parameter.1
— PartBody
   — Manifold Solid #1386
   — Recognize.1
— Geometrical Set.1

Figure 8–9

The sheet metal parameters are also created for the model. The thickness of the model is based on the thickness of the reference wall. The default bend radius is automatically set to two times the thickness of the model. Parameters can be edited by double-clicking on the Sheet Metal Parameter element in the specification tree.

8.2 Checking for Overlap

Overlap occurs when two walls intersect each other in the Unfolded view and it needs to be corrected so that the model can be manufactured correctly. Using the Overlapping analysis, a curve is generated indicating the area of overlap. This curve can be used as the profile for additional sheet metal features, such as cutouts, to resolve the issue.

General Steps

Use the following general steps to check for overlap:

1. Unfold the model.
2. Run the analysis.
3. Generate curves to represent areas of overlap.

Step 1 - Unfold the model.

To check for overlap, the model must be in the unfolded view.

Click [icon] (Unfold) to unfold the model, as shown in Figure 8–10.

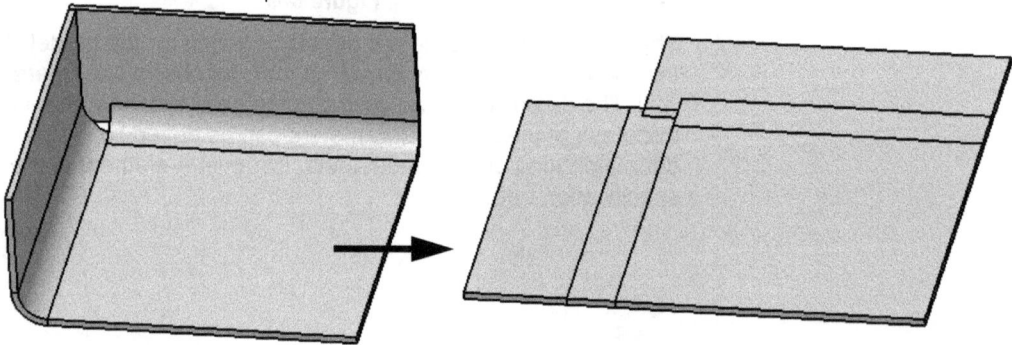

Figure 8–10

Step 2 - Run the analysis.

Click ![icon] (Check Overlapping) in the Manufacturing preparation toolbar to start the analysis. The Overlapping detection dialog box opens when the analysis is complete. The dialog box indicates how many overlapping areas were detected, as shown in Figure 8–11. If no overlapping areas are detected, the dialog box reports "No overlapping detected".

Figure 8–11

Step 3 - Generate curves to represent areas of overlap.

Click **OK** to close the Overlapping Detection dialog box. A curve is generated on the model of the overlapping area, as shown in Figure 8–12.

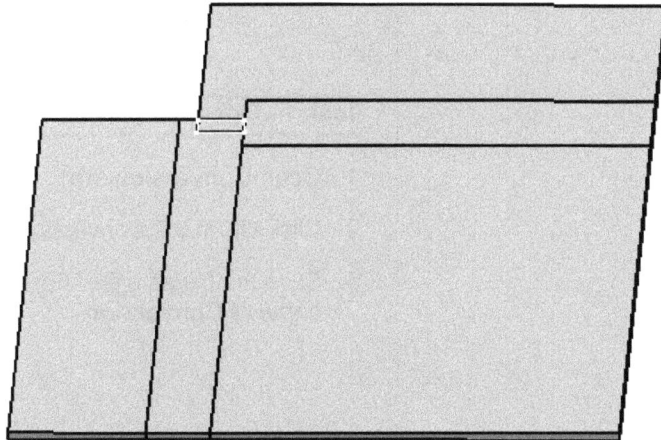

Figure 8–12

Practice 8a | Part Conversion

Practice Objectives

- Open an imported file format.
- Convert a part model to sheet metal.
- Create bends.
- Unfold a model.

In this practice, you will open an STEP file that you have received and convert it into a sheet metal part. The model will have all required walls, cutouts, and bends, as well sheet metal parameters generated for it. The final sheet metal model created at the end of the practice displays as shown in Figure 8–13.

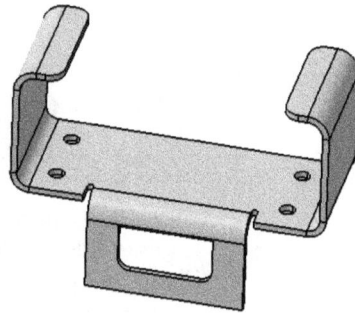

Figure 8–13

Task 1 - Open the part.

1. Open **Conversion.stp**.

2. Click **OK** in the Conversion.stp dialog box.

3. Save the file as a CATPart file and accept the default model name of **Conversion**.

The part body contains only one feature because this model is an imported file, as shown in Figure 8–14. The individual features of this part are not available.

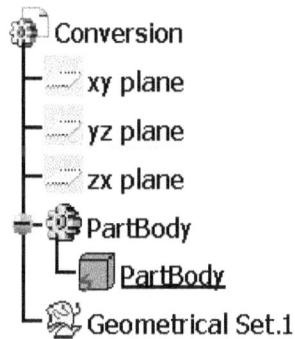

Figure 8–14

Task 2 - Convert the model.

1. Activate the Generative Sheet Metal Design workbench if it is not already active.

2. Click ![icon] (Recognize). Select the surface shown in Figure 8–15 for the reference wall. This wall remains fixed when the part is unfolded.

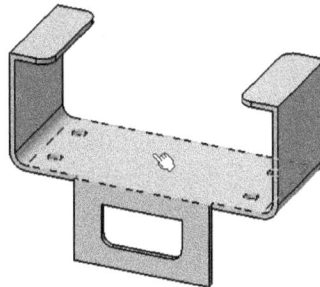

Figure 8–15

3. Note that all features are set to ⬚ (Full Recognition) to recognize all sheet metal features, as shown in Figure 8–16.

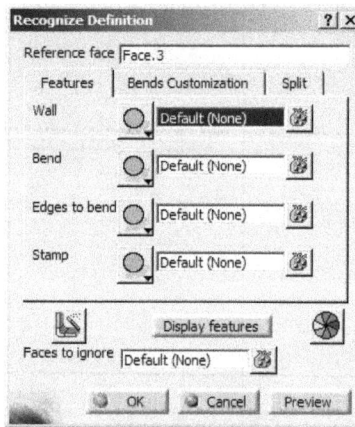

Figure 8–16

4. Click **Display features**. A preview of the model displays all of the faces that will be recognized as walls in blue and all of the faces that will be recognized as bends in green. Note that bends are not being created between the top horizontal walls and the vertical walls and between the referenced wall and the lower vertical wall, as shown in Figure 8–17. This is because the original model had sharp corners between these walls and bends were not automatically generated at these intersections during the Recognize operation.

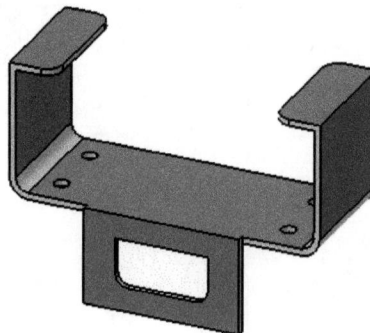

Figure 8–17

5. Click **OK** and click **Close** in the Warnings dialog box.

*You can also update the model by selecting **Edit>Update**.*

6. If required, click ⊚ (Update All). The model is converted into a sheetmetal model, as shown in Figure 8–18.

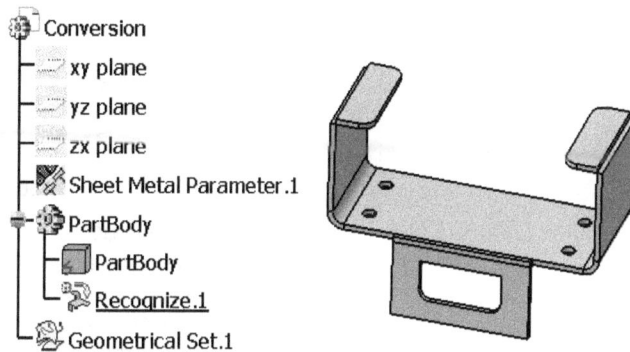

Figure 8–18

7. Click ⊠ (Unfold). What happens to the model when it is unfolded? Fold the model.

Task 3 - Create additional bends.

Because the original model had sharp corners between some walls, bends were not automatically generated at these intersections during the Recognize operation.

1. Click ⌐ (Bend) and create bends between the walls as shown in Figure 8–19.

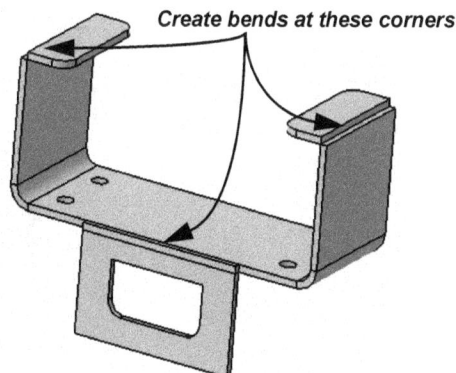

Figure 8–19

2. Unfold the part. The unfolded part displays as shown in Figure 8–20.

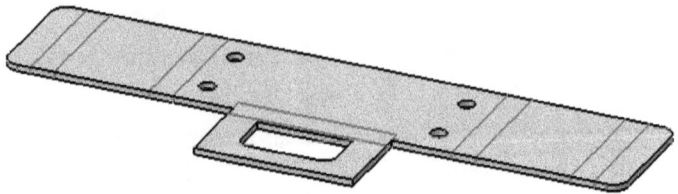

Figure 8–20

During the previous unfold operation, no bend feature existed between the first wall and the additional vertical wall. The system does not know how to unfold converted geometry if there is no bend. With the bend features, all walls can be unfolded correctly.

3. Click [icon] again to return the model to its formed state.

Task 4 - Edit the sheet metal parameters.

---

1. Double-click on **Sheet Metal Parameter.1** in the specification tree.

2. Select the *Bend Extremities* tab.

3. Select **Round Relief** in the drop-down list and enter the following parameter values:

   - *L1:* **1mm**
   - *L2:* **2mm**

4. Click **OK**. The model displays as shown in Figure 8–21.

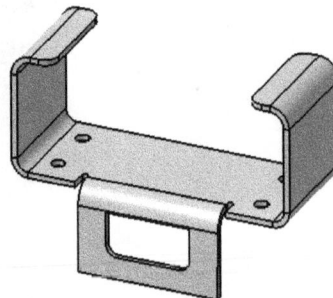

Figure 8–21

5. Save and close the file.

Practice 8b

Part Conversion II

Practice Objectives

- Convert a part model to sheet metal.
- Create bends.
- Solve ambiguities.

In this practice, you will convert a tray into a sheet metal model. This conversion requires you to select the correct required walls and solve some ambiguities when creating the bends. At the end of this practice, the model will display as shown in Figure 8–22.

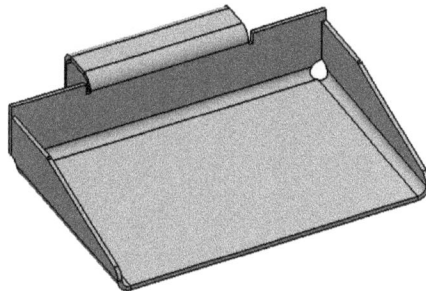

Figure 8–22

Task 1 - Open the part.

1. Open the **Tray.CATPart** file. The model displays as shown in Figure 8–23. This model was created in the Part Design workbench.

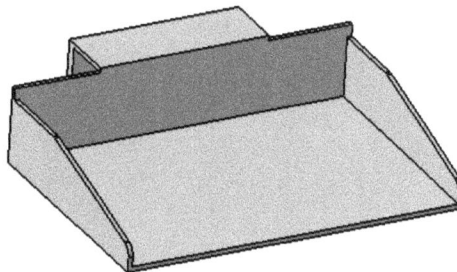

Figure 8–23

Task 2 - Recognize sheet metal features.

1. Activate the Generative Sheet Metal Design workbench if it is not already active.

2. Click ![icon] (Recognize).

3. Select the wall shown in Figure 8–24 to act as the reference wall.

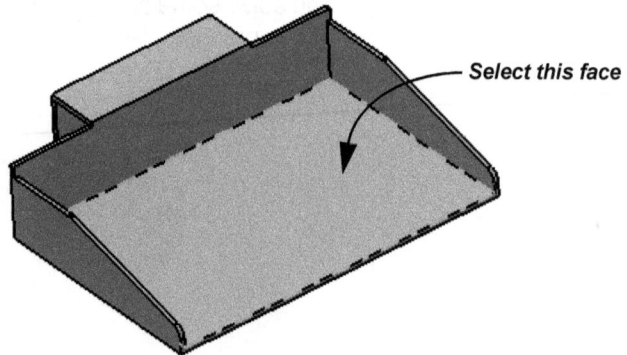

Select this face

Figure 8–24

4. Verify that the ![icon] (Full Recognition) options are set as shown in Figure 8–25.

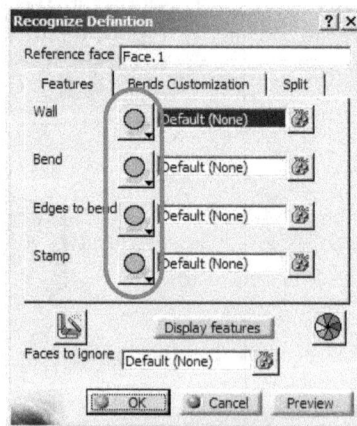

Figure 8–25

5. Click **OK**. An Update Error message box opens.

6. Click **OK**.

7. Click **Yes** in the Recognize build warning dialog box to continue the operation.

8. Click **OK** and close the Warnings dialog box. The model could not be converted completely because one of the walls is missing as shown in Figure 8–26. This is because the wall's thickness value did not match the thickness value of the reference wall.

Additional wall has not been recognized ——

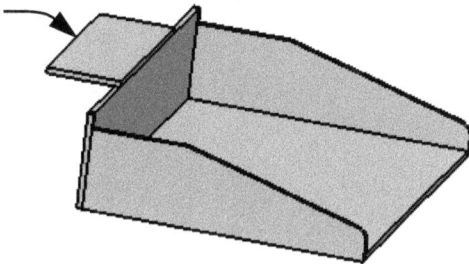

Figure 8–26

9. Click (Undo) until the wall recognition operation is undone.

Task 3 - Correct the wall thickness.

---

1. Double-click on **Pad.4**, as shown in Figure 8–27.

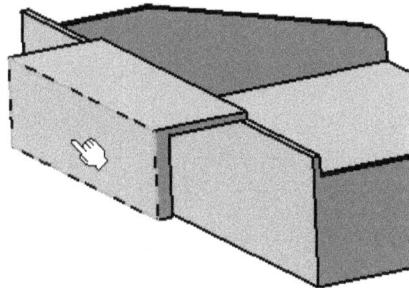

Figure 8–27

2. Change the length of the wall to **2mm**. The thickness of modified wall matches the thickness value for the model.

3. Click **OK**.

Task 4 - Recognize sheet metal features with a new reference.

1. Click ![Recognize icon] (Recognize) to recognize the walls again. Select the same surface as the reference wall.

2. Click **OK** and close the Warnings dialog box. If required, select **Edit>Update** to update the model. This new conversion is improved, but still not what is required. The back surface should have extended the full width of the tray; however, it stops at the inside of the side walls, as shown in Figure 8–28. This is because CATIA selected the inside of the back wall to keep instead of the outside. It also selected the outer surface of the side walls instead of the inside. To solve this issue, you need to select some compulsory walls.

The back wall should be rectangular and coincident with the edges of the side walls.

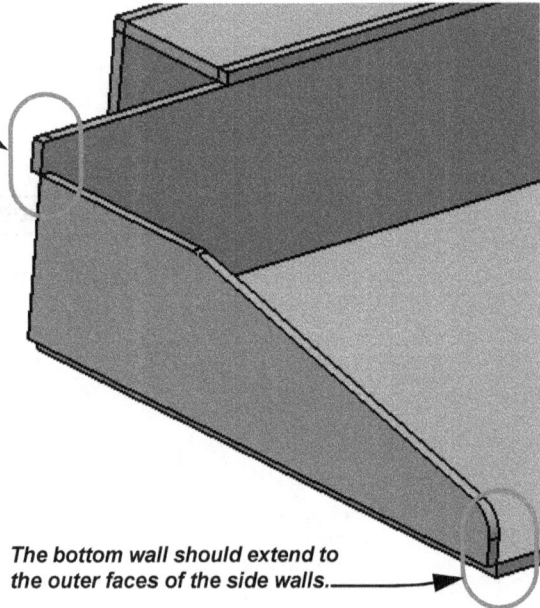

The bottom wall should extend to the outer faces of the side walls.

Figure 8–28

Task 5 - Convert the model with compulsory walls.

1. Edit the **Recognize.1** feature in the specification tree.

2. Select the *Reference face* field and select the bottom surface as the reference wall, as shown in Figure 8–29.

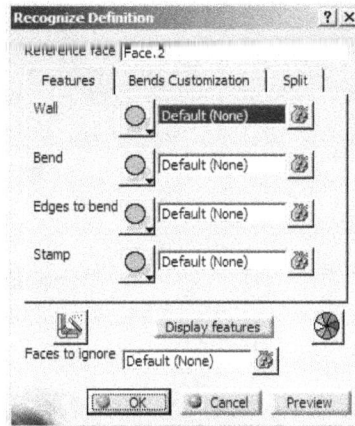

Figure 8–29

3. Click next to the *Wall* field and select the outer side of the back wall, as shown in Figure 8–30.

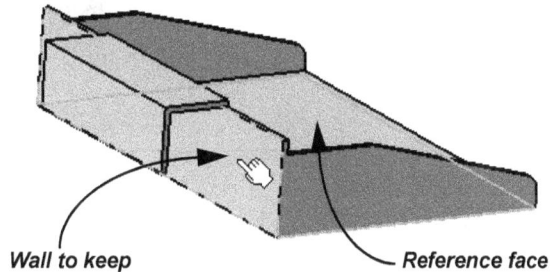

Wall to keep   — *Reference face*

Figure 8–30

4. Select the two inner surfaces of the side walls, as shown in Figure 8–31. These walls are also walls to keep.

Select the inside surfaces of the two side walls.

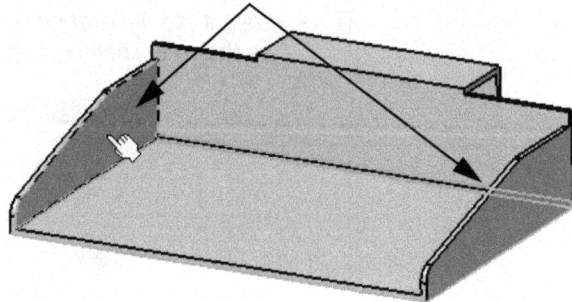

Figure 8–31

5. Click **Close** and then click **OK**. Close the Warnings dialog box. The model displays as shown in Figure 8–32.

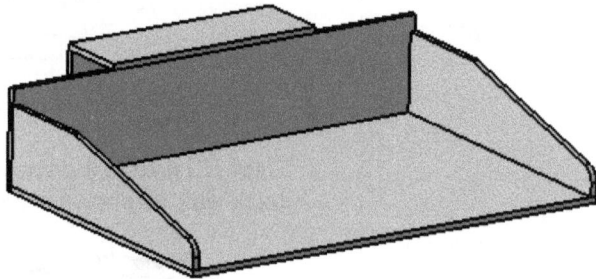

Figure 8–32

Task 6 - Create bends.

1. Use ![bend icon] (Bend) to create bends between the bottom wall and the three side walls as shown in Figure 8–33.

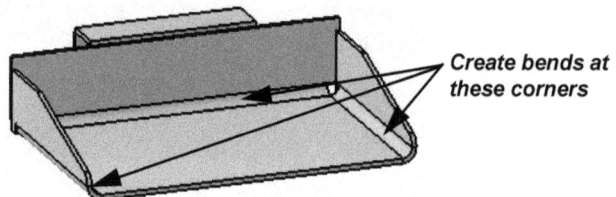

Create bends at these corners

Figure 8–33

2. Create two more bends as shown in Figure 8–34.

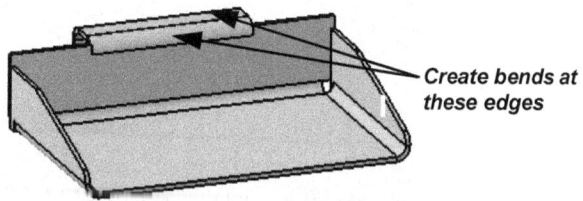

Create bends at
these edges

Figure 8–34

Task 7 - Apply bend relief.

1. Double-click **Sheet Metal Parameters** in the specification tree.

2. Select **Square Relief** in the drop-down list in the *Bend Extremities* tab. Enter **1** for **L1** and **2** for **L2**.

3. Click **OK**. The model updates as shown in Figure 8–35.

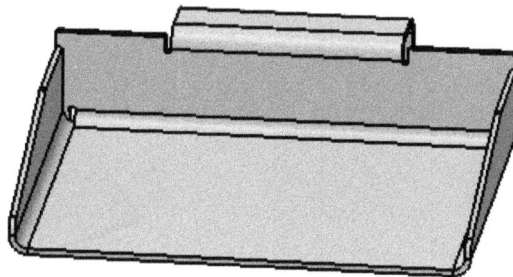

Figure 8–35

Task 8 - (Optional) Create corner relief.

In this task, you will add relief to the corners of the model.

1. Click 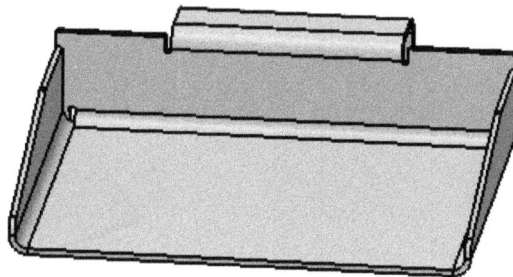 to unfold the part.

2. Click (Corner Relief) and select **Circular** in the Type drop-down list. Right-click in the *Support* field and select **Select All**. The dialog box opens as shown in Figure 8–36.

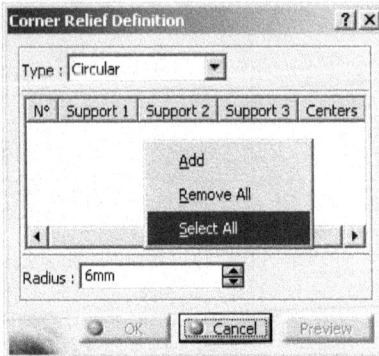

Figure 8–36

3. Enter **6mm** as the radius and click **OK**. The model displays as shown in Figure 8–37

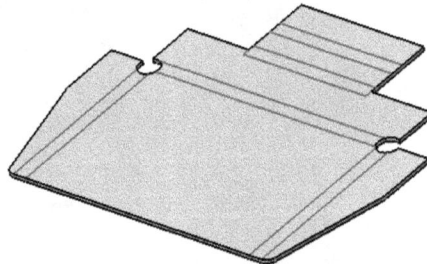

Figure 8–37

4. Fold the part. The model displays as shown in Figure 8–38.

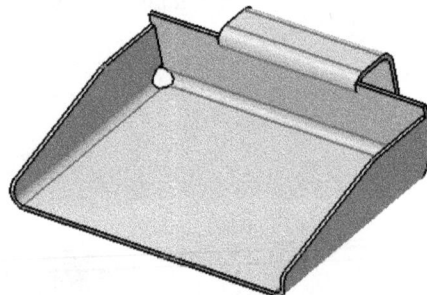

Figure 8–38

5. Save and close the file.

Chapter 9

Output

You can document a sheet metal part by outputting it to a DXF file or creating a drawing. A DXF file is a 2D file format that many industry applications can open, and that can be used to manufacture the product. Drawings enable you to show multiple conditions of a model in the same drawing.

Learning Objectives in this Chapter

- Understand how to output to DXF.
- Understand how to output to a Drawing.

9.1 Output to DXF

A DXF file is a 2D file format that many industry applications can open. The DXF operation outputs the unfolded view of the drawing, including all bend axes and flanges. This can be used to manufacture the product.

To save the unfolded view as a DXF file, click (Save as DXF) in the Manufacturing preparation toolbar. The Save as Dxf dialog box opens, as shown in Figure 9–1.

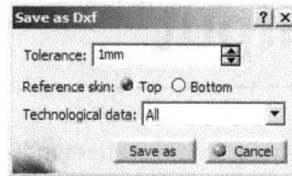

Figure 9–1

To define the included geometry, select one of the following options from the Technological data drop-down list.

*   **All:** All the geometries that can be represented are shown in different colors in the drawing.

*   **None:** No geometry is represented in the drawing.

*   **Bend lines:** Only bend lines are represented in the drawing.

*   **Stamp lines:** Only stamps lines are represented in the drawing.

You can control the coarseness of lines and circles by editing the **Tolerance**. The closer the tolerance is to zero, the smoother the lines and circles will be.

To complete the DXF, click **Save as** and save the DXF to the name and location required.

To view the saved DXF file, click (Open) and select the file in the File Section dialog box. Select **dxf (*.dxf)** in the Files of type drop-down list to quickly find the correct file, as shown in Figure 9–2. Click **Open** to open the file.

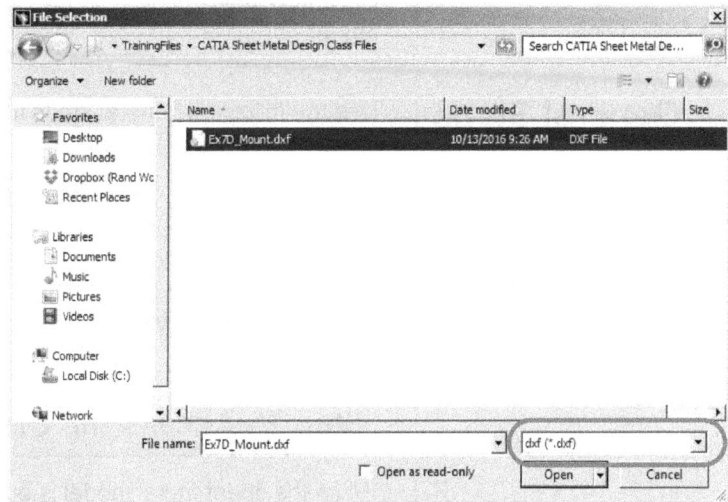

Figure 9–2

The DXF is automatically opened in the drafting workbench. Select **File>Page Setup** to change the sheet size and orientation, if required. The Unfolded DXF file is shown in Figure 9–3.

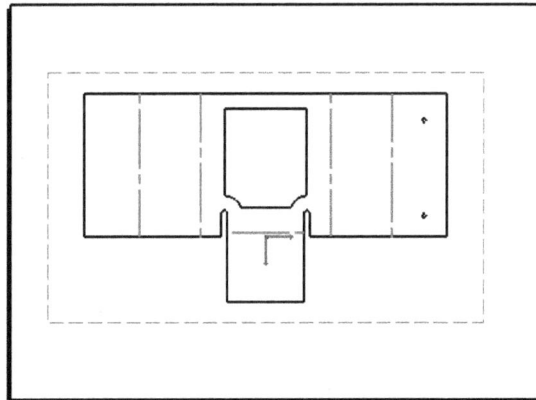

Figure 9–3

9.2 Output to a Drawing

Sheet metal models can be output to drawings using the same technique as an assembly or part model. It is possible to use all types of drawing views with Sheet metal models, including the **Unfolded view** option. This option creates a view of the unfolded model.

General Steps

Use the following general steps to start a drawing of a sheet metal model.

1. Access the Drafting workbench.
2. Create an unfolded view of the model.
3. Select the 3D model.
4. Place the view.
5. Generate the view.

Step 1 - Access the Drafting workbench.

While the sheet metal model is active, select **Start>Mechanical Design>Drafting**. The New Drawing Creation dialog box opens. Select the required type of layout, as shown in Figure 9–4.

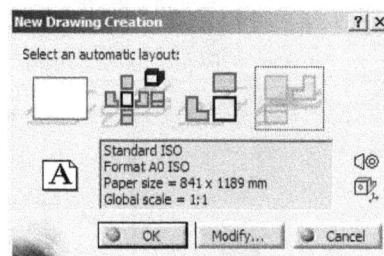

Figure 9–4

Click **Modify** to change to sheet size, orientation, or format in the New Drawing dialog box, as shown in Figure 9–5.

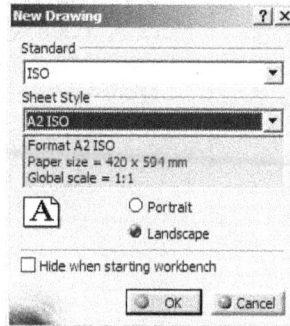

Figure 9–5

Once satisfied with the initial drawing setup, click **OK** to generate the drawing, as shown in Figure 9–6.

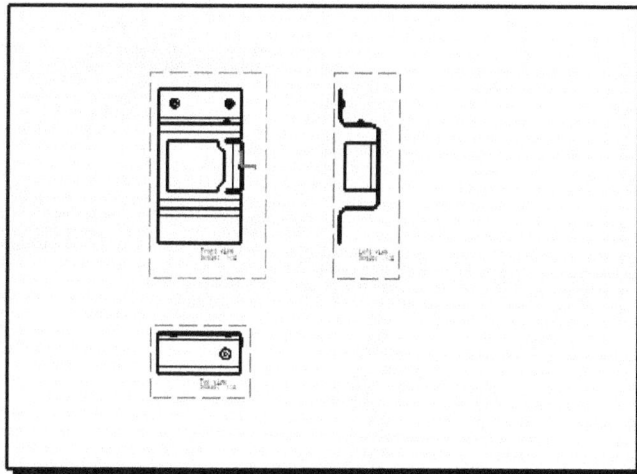

Figure 9–6

Step 2 - Create an unfolded view of the model.

Click [icon] (Unfolded View) to create an unfolded view of the model.

Step 3 - Select the 3D model.

Select **Window>Tile Horizontally** to view the model and the drawing at the same time. Select a planar surface for the reference for the drawing view in the model window, as shown in Figure 9–7.

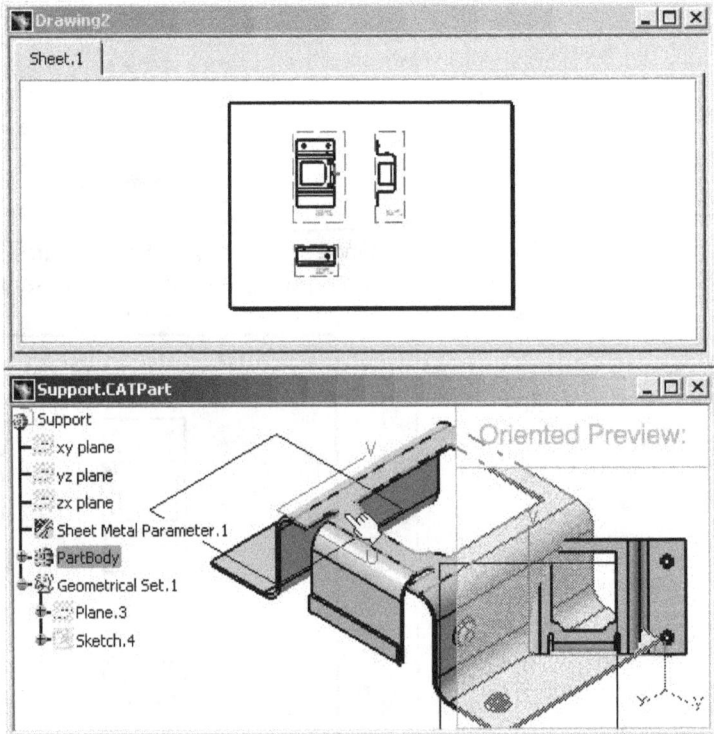

Figure 9–7

Step 4 - Place the view.

In the drawing window, use the green border around the unfolded view to move the view in the drawing, and use the compass to rotate the view to the correct orientation, as shown in Figure 9–8.

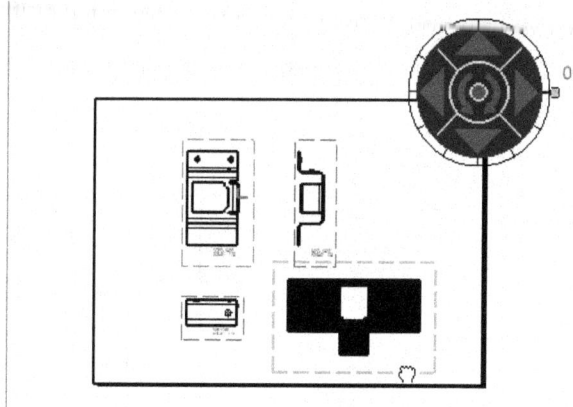

Figure 9–8

Step 5 - Generate the view.

Once the view is correct, click anywhere in the drawing to generate the view, as shown in Figure 9–9.

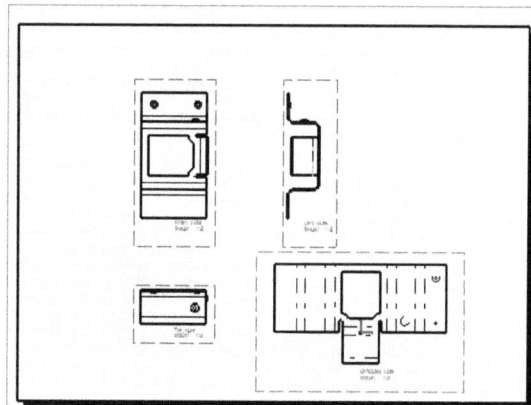

Figure 9–9

Continue creating additional views, and dimension and detail the drawing fully using the drawing tools.

Practice 9a

Output a Model to DXF

Practice Objective

- Output a sheet metal flat pattern to DXF.

In this practice, you will export an unfolded view of the mounting bracket you have created throughout this course. You will then open the DXF file and view the output. The DXF output will display as shown in Figure 9–10.

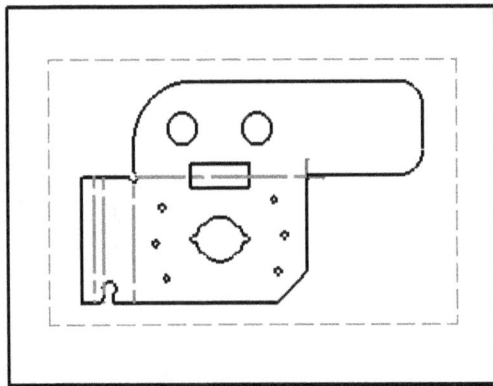

Figure 9–10

Task 1 - Open the part.

1. Open **Ex9A_Mounting_Bracket_2.CATPart**.

   If you completed **Practice 7a**, open **Mounting_Bracket_2.CATPart** instead. The model displays as shown in Figure 9–11.

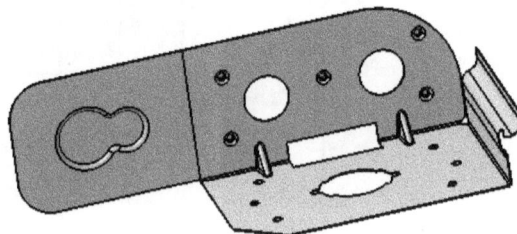

Figure 9–11

Task 2 - Output the model to DXF.

1. Activate the Generative Sheetmetal Design workbench, if required.

2. Click (Save As DXF) in the Manufacturing preparation toolbar.

3. In the Save as Dxf dialog box, select **All** from the Technological data drop-down list, as shown in Figure 9–12.

Figure 9–12

4. Click **Save as**.

5. Save the DXF file with the name **Mounting_Bracket** in the same directory as the Mounting Bracket model file, as shown in Figure 9–13.

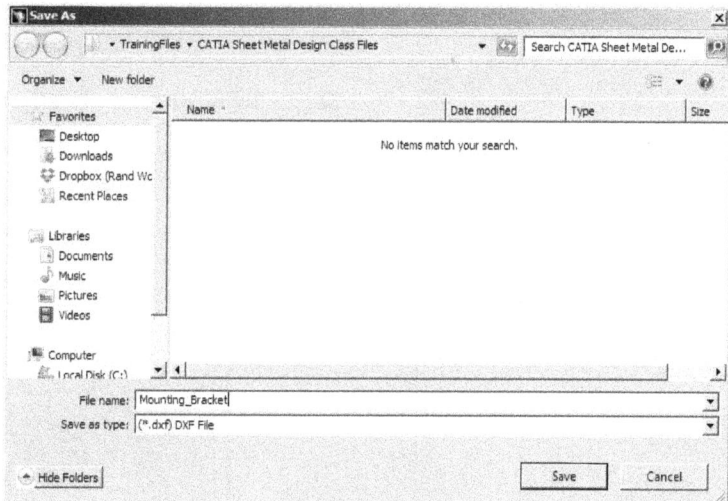

Figure 9–13

6. Click **Save**.

Task 3 - Open the DXF file.

1. Click 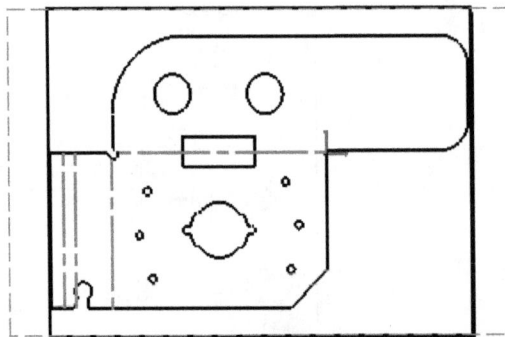 (Open).

2. Select **dxf (*.dxf)** in the Files of type drop-down list, as shown in Figure 9–14.

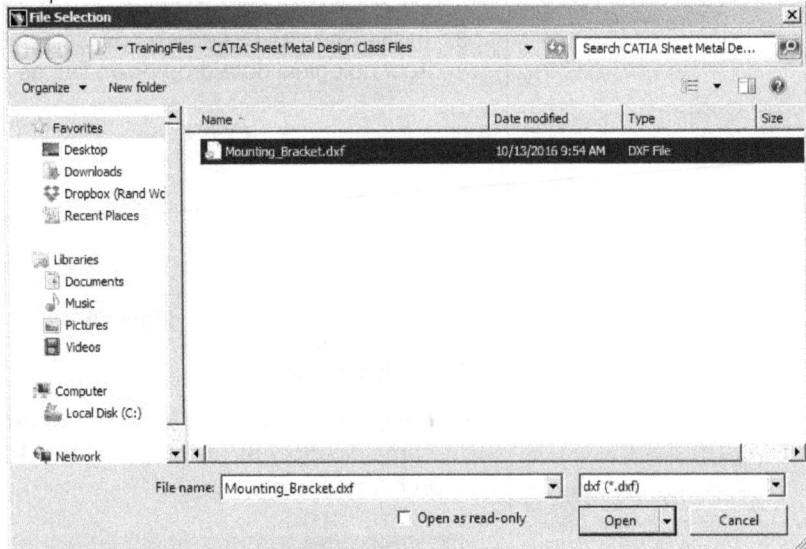

Figure 9–14

3. Select the **Mounting_Bracket.dxf** file.

4. Click **Open**. The file opens in the Drafting workbench, as shown in Figure 9–15.

Your default sheet size and/or draft orientation might not be the same.

Figure 9–15

Task 4 - Reformat the drawing page.

1. Select **File>Page Setup**.

2. Set up the page as shown in Figure 9–16:

   - *Standard:* **ISO**
   - *Format:* **A1 ISO**
   - *Orientation:* **Landscape**

Figure 9–16

3. Select the border of the view. While holding the left mouse button down, drag the view to the center of the drawing, as shown in Figure 9–17.

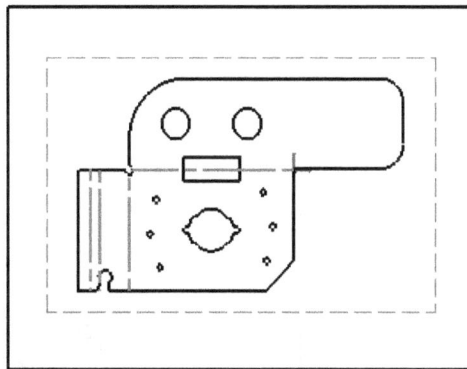

Figure 9–17

4. Save the drawing as **Mounting_Bracket.CATDrawing** and close all files.

Practice 9b | Create Unfolded View

Practice Objective

- Add an unfolded view of the sheet metal model to a drawing.

In this practice, you will create a new drawing with three default views, using the mount model you have been creating throughout the course. You will then add an unfolded view to the drawing. At the end of this practice, the drawing will display as shown in Figure 9–18.

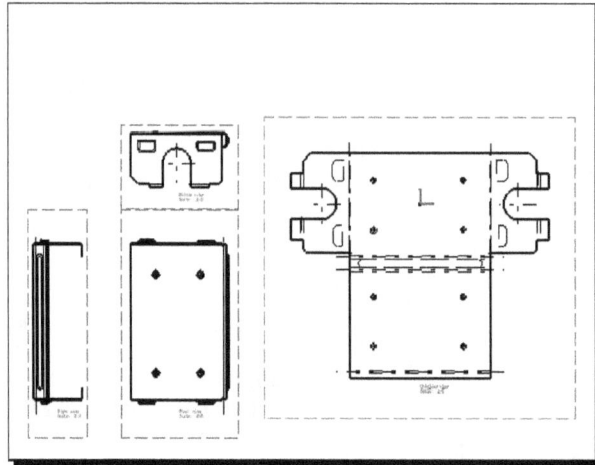

Figure 9–18

Task 1 - Open the part.

1. Open **Ex9B_Mount.CATPart**. If you completed Practice 7d, open **Mount.CATPart** instead. The model displays as shown in Figure 9–19.

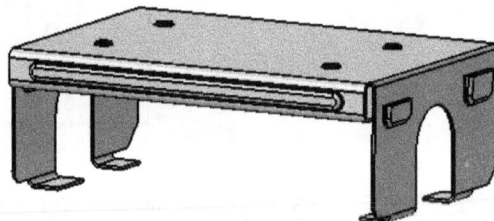

Figure 9–19

Task 2 - Create a new drawing.

1. Select **Start>Mechanical Design>Drafting**.

2. Click **Modify** in the New Drawing Creation dialog box.

3. Create the new drawing using the following conditions:

   - *Standard:* **ISO**
   - *Format:* **A1 ISO**
   - *Orientation:* **Landscape**

4. Click **OK** to close the New Drawing dialog box.

5. Click [icon] (Front, Bottom, and Right) as the layout in the New Drawing Creation dialog box, as shown in Figure 9–20.

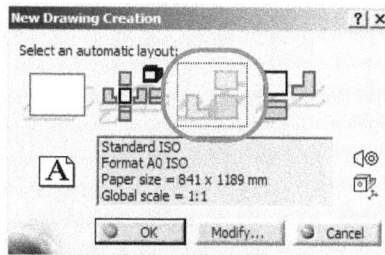

Figure 9–20

6. Click **OK** to generate the drawing.

7. Right-click on **Sheet.1** in the specification tree and select **Properties**.

8. Change the scale to **1:2** as shown in Figure 9–21.

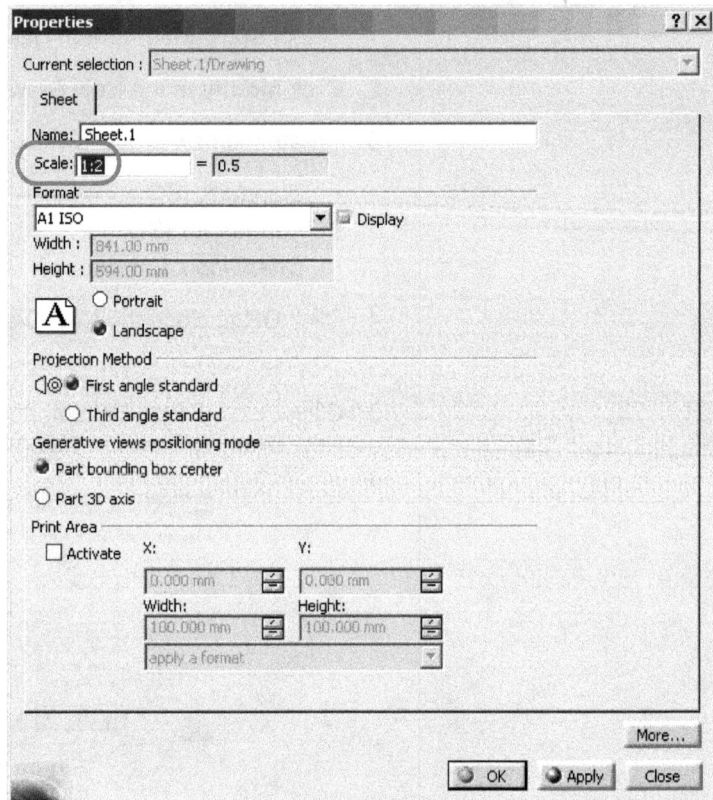

Figure 9–21

9. Click **OK** to apply the changes and close the dialog box.

10. Move the views to the position shown in Figure 9–22.

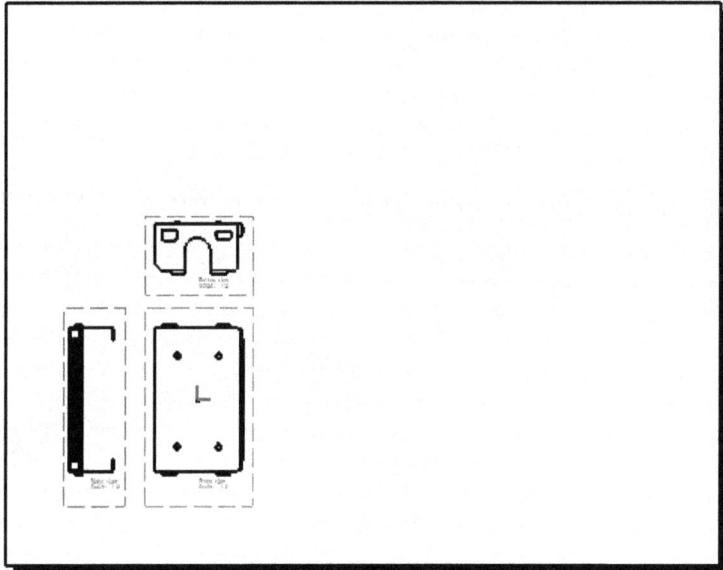

Figure 9–22

Task 3 - Create an unfolded view of the model.

1. Click (Unfolded View).

2. Activate the model in the **Window** menu, as shown in Figure 9–23.

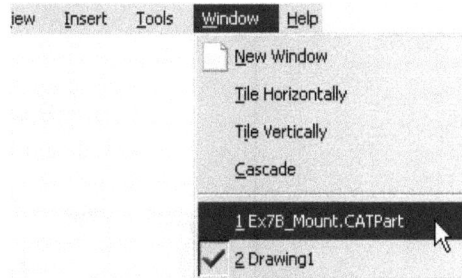

Figure 9–23

3. Select the surface shown in Figure 9–24.

Mount
— xy plane
— yz plane
— zx plane
— PowerCopy
— Sheet Metal Parameter.1
— PartBody
— Geometrical Set.1
  — Plane.1
  — Plane.2

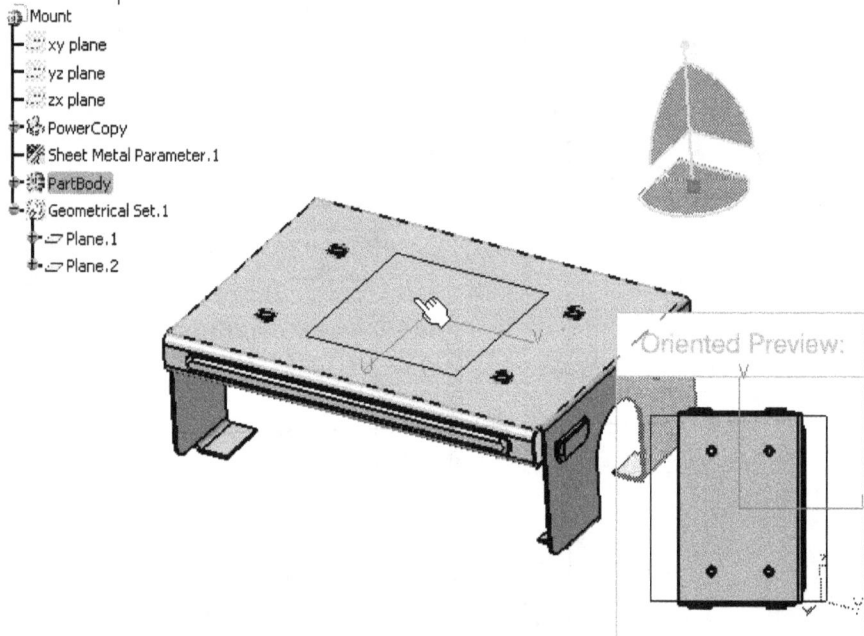

Oriented Preview:

Figure 9–24

4. Use the compass to orient the model, as shown in Figure 9–25.

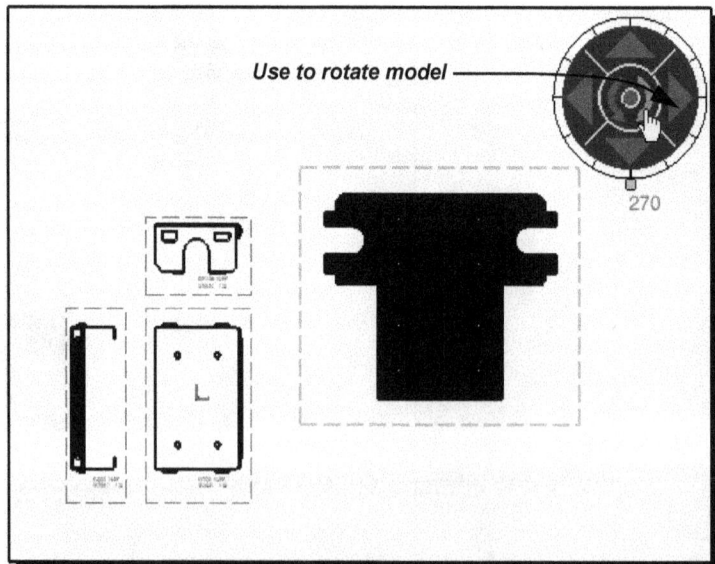

Use to rotate model

270

Figure 9–25

5. Select anywhere in the drawing to generate the view. The model displays as shown in Figure 9–26.

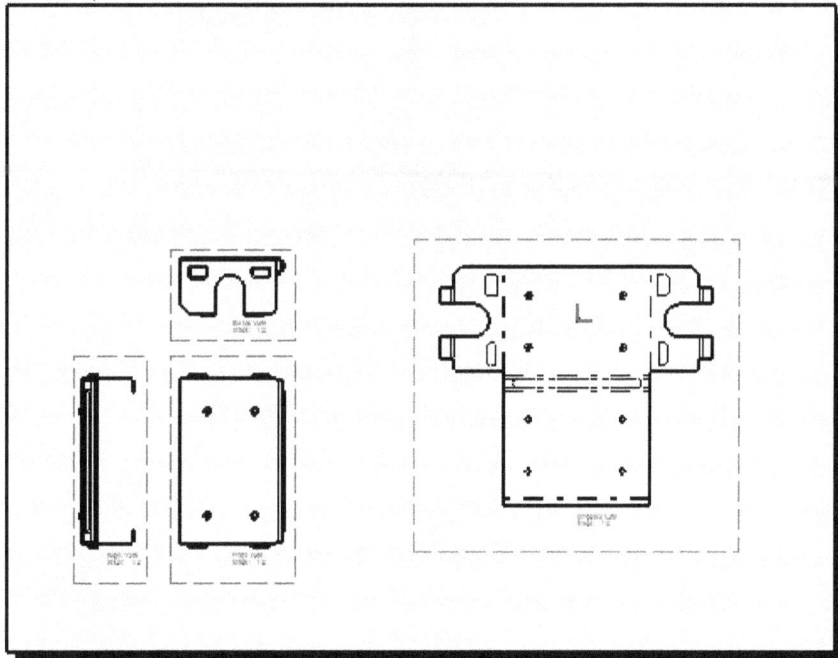

Figure 9–26

6. Select the **Unfolded** view in the specification tree, right-click and select **Properties**.

7. Select the *View* tab and change the scale to **1:1**, as shown in Figure 9–27.

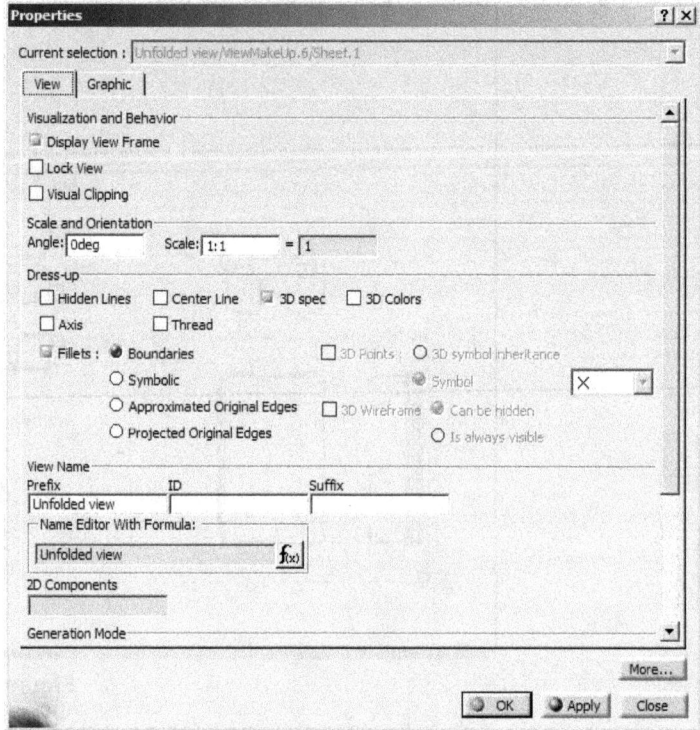

Figure 9–27

8. Click **OK** to apply the changes and close the dialog box. The model displays as shown in Figure 9–28.

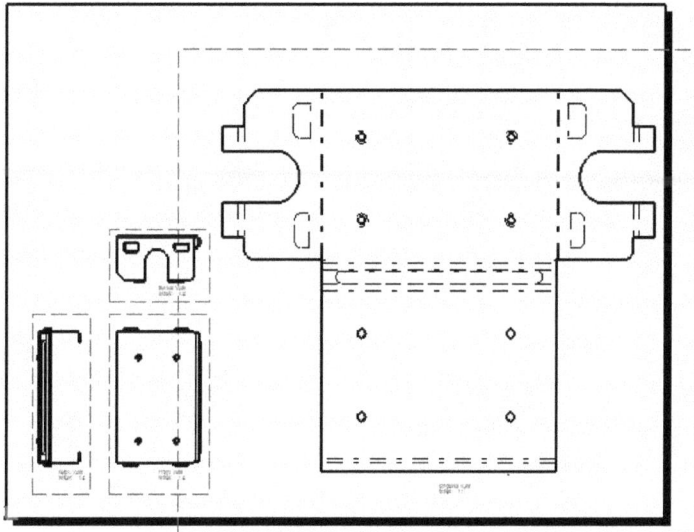

Figure 9–28

9. Name the drawing **Mount.CATDrawing**.

10. Save and close the file.

Standard Tables

Standard tables are typically developed to comply with the company standard and are stored in a centralized folder, from which they can be used by all of the designers. Information (such as standard thickness, default bend radii, and bend tables) can be stored in the standard files.

Learning Objectives in this Chapter

- Creating Standard Tables.
- Using Standard Tables.

A.1 Creating Standard Tables

A sheet metal standard file is an Excel spreadsheet file (*.XLS) or a text file (*.txt) that can be read into a CATIA sheetmetal model to create parts in company standards. Information (such as bend deduction) that is used to calculate flat pattern length, standard thickness, and bend radii is stored in the standard files.

Main Sheet Metal Standards File

It is important that the column headings of the tables are correct. The headings are matched with system generated parameters. If the headers are not correct, they do not match the parameters.

Sheetmetal standard tables are multi-tiered. The first tier is the Main Sheet Metal Standards file. This contains links to other files from which the information is retrieved. Figure A–1 shows an example of a Main Standards file.

The example contains four columns:

- The first column in the table lists all of the available company standards (or materials).

- The second column lists the available thicknesses. This column must exist for the table to be valid.

- The third column lists the default bend radius.

- The forth column refers CATIA to the document containing the bend table information.

	A	B	C		D
1	SheetMetalStandard	Thickness (mm)	DefaultBendRadius (mm)		BendTable
2	AL - 3003	2		1	BendTable_T2R1.xls
3	AL - 3003	3		2	BendTable_T3R2.xls
4	AL - 3003	5		3	BendTable_T5R3.xls
5	AL - 3003	6		6	BendTable_T6R6.xls
6					

Figure A–1

If you are using a bend table the K Factor is ignored.

Additional columns can be added to the main sheet metal standards file that provide information for K Factor, as well as paths to additional tables for available hole and stamp standards. See the CATIA help documentation Generative Sheetmetal Design>User Tasks>Managing the Default Parameters>*Editing the Sheet and Tool Parameters* for more information on the available sheetmetal standard files that can be defined.

Bend Table

Bend allowance is calculated based on the material thickness, bend radius, bend angle, and K-factor. However, you can override this equation and use bend tables. Bend tables are an alternative method of determining the flat pattern length of a model. A bend table is a collection of data in a specific format used to determine bend deduction. This bend deduction value can then be used by CATIA to calculate the unfolded length of a sheet metal model. Figure A–2 shows the difference between bend allowance and bend deduction (used in the bend table).

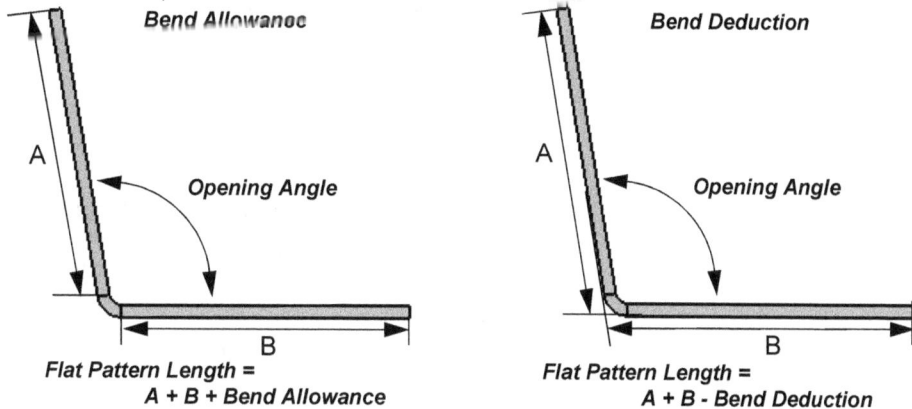

Bend Allowance

A

Opening Angle

B

Flat Pattern Length =
A + B + Bend Allowance

Bend Deduction

A

Opening Angle

B

Flat Pattern Length =
A + B - Bend Deduction

Figure A–2

Bend tables are only used when the default bend radius for bend and bend from flat features is used. If the bend radius is overridden (or a feature is created other than a bend or bend from flat feature), K Factor is used instead.

The *BendTable* column in the main sheetmetal standards file provides a path to the file containing the bend deduction table. This table contains the bend deduction values at given open angles. If a bend is created at an angle other than what is defined in the Bend table, the Bend Deduction value is interpolated from the known values. Figure A–3 shows an example of a bend table.

	A	B
1	OpenAngle (deg)	Deduction(mm)
2	25	-6.529
3	90	-3.644
4	160	-0.535
5		

Figure A–3

A.2 Using Standard Tables

A sheetmetal standard file is an Excel spreadsheet file (*.XLS) or a text file (*.txt) that can be read into a CATIA sheetmetal model to create parts in company standards. Standard tables can be used in any sheet metal model once they have been created.

General Steps

Use the following general steps to define the sheetmetal parameters based on standard tables:

1. Access the Sheet Metal Parameters.
2. Load the table.
3. Select the correct values.

Step 1 - Access the Sheet Metal Parameters.

Click (Sheet Metal Parameters). The dialog box opens as shown in Figure A–4.

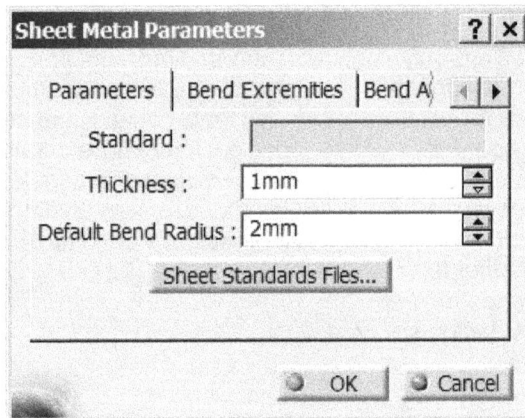

Figure A–4

Step 2 - Load the table.

Click **Sheet Standards Files**. Select the main sheetmetal standards file in the File Selection dialog box, as shown in Figure A–5, and click **Open**.

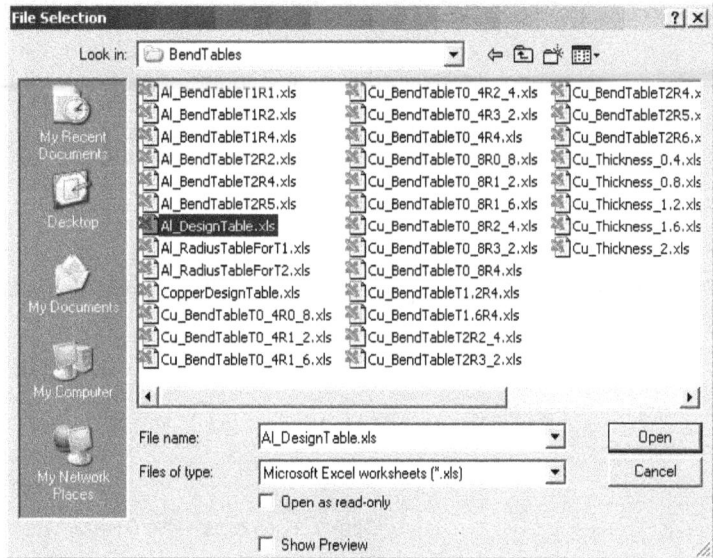

Figure A–5

Parameters inside the Sheet Metal Parameters dialog box are grayed out, as shown in Figure A–6.

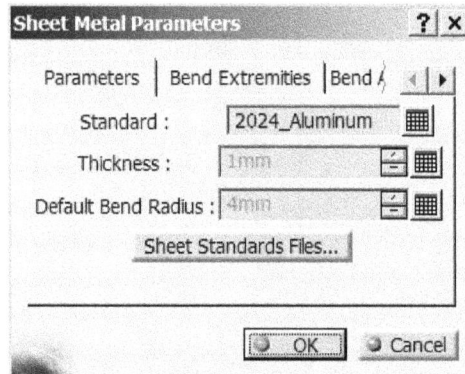

Figure A–6

Step 3 - Select the correct values.

Click ▦ next to the sheetmetal parameter field that you want to modify to select a different row in the selected table. For

example, click ▦ next to the *Standard* field to select the appropriate standard, as shown in Figure A–7, and click **OK**. The *Thickness and Default Bend Radius* fields automatically populate with the appropriate values.

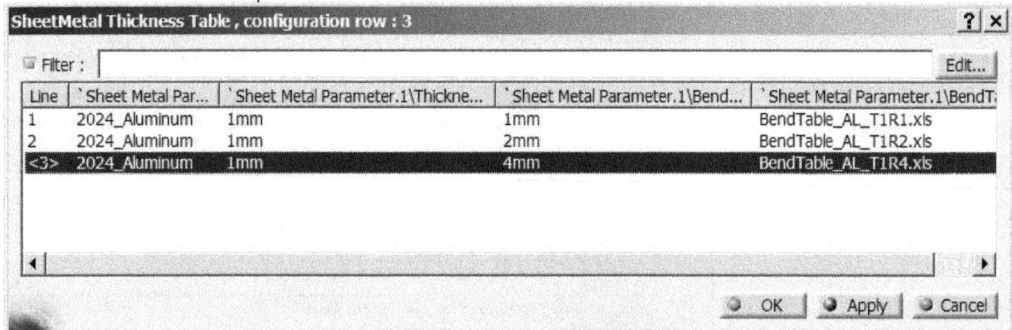

Line	` Sheet Metal Par...	` Sheet Metal Parameter.1\Thickne...	` Sheet Metal Parameter.1\Bend...	` Sheet Metal Parameter.1\BendT:
1	2024_Aluminum	1mm	1mm	BendTable_AL_T1R1.xls
2	2024_Aluminum	1mm	2mm	BendTable_AL_T1R2.xls
<3>	2024_Aluminum	1mm	4mm	BendTable_AL_T1R4.xls

SheetMetal Thickness Table , configuration row : 3 ? ×

Filter : Edit...

OK   Apply   Cancel

Figure A–7

Click **OK** to close the Sheet Metal Parameters dialog box.